DECLARING

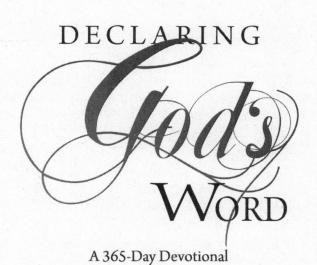

WORD

A 365-Day Devotional

DECLARING

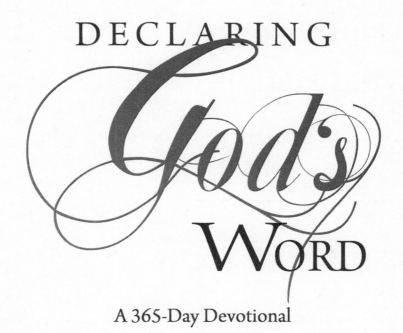

God's

WORD

A 365-Day Devotional

DEREK PRINCE

WHITAKER
HOUSE

Publisher's note:
This devotional was compiled from the extensive archive of Derek Prince's published and recorded materials and has been approved by the Derek Prince Ministries editorial team.

DECLARING GOD'S WORD: A 365-Day Devotional

Derek Prince Ministries
P.O. Box 19501
Charlotte, North Carolina 28219-9501
www.derekprince.org

ISBN: 978-1-60374-067-8 • eBook ISBN: 978-1-60374-196-5
Printed in the United States of America
© 2008 by Derek Prince Ministries–International

Whitaker House
1030 Hunt Valley Circle
New Kensington, PA 15068
www.whitakerhouse.com

Library of Congress Cataloging-in-Publication Data
Prince, Derek.
  Declaring God's word : a 365-day devotional / by Derek Prince.
    p. cm.
  Summary: "Provides believers with a full year of daily devotions on the implications of Christ's death and resurrection, including freedom from sin and adoption as God's children, and scriptural declarations to build faith"—Provided by publisher.
  ISBN 978-1-60374-067-8 (trade pbk. : alk. paper) 1. Devotional calendars. I. Title.
  BV4811.P76 2008
  242'.2—dc22
                              2008035501

9 10 11 12 13 14 15 **W** 24 23 22 21 20

Believers overcame Satan by the blood of Jesus Christ, and they testified to what the Word of God says the blood of Jesus does for us.

—Derek Prince paraphrase of Revelation 12:11

Introduction to
DECLARING GOD'S WORD:
A 365-Day Devotional

The International Publishing Team of Derek Prince Ministries is excited to bring you this unique book by renowned Bible scholar Derek Prince, *Declaring God's Word: A 365-Day Devotional*. We believe it has the potential to change not only your life, but the world, as well.

We realize that is a sweeping statement—one that might seem to "oversell" the book. However, we stand by the statement, and here's why. This book is far more than your ordinary devotional.

Like you, we enjoy a variety of devotionals written by great men and women of God. Similar to this book, those works consist of daily entries with a brief insight into a passage from God's Word, followed by a prayer designed to inspire the reader for that day. That's where the similarity ends.

One additional component makes this book powerfully unique. That component is "proclamation"—*Declaring God's Word*, as the title states. Proclamation turns this book into a powerful tool in your hands—actually, a weapon of spiritual warfare. Your proclamation will represent a daily declaration of war on the kingdom of Satan and a daily announcement of your intention to stand with the King of kings. But that's only a part of it.

The most exciting thought of all is that you will join with thousands of Christians all over the world in reading this book, declaring the same proclamations, and praying the same prayers—on the very same day, maybe even simultaneously. Take a moment to think about how powerful that will be! The impact of this corporate action will have positive spiritual implications far beyond what we can imagine.

In a teaching on the release of authority when God's Word is spoken by believers, Derek quoted Jeremiah 1:9—*"Behold, I have put My words in your mouth"*—then made this bold claim: when we declare the Word that God puts in our mouths, our proclamation carries as much authority as if God Himself were declaring it. That is the unique power and authority set in motion through *Declaring God's Word.*

Derek Prince was a man of prayer and proclamation—and He was practical. He always gave his listeners the opportunity to respond. This book is no different.

Each day, you will have the chance to respond to the daily teaching, which begins with a proclamation Derek originated. (At the start of most of Derek's teachings on CD, you will hear Derek and his wife begin in unison with a proclamation of a particular Scripture passage or scriptural thought. In this devotional, each entry begins the same way.)

Each day's teaching is pure Derek, in his exact words. Though Derek is no longer with us on earth, his powerful teaching remains, and, as Hebrews 11:4 says that *"...through faith, though he is dead, he still speaks"* (NASB). How we thank the Lord for the legacy of teaching Derek has left for us.

The section that follows the teaching summarizes what Derek has taught with a prayer and proclamation related to the day's topic. You will notice that each prayer begins with an expression of thanks to God. Along with Derek's amazing teaching gift, one of the traits we most admired about him was his constant attitude of thanksgiving. At many of his teaching sessions, Derek would close his message by asking the audience to wait upon the Lord in silence. During those moments, it was very common to hear Derek uttering over and over again, "Thank You, Lord. Thank You, Jesus. Oh, we thank You, Lord." Derek was a thankful man, and the prayers reflect that fact.

Rather than assuming you would naturally pray and proclaim on your own, we have provided specific responses as a help to you. Here is where you will experience the unique individual and corporate power that comes from declaring the same prayer and proclamation with other people on the same day.

Each entry ends with a repetition of the same proclamation that appears under the title of the entry at the top of the page. That's no mistake. Repetition is a common yet powerful biblical principle, as well as a means of affirming the truth of God's Word. An excellent scriptural example of the usefulness of repetition is found in Psalm 124:1–2: *"'If it had not been the* LORD *who was on our side,' let Israel now say* [in other words, "Let's have everyone repeat this together"], *'If it had not been the* LORD *who was on our side....'"* For additional New Testament "reminders by repetition," see Philippians 3:1, Hebrews 2:1, and 2 Peter 1:12–15.

May *Declaring God's Word* be a daily source of spiritual power and growth for you. May its teachings establish a foundation of truth in your life, making you increasingly unshakable in these increasingly shaky modern times. May you grow in faith as you absorb Derek's teachings, proclaim the truth of God's Word, and pray to your Father in heaven, confident that you are joining with Christians everywhere, powerfully declaring God's Word and advancing His gospel.

And lastly, may this book fulfill the prayer Jesus Himself taught us: *"Thy kingdom come. Thy will be done in earth, as it is in heaven"* (Matthew 6:10 KJV).

—The International Publishing Team
of Derek Prince Ministries

WEEK 1:

I testify to Satan personally as to what the Word says the blood of Jesus does for me.

And they overcame him by the blood of the Lamb and by the word of their testimony, and they did not love their lives to the death.

—Revelation 12:11

JANUARY 1

Knowing the Word

*I testify to Satan personally as to what the Word says
the blood of Jesus does for me.*

I believe the Lord showed me through an insight into Scripture how we can overcome Satan. Most Christians know that we are to overcome him by the blood of the Lamb and by the word of our testimony. But many tend to make it a kind of repetitive phrase: "I plead the blood...I plead the blood." I don't want to discount the value of that practice, but I have observed that sometimes it does not impress the devil. I think we have to apply it more purposefully.

How do we overcome Satan by the blood of the Lamb and by the word of our testimony? Three elements are involved: the blood, the Word of God, and our testimony. And this is how I interpret the application of Revelation 12:11: We overcome Satan when we testify personally as to what the Word says the blood of Jesus does for us.

It is very clear that if we are going to testify to what the Word says the blood does for us, we will have to *know* what the Word says the blood does. Over the next several weeks, we will be looking at what the Word of God says the blood of Jesus accomplishes for us.

Thank You, Lord, for the blood of Jesus. Because of what the Word says, I proclaim that I have overcome Satan by testifying to what the blood of Jesus has done for me. I testify to Satan personally as to what the Word says the blood of Jesus does for me. Amen.

The Fullness of the Cross, Vol. 4: The Sevenfold Power of the Blood (audio)
The Roman Pilgrimage, Vol. 1: Romans 1:1–1:17 (audio, video)

Applying the Blood

*I testify to Satan personally as to what the Word says
the blood of Jesus does for me.*

In looking at this confession, we can see that we have to know what the blood of Jesus does for us. Then, we have to take it from the "blood bank" and get it into our lives. There is a parallel for this application in the Passover ceremony, which was God's provision of deliverance and salvation for Israel. (See Exodus 12:21–27.) The father of each family had to kill a lamb (the sacrifice) and catch its blood in a basin. This act demonstrates the tremendous responsibility of fathers to be priests of their families.

The blood in the basin, however, did not protect any Israelite family; it had to be transferred from the basin to where the family lived. Only one means was provided, and that was hyssop. This plant is common in the Middle East; it grows everywhere there. So they had to pick a bunch of hyssop, dip it in the blood, and strike it on the lintel and two doorposts of their dwelling, but never on the threshold. You are never to walk over the blood.

With that done, the destroying angel could not enter the dwelling. But only those Israelites who were in their homes, safe behind the blood, were protected. That was the only place of safety in Egypt that night.

Thank You, Lord, for the blood of Jesus. I proclaim that I am
protected from the adversary by applying the blood to myself and
my family. I testify to Satan personally as to what the Word says the
blood of Jesus does for me. Amen.

The Fullness of the Cross, Vol. 4: How to Appropriate the Blood (audio)

Walking in Obedience

*I testify to Satan personally as to what the Word says
the blood of Jesus does for me.*

In the Passover ceremony, the blood of lambs was collected in basins. Once the blood was transferred from the basins to the Israelites' dwelling places, they were safe, on one condition: they had to stay inside their houses.

This truth is very important: the blood protects only the obedient. You are safe while you obey. Let's look at 1 Peter 1:2. Peter was greeting the *"pilgrims of the Dispersion* [in Greek, *diaspora*]" (verse 1). He was specifically addressing the Jews outside the land of Israel, who were *"elect* [or chosen] *according to the foreknowledge of God the Father, in sanctification of the Spirit, for obedience and sprinkling of the blood of Jesus Christ."*

Notice that *obedience* comes before *sprinkling*. The blood is not sprinkled on the disobedient. The blood does not protect those who go out of the house. It protects only those who are behind the blood or covered by it. So, bear in mind, although there is perfect protection in the blood, it is for the obedient alone.

Thank You, Lord, for the blood of Jesus. I proclaim this day that I will walk in obedience to You. I testify to Satan personally as to what the Word says the blood of Jesus does for me. Amen.

The Fullness of the Cross, Vol. 4: The Sevenfold Power of the Blood (audio)

Eliminating Sin

*I testify to Satan personally as to what the Word says
the blood of Jesus does for me.*

Looking once again at the Passover ceremony for Israel, we find one burning question for our application today: How do we get the shed blood—after the sacrifice is complete—to the places where we live? As long as the blood remains in the basin, it is not doing any good. It is available, but it does nothing. The Israelites had to take this simple plant called hyssop, dip it in the blood, and strike it on the outside of their houses on the doorposts and above the doors. Only then were they protected. Yet in the Passover ceremony, something else preceded the application of the blood.

Let's look at 1 Corinthians, where Paul applied the teaching of the Passover and the Feast of Unleavened Bread to Christians. Every Jewish family had to eliminate everything that was leavened from their house for seven days. The Orthodox Jews still observe this practice today.

> *Therefore purge out the old leaven, that you may be a new lump, since you truly are unleavened. For indeed Christ, our Passover, was sacrificed for us. Therefore let us keep the feast, not with old leaven, nor with the leaven of malice and wickedness, but with the unleavened bread of sincerity and truth.*　(1 Corinthians 5:7–8)

We, too, must purge the old leaven—sin—from our lives in order to live in obedience to God. This enables the blood to protect every area of our lives.

Thank You, Lord, for the blood of Jesus. I proclaim that as I apply it to my life, I am purging any sin that may be present in me. I testify to Satan personally as to what the Word says the blood of Jesus does for me. Amen.

The Fullness of the Cross, Vol. 4: The Sevenfold Power of the Blood (audio)

Relying on the Lamb

I testify to Satan personally as to what the Word says
the blood of Jesus does for me.

In 1 Corinthians 5:7, Paul connected the Passover of the Old Testament with the crucifixion of Jesus:

> *For indeed Christ* [the Messiah], *our Passover, was sacrificed for us.*

There is a very clear application of the Passover to the sacrifice of Jesus on the cross. We can say that the Passover Lamb was killed almost twenty centuries ago, and His blood is in the basin. His blood has been shed, but the blood cannot protect us while it remains in the basin. We have to transfer the blood from the basin to the places where we live.

Under the old covenant, hyssop was used, but what do we use under the new covenant? The answer is our testimonies. Our personal testimonies take the blood out of the basin and apply it to our "houses"—to our lives, our situations, and our families. We overcome Satan when we testify personally to what the Word says the blood of Jesus does for us.

Thank You, Lord, for the blood of Jesus. I proclaim that Jesus was sacrificed for me, and I rely on His blood to make me clean and free from sin. I testify to Satan personally as to what the Word says the blood of Jesus does for me. Amen.

The Fullness of the Cross, Vol. 4: The Sevenfold Power of the Blood (audio)

A Complete Sacrifice

I testify to Satan personally as to what the Word says the blood of Jesus does for me.

The most important day in the religious year of the Jewish people was the Day of Atonement, known today as Yom Kippur. On that day alone, the high priest went into the Holy of Holies with the blood of the sacrifices that covered the sins of Israel for one more year.

> He [the high priest] *shall take some of the blood of the bull and sprinkle it with his finger on the mercy seat on the east side; and before the mercy seat he shall sprinkle some of the blood with his finger seven times.* (Leviticus 16:14)

The blood alone could offer propitiation for the sins of God's people, and it had to be brought into the presence of Almighty God in the Holy of Holies. I want you to notice in particular that the blood was sprinkled *seven* times. This frequency was no coincidence, for in the Bible, seven is the number that indicates the work of the Holy Spirit. Seven is also the number of completeness, or perfection. This regulation was exactly fulfilled in the way that Jesus shed His blood. His blood was shed precisely seven times before the sacrifice was complete.

Thank You, Lord, for the blood of Jesus. I proclaim that His complete work on the cross has taken away my sins. I testify to Satan personally as to what the Word says the blood of Jesus does for me. Amen.

Extravagant Love (audio)

The Measure of His Love

*I testify to Satan personally as to what the Word says
the blood of Jesus does for me.*

On the Day of Atonement, the blood of the sacrifices had to be sprinkled seven times before God the Father. (See Leviticus 16:14.) We see this regulation exactly fulfilled in the sacrifice of Jesus on the cross in the New Testament.

First, His sweat became blood. Second, the Roman soldiers struck Him in the face with their fists and with rods. Third, they flogged Him with a Roman scourge. Fourth, His beard was pulled out. Fifth, thorns were pressed deep into His scalp. Sixth, His hands and feet were pierced with nails. Seventh, His side was pierced with a spear.

That is the measure of Christ's love. It cost Him literally all He had. He did not simply give up His glory, His throne, and His majesty as God. He did not simply give up His few earthly possessions as a man on earth. He gave up Himself. It was His own life that He poured out in His blood as the redemptive price. Think about that staggering reality and know that it is the measure of God's love. It is extravagant, to say the least.

Thank You, Lord, for the blood of Jesus. I proclaim that He gave
all He had—poured out His life completely—so that I may be free
from sin. I testify to Satan personally as to what the Word says the
blood of Jesus does for me. Amen.

Extravagant Love (audio)

Through the blood of Jesus, I am redeemed out of the hand of the devil.

Let the redeemed of the LORD say so, whom He has redeemed from the hand of the enemy.

—Psalm 107:2

True Believers

Through the blood of Jesus, I am redeemed
out of the hand of the devil.

Let the **redeemed of the LORD say so**, *whom He has redeemed*
from the hand of the enemy.   (Psalm 107:2, emphasis added)

This statement of Scripture is one that concerns what the blood of Jesus does for us as believers. Let us also look at this verse in Ephesians:

In Him [Christ] *we have redemption through His blood, the forgiveness of sins, according to the riches of His grace.*
(Ephesians 1:7)

Notice, first of all, that to receive these benefits, we have to be in Christ. We have to be true believers in Christ. When we are in Christ, the first thing that we gain is redemption through His blood.

To redeem means "to buy back," or "to pay a ransom price." We were formerly in the hands of the devil and we belonged to him. But Jesus paid the ransom price of His blood on the cross to buy us back.

Thank You, Lord, for the blood of Jesus. I proclaim that through His blood, I have been ransomed—bought back—and am a true believer in Christ. Through the blood of Jesus, I am redeemed out of the hand of the devil. Amen.

Spiritual Conflict, Vol. 3: God's People Triumphant: Spiritual Weapons—The Blood, The Word, Our Testimony (audio)

The Sinless Lamb

*Through the blood of Jesus, I am redeemed
out of the hand of the devil.*

We were redeemed, or bought back, from our old, evil, ungodly ways of living, from the grip of Satan, from the condemnation of sin, and from being open to the attacks of the devourer and the destroyer. But *how* were we bought back?

> *Knowing that you were not redeemed with corruptible things, like silver or gold, from your aimless conduct received by tradition from your fathers, but with the precious blood of Christ, as of a lamb without blemish and without spot.* (1 Peter 1:18–19)

We are redeemed by the precious blood of Jesus Christ—without blemish, without original sin; without spot, without personal sin—the sinless Lamb of God who took away the sins of the world. It is only through His blood that we are redeemed. There was no other amount that could pay the price to purchase our redemption.

Thank You, Lord, for the blood of Jesus. I proclaim that Jesus, the sinless Lamb of God, has taken away my sins. Through the blood of Jesus, I am redeemed out of the hand of the devil. Amen.

Spiritual Conflict, Vol. 3: God's People Triumphant: Spiritual Weapons—The Blood, The Word, Our Testimony (audio)

JANUARY 10

An Effective Transfer

Through the blood of Jesus, I am redeemed
out of the hand of the devil.

Let the redeemed of the LORD say so, whom He has redeemed
from the hand of the enemy. (Psalm 107:2)

Some people may know that they were redeemed out of the hand
of the devil; others do not. But I know full well where I was before
Jesus came into my life; I have no doubt about it. I know what it is
like to be in the devil's hand, and I never want to be there again. I
also know, by what Scripture says, that it was the blood of Jesus that
got me out of the hand of the devil and into the hand of the Good
Shepherd. Jesus said of His people, *"I give unto them eternal life; and
they shall never perish, neither shall any man pluck them out of my hand"*
(John 10:28 KJV). That was the transfer from the devil's hand to the
hand of the Lord.

But notice that this transfer is effective and able to benefit us
only when we do one thing: when we *"say so."* *"Let the redeemed of the
LORD say so."* If you are redeemed, say it! If you do not say it, your
redemption is not effective. It is the word of your testimony that
makes the blood effective.

Thank You, Lord, for the blood of Jesus. I declare that by His blood,
I have been transferred from the enemy's hand to the hand of the
Lord. Through the blood of Jesus, I am redeemed out of the hand of
the devil. Amen.

---

*Spiritual Conflict, Vol. 3: God's People Triumphant: Spiritual Weapons—The Blood, The Word,
Our Testimony* (audio)

The Protection of the Almighty

*Through the blood of Jesus, I am redeemed
out of the hand of the devil.*

Psalm 91 has been called the "atomic age psalm." This is a psalm of perfect protection from every kind of evil, danger, and harm—however it may come, by whatever means, and at whatever time. Many Christians know this passage well. But let's just look at the first two verses:

> *He who dwells in the secret place of the Most High shall abide
> under the shadow of the Almighty.* (Psalm 91:1)

The word *abide* in Hebrew normally means "to pass the night." It is a word that is frequently used to describe the act of spending the night. So, this tells us that during the hours of darkness, the true believer will be under the shadow, or protection, of the Almighty. Notice the second verse:

> *I will say of the LORD, "He is my refuge and my fortress; my God,
> in Him I will trust."* (verse 2)

This is the antechamber, the entranceway, into the complete protection of the remaining verses of that psalm. It is your testimony: *"I will say."* If you do not say it, you will not have it. And it takes some courage to say what follows in Psalm 91. But only those who say it have the scriptural right to live in it. It is the word of our testimony that makes it effective.

Thank You, Lord, for the blood of Jesus. I declare that by His blood,
I now live under the protection of Almighty God. Through the blood
of Jesus, I am redeemed out of the hand of the devil. Amen.

---

*Spiritual Conflict, Vol. 3: God's People Triumphant: Spiritual Weapons—The Blood, The Word,
Our Testimony* (audio)

Bought at a Price

*Through the blood of Jesus, I am redeemed
out of the hand of the devil.*

The term *redemption* means "to buy back." We were slaves, exposed for sale in Satan's slave market. The apostle Paul said, *"I am carnal, sold under sin"* (Romans 7:14). In the Roman culture of his day, to sell somebody as a slave was to sell him under a spear. He would stand on a block with a spear extended out over his head. When you saw him standing there like that, you knew that he was being sold as a slave.

Paul was saying in this statement, "My sin is the spear over my head, which has caused me to be sold as a slave in the slave market." And there, too, were we—all of us, sold with Paul as slaves because of our sins.

But one day, Jesus walked into the market and said, "I'll buy them." What's the price? The blood of Jesus. We were bought out of Satan's kingdom and brought into God's kingdom.

A slave has no choice about the type of job that he or she will perform for his or her master. One slave may be a cook, another a prostitute—it is the slave owner's decision. That is how we were. Some may have been respectable slaves, but they were no better than those who were not so respectable. Do not despise prostitutes or alcoholics, for it was the slave owner's decision that made them what they are. Satan decided what they would be, but Jesus' blood breaks his hold and sets them free from the devil's designs.

Thank You, Lord, for the blood of Jesus. I proclaim that I have been bought out of Satan's kingdom and brought into God's kingdom. Through the blood of Jesus, I am redeemed out of the hand of the devil. Amen.

The Good News of the Kingdom, Vol. 1: The Kingdom for All Nations (audio)

Made and Bought by Him

*Through the blood of Jesus, I am redeemed
out of the hand of the devil.*

Here is a parable I told to a group of Polynesian Maoris, who are great wood carvers, to illustrate the price Jesus paid to redeem us from our sins.

There was once a boy who carved a beautiful little wooden sailboat. One day he took it down to the ocean to sail, but the wind changed and carried his boat out to sea. Since he could not recover his boat, he went home without it.

The next high tide brought the boat back again, and it was found by a man walking along the seashore. He inspected the boat and saw that it was beautifully made, so he sold it to a shopkeeper who cleaned it up and put it in his window, priced to sell.

Some while later, the boy passed by the shop and saw his boat. He knew immediately that it was his, but he had no way to prove it. So, if he wanted it back, he knew he would have to buy it.

He set to work to earn the money by washing cars, mowing lawns, and other tasks. When he finally raised the necessary funds, he walked into the shop and bought back his boat. He took it in his hands, and, holding it to his breast, said, "Now you're mine! I made you and I bought you."

Picture yourself as that boat. You may feel inadequate or worthless; you may wonder if God really cares. But the Lord is saying to you, "Now you're doubly Mine—I made you and I bought you; you're fully Mine."

Thank You, Lord, for the blood of Jesus. I proclaim that the Lord made me and bought me, and I am fully His. Through the blood of Jesus, I am redeemed out of the hand of the devil. Amen.

The Good News of the Kingdom, Vol. 1: The Kingdom for All Nations (audio)

Out of One Kingdom—into Another

*Through the blood of Jesus, I am redeemed
out of the hand of the devil.*

The Lord redeemed us so that we are no longer in the hand of the enemy but in the Lord's hand.

> *Giving thanks to the Father who has qualified us to be partakers of the inheritance of the saints in the light. He has delivered us from the power of darkness and conveyed us into the kingdom of the Son of His love.* (Colossians 1:12–13)

It is a fact that God has delivered us from the power of darkness—that is, Satan's kingdom—and conveyed us into the kingdom of Christ. Thus, we have redemption—our sins are forgiven. We are no longer in Satan's territory, nor are we under his authority. The unbelieving, those who reject Christ, the rebellious, and the disobedient are under Satan's legitimate authority, but we Christians are not.

The fact is that when we repented and surrendered to Jesus Christ and made Him Lord of our lives, we were conveyed (translated, or carried over)—spirit, soul, and body—out of the kingdom of Satan and into the kingdom of Christ. These are facts. We believe facts from the invisible realm of God's Word because we no longer go by our feelings. The shield of faith covers every area of our lives. No fiery dart need ever get past it. (See Ephesians 6:16.)

Thank You, Lord, for the blood of Jesus. I proclaim that by His blood, I have been delivered from darkness and translated into the kingdom of the Son of God's love. Through the blood of Jesus, I am redeemed out of the hand of the devil. Amen.

The Good News of the Kingdom, Vol. 1: The Kingdom for All Nations (audio)

WEEK 3:

Through the blood of Jesus, all my sins are forgiven.

In Him we have redemption through His blood, the forgiveness of sins, according to the riches of His grace.

—Ephesians 1:7

Full Rights of Redemption

Through the blood of Jesus, all my sins are forgiven.

In Ephesians 1:7, we see this provision of the blood of Jesus:

> In Him [Christ] *we have redemption through His blood, the forgiveness of sins, according to the riches of His grace.*

The forgiveness of our sins is purchased for us by the blood of Jesus. Compare this verse with what Jesus said at the Last Supper in Matthew 26:28 as He gave the disciples the cup, which was the emblem of His blood:

> For this is My blood of the new covenant [testament], *which is shed for many for the remission* [forgiveness] *of sins.*
> (Matthew 26:28)

Hebrews 9:22 says that without shedding of blood, there is no remission of sin. So the blood of Jesus was shed that our sins might be forgiven.

You will notice that in Ephesians 1:7, Paul made these two things coextensive: redemption through the blood of Jesus and the forgiveness of sins. This is very important to understand because we have the full legal rights of redemption only insofar as our sins are forgiven.

Thank You, Lord, for the blood of Jesus. I proclaim that because all my sins are forgiven by His blood, I now have the full legal rights of redemption. Through the blood of Jesus, all my sins are forgiven. Amen.

Spiritual Conflict, Vol. 3: God's People Triumphant: Spiritual Weapons—The Blood, The Word, Our Testimony (audio)

Settling All Claims

Through the blood of Jesus, all my sins are forgiven.

If all our sins are forgiven, we have total rights of redemption. But if there is any sin in our lives that is not confessed—and is therefore not forgiven—we do not have full legal rights of redemption in that area. Satan still has a claim in that area. I have proved this many times in the ministry of deliverance. If Satan has any claim, he will not give it up. You can shout in his face or fast for a week, but you will not change the situation because Satan knows that he has a legal claim that still has not been settled.

Another common way in which believers give Satan a legal claim in their lives is by failing to forgive others. Jesus taught us that we are forgiven by God in the same measure in which we forgive others. We are to pray, *"Forgive us our debts* [trespasses], *as we forgive our debtors* [those who trespasses against us]" (Matthew 6:12). We are not entitled to claim forgiveness from God above the measure in which we forgive others. (See verses 14–15.) Therefore, if there are any people we have not forgiven, in that measure, we are not forgiven by God. In other words, any area of unforgiveness in our lives is an area to which Satan still has legal claim. Do what you will; you cannot dislodge him until you have forgiven whomever you need to forgive.

Thank You, Lord, for the blood of Jesus. I proclaim that I am fully forgiven, because I confess all my sins and now forgive those who have hurt me (list specific names). Through the blood of Jesus, all my sins are forgiven. Amen.

Spiritual Conflict, Vol. 3: God's People Triumphant: Spiritual Weapons—The Blood, The Word, Our Testimony (audio)

Two Directions of Forgiveness

Through the blood of Jesus, all my sins are forgiven.

Forgiveness is one of the most beautiful words in any language. What makes it such a special and beautiful word? Consider some of the results that flow from forgiveness: reconciliation, peace, harmony, understanding, fellowship. How our world today stands in such dire need of these things!

In contrast, consider some of the consequences that flow from our failure to give and receive forgiveness: bitterness, strife, disharmony, hatred, and war. At times, it seems as though the entire human race is in danger of being overwhelmed by these evil, negative forces. If we are ever to rise above these conditions, it will be only as we learn and apply the principles of forgiveness.

There are two directions of forgiveness presented in the Bible. These two directions are portrayed by that great symbol of our Christian faith: the cross. The cross has two beams—one vertical, one horizontal—that represent the two directions of forgiveness. The vertical beam represents the forgiveness that we all need to receive from God and can be received only through our identification with the sacrifice and resurrection of Jesus Christ. The horizontal beam represents our relationships with our fellow men, and it speaks of the forgiveness that, in this case, has two directions: the forgiveness we need to receive from others, and the forgiveness we need to extend to others. Once again, the only place where we can receive the grace for that kind of forgiveness is the cross.

Thank You, Lord, for the blood of Jesus. I proclaim that I not only receive God's forgiveness; I also open myself up to receive the forgiveness of others, and I extend my forgiveness to them, as well. Through the blood of Jesus, all my sins are forgiven. Amen.

The Three Most Powerful Words (booklet)

DECLARING GOD'S WORD

A Clean Slate

Through the blood of Jesus, all my sins are forgiven.

O ne of the most wondrous aspects of God's nature is that when He forgives, He does so completely and in full. The book of Micah states this truth beautifully:

> *Who is a God like you, who pardons sin and forgives the transgression of the remnant of his inheritance? You do not stay angry forever but delight to show mercy. You will again have compassion on us; you will tread our sins underfoot and hurl all our iniquities into the depths of the sea.* (Micah 7:18–19 NIV)

Isn't that beautiful? Every wrong thing that we have ever done—everything that could ever make us feel guilty, every accusation that the enemy could ever bring against us—God treads underfoot, then hurls it into the depths of the sea.

Someone has remarked that when God casts your sins into the sea, He puts up a notice that reads, "NO FISHING!" Don't ever try to go back and resurrect something that God has buried. If God has forgiven you, you are forgiven. There are no further questions. God's forgiveness is total. In Isaiah, God speaks to His people,

> *I, even I, am He who blots out your transgressions for My own sake; and I will not remember your sins.* (Isaiah 43:25)

When God forgives us, He blots out the record of our sins; our slates are clean. God does not have a poor memory, but He does have the ability to choose to forget. And when He forgives, He forgets!

Thank You, Lord, for the blood of Jesus. I proclaim that You have forgiven me fully, blotting out the record of my sins. You have forgotten them, and I will, as well. Through the blood of Jesus, all my sins are forgiven. Amen.

The Three Most Powerful Words (booklet)

The Countless Blessings of Forgiveness

Through the blood of Jesus, all my sins are forgiven.

The type of forgiveness that we need, and can receive only from God Himself, is the vertical aspect of forgiveness. There is such blessedness in being forgiven by God. This truth was articulated perhaps most beautifully by David in Psalm 32:

> *Blessed is he whose transgressions are forgiven, whose sins are covered. Blessed is the man whose sin the LORD does not count against him and in whose spirit is no deceit.*
>
> (verses 1–2 NIV)

In the Hebrew language, this psalm begins with a plural noun: *blessednesses*. "Oh, the blessednesses of the one whose transgressions are forgiven, whose sins are covered." The implication is that there are innumerable blessings attached to having our sins forgiven by God.

It is important to see that the Bible does not talk about a man who does not need forgiveness. The Bible clearly indicates that all of us need forgiveness from God; there are no exceptions. In other psalms, David said that there is no man who does not sin. We have all sinned. Therefore, we all need forgiveness. It is not a question of whether we need forgiveness but whether we receive it.

Thank You, Lord, for the blood of Jesus. I proclaim that I need Your forgiveness, and that as You forgive me, You bring great blessing to me, as well. Through the blood of Jesus, all my sins are forgiven.
Amen.

The Three Most Powerful Words (booklet)

DECLARING GOD'S WORD

Acknowledging Our Sin

Through the blood of Jesus, all my sins are forgiven.

In Psalm 32, King David wrote out of his own personal experience:

> *When I kept silent, my bones wasted away through my groaning all day long. For day and night your hand was heavy upon me; my strength was sapped as in the heat of summer. Then I acknowledged my sin to you and did not cover up my iniquity. I said, "I will confess my transgressions to the LORD"—and you forgave the guilt of my sin.*   (verses 3–5 NIV)

I believe that when David wrote this, he had in mind the matter of Bathsheba, the wife of Uriah the Hittite. It was a terrible situation in which David had committed adultery, then committed murder to cover up his adultery. David obviously had been like many of us. For a long while, he had refused to face the fact of his sin. He tried to ignore it.

In the next verses, David makes a personal application:

> *Therefore let everyone who is godly pray to you while you may be found; surely when the mighty waters rise, they will not reach him. You are my hiding place; you will protect me from trouble and surround me with songs of deliverance.*   (verses 6–7 NIV)

It is never too late to confess our sins to God and seek refuge in His salvation. He will deliver us from our sins if we'll only acknowledge them and repent.

Thank You, Lord, for the blood of Jesus. I proclaim that because I readily confess any sin that I may have tried to hide, You have forgiven the guilt of my sin. You protect me from trouble and surround me with deliverance. Through the blood of Jesus, all my sins are forgiven. Amen.

The Three Most Powerful Words (booklet)

Testifying Personally

Through the blood of Jesus, all my sins are forgiven.

In Him [Christ] we have redemption through His blood, the forgiveness of sins, according to the riches of His grace.

(Ephesians 1:7)

Looking at this statement from the Word of God about the blood of Jesus, I will show you how to apply it with the hyssop of your personal testimony to your own life situation and need.

This verse tells us two things that we have through the blood of Jesus when we are in Christ. Remember, if we are outside of Christ, it does not avail. During the first Passover in Egypt, the blood did not protect those who were not inside their houses. It was only inside their houses that the Israelites were protected, and it is only inside Christ that we have redemption and forgiveness of sins.

I know the above verse by heart. If I stood upside down in a corner of a dark room on a dark night, I could quote this Scripture without the least problem. I live by this Scripture. I keep my hyssop in my hand. Believe me, not many days pass that I am not using the hyssop in my own life. I have discovered it does the job.

Thank You, Lord, for the blood of Jesus. I apply it with the hyssop of my personal testimony, proclaiming that by His blood, I have redemption and forgiveness of sins. Through the blood of Jesus, all my sins are forgiven. Amen.

Praying to Change History: God's Atomic Weapon: The Blood of Jesus (audio)

A free Derek Prince resource for you!

To further introduce you to the unique ministry of one of the great Bible teachers of our time, Derek Prince Ministries would like to send you one of his most acclaimed, timeless teachings.

Derek Prince's message on audio CD entitled *Do You Realize How Valuable You Are?* has helped countless people around the world discover the freedom, power and purpose that flow from a revelation of your worth to your heavenly Father. Simply fill out and return this card, and we'll get it right out to you!

☐ **Yes**, please send me the Derek Prince teaching *Do You Realize How Valuable You Are?* on audio CD. CD4411

name: _____

address: _____

city: _____ state: _____ zip: _____

e-mail: _____

www.derekprince.org   f www.facebook.com/dpmlegacy   ▸ @DPMUSA

▶ youtube.com/DerekPrinceMinistry   ⓟ pinterest.com/derekprinceusa

BUSINESS REPLY MAIL
FIRST-CLASS MAIL   PERMIT NO. 705   CHARLOTTE, NC

POSTAGE WILL BE PAID BY ADDRESSEE

DEREK PRINCE MINISTRIES
PO BOX 19501
CHARLOTTE NC 28219-9932

WEEK 4:

The blood of Jesus Christ, God's Son, continually cleanses me from all sin.

But if we walk in the light as He is in the light, we have fellowship with one another, and the blood of Jesus Christ His Son cleanses us from all sin.

—1 John 1:7

A Continuing Process

The blood of Jesus Christ, God's Son,
continually cleanses me from all sin.

O ne provision of the precious blood of Jesus is cleansing.

> But if we walk in the light as He [Jesus] is in the light, we have
> fellowship with one another, and the blood of Jesus Christ His
> Son cleanses us from all sin.   (1 John 1:7)

In this verse, there are three verbs in the continuing present tense: *walk, fellowship,* and *cleanse.* We must take note of that. If we *continue* walking in the light, we *continue* having fellowship with one another, and the blood of Jesus *continues* to cleanse us.

It is very important to see that this is conditional. If we continue to walk in the light of God's Word by obeying what it says, then the first result is that we have fellowship with one another. If we are not walking in the light, we will not have fellowship. And if we do not have fellowship, we are not walking in the light. But, if we walk in the light and have fellowship, then the blood of Jesus continually keeps us clean.

Thank You, Lord, for the blood of Jesus. I proclaim that I continue
to walk in the light, have fellowship with other believers, and receive
cleansing from sin. The blood of Jesus Christ, God's Son, continually
cleanses me from all sin. Amen.

The Roman Pilgrimage, Vol. 1: Romans 1:1–1:17 (audio, video)

Cleansing Here and Now

The blood of Jesus Christ, God's Son,
continually cleanses me from all sin.

My personal testimony based on the statement above would be, "While I am walking in the light, the blood of Jesus is cleansing me, now and continually, from all sin." I say it is "cleansing me now" because that makes it a here-and-now statement, not just a vague generalization. It is for me in the here and now, but it is also continual—indefinitely into the future as I continue to walk in the light.

The Swahili language of East Africa has a special tense to describe things that are complete and permanent. In that well-known song, "The Blood of Jesus Cleanses Us from All Sin," they sing, "The blood of Jesus completely cleanses us absolutely." These lyrics have stuck with me because they say it so perfectly. So, consider this confession in the light of something that is continual and complete.

There is a beautiful commentary on this truth in Psalm 51, which is the great penitent psalm David penned after he was convicted of his sins of adultery and murder. It is one of the most beautiful psalms—a psalm every one of us would do well to read from time to time, making it our own prayer. I believe in making the psalms my prayers; I don't just read them, but I read them as my prayers.

"Purge me with hyssop, and I shall be clean; wash me, and I shall be whiter than snow" (Psalm 51:7). You will notice that David introduces the hyssop. The implication is that hyssop is the substance that brings the blood to where I am. It is a beautiful, prophetic preview of being cleansed with the blood of Jesus.

Thank You, Lord, for the blood of Jesus. I proclaim that His blood is cleansing me, now and continually, from all sin. The blood of Jesus Christ, God's Son, continually cleanses me from all sin. Amen.

The Roman Pilgrimage, Vol. 1: Romans 1:1–1:17 (audio, video)

Fulfilling the Conditions

The blood of Jesus Christ, God's Son,
continually cleanses me from all sin.

L et's look more closely at the statement about the blood that is
found in 1 John 1:7: *"But if we walk in the light as He* [Jesus] *is in the
light, we have fellowship with one another, and the blood of Jesus Christ
His Son cleanses us from all sin."*

We have already seen how these three elements are interrelated
and bound together in the Word of God: walking in the light, fellowship
with one another, and the cleansing of the blood. Scores of people claim
the cleansing and protection of the blood but do not meet the conditions that entitle them to receive it. Cleansing by the blood of Jesus
Christ is a consequence that follows from something that is preceded
by an "if"—it is a conditional statement, contingent upon our fulfilling a premise—*if* we walk in the light as He is in the light. Then, two
results follow—not one, but two. The cleansing of the blood is the second result; the first result is that we have fellowship with one another.

Logically, if we are not in fellowship with one another, it is proof
that we are not walking in the light. If we are not walking in the light,
it logically follows that we cannot claim the cleansing of the blood
of Jesus. So, we come to this conclusion: if we are out of fellowship,
we are out of the light. If we are out of the light, the blood no longer
cleanses us. The blood of Jesus cleanses only in the light. This is one
of the most important principles we can understand.

Thank You, Lord, for the blood of Jesus. I proclaim my wholehearted
intention to walk in the light, as Jesus is in the light, and to enter fully
into fellowship and cleansing from sin. The blood of Jesus Christ,
God's Son, continually cleanses me from all sin. Amen.

Spiritual Conflict, Vol. 3: God's People Triumphant: Spiritual Weapons—The Blood, The Word,
Our Testimony (audio)

Bringing Sin to the Light

*The blood of Jesus Christ, God's Son,
continually cleanses me from all sin.*

Fellowship is the place of light. This is why fellowship is a place of testing. The closer the fellowship, the brighter the light, until you come to the place where there are no hidden corners. There are no shadows; nothing is swept under the rug, nothing is covered up. It can be a frightening place for the natural man. But it is the only place where the blood of Jesus fully fulfills its function of cleansing. If you desire cleansing, it comes in the light. If you are in any way wrong before God, or wrong with your neighbor, you are not fully in the light. And the blood will never be applied except in the light.

What do you have to do? Come to the light. What is "coming to the light"? Confessing your sins, acknowledging them openly before God. Now, that is the hardest thing for natural man to do. The light seems so bright. You may think, *Oh, I couldn't bring that terrible thing, that awful memory, that guilty secret; I couldn't expose it to the light.* The natural man shrinks from it. But the truth is that when it gets to the light, it disappears because, then, the blood cleanses it. But if you do not bring it to the light, you keep it. This is a tremendous principle. The blood operates only in the light.

Supposing that we have met the condition of walking in the light. If this is the case, then we are in fellowship with our fellow believers, and we have the right to make this our testimony.

Thank You, Lord, for the blood of Jesus. I proclaim now that I bring to the light any awful memories or hidden sins (state them here), and I expose them to the light of Jesus and the cleansing of His blood. The blood of Jesus Christ, God's Son, continually cleanses me from all sin. Amen.

Spiritual Conflict, Vol. 3: God's People Triumphant: Spiritual Weapons—The Blood, The Word, Our Testimony (audio)

Obedience and Truth

The blood of Jesus Christ, God's Son,
continually cleanses me from all sin.

Fellowship is the first test of whether we are walking in the light. If we are not enjoying fellowship with our fellow believers and with the Lord, then we are not in the light, and if we are not in the light, the blood of Jesus does not cleanse us.

The next question, then, concerns *how* we walk in the light. The first condition is that we must walk in obedience to the Word of God. Psalm 119:105 says, *"Your word is a lamp to my feet and a light to my path."* The second requirement is summed up by Paul in Ephesians 4:15, where he wrote, *"Speaking the truth in love, may* [we] *grow up in all things into Him who is the head; Christ."*

In this passage, "walking in the light" is defined as relating to our fellow believers in truth and in love. We must be willing to act in truth in our relationships with one another, but we have to do so in love.

Thus, walking in the light consists of two things put together: walking in obedience to the Word of God and walking in truth and love with our fellow believers. When we meet those conditions, then we can say with full assurance that the blood of Jesus is cleansing us from all sin.

Today we are very conscious of the physical pollution of the atmosphere around us, but the spiritual atmosphere is also polluted by sin, corruption, and ungodliness. In order to be kept clean, we need the continual cleansing of the blood of Jesus.

Thank You, Lord, for the blood of Jesus. I proclaim that I am cleansed by His blood, because I have set my face to walk in obedience to His Word and in right relationship with others. The blood of Jesus Christ, God's Son, continually cleanses me from all sin. Amen.

Spiritual Conflict, Vol. 3: God's People Triumphant: Spiritual Weapons—The Blood, The Word, Our Testimony (audio)

The Blood *"Speaks"*

The blood of Jesus Christ, God's Son,
continually cleanses me from all sin.

There is another precious provision made for us by the blood of
Jesus, one of which many Christians are not aware. Hebrews 12:22,
24 reads, *"You* [all true believers] *have come to Mount Zion...to the blood
of sprinkling that speaks better things than that of Abel."*

In the heavenly Mount Zion, the blood of Jesus was sprinkled
on our behalf in the Holy of Holies before the very presence of God.
Christ entered this place as our forerunner, having obtained our eternal redemption through His sacrifice, and He sprinkled the evidence
of that redemption in the very presence of Almighty God the Father.

We should notice an important contrast here. Early in history,
Cain, the first son of Adam and Eve, murdered his brother, Abel. Cain
then tried to deny responsibility, but the Lord challenged him and
said, "There is no way you can conceal your guilt, because the blood of
your brother that you shed on the earth is crying out to Me for vengeance." (See Genesis 4:1–15.) In contrast, the blood of Jesus sprinkled in heaven cries out not for vengeance but for mercy. The blood is
a continual plea in the very presence of God for His mercy.

Once we have testified personally to the power of the blood
of Jesus, we do not have to repeat those words every few minutes,
because the blood of Jesus is speaking all the time on our behalf in
the very presence of God. Every time we are troubled, tempted, fearful, or anxious, we should remind ourselves, *The blood of Jesus is speaking in God's presence on my behalf at this very moment.*

Thank You, Lord, for the blood of Jesus. I proclaim that His blood
is speaking for mercy in God's presence on my behalf right now. The
blood of Jesus Christ, God's Son, continually cleanses me from all sin.
Amen.

Spiritual Conflict, Vol. 3: God's People Triumphant: Spiritual Weapons—The Blood, The Word,
Our Testimony (audio)

Smooth Stones

The blood of Jesus Christ, God's Son,
continually cleanses me from all sin.

The fact that a person has repented of his sins and claimed salvation in Christ does not mean that his whole character has been instantly transformed. Certainly, a vitally important process of change has been set in motion, but it may take many years for that change to be worked out in every area of his character.

When David needed smooth stones to fit in his sling so that he could slay Goliath, he went down to the valley—the lowly place of humility. There in the brook he found the kind of stones he needed. What had made them smooth? Two pressures: first, the water flowing over them; second, their continual jostling against one another.

This is a picture of how Christian character is formed. First, there is the continual washing of water by the Word (see Ephesians 5:26). Second, as we "jostle" one another in personal relationships, our rough edges are gradually worn down until they become smooth. We are "living stones" who need continual smoothing. (See 1 Peter 2:5.)

Let me add a side comment that when Jesus needs "living stones" for His sling, He, too, goes to the valley—the place of humility. There, He chooses stones that have been made smooth by the action of God's Word and by the pressures of regular fellowship with other believers. It is a mark of spiritual maturity to sincerely love our fellow Christians, not simply for what they are in themselves, but for what they mean to Jesus, who shed His lifeblood for each of them.

Thank You, Lord, for the blood of Jesus. I proclaim that I submit humbly to the washing of the Word and commit myself to love my fellow Christians with sincerity. The blood of Jesus Christ, God's Son, continually cleanses me from all sin. Amen.

Spiritual Conflict, Vol. 3: God's People Triumphant: Spiritual Weapons—The Blood, The Word, Our Testimony (audio)

WEEK 5:

Through the blood of Jesus, I am justified, made righteous, just-as-if-I'd never sinned.

Much more then, having now been justified by His blood, we shall be saved from wrath through Him.

—Romans 5:9

A Hunger and Thirst for Righteousness

Through the blood of Jesus, I am justified, made righteous,
just-as-if-I'd never sinned.

The word *justification* is a rather tiresome theological term whose true meaning is often obscured. We will first look at the word, then I will try to explain its meaning. The central theme of Romans is righteousness. Many centuries before, Job had asked the question, *"How then can man be righteous before God?"* (Job 25:4). The book of Romans presents God's answer. If we are interested in righteousness, we will be interested in Romans. Jesus said, *"Blessed are those who hunger and thirst for righteousness, for they shall be filled"* (Matthew 5:6). We can hunger and thirst for healing or prosperity without being blessed. But when we become hungry and thirsty for righteousness, then we will be blessed.

> *Much more then, having now been justified by His blood, we shall*
> *be saved from wrath through Him.* (Romans 5:9)

Notice that we have been justified by His blood. In both the Hebrew and Greek languages, there is one word that is translated as either "just" or "righteous." In Hebrew, the word is *tsadaq*, and in Greek, it is *dikaioō*. But no matter how it is translated, it is the same word. In English, we tend to refer to *just* in terms of legality and law, but *righteousness* in terms of character and conduct. There is no such division in the languages of the Bible. "Having been justified by His blood" means the same thing as "having been made righteous by His blood."

Thank You, Lord, for the blood of Jesus. I proclaim my desire to
hunger and thirst for righteousness and justification by His blood.
Through the blood of Jesus, I am justified, made righteous,
just-as-if-I'd never sinned. Amen.

The Roman Pilgrimage, Vol. 1: Romans 1:1–1:17 (audio, video)

What Justification Means

Through the blood of Jesus, I am justified, made righteous, just-as-if-I'd never sinned.

Much more then, having now been justified by His blood, we shall be saved from wrath through Him. (Romans 5:9)

The word translated "*justified*" has a whole slew of related meanings. First, it has a legal meaning. Legally speaking, it means that we are acquitted, absolved of all wrongdoing. We were on trial, but we were acquitted. That is very good news. Think of what a person being tried for murder might feel to find that he has been acquitted. Just try to imagine it. We also should feel that happy.

Second, we are not guilty.

Third, we are reckoned righteous.

Many people stop there. But I assure you that the full meaning of the word is more than that. We are also made righteous. The blood of Jesus not only causes us to be reckoned righteous, it actually *makes* us righteous.

Then, we are justified. This means it is "just-as-if-I'd" never sinned. We have been made righteous with the righteousness of Christ, which has no evil past and no shadow of guilt, and against which Satan cannot accuse us. We are made righteous with the righteousness of Jesus. It is by Christ's righteousness that we are justified. There is no guilt, no problem with the past. It has all been erased.

Thank You, Lord, for the blood of Jesus. I proclaim that through His blood, I am justified, made righteous, just-as-if-I'd never sinned. Amen.

The Roman Pilgrimage, Vol. 1: Romans 1:1–1:17 (audio, video)

Righteous and Just

*Through the blood of Jesus, I am justified, made righteous,
just-as-if-I'd never sinned.*

*Much more then, having now been justified by His blood, we shall
be saved from wrath through Him.* (Romans 5:9)

Whenever we find the word *just* in the Bible, we can substitute the word *righteous*. This is true in both Old Testament Hebrew and New Testament Greek. The translators of the King James Version alternately translated the same word as either "righteous" or "just." They tended to use the word *just* in the context of legal processes and the word *righteous* in the context of practical living. But it is one and the same word.

The problem comes with the use of the word *justified*, which is often reserved for a type of legal transaction in the courts of heaven. But this practice means using only half of the signification of the word. To be justified means to be made just, or righteous. The word *righteous* comes right down to where we live—our homes, workplaces, or personal relationships. *Just* conveys a legal formality transacted in a remote courtroom. Scripture says (and this is a perfectly legitimate and correct translation) that we have been made righteous by the blood of Jesus. We cannot consider ourselves justified if we have not been made righteous. Justification is more than a legal ceremony or a change of labels. It is a change of character and life, and it is produced by the blood of Jesus. We have been made righteous with a righteousness that is not our own—the righteousness of Jesus Christ.

Thank You, Lord, for the blood of Jesus. I proclaim that by His blood, I have been made righteous with a righteousness not my own. Through the blood of Jesus, I am justified, made righteous, just-as-if-I'd never sinned. Amen.

Spiritual Conflict, Vol. 3: God's People Triumphant: Spiritual Weapons—The Blood, The Word, Our Testimony (audio)

Justified Freely

*Through the blood of Jesus, I am justified, made righteous,
just-as-if-I'd never sinned.*

*Being justified freely by His grace through the redemption that
is in Christ Jesus, whom God set forth as a propitiation by His
blood, through faith, to demonstrate His righteousness.*

(Romans 3:24–25)

I am glad the word *"freely"* is included in this passage. The problem
with religious people is that they are always trying to earn redemption and they never arrive. They are never satisfied and never relaxed
because they think they have to do just a little bit more to be made
righteous. It never will work.

We are justified only through faith in the blood of Jesus. Let's
look at Romans 4:4: *"Now to him who works* [the religious person], *the
wages are not counted as grace but as debt."*

Many people think that if they have always lived rightly and
done their duty, God owes them righteousness or justification—that
it is a debt they're due. But in actual fact, God doesn't owe anything
to anybody. Notice verse 5: *"But to him who does not work but believes on
Him who justifies the ungodly, his faith is accounted for righteousness."*

The first thing we have to do is stop trying to make ourselves
righteous. Stop trying to be a little better. Call a halt to all that. What
we need to do is just *believe*. It is that simple. Otherwise, we will never
make it.

Thank You, Lord, for the blood of Jesus. I proclaim that I have been
justified freely by His grace. I believe on Him who justifies me, and
my faith is counted as righteousness. Through the blood of Jesus, I am
justified, made righteous, just-as-if-I'd never sinned. Amen.

*Spiritual Conflict, Vol. 3: God's People Triumphant: Spiritual Weapons—The Blood, The Word,
Our Testimony* (audio)

Boldness by Righteousness

Through the blood of Jesus, I am justified, made righteous,
just-as-if-I'd never sinned.

God makes unrighteous people righteous. Scripture says it, and I believe it. Let's look at one simple verse that affirms this truth: *"For He made Him who knew no sin to be sin for us, that we might become the righteousness of God in Him"* (2 Corinthians 5:21).

In this verse, I like to insert names in place of the pronouns: "For God made Jesus, who knew no sin, to be sin for you and me, that we might become the righteousness of God in Jesus." There is a complete exchange: Jesus was made sin with our sinfulness so that we might be made righteous with His righteousness. This righteousness is available through faith in His blood.

Righteousness produces certain immediate and definite observable results. Let's look at one of those results as stated in Scripture. Actually, our ways of living, our attitudes, our relationships, and the effectiveness of our Christian lives and acts of service will depend on how far we realize that we have been made righteous. We read in Proverbs 28:1, *"The wicked flee when no one pursues, but the righteous are bold as a lion."*

Many Christians today lack boldness. They are timid and apologetic; they tend to back down when confronted with evil or with the devil. The real root cause is their failure to appreciate the fact that they are righteous in God's sight—as righteous as Jesus Christ Himself. When we appreciate that truth, it makes us bold.

Thank You, Lord, for the blood of Jesus. I proclaim that I have been made righteous with His righteousness, and I step by faith into the boldness that this realization brings. Through the blood of Jesus, I am justified, made righteous, just-as-if-I'd never sinned. Amen.

Spiritual Conflict, Vol. 3: God's People Triumphant: Spiritual Weapons—The Blood, The Word, Our Testimony (audio)

Peace and Assurance

Through the blood of Jesus, I am justified, made righteous,
just-as-if-I'd never sinned.

In the book of Isaiah, we read about another result of righteousness in the Christian life: *"The work of righteousness will be peace, and the effect of righteousness, quietness and assurance forever"* (Isaiah 32:17).

Three products of righteousness are given in that verse: peace, quietness, and assurance. They all come from the realization that we have been made righteous with the righteousness of Jesus Christ.

Another result is described in Romans 14:17: *"For the kingdom of God is not eating and drinking, but righteousness and peace and joy in the Holy Spirit."*

Yesterday's reading showed us that righteousness brings boldness; today, we add to that peace, quietness, assurance, and joy. All these things are products of righteousness. If we do not receive Christ's righteousness by faith, we will struggle and try to attain all these other characteristics without ever achieving them. It is pathetic to see Christians *trying* to be joyful or peaceful, or trying to be relaxed or assured. Someone has told them they ought to be. But it is my experience that when they really get the assurance of sin's forgiveness and righteousness by faith, they will find it just happens. Joy flows naturally. Peace comes without effort. Assurance is present. Boldness expresses itself. The root problem is getting people to realize that they have been made righteous with the righteousness of Jesus Christ.

Thank You, Lord, for the blood of Jesus. I proclaim that I have been made righteous with His righteousness, and I step by faith into the peace, quietness, assurance, and joy that this realization brings. Through the blood of Jesus, I am justified, made righteous, just-as-if-I'd never sinned. Amen.

Spiritual Conflict, Vol. 3: God's People Triumphant: Spiritual Weapons—The Blood, The Word, Our Testimony (audio)

A Good Confession

*Through the blood of Jesus, I am justified, made righteous,
just-as-if-I'd never sinned.*

Religious people think they are pretty holy if they point out how sinful they are. The general attitude is that we would be conceited if we claimed to be righteous, that we would be religious if we kept speaking about our failures, our inconsistencies, and the wrongs we've committed.

Every Sunday morning in the church where I was brought up, we had to say, "Pardon us, miserable offenders." I always felt that I didn't want to be a miserable offender, but when I looked at the other offenders, I could surely agree that we were all miserable. Eventually, I said to myself, *If all religion can do is make me miserable, I can be an offender without religion and not be half as miserable.* And that is what I became until I met the Lord.

The language of religion continually states, "We are miserable offenders; we have erred and strayed from God's ways like lost sheep; we have committed the things we ought not to have done and we have left undone the things we ought to have done."

I could not say those words now; I would be a hypocrite. How could I pray for victory over sin on a Monday morning if I knew that the following Sunday I would be saying that I had erred and strayed, that I had done those things I should not have done and left undone those things I should have done? It would completely undermine the basis of my faith. Yet it sounds so good, so pious.

Let's make our confession in line with God's Word and believe it: Through the blood of Jesus, I am justified, made righteous, "just-as-if-I'd" never sinned.

Thank You, Lord, for the blood of Jesus. I bring my confession into line with God's Word and proclaim: Through the blood of Jesus, I am justified, made righteous, just-as-if-I'd never sinned. Amen.

Spiritual Conflict, Vol. 3: God's People Triumphant: Spiritual Weapons—The Blood, The Word, Our Testimony (audio)

WEEK 6:

Through the blood of Jesus, I am sanctified, made holy, set apart to God.

Therefore Jesus also, that He might sanctify the people with His own blood, suffered outside the gate.

—Hebrews 13:12

What Sanctification Means

*Through the blood of Jesus, I am sanctified, made holy,
set apart to God.*

Sanctification is another one of these long, theological words. Let's break it down. *To sanctify* is directly related in the original biblical languages to the word for "holy." So, "to sanctify" means "to make holy." The English word *sanctify* is related to the word *saint*. Sanctification is the process of making something saintly, or holy.

> *Therefore Jesus also, that He might sanctify the people with His own blood, suffered outside the gate.* (Hebrews 13:12)

Jesus went outside the city as a sin offering. (See, for example, John 19:16–20.) We learn from the Old Testament that sin offerings could not be offered within the compound of God's people. (See, for example, Exodus 29:14.) Sanctification always includes separation.

To make ourselves holy, we must offer the right testimony: "Through the blood of Jesus, I am sanctified, made holy, set apart to God, separated from all that is evil. Between all evil and me is the blood of Jesus."

The one who is sanctified is in an area where God has access to him, but the devil does not. To be sanctified is to be removed from the area of Satan's visitation and reach and to be placed in an area where we are available to God, but not at home when the devil calls. That is what it is to be sanctified, made holy, set apart to God.

Thank You, Lord, for the blood of Jesus. I proclaim that through the blood of Jesus, I am sanctified, made holy, set apart to God. Amen.

The Roman Pilgrimage, Vol. 1: Romans 1:1–1:17 (audio, video)

Respect for the Blood

Through the blood of Jesus, I am sanctified, made holy,
set apart to God.

I n looking at the sanctifying power of the blood of Jesus, we want to examine a passage from Hebrews that speaks about the apostate—the person who turns away from the Christian faith, having known it, into a deliberate denial and rejection of the Lord Jesus Christ. It speaks about all the sacred things that he renounces and, in a sense, defiles:

> *Of how much worse punishment, do you suppose, will he be thought worthy who has trampled the Son of God underfoot, counted the blood of the covenant by which he was sanctified a common* [or unholy] *thing, and insulted the Spirit of grace?*
>
> (Hebrews 10:29)

It is plain to see from this verse that we are sanctified by the blood of the covenant. But here is a person who has been sanctified by the blood of the New Covenant and then turns back. Let's look closely at the meaning of trampling underfoot the blood of Jesus. This reference is in relation to the Passover ceremony, where the blood was applied to the lintel and the doorposts, but never to the threshold. We are never to show disrespect for the blood of Jesus.

Thank You, Lord, for the blood of Jesus. I proclaim my profound respect for the blood of the covenant, through which I am sanctified, made holy, set apart to God. Amen.

Spiritual Conflict, Vol. 3: God's People Triumphant: Spiritual Weapons—The Blood, The Word, Our Testimony (audio)

A Total Transfer

Through the blood of Jesus, I am sanctified, made holy,
set apart to God.

Just like righteousness, sanctification does not come by effort or by religion, but only by faith in the blood of Jesus. To be sanctified is to be set apart to God. We now belong to God; we are under God's control and available to Him. Anything that is not of God has no right to approach us; it is kept away by the blood.

> *Giving thanks to the Father who has qualified us to be partakers of the inheritance of the saints in the light. He has delivered us from the power* [or authority] *of darkness and conveyed us into the kingdom of the Son of His love.* (Colossians 1:12–13)

Through faith in the blood of Jesus, we have been removed from the area of Satan's authority and conveyed into the kingdom of God. The word *"conveyed* [*"translated"* KJV]*"* means "carried over from one place to another." In Scripture, the word is used for a total transfer. In the Old Testament, there were two men, Enoch and Elijah, who were translated from earth to heaven. And both of them went entirely. All that Elijah left behind was his mantle, but his body was gone.

As I understand Scripture, this is true for us, too. We have been totally translated. We aren't *going to be* translated; rather, we *have been*—spirit, soul, and body. We are no longer in the devil's territory, no longer under the devil's laws. We are in the territory of the Son of God and under His laws.

Thank You, Lord, for the blood of Jesus. I proclaim that I have been made holy by faith in the blood of Jesus, transferred totally from the devil's territory into the territory of the Son of God. Through the blood of Jesus, I am sanctified, made holy, set apart to God. Amen.

Spiritual Conflict, Vol. 3: God's People Triumphant: Spiritual Weapons—The Blood, The Word, Our Testimony (audio)

FEBRUARY 8

Bought Back Totally

Through the blood of Jesus, I am sanctified, made holy,
set apart to God.

In Romans, we read about two kingdoms with their opposing laws of operation. The devil's law is the law of sin and death; the law of God's kingdom is the law of the Spirit of life in Christ Jesus. *"For the law of the Spirit of life in Christ Jesus has made me free from the law of sin and death"* (Romans 8:2).

We are no longer in the devil's territory, no longer under the devil's law. His kingdom does not apply to us because we are in another kingdom. We have been translated, carried over—spirit, soul, and body. And this transaction occurs through the blood of Jesus—we are sanctified, set apart to God, by the blood of Jesus.

Now, let's consider the implications in relation to the body of the believer. I can say by experience that this is where it really begins to operate, when we bring it down to the realm of our physical bodies. Consider this: *"Or do you not know that your body is the temple of the Holy Spirit who is in you, whom you have from God, and you are not your own? For you were bought at a price; therefore glorify God in your body and in your spirit, which are God's"* (1 Corinthians 6:19–20).

The words *"bought at a price"* take us back to the theme of redemption. We are bought back out of the hand of the devil with the blood of Jesus. How much of us was bought back? Just our spirits? No, both our spirits and our bodies belong to God because Jesus paid the total redemption price of His blood.

Thank You, Lord, for the blood of Jesus. I proclaim that I have been bought back totally from the devil's kingdom and brought into the kingdom of God. My spirit and body belong to God, because Jesus paid the total redemption price of His precious blood. Through the blood of Jesus, I am sanctified, made holy, set apart to God. Amen.

Spiritual Conflict, Vol. 3: God's People Triumphant: Spiritual Weapons—The Blood, The Word, Our Testimony (audio)

His Plan to Make Us Holy

*Through the blood of Jesus, I am sanctified, made holy,
set apart to God.*

We know that the word *sanctify* is related to the word *saint*, and is directly related in the original biblical languages to the word for "holy." So, sanctification means being made holy. God has planned for us to be made holy.

Holiness is a unique attribute among the attributes of God. God has many wonderful attributes—love, power, wisdom, and so forth—but all those have a quality that we could say is remotely reflected in human beings. We have experienced love from human beings. We know of those who are powerful. We have met human beings who are wise. Of course, these qualities appear in humans to a degree immeasurably less than they do in God, but at least we have an idea of what these qualities are. But when we talk about holiness, there is nothing else to compare it to. God is uniquely holy.

Holiness is something that is not found outside of God. Really, in some ways you can measure how much you know God by how much you know holiness. I relate it this way: We thank God for His goodness, we praise God for His greatness, but we worship God for His holiness. *Worship* is the response to the holiness of God.

In the Old Testament, God said, *"You shall be holy; for I am holy"* (Leviticus 11:44), and, in the New Testament, Peter restated the Lord's words, saying, *"Be holy, for I am holy"* (1 Peter 1:16). Yet two different ways of attaining holiness were being referred to. I will compare these two ways—one by the old covenant, and the other by the new covenant—over the next few days.

Thank You, Lord, for the blood of Jesus. I proclaim that God is holy, deserving of worship—and that through the blood of Jesus, I am sanctified, made holy, set apart to God. Amen.

Holiness the Jesus Way (audio)

DECLARING GOD'S WORD

Not a Set of Rules

Through the blood of Jesus, I am sanctified, made holy, set apart to God.

Let us look at the way holiness was to be attained under the old covenant. God said, *"You shall be holy; for I am holy"* (Leviticus 11:44). All of Leviticus 11 enumerates complicated regulations regarding what to eat, what to wear, and what makes one clean or unclean.

God's requirement was to *"consecrate yourselves"* (Leviticus 11:44). But you find out from this chapter that maintaining holiness was very complicated. There was a series of the most involved regulations.

> *These also shall be unclean to you among the creeping things that creep on the earth: the mole, the mouse, and the large lizard...; the gecko, the monitor lizard, the sand reptile, the sand lizard, and the chameleon....Whoever touches them when they are dead shall be unclean until evening.* (Leviticus 11:29–31)

According to this regulation, for instance, if a mouse died and someone picked it up by the tail, he would be unclean until that evening. But Scripture goes on to give further regulations about the container the mouse might fall in and the article of clothing it might touch, then gives instructions on how to deal with the uncleanness. Observing all of these regulations would be a full-time job.

God said that if you succeeded in following these rules, you would be holy. But if you were going to attain holiness by keeping a set of rules, you would have to keep *all the rules all the time*. You could not omit one at any time. But thank God that He provided a better way—because keeping all these rules is impossible for sinful humans.

Thank You, Lord, for the blood of Jesus. I proclaim that God's plan is to make me holy—not by observance of a set of rules, but through the blood of Jesus, by which I am sanctified, made holy, set apart to God. Amen.

Holiness the Jesus Way (audio)

Holiness by Faith

Through the blood of Jesus, I am sanctified, made holy,
set apart to God.

We can tell that revival is here when God's people are more interested in being holy than being healed. Our standard of priority is wrong. If I were to organize a healing meeting, people would come streaming in, but if I were to teach about holiness, the attendance would drop. In actual fact, holiness is much more important than healing. Healing is temporary and will help you to get through this life only. Thank God for it. But holiness is eternal; it will be with you forever in heaven. Something has to happen by the power of the Holy Spirit to change our sense of values.

> *So now, brethren, I commend you to God and to the word of His*
> *grace, which is able to build you up and give you an inheritance*
> *among all those who are sanctified.* (Acts 20:32)

The inheritance is for those who have been sanctified. This passage says the Word of God can bring you into that inheritance. Yet how is sanctification attained under God's better way, the new covenant? Jesus commissioned Saul of Tarsus when He first revealed Himself to Saul (who later became Paul). He said,

> *I will deliver you from the Jewish people, as well as from the Gentiles, to whom I now send you, to open their eyes, in order to turn*
> *them from darkness to light, and from the power of Satan to God,*
> *that they may receive forgiveness of sins and an inheritance among*
> *those who are sanctified by faith in Me.* (Acts 26:17–18)

We can be sanctified by keeping all the rules of the Old Testament—if we keep them all the time. Again, this is impossible for sinful humans. The other way is completely different—not by keeping a set of rules, but by faith in Jesus.

Thank You, Lord, for the blood of Jesus. I proclaim my faith in Jesus Christ, affirming that through the blood of Jesus, I am sanctified, made holy, set apart to God. Amen.

Holiness the Jesus Way (audio)

DECLARING GOD'S WORD

WEEK 7:

My body is a temple of the Holy Spirit, redeemed, cleansed, by the blood of Jesus.

Or do you not know that your body is the temple of the Holy Spirit who is in you, whom you have from God, and you are not your own?

—1 Corinthians 6:19

The Indwelling Holy Spirit

My body is a temple of the Holy Spirit, redeemed,
cleansed, by the blood of Jesus.

A very distinctive mark of personality is the ability to speak. At Pentecost, when the Holy Spirit descended from heaven, He spoke in *"other tongues"* (Acts 2:4) through the disciples. By this He signified that He had come, as a Person, to take up His dwelling on earth. He is now the permanent, personal representative of the Godhead residing on earth.

From Pentecost on, each time the Holy Spirit comes to take up His residence as a Person in the body of a believer, it is appropriate that He should manifest His presence by speaking out of that believer in a new language that is supernaturally imparted. In effect, He is saying, "Now you know that I am here as a Person to indwell your body."

For this reason, in 1 Corinthians 6:19, Paul said, *"Do you not know that your body is the temple of the Holy Spirit?"* He emphasized that speaking in tongues is not merely a brief, supernatural experience; beyond that, it is a divinely given sign that the Holy Spirit, as a Person, has taken up His dwelling in the believer's body, thereby making it a sacred temple. This truth places a solemn obligation upon each believer to keep his body in a condition of holiness that is appropriate for God's temple.

Thank You, Lord, for the blood of Jesus and the work of Your
Holy Spirit. I proclaim that my body is a temple of the Holy Spirit,
redeemed, cleansed, by the blood of Jesus.

Who Is the Holy Spirit? (Teaching Legacy Letter)

FEBRUARY 13

My Body: The Lord's Temple

*My body is a temple of the Holy Spirit, redeemed,
cleansed, by the blood of Jesus.*

*However, the Most High does not dwell in temples made with
hands, as the prophet says: "Heaven is My throne, and earth is
My footstool. What house will you build for Me? says the LORD,
or what is the place of My rest? Has My hand not made all these
things?"* (Acts 7:48–50)

God dwells in a temple made not by hands but by divine workmanship, according to divine purpose. That temple is the body of the believer, redeemed by the blood of Jesus Christ. As Paul explained in 1 Corinthians 6:13, *"Foods for the stomach and the stomach for foods, but God will destroy both it and them. Now the body is not for sexual immorality but for the Lord, and the Lord for the body."* This verse talks about food for the stomach and the stomach for food. In Proverbs, it says, *"The righteous eats to the satisfying of his soul"* (Proverbs 13:25). We who are righteous do not overeat. Why? Because our bodies are the Lord's temple, and we are not to defile them by gluttony, drunkenness, immorality, or any other form of misuse. The body is for the Lord, and the Lord is for the body. When I present my body to the Lord, then I have the rights of the Lord for my body.

Let's use this analogy: If I purchase a piece of property, I become responsible for its maintenance; but if I live in a rented property, the landlord is responsible. If we just let Jesus have a temporary right over our bodies, He does not accept responsibility for their maintenance. But if He owns them, He is responsible to maintain them. That is the relationship He desires.

Thank You, Lord, for the blood of Jesus and the work of Your Holy Spirit. I proclaim that my body is a temple of the Holy Spirit and the Lord has all rights to my body. Thus, I will not defile it with gluttony, drunkenness, immorality, or any other misuse. My body is a temple of the Holy Spirit, redeemed, cleansed, by the blood of Jesus. Amen.

Spiritual Conflict, Vol. 3: God's People Triumphant: Spiritual Weapons—The Blood, The Word, Our Testimony (audio)

God's Property

My body is a temple of the Holy Spirit, redeemed,
cleansed, by the blood of Jesus.

The Bible says that we are to glorify God in both our bodies and our spirits (see 1 Corinthians 6:20), for both belong to God; both have been redeemed out of the hand of the devil by the blood of Jesus. No part of me—spirit, soul, or body—is under the dominion or control of Satan.

Let me say clearly that I do not have a resurrection body but a mortal body. But that mortal body—all its fibers, cells, and tissues—is God's property, not the devil's. If the devil encroaches on that territory, he is a trespasser. By application of our rights in Jesus, we can put up a sign that says "No Trespassing." Legally, our bodies do not belong to the devil but to Jesus, who has a special purpose for them. They are to be places of personal residence of the third Person of the Godhead, the Holy Spirit. Our bodies are sacred because they are the appointed dwelling places of the Holy Spirit.

Scripture says clearly many times that God does not dwell in temples made with hands. (See, for example, Acts 7:48.) Neither does He dwell in church buildings, chapels, synagogues, or other physical houses of worship. He dwells in His people.

Thank You, Lord, for the blood of Jesus and the work of Your Holy Spirit. I proclaim that my body is God's property, not the devil's. Legally, my body does not belong to the devil, but to Jesus—and He has a special purpose for my body. My body is a temple of the Holy Spirit, redeemed, cleansed, by the blood of Jesus. Amen.

Spiritual Conflict, Vol. 3: God's People Triumphant: Spiritual Weapons—The Blood, The Word, Our Testimony (audio)

Listening to God's Voice

My body is a temple of the Holy Spirit, redeemed,
cleansed, by the blood of Jesus.

Our destinies, for good or ill, are settled by the voice we choose to heed. Listening to the voice of the Lord and obeying what He says will bring blessings. Ignoring the voice of the Lord will bring many curses. It is impossible to obey God without first hearing His voice, for His voice tells us what He requires.

Many professing Christians are insensitive to the voice of God. We may continue our religious activities and duties, but they are habitual and formal—just patterns we have cultivated that lack a constant awareness of God's voice. Through all dispensations, God asks His people to listen to His voice.

In Jeremiah 7, God explained what He really required of Israel when He redeemed them from Egypt. The first thing He had in mind was not keeping the Law for the offering of sacrifices but listening to His voice. It was His voice that would lead them to keep the Law and offer the necessary sacrifices. Merely observing the externals of the Law was of no avail if they were not doing so as a result of hearing the voice of the Lord. The key requirement of God is that we listen to His voice.

> *For I did not speak to your fathers, or command them in the day that I brought them out of the land of Egypt, concerning burnt offerings or sacrifices. But this is what I commanded them, saying, "Obey My voice, and I will be your God, and you shall be My people."* (Jeremiah 7:22–23)

The simple requirement is, *"Obey My voice, and I will be your God."* That sums it up as simply as possible.

Thank You, Lord, for the blood of Jesus and the work of Your Holy Spirit. I proclaim that I will listen to the voice of the Lord and obey what He says. I proclaim His truth for me: *"Obey My voice, and I will be your God."* My body is a temple of the Holy Spirit, redeemed, cleansed, by the blood of Jesus. Amen.

Claiming Our Inheritance (audio)

His Holy Spirit within Us

*My body is a temple of the Holy Spirit, redeemed,
cleansed, by the blood of Jesus.*

*For if you live according to the flesh you will die; but if by the
Spirit you put to death the deeds of the body, you will live.*

(Romans 8:13)

Paul said to "spiritual Christians" that if we live according to the flesh, we will die, for we are nurturing that which is corrupt. All you get is corruption when you live according to the flesh.

There is total opposition between the flesh and the Spirit; there is no reconciliation between them. God's plan of redemption is to put to death the old, fleshly nature and bring into being a totally new nature by His Holy Spirit within us. Although God has made total provision for this transformation, we have to work it out in our lives. We have to put to death the deeds of the body. God does not do it for us; He has given us the legal right, authority, and power, but we must exercise them.

Scripture says, *"But as many as received Him [Jesus], to them He [God] gave the right [authority] to become children of God"* (John 1:12). We receive authority when we are born again. But authority is useless unless exercised. The new birth is just a potential—the opportunity to develop into something wonderful if we will exercise our authority. If we never take steps to exercise authority in a scriptural way over the problems and sins that confront and beset us, we will make no progress at all.

We must move out of one way of thinking—the area of the flesh—into a totally different one. We need the help of the Holy Spirit. *"For as many as are [being] led by the Spirit of God, these [and these only] are sons of God"* (Romans 8:14).

Thank You, Lord, for the blood of Jesus and the work of Your Holy Spirit. I proclaim that by faith, I am putting to death the deeds of the body and opening myself up to the totally new nature Your Holy Spirit creates within me. My body is a temple of the Holy Spirit, redeemed, cleansed, by the blood of Jesus. Amen.

The Roman Pilgrimage, Vol. 2: Romans 7:25–8:4 (audio, video)

Washing and Regeneration

My body is a temple of the Holy Spirit, redeemed,
cleansed, by the blood of Jesus.

The process of salvation involves washing and regeneration. *"He [God] saved us, not on the basis of deeds which we have done in righteousness, but according to His mercy, by the washing of regeneration and renewing by the Holy Spirit"* (Titus 3:5 NASB).

Let's look at these concepts briefly, starting with *washing*, or *cleansing*. Sin defiles. We are inwardly dirty, and we need to be cleansed. Only the blood of the Lord Jesus Christ can cleanse the sinner from all sin. How can we receive that cleansing? *"If we confess our sins, He is faithful and righteous to forgive us our sins and to cleanse us from all unrighteousness"* (1 John 1:9 NASB). God not only forgives the past, but He also cleanses us from all the defilement of sin. In the same chapter, John said that it's the blood of Jesus, God's Son, that cleanses us. (See verse 7.)

The second phase of this process is *regeneration*, or *rebirth*. Jesus said to Nicodemus, *"Truly, truly, I say to you, unless one is born again, he cannot see the kingdom of God"* (John 3:3 NASB). This is a birth that comes from God's realm above. A little further on, Jesus said, *"That which is born of the flesh is flesh, and that which is born of the Spirit is spirit"* (John 3:6 NASB).

When we were born of our mothers, it was a birth of our physical bodies and our fleshly nature. That is not the kind of birth that brings salvation. We have to receive a totally new life born into us by the Spirit of God from above. That is regeneration, or rebirth.

Thank You, Lord, for the blood of Jesus and the work of Your Holy Spirit. I proclaim that the Lord Jesus Christ is cleansing me from all sin by His blood, and I receive regeneration and rebirth—a totally new life born into me by the Spirit of God. My body is a temple of the Holy Spirit, redeemed, cleansed, by the blood of Jesus. Amen.

The Roman Pilgrimage, Vol. 2: Romans 7:25–8:4 (audio, video)

Renewal by the Spirit

*My body is a temple of the Holy Spirit, redeemed,
cleansed, by the blood of Jesus.*

The process of salvation includes renewing. In Titus 3:5, we read, *"He [God] saved us, not on the basis of deeds which we have done in righteousness, but according to His mercy, by the washing of regeneration and renewing by the Holy Spirit"* (NASB).

The last aspect that Paul mentioned in this verse is *renewing*. We must become new creations. Paul said, *"Therefore, if anyone is in Christ, he is a new creation; the old has gone, the new has come!"* (2 Corinthians 5:17 NIV).

The word *"creation"* is important, as there is only one who creates—God. Man can manufacture, repair, or produce, but man cannot create. Our hearts and our whole inner beings have been so defiled and distorted by the effects of sin that repairing or patching up is no good. A new creation alone will be good.

In the Old Testament, after David had fallen into adultery, committed murder, and finally been confronted with the awful condition of his own heart, he cried out to God in agony, *"Create in me a clean heart, O God"* (Psalm 51:10). He knew that creation had to come from God; it could not come about by any human process.

In Titus 3:5, we have seen the three aspects of the process of being saved—a washing, or cleansing; a regeneration, or rebirth; and a renewing, or new creation. God does something that man absolutely cannot do. All of this is by God's mercy, not His justice. It is not according to our deeds of righteousness—those won't achieve anything. Salvation has to come from God's sovereign mercy.

Thank You, Lord, for the blood of Jesus and the work of Your Holy Spirit. I proclaim that I am being renewed by the Holy Spirit. I am a new creation, not by my own deeds of righteousness, but by God's sovereign mercy to me. My body is a temple of the Holy Spirit, redeemed, cleansed by the blood of Jesus. Amen.

The Roman Pilgrimage, Vol. 2: Romans 7:25–8:4 (audio, video)

Satan has no place in me, no power over me, no unsettled claims against me. All has been settled by the blood of Jesus!

Who shall bring a charge against God's elect? It is God who justifies. Who is he who condemns? It is Christ who died, and furthermore is also risen, who is even at the right hand of God, who also makes intercession for us.

—Romans 8:33–34

Forgiving Others

Satan has no place in me, no power over me, no unsettled claims against me. All has been settled by the blood of Jesus!

One common way in which believers give Satan a legal claim in their lives is failing to forgive others. Jesus taught us that we are forgiven by God in the same measure in which we forgive others. He said, *"If you forgive men their trespasses, your heavenly Father will also forgive you. But if you do not forgive men their trespasses, neither will your Father forgive your trespasses"* (Matthew 6:14–15). We are not entitled to claim forgiveness from God in a measure greater than that with which we forgive others. If there is any person whom we do not forgive, in a corresponding measure, we are not forgiven by God. That means the area of unforgiveness in our own lives is an area over which Satan still has a legal claim. We cannot dislodge him until we have forgiven whomever it may be who needs to be forgiven.

Redemption is coextensive with the forgiveness of sins. If all our sins are forgiven, then we have the total rights of redemption. Satan has no legal claim outstanding against us. But if there is any area in our lives in which sin has not been totally dealt with, Satan still has a legal claim in that area. We can get all the preachers in America to preach and pray over us, but we will not dislodge the devil, because he knows he has a legal claim. We need to remember that the devil is a legal expert. He knows it, too. However, God's Word offers us total forgiveness of sin. It is crucial that we hold on to the total forgiveness and leave no offense unforgiven.

Thank You, Lord, for the blood of Jesus. I ask God to forgive every sin, and I forgive every person whom I need to forgive (give specific names). Having done that, I proclaim that Satan has no place in me, no power over me, no unsettled claims against me. All has been settled by the blood of Jesus! Amen.

Spiritual Conflict, Vol. 3: God's People Triumphant: Spiritual Weapons—The Blood, The Word, Our Testimony (audio)

Say It Again!

Satan has no place in me, no power over me, no unsettled claims against me. All has been settled by the blood of Jesus!

I can well remember when I first began to make this kind of testimony. I thought, *I wonder where the devil will hit me next.* I know of people who will not testify because they are afraid of what will happen when they do, but that is just playing the devil's game. Remember, this is his way of keeping you from doing what will put you beyond his reach. It is only by the word of your testimony that you will get the benefits of the blood.

The first time you say it, all hell may break loose. Well, praise the Lord! Say it again. The Bible says, *"Let us hold fast our confession"* (Hebrews 4:14). And then, when everything really turns loose, Scripture says, *"Let us hold fast the confession of our hope without wavering"* (Hebrews 10:23). Keep on saying it. It does not depend on our feelings. It does not depend on our situations, symptoms, or circumstances. It is as eternally true as the Word of God.

Forever, God's Word is settled in heaven. (See Psalm 119:89.) Satan has no place in us, no power over us, and no unsettled claims against us.

Thank You, Lord, for the blood of Jesus. I proclaim that Satan has no place in me, no power over me, no unsettled claims against me. All has been settled by the blood of Jesus! And I intend to declare this over and over again. Amen.

Spiritual Conflict, Vol. 3: God's People Triumphant: Spiritual Weapons—The Blood, The Word, Our Testimony (audio)

Jesus the Deliverer

Satan has no place in me, no power over me, no unsettled claims against me. All has been settled by the blood of Jesus!

The same Christ who is the only Savior is also the only Deliverer. Only Jesus can break the power of demonic bondage in people's lives and set them free. I want us to be introduced to the Deliverer in just the same way.

For those of us who desire deliverance, we need to make direct, personal contact with Christ. Here are four simple conditions we need to meet:

Be sure we have repented. That is, know that we have turned away from every form of sin.

Look only to Jesus, for He alone is the Deliverer.

Base our appeals solely on what Jesus did for us through His death on the cross rather than on any "good works" of our own.

Be sure that, by an act of our wills, we have forgiven every person who ever harmed or wronged us.

When I personally received deliverance from the demon of depression, I received this promise: *"Whoever calls on the name of the LORD shall be saved"* (Joel 2:32). I also remembered these words of Jesus: *"In My name they* [the disciples] *will cast out demons"* (Mark 16:17). In the name of Jesus, we, too, have the authority to expel demons.

Thank You, Lord, for the blood of Jesus. I proclaim that He alone is my Deliverer, and that *"whoever calls on the name of the Lord shall be saved."* Satan has no place in me, no power over me, no unsettled claims against me. All has been settled by the blood of Jesus! Amen.

They Shall Expel Demons (book)

Understanding the Battleground

Satan has no place in me, no power over me, no unsettled claims against me. All has been settled by the blood of Jesus!

For though we walk in the flesh, we do not war according to the flesh. For the weapons of our warfare are not carnal [fleshly or physical] but mighty in God for pulling down strongholds, casting down arguments and every high thing that exalts itself against the knowledge of God, bringing every thought into captivity to the obedience of Christ. (2 Corinthians 10:3–5)

Our warfare against Satan is waged in the spiritual realm; therefore, the weapons are spiritual and appropriate to the realm of the warfare.

It is tremendously important that we understand where the battle is taking place. Paul used various words in 2 Corinthians to speak of the battleground and our objectives. In different translations, we find the following words: *"imaginations," "reasonings," "speculations," "arguments," "knowledge,"* and *"thought."* Notice that every one of those words refers to the realm of the mind. We absolutely must understand that the battleground is in our minds. Satan is waging an all-out war to captivate the minds of the human race. He is building strongholds and fortresses in our minds, and it is our responsibility, as God's representatives, to use our spiritual weapons to break down these strongholds, to liberate the minds of men and women, and then to bring them into captivity to the obedience of Christ. What a staggering assignment that is!

Satan deliberately and systematically builds strongholds in people's minds. These fortresses resist the truth of the gospel and the Word of God and prevent us from being able to receive the message of the gospel.

Thank You, Lord, for the blood of Jesus. I proclaim that by His blood, I am breaking down the strongholds Satan has built in my mind. I declare that Satan has no place in me, no power over me, no unsettled claims against me. All has been settled by the blood of Jesus! Amen.

Derek Prince on Experiencing God's Power (book)

The Power of Fasting

Satan has no place in me, no power over me, no unsettled claims against me. All has been settled by the blood of Jesus!

In fact, in the day of your fast you find pleasure, and exploit all your laborers. Indeed, you fast for strife and debate, and to strike with the fist of wickedness....Is it a fast that I have chosen, a day for a man to afflict his soul? Is it to bow down his head like a bulrush? (Isaiah 58:3–5)

F or the people here described, fasting was merely an accepted part of religious ritual, the kind of fasting practiced by the Pharisees in Jesus' day. Instead of real repentance or self-humbling, they continued with normal secular affairs and retained evil attitudes of greed, selfishness, pride, and oppression.

The kind of fast that is well pleasing to God, on the other hand, springs from totally different motives and attitudes: *"To loose the bonds of wickedness, to undo the heavy burdens, to let the oppressed go free, and that you break every yoke"* (verse 6). Scripture and experience alike confirm that there are many bonds that cannot be loosed, burdens that cannot be undone, yokes that cannot be broken, and many oppressed who will never go free until God's people—and especially their leaders—obey God's call to true fasting and prayer.

Isaiah continues to describe our proper attitudes toward the needy and oppressed: *"To share your bread with the hungry, and that you bring to your house the poor who are cast out; when you see the naked, that you cover him, and not hide yourself from your own flesh"* (verse 7). Fasting must be united with sincere and practical charity in our dealings with those around us—particularly, those who need our help in material and financial matters.

Thank You, Lord, for the blood of Jesus. I will obey God's call to fasting and praying as God's chosen way to loose bonds, undo burdens, free the oppressed, and break yokes. I proclaim that Satan has no place in me, no power over me, no unsettled claims against me. All has been settled by the blood of Jesus! Amen.

Shaping History through Prayer and Fasting (book)

The Ruthless Cross

Satan has no place in me, no power over me, no unsettled claims against me. All has been settled by the blood of Jesus!

Some people struggle with fear, depression, loneliness, lust, or anger. A counselor can help us just so far; but in the last resort, the solution is in our hands: the cross. We must identify this nature in us when and where it rises up. In the ministry of deliverance, there are two demons that are the gatekeepers. They swing the door open for the next demon to come. These gatekeepers are self-pity and resentment. Self-pity is a tremendously powerful tool of Satan, and nobody can afford to indulge resentment.

At some point, we must be ruthless. The cross is entirely ruthless—there is nothing comfortable, attractive, or sweet about it. But we thank God for it because it is the way out; it is God's provision.

Most of us have a "besetting sin"—a sin we are so accustomed to that we think it is a part of ourselves. We find it hard to hate because it is almost like hating ourselves. Interestingly enough, my besetting sin was my father's problem before me. Children inherit a lot from their parents, and certain patterns of behavior are set before us. I see behaviors in me that are direct reproductions of my father's behavior.

We need to ask the Holy Spirit to identify the nature of our problems. Call them by their right names (they probably won't be pretty)—maybe lust, lying, or pride. Then, we must say, "In Jesus, it has been crucified. I put it to the cross. I will not let it dominate me. I am free from it through the cross."

Thank You, Lord, for the blood of Jesus. I proclaim that in Jesus, the besetting sin in my life (name it here) has been crucified. I put it on the cross. I will not let it dominate me any longer. Satan has no place in me, no power over me, no unsettled claims against me. All has been settled by the blood of Jesus! Amen.

The Fullness of the Cross, Vol. 3: Deliverance from the Fleshly Nature (audio)

Keep Saying It!

Satan has no place in me, no power over me, no unsettled claims against me. All has been settled by the blood of Jesus!

The first time we make this declaration, Satan will laugh at us. We need to *keep* saying it. Satan is the tempter, but he is very methodical and wastes no time. He will tempt you as long as he gets any response from you. When there is no more response, he won't bother to tempt you.

So, we can be tempted in the area of, let's say, resentment. We must keep saying, "It was crucified. It has no power in me. It has no place in me." The devil says, "That isn't really true. That's just something Brother Prince said." But we keep saying it. And after a while, it becomes so real that the devil doesn't waste his time trying to tempt us any longer.

One of the things we have to do is build the walls of our character. The Bible says that the person who has no control over his own spirit is like a city that is broken down and without walls. (See Proverbs 25:28.) In our culture today, many people are growing up like broken-down walls because of bad homes, drugs, or evil influences. Anybody who has been deep in drugs is definitely a city without protective walls. We build the walls by strengthening our wills and asserting our rights bought by the cross. We may think of this process as a terrible experience. But we don't realize how much good it is doing us; at the end of it, we have built strong character. Gifts are temporary, for this life only; character is permanent—it goes into eternity with us. God is infinitely more interested in your character than in your gifts.

Thank You, Lord, for the blood of Jesus. I proclaim that I intend to strengthen my will and assert my rights bought by the cross, declaring over and over again: Satan has no place in me, no power over me, no unsettled claims against me. All has been settled by the blood of Jesus! Amen.

The Fullness of the Cross, Vol. 3: Deliverance from the Fleshly Nature (audio)

WEEK 9:

My body is a temple for the Holy Spirit, redeemed, cleansed, and sanctified by the blood of Jesus.

Or do you not know that your body is the temple of the Holy Spirit who is in you, whom you have from God, and you are not your own?

—1 Corinthians 6:19

Glorifying God in My Body

My body is a temple for the Holy Spirit, redeemed,
cleansed, and sanctified by the blood of Jesus.

Or do you not know that your body is the temple of the Holy
Spirit who is in you, whom you have from God, and you are not
your own? For you were bought at a price; therefore glorify God
in your body and in your spirit, which are God's.

(1 Corinthians 6:19–20)

There are many ways in which we use our bodies. One primary activity consists of nourishing ourselves—eating and drinking. Paul said that we need to do those activities in a way that glorifies God:

Therefore, whether you eat or drink, or whatever you do, do all to
the glory of God. (1 Corinthians 10:31)

What does it mean to *"eat...to the glory of God"*? I leave it to you to answer this question. Some people cannot even imagine they can give God glory by the way they eat. But God has said He is a jealous God (see, for example, Exodus 34:14), and He wants to be glorified in every aspect of life—especially the simple, daily, down-to-earth activities.

But let me ask you one more question. Is it possible to overeat to the glory of God? I can't see that it is possible, since overeating is a form of self-indulgence. Proverbs 13:25 says, *"The righteous eats to the satisfying of his soul."* We are entitled to satisfaction, but if we go beyond that—beyond meeting our legitimate needs—then we are being self-indulgent.

Thank You, Lord, for the blood of Jesus and the work of Your Holy Spirit. I proclaim that my body is a temple for the Holy Spirit, redeemed, cleansed, and sanctified by the blood of Jesus. My body belongs to God, and I intend to use it in a way that glorifies Him—including what I eat and drink. Amen.

Update 92 – July 2000 (audio)

"Fearfully and Wonderfully Made"

My body is a temple for the Holy Spirit, redeemed,
cleansed, and sanctified by the blood of Jesus.

In Psalm 139:13–14, David spoke to the Lord, saying,

For You formed my inward parts; You covered me in my mother's
womb. I will praise You, for I am fearfully and wonderfully made;
marvelous are Your works, and that my soul knows very well.

He was telling God, in other words, "You were there when I was still in my mother's womb; You were fashioning me together."

I wonder if we realize that we are fearfully and wonderfully made. When I think of what was involved in God creating my body and providing me with a body, I feel a sense of awe. I am fearfully and wonderfully made, and I have to give account to God for what I have done with the body He gave me.

We are so occupied with computers today—and they are really wonderful implements. But I want to point out that, by far, the most wonderful computers we will ever encounter are our own bodies. Many Christians give much more careful attention to their computers than they do their own bodies. After all, if a computer fails or crashes or becomes obsolete, with a little extra money, we can buy another. But when the human body fails, when that computer breaks down, that is the end. There is nothing more that can be done.

Thank You, Lord, for the blood of Jesus and the work of Your Holy Spirit. I proclaim with awe that I am fearfully and wonderfully made. My body is a temple for the Holy Spirit, redeemed, cleansed, and sanctified by the blood of Jesus. Amen.

Update 92 – July 2000 (audio)

The Importance of Diet

My body is a temple for the Holy Spirit, redeemed,
cleansed, and sanctified by the blood of Jesus.

Diet, or daily regimen, is a vital facet of life. Everybody follows a diet, whether he knows it or not. Various methods of dietary management are advocated, and among them is vegetarianism. I have met many people who are disposed to be vegetarians. I am not critical of them; I respect them. However, I think there are certain cautions they must keep in mind. Consider what Paul wrote:

> *Receive one who is weak in the faith, but not to disputes over doubt-ful things. For one believes he may eat all things, but he who is weak eats only vegetables. Let not him who eats despise him who does not eat, and let not him who does not eat judge him who eats; for God has received him.* (Romans 14:1–3)

Paul said that we should be careful about our attitudes toward other people. Regarding vegetarianism, he said of the one who eats only vegetables that his faith is weak, for he eschews meat as a means of trying to attain righteousness.

Then, there is another diet solution advocated and espoused by many people: abstaining completely from alcohol. But Scripture tells us that the Lord *"causes the grass to grow for the cattle, and vegetation for the service of man, that he may bring forth food from the earth, and wine that makes glad the heart of man, oil to make his face shine, and bread which strengthens man's heart"* (Psalm 104:14–15).

God brings forth from the earth various things for us to con-sume, including wine, which *"makes glad the heart of man."* Obviously, God does not demand that we be teetotalers.

Thank You, Lord, for the blood of Jesus and the work of Your Holy Spirit. I will glorify God even in what I eat and how often I do so. My body is a temple for the Holy Spirit, redeemed, cleansed, and sanctified by the blood of Jesus. Amen.

Update 92 – July 2000 (audio)

Cooperating with the Spirit

My body is a temple for the Holy Spirit, redeemed, cleansed, and sanctified by the blood of Jesus.

Now the Spirit expressly says that in latter times some will depart from the faith, giving heed to deceiving spirits and doctrines of demons, speaking lies in hypocrisy, having their own conscience seared with a hot iron, forbidding to marry, and commanding to abstain from foods which God created to be received with thanksgiving by those who believe and know the truth. For every creature of God [every kind of food] is good, and nothing is to be refused if it is received with thanksgiving; for it is sanctified by the word of God and prayer. (1 Timothy 4:1–5)

In this passage, Paul was saying, first of all, that abstaining from the marriage relationship (i.e., celibacy) is not an automatic condition of holiness; it does not necessarily lead to holiness. In fact, if we look at the history of the church, in cases where the clergy were required to be celibate, it is apparent that celibacy did not always produce holiness.

Regarding diets, what Paul was saying is, "Everything that God has created as food is good." But we have to bear in mind that the good food that God created may be corrupted by what we mix with it or the way we prepare it. So, take the time and effort to distinguish between things that are helpful and things that are harmful. Cooperate with the Holy Spirit.

Thank You, Lord, for the blood of Jesus and the work of Your Holy Spirit. I proclaim that I will cooperate with the Holy Spirit to distinguish what is helpful or harmful for my body, because it is a temple of the Holy Spirit, redeemed, cleansed, and sanctified by the blood of Jesus. Amen.

Update 92 – July 2000 (audio)

Taking Care of the Temple

*My body is a temple for the Holy Spirit, redeemed,
cleansed, and sanctified by the blood of Jesus.*

Scripture has led me to some practical conclusions regarding my body. I do not seek to impose these on anybody, but I have given a lot of care and prayer to this subject, and I have been prepared to make radical changes in my own lifestyle, if they are God's will.

My first conclusion, the basis of all the other conclusions, is that I must treat my body with reverence and attune to it as a temple of the Holy Spirit. Again, Paul said, *"Do you not know that your body is the temple of the Holy Spirit?"* (1 Corinthians 6:19). If we take this passage seriously, then we are going to deal with our bodies as with a temple, for that is what they are.

Suppose for a moment that God put us in charge of a material temple—a building of stone, timber, and glass. If we were conscientious, we would be concerned about looking after it—keeping it clean and free from dust, with no broken windows or clogged toilets. We would feel tremendous responsibility to keep that building in the best possible condition. As Christians, you and I have an even greater responsibility to keep our bodies, which are the temple of Holy Spirit, in the best possible condition, and we need to find out what is involved in doing that.

In his second letter to Timothy, Paul wrote, *"For God did not give us a spirit of timidity* [or fear], *but a spirit of power, of love and of self-discipline"* (2 Timothy 1:7 NIV). We see here that the Holy Spirit is a Spirit of self-discipline. But there is a subtle balance: He won't discipline us if we are not willing to be disciplined. If we seek the help of the Holy Spirit in cultivating self-discipline, He will help us.

Thank You, Lord, for the blood of Jesus and the work of Your Holy Spirit. I will seek the help of the Holy Spirit in cultivating self-discipline to keep my body in the best possible condition, for it is a temple of the Holy Spirit, redeemed, cleansed, and sanctified by the blood of Jesus. Amen.

Update 92 – July 2000 (audio)

Radical Obedience

*My body is a temple for the Holy Spirit, redeemed,
cleansed, and sanctified by the blood of Jesus.*

In making this confession, we need to be radical. Christianity is a radical religion. The word *radical* means "dealing with the root." When John the Baptist introduced the gospel and Jesus, he said, *"And even now the ax is laid to the root of the trees. Therefore every tree which does not bear good fruit is cut down and thrown into the fire"* (Matthew 3:10). God is not going to lop off a few branches or even cut off the trunk. He is going to go straight to the root. He requires that a tree bring forth good fruit. If a tree does not bring forth good fruit, God says to chop it down.

Among the younger generation, there is a tendency to be pretty radical. I think this inclination needs to be encouraged—in the right direction. To be honest, we older generations have often compromised rather than be radical. We need to cooperate with the Holy Spirit, who often calls for apparently radical things.

> *But if the Spirit of Him who raised Jesus from the dead dwells in you, He who raised Christ from the dead will also give life to your mortal bodies through His Spirit who dwells in you.*
>
> (Romans 8:11)

Paul was making a remarkable statement here. He said that it was the Holy Spirit, the Spirit of God, who raised the dead body of Jesus from the tomb. And if you have that same Holy Spirit in your body, then He can do much that you need in your body through His power. What a radical truth!

Thank You, Lord, for the blood of Jesus and the work of Your Holy Spirit. I proclaim that I will pursue radical obedience in cooperating with the Holy Spirit, because my body is a temple for the Holy Spirit, redeemed, cleansed, and sanctified by the blood of Jesus.
Amen.

Update 92 – July 2000 (audio)

Finishing His Work

My body is a temple for the Holy Spirit, redeemed,
cleansed, and sanctified by the blood of Jesus.

Here are a few suggestions regarding how to treat your body as a temple for the Holy Spirit.

First of all, treat your body with reverence because it is a temple of the Holy Spirit, whom we revere. Among contemporary Christians, I find there is very little reverence for the body.

Second, seek the help of the Holy Spirit in cultivating self-discipline.

Third, take the time and make the effort to distinguish between that which is helpful and that which is harmful.

Fourth, be willing to be radical because your life is at stake.

Fifth, seek to cooperate with the Holy Spirit.

There are many other steps I could add to this list, but these I have acquired through experience. I was challenged by the Lord to consider whether I was leading a life of self-indulgence. I was challenged by the Lord to consider these questions: Do I want to go on living? Do I want to finish my assigned task? Jesus said to His disciples, *"My food is to do the will of Him who sent Me, and to finish His work"* (John 4:34).

That is the best diet: to do the will of Him who sent us—and to finish His work. Even after spending more than fifty years in the Lord's service, I believed there were certain tasks assigned to me by God that I had not yet fulfilled. I never took it for granted that I would fulfill them. I always took care of my body, knowing the importance of keeping myself in good physical condition so my life would not be cut short before I had finished God's work.

Thank You, Lord, for the blood of Jesus and the work of Your Holy Spirit. I proclaim that I will cooperate with the Holy Spirit, keeping myself in good physical condition to finish His work. My body is a temple of the Holy Spirit, redeemed, cleansed, and sanctified by the blood of Jesus. Amen.

Update 92 – July 2000 (audio)

My members, the parts of my body, are instruments of righteousness, yielded to God for His service and for His glory.

Do not present your members as instruments of unrighteousness to sin, but present yourselves to God as being alive from the dead, and your members as instruments of righteousness to God.

—Romans 6:13

Presenting Ourselves to God

My members, the parts of my body, are instruments of
righteousness, yielded to God for His service and for His glory.

God's solution for the old nature can be summed up in one word: *execution*. Execution is what took place on the cross, when Jesus died and our old man was crucified with Him. How do we apply God's solution in our own lives?

> *Therefore do not let sin reign in your mortal body that you should obey its lusts, and do not go on presenting the members of your body to sin as instruments of unrighteousness; but present yourselves to God as those alive from the dead, and your members as instruments of righteousness to God. For sin shall not be master over you, for you are not under law, but under grace.* (Romans 6:12–14 NASB)

Paul's instructions can be followed only by those who have put their faith in Jesus and accepted His substitutionary sacrifice on their behalf. Someone once said, "If you ever want to get to heaven, you've got to learn to say no." That is certainly the truth. Paul said that we must make up our minds and take a firm stand against sin. Both sin and Satan can tell the difference between when we are just saying words and when we really mean them. We must proclaim these words with conviction. Then, through faith in Jesus, our wills are liberated from the dominion of sin. It then becomes our responsibility to exercise our wills aright. God is not going to do that for us. This is the point at which we have to recognize our responsibility to monitor our wills.

Thank You, Jesus, for Your victory on the cross. I take a stand now and proclaim that sin and Satan have no claim and no power over me. I proclaim that my members, the parts of my body, are instruments of righteousness, yielded to God for His service and for His glory.
Amen.

The Roman Pilgrimage, Vol. 2: Romans 6:23–7:16 (audio, video)

Declaring God's Word

Release from Torment

My members, the parts of my body, are instruments of
righteousness, yielded to God for His service and for His glory.

For several years, while I was a pastor in London, I had a tremendous struggle against depression that would come over me, weigh upon me, and shut me in. It gave me a sense of hopelessness and failure. Maybe you can identify with this. I fought this situation in every way that I knew, but I made no progress. Then, I came across Isaiah 61:3: *"To console those who mourn in Zion, to give them...the garment of praise for the spirit of heaviness."*

As I read those words, the Holy Spirit showed me, "That's your problem!" It was like a flood of light coming in. I realized I was not fighting against myself but another being—an evil spirit that was tormenting and oppressing me. When I realized that, I was probably 80 percent of the way to victory. I actually needed only one other Scripture: *"Whoever calls on the name of the LORD shall be saved ["delivered" KJV]"* (Joel 2:32).

Putting those two Scriptures together, I prayed, "God, You've shown me that I'm oppressed by a spirit of heaviness. I come to You now, calling on the name of the Lord Jesus. Deliver me." He liberated my mind from that oppressing spirit.

Now, it was up to me to reprogram my own mind. I had habitually negative thought patterns, which God showed me to be a denial of my faith in Jesus. It was up to me to retrain my mind. Over a period of several years, every time a negative, pessimistic thought came to me, I would reject it, replacing it with a positive confession from Scripture. Several years later, my whole inner working had changed completely. I was a totally different person.

Thank You, Jesus, for Your victory on the cross. I proclaim that I have been released from all torment, and that my members, the parts of my body, are instruments of righteousness, yielded to God for His service and for His glory. Amen.

The Roman Pilgrimage, Vol. 2: Romans 6:23–7:16 (audio, video)

MARCH 7

Yielded to God

My members, the parts of my body, are instruments of
righteousness, yielded to God for His service and for His glory.

Paul said, *"Do not let sin reign in your mortal body that you should obey its lusts, and do not go on presenting your members to sin as instruments of unrighteousness; but present yourselves to God as those alive from the dead, and your members as instruments of righteousness to God"* (Romans 6:12–13 NASB). We have been set free. Sin must not control our hands, our feet, or our tongues. On the contrary, Paul said, we should yield ourselves to God and our members as instruments of righteousness to God. There's a double yielding.

First, we yield our wills to God by saying, "Not my will, but Yours, be done." In the Lord's Prayer, the second petition is, *"Your will be done on earth as it is in heaven"* (Matthew 6:10). When we pray "Your will be done," it begins with the will of the one who is praying—one who wills for God's will to be done.

Once we have yielded our wills, we then yield our physical members to God as instruments of righteousness. In Greek, the word *"instruments"* literally means "weapons," implying spiritual conflict. These are not just any instruments, like a hoe or plow—they are fighting instruments, like a sword.

The baptism in the Holy Spirit is key because in that experience we first yield our wills to God; we then yield the one unruly member that we are powerless to control: the tongue. When we are baptized in the Holy Spirit, we actually fulfill the instruction to yield our members to God as instruments (weapons) of righteousness. Certainly, when the tongue has been yielded to God and taken over by the Holy Spirit, it becomes a weapon: in prayer, in testimony, and in preaching.

Thank You, Jesus, for Your victory on the cross. I yield myself and my will to God, proclaiming that my members, the parts of my body, are instruments of righteousness, yielded to God for His service and for His glory. Amen.

The Roman Pilgrimage, Vol. 2: Romans 6:23–7:16 (audio, video)

Moving Forward

My members, the parts of my body, are instruments of
righteousness, yielded to God for His service and for His glory.

W e have a choice to make. Something is going to control us.
Which will it be: sin or righteousness? If we say righteousness,
we can believe we will be tested! The devil will not give up as long as
he thinks he has a chance of succeeding.

When an individual is tested and tempted, the devil will go on
until that person has come to the place where the temptation just
doesn't affect him. He does not even entertain the thought. The devil
is clever enough not to waste his time on people like that. But if any
double-mindedness exists in us, the devil will exploit it. We must
make a firm decision.

> *I am speaking in human terms because of the weakness of your*
> *flesh. For...you presented your members as slaves to impurity and*
> *to lawlessness, resulting in further lawlessness.*
>
> (Romans 6:19 NASB)

If we choose lawlessness, it will increase. We will become more
and more lawless. Many of us can trace that reality in our lives.

Instead of increasing in lawlessness, *"now present your members*
as slaves to righteousness, resulting in sanctification [holiness]*"* (verse 19
NASB).

It is almost impossible to stand still in the spiritual life. We are
either going to go forward or backward. We are either going to progress in holiness or go further into rebellion.

Thank You, Jesus, for Your victory on the cross. I present myself as a
slave to righteousness and proclaim that my members, the parts of my
body, are instruments of righteousness, yielded to God for His service
and for His glory. Amen.

The Roman Pilgrimage, Vol. 2: Romans 6:23–7:16 (audio, video)

Choosing Grace

*My members, the parts of my body, are instruments of
righteousness, yielded to God for His service and for His glory.*

*I beseech you therefore, brethren, by the mercies of God, that you
present your bodies a living sacrifice, holy, acceptable to God.*
(Romans 12:1)

It is a question of setting our wills, then yielding—in that order. If
we don't *will*, then, by habit, we will yield to the wrong thing. We
must stop presenting our bodies, our members, to sin. When we were
still unbelievers, we did just that for a long while. But we have to stop
and say, "That's the end of that!" Once we yield our wills to God, we
don't have to yield our members to Satan.

*"For sin shall not have dominion over you, for you are not under law
but under grace"* (Romans 6:14). The implications of this statement are
far-reaching. Paul said that we are not under law but under grace. It
is either one or the other—it cannot be both at the same time. If we
are under law, we are not under grace. If we are under grace, we are
not under law.

Moreover, Paul said that sin shall not have dominion over us, for
we are not under the law. The corollary is that if we are under the law,
sin *will* have dominion over us. That is a shocking statement to many
people, but that is what the Bible consistently says.

We are not governed by a set of rules. We have become sons of
God, and we obey Him because we love Him. From now on, love, not
fear, is our motivation for obedience. God does not make us slaves;
the Law does that. God makes us His sons and daughters. We have to
choose the Law or God's grace.

Thank You, Jesus, for Your victory on the cross. I choose grace and
yield my will to God, proclaiming that my members, the parts of my
body, are instruments of righteousness, yielded to God for His service
and for His glory. Amen.

The Roman Pilgrimage, Vol. 2: Romans 6:23–7:16 (audio, video)

Whom Will We Serve?

My members, the parts of my body, are instruments of righteousness, yielded to God for His service and for His glory.

> *Do you not know that to whom you present yourselves slaves to obey, you are that one's slaves whom you obey, whether of sin leading to death, or of obedience leading to righteousness?*
> (Romans 6:16)

Paul said that when we yield ourselves to someone, we become slaves of the one we obey. If we yield to, let's say, immorality, we become slaves of immorality. We cannot yield to sin without becoming its slaves. Thus, we must decide to whom and to what we want to yield. Some of us don't like choices, but in the spiritual life, we cannot avoid them.

At the end of his career, Joshua gave Israel a choice:

> *Now therefore, fear the LORD, serve Him in sincerity and in truth....And if it seems evil to you to serve the LORD, choose for yourselves this day whom you will serve, whether the gods which your fathers served that were on the other side of the River, or the gods of the Amorites, in whose land you dwell. But as for me and my house, we will serve the LORD.* (Joshua 24:14–15)

Joshua challenged the Israelites to make a choice, and this choice has never changed. It is not *whether* we will serve; it is *whom* we will serve. Serve we will. Before we were redeemed, we had no choice. We could not keep from sinning; there was no other option but to be slaves to sin and servants of Satan. After we experience redemption through faith in Jesus Christ, though, we have another option: we can choose to serve God and be "slaves" to righteousness.

Thank You, Jesus, for Your victory on the cross. I choose to serve the Lord, and I proclaim that my members, the parts of my body, are instruments of righteousness, yielded to God for His service and for His glory. Amen.

The Roman Pilgrimage, Vol. 2: Romans 6:23–7:16 (audio, video)

My Body Is for the Lord

My members, the parts of my body, are instruments of
righteousness, yielded to God for His service and for His glory.

Present yourselves to God as being alive from the dead, and your
members as instruments of righteousness to God. (Romans 6:13)

We give our physical members to God and say, "God, You use them." Then, we also have to keep the temple holy. Paul wrote, *"Now the body is not for sexual immorality but for the Lord, and the Lord for the body"* (1 Corinthians 6:13). Today, we call sexual immorality "premarital sex." But God has not changed His estimate of this sin. The body is not for premarital sex; the body is for the Lord. And then, *"the Lord* [is] *for the body,"* too. Isn't that wonderful? If we give our bodies to the Lord, then the Lord is for our bodies.

Paul was a down-to-earth man who talked to people about things that really concerned them. He continued, *"Flee sexual immorality. Every sin that a man does is outside the body, but he who commits sexual immorality sins against his own body"* (verse 18).

Many people interpret this passage as a warning about sexually transmitted diseases, such as HIV, gonorrhea, or syphilis. These may certainly be consequences of sexual immorality, but Paul's teaching means much more than that. We endanger the health of our bodies when we commit any kind of immorality. Many times when Christians seek healing and do not receive it, the root cause is immorality. In most cases, God demands that we go to the root cause, repent of it, and set it aright before we can receive healing from Him.

Thank You, Jesus, for Your victory on the cross. I give my body to the Lord, proclaiming that my members, the parts of my body, are instruments of righteousness, yielded to God for His service and for His glory. Amen.

Who Am I?: Why You Have a Body (audio)

I overcome Satan by the blood of the Lamb and the word of my testimony, and I do not love my life to the death.

They overcame him [Satan] by the blood of the Lamb and by the word of their testimony, and they did not love their lives to the death.

—Revelation 12:11

Resurrection Life

I overcome Satan by the blood of the Lamb and the word of my testimony, and I do not love my life to the death.

Leviticus 17:11 says, *"The life of the flesh is in the blood."* When Jesus poured out His blood, He poured out His life. As I understand it, the life of God was released into the universe. And no mind can really comprehend the fullness of what that means.

> *Then Jesus said to them, "Most assuredly* [of utmost importance], *I say to you, unless you eat the flesh of the Son of Man and drink His blood, you have no life in you. Whoever eats My flesh and drinks My blood has eternal life, and I will raise him up at the last day."* (John 6:53–54)

Bear in mind that our redemption is not complete until the resurrection. In Philippians 3:12, Paul said, *"Not that I have already attained, or am already perfected; but I press on, that I may lay hold of that for which Christ Jesus has also laid hold of me,"* which is *"the resurrection from the dead"* (verse 11).

Some people have the impression that their bodies are not very important. But God says our bodies are very important—they are temples for the Holy Spirit. They are *"fearfully and wonderfully made"* (Psalm 139:14). And God is not going to leave our bodies in a state of decay. He is going to resurrect them with glory like that of Jesus. Redemption is the full outworking of Jesus' sacrifice, and it is consummated by the resurrection.

Thank You, Lord, for the blood of the Lamb. Like Paul, *"I press on...that I may attain to the resurrection from the dead."* I proclaim that I overcome Satan by the blood of the Lamb and the word of my testimony, and I do not love my life to the death. Amen.

The Fullness of the Cross, Vol. 4: The Sevenfold Power of the Blood (audio)

The Glory to Be Revealed

*I overcome Satan by the blood of the Lamb and the word of my
testimony, and I do not love my life to the death.*

> *For I consider that the sufferings of this present time are not worthy
> to be compared with the glory which shall be revealed in us* [at the
> resurrection]. *For the earnest expectation of the creation eagerly
> waits for the revealing of the sons of God.* (Romans 8:18–19)

Many Christians do not seem to grasp the significance of Christ's
resurrection for us. The sons of God are revealed at the resurrection; all of creation is waiting expectantly for it on tiptoe. The trees, seas,
rivers, and mountains are all waiting. It is extraordinary that creation
has so much excitement—and that much of the church has so little.

> *For the creation was subjected to futility, not willingly, but
> because of Him who subjected it in hope; because the creation
> itself also will be delivered from the bondage of corruption into
> the glorious liberty of the children of God.* (verses 20–21)

The entirety of creation suffered because of man's sin. Before
man sinned, there were no thorns and thistles; nothing ever died
or rotted. And we see that we're not the only ones who are going to
come into a glorious resurrection; creation is, too. However, God has
assigned this priority: creation does not come in until we come in. As
Paul wrote, *"For we know that the whole creation groans and labors with
birth pangs together until now"* (verse 22).

Paul often used the phrase "we know," yet most contemporary
Christians *don't* know. Do we know that the whole creation is in labor
pains, waiting for the revelation of the sons of God, the birth of a new
age, and deliverance from corruption?

Thank You, Lord, for the blood of the Lamb. I proclaim that I am
coming into the glory destined for the sons of God. I overcome Satan
by the blood of the Lamb and the word of my testimony, and I do
not love my life to the death. Amen.

The Fullness of the Cross, Vol. 4: The Sevenfold Power of the Blood (audio)

The Blood of Jesus

*I overcome Satan by the blood of the Lamb and the word of my
testimony, and I do not love my life to the death.*

Four times in John 6, Jesus said about the believer, *"I will raise him
up at the last day."* (See verses 39, 40, 44, and 54.) Resurrection is a
part of salvation.

> *Whoever eats My flesh and drinks My blood has eternal life, and
> I will raise him up at the last day. For My flesh is food indeed*
> [true food], *and My blood is drink indeed* [true drink]. *He who
> eats My flesh and drinks My blood abides in Me, and I in him.*
> (John 6:54–56)

The words *eats*, *drinks*, and *abides* are in the continuing present
tense: "He who continually feeds on My flesh, and continually drinks
My blood, continually abides in Me and I in him."

It is very clear that the Lord attaches tremendous importance
to feeding on His flesh and drinking His blood. I am not the final
authority, but I really believe He is talking about the sacrament of the
Lord's Supper, or Communion.

At one time, I lived in an Arab town with Arab Christians. When
they took the Lord's Supper, they said, "Let us drink the blood of
Jesus." I believe those Arab Christians got the right picture. Drinking
the blood of Jesus is Communion.

Something in us says, "I don't like the thought of drinking blood."
I remember that it took me years to come to grips with this statement. But to have eternal life, we have to drink Jesus' blood and feed
on His flesh.

Thank You, Lord, for the blood of the Lamb. I partake of His eternal
life by drinking His blood and feeding on His flesh, and I proclaim
that I overcome Satan by the blood of the Lamb and by the word of
my testimony, and I do not love my life to the death. Amen.

The Fullness of the Cross: The Sevenfold Power of the Blood (audio)

Declaring God's Word

The Importance of Communion

I overcome Satan by the blood of the Lamb and the word of my testimony, and I do not love my life to the death.

We have noted that the life is in the blood. (See Leviticus 17:11.) If we want the life, we must appropriate the blood. We do that by taking Communion, as well as by the word of our testimony.

To me, this matter of taking Communion has become extremely important. Paul quoted Jesus in 1 Corinthians 11:25, saying, *"This do, as often as you drink it, in remembrance of Me."* Many churches think that says, "As seldom as you do it." Some of the most beautiful services I have ever attended were liturgical Communion services; they were so beautiful because they held on to that fact.

At one point, my wife, Ruth, and I came to the conclusion that we were not taking Communion as often as we should. As the priest of our home, I decided we would have Communion every morning during our time with the Lord. I am not saying that every Christian should do this, but I am thankful that we did. We would have felt that something had dropped out of our lives if we had omitted it.

Every day, when we took Communion, we would say, "We receive this bread as Your flesh, Lord, and this wine as Your blood." I would do this in a simple, specific way, saying, "Lord, we are doing this in remembrance of You; we are proclaiming Your death until You come." In Communion, we have no past but the cross, no future but the coming. We do it in remembrance of the cross until Jesus comes. Let this compel us to consider whether we are really availing ourselves of the life that is in the blood.

Thank You, Lord, for the blood of the Lamb. I avail myself of the life that is in the blood through Communion, and I proclaim that I overcome Satan by the blood of the Lamb and by the word of my testimony, and I do not love my life to the death. Amen.

The Fullness of the Cross, Vol. 4: The Sevenfold Power of the Blood (audio)

Laying Down Our Lives

I overcome Satan by the blood of the Lamb and the word of my testimony, and I do not love my life to the death.

In order to experience the full effects of the blood of Jesus, we need to know how to appropriate His blood. Today's Scripture and our confession for this week refer to a great end-time conflict that involves both heaven and earth—the angels of God, Satan and his angels, and God's believing people on earth. The statement is made by God's angels: *"They overcame him by the blood of the Lamb and by the word of their testimony, and they did not love their lives to the death"* (Revelation 12:11).

"They" are people like you and me, believers in Jesus Christ. *"Him"* refers to Satan. There is a direct conflict between us and Satan; there is no one in between. This verse tells us how the believers overcame him, further describing them as committed—totally committed. A committed Christian is the only kind that frightens Satan. When it says *"they did not love not their lives to the death,"* it means that staying alive was not their first priority. Priority number one was to be faithful to the Lord and to do His will.

When talking about "soldiers in the Lord's army," many of us have a vague and sentimental idea about what that means. When I was a soldier in the British army, I did not receive a certificate from the commanding officer guaranteeing that I would not lose my life. Any soldier knows he may be killed; serving may cost his life. It is the same in the Lord's army. There is no guarantee that we will not have to lay down our lives. The people Satan fears are those who are not afraid to lay down their lives. After all, this life is brief compared with life eternal.

Thank You, Lord, for the blood of the Lamb. I proclaim that "staying alive" is not my first priority, and also that I overcome Satan by the blood of the Lamb and the word of my testimony, and I do not love my life to the death. Amen.

How to Apply the Blood (audio)

MARCH 17

The Weapons of Our Warfare

I overcome Satan by the blood of the Lamb and the word of my testimony, and I do not love my life to the death.

In Revelation 12:7–9, we see that heaven has been purged of the dragon (Satan) and his angels. Rejoice, heaven; look out, earth! Now the devil is right down here on earth, and he knows he has only a few short years to do mischief and cause harm. It is clear to me that this period is closely related to all (or part) of the seventieth week of Daniel. (See Daniel 9:21–24.) It is a specific time period—one that the devil, who is a student of prophecy, knows well. And Jesus has said those days will be cut short. (See, for example, Matthew 24:21–22.) Though theoretically the Bible says three and a half years, there will be at least a few "days" taken off at the end. Then, the devil will be bound and imprisoned in the bottomless pit.

The devil wants to keep us ignorant of this fact, because as long we are ignorant, we cannot do what God has appointed. But God has given us the spiritual weapons to cast down Satan from his place in the heavenlies.

> *For the weapons of our warfare are not carnal but are mighty in God for pulling down strongholds, casting down arguments ["imaginations" KJV] and every high thing that exalts itself against the knowledge of God.* (2 Corinthians 10:4–5)

The spiritual weapons given to us will enable us to cast down every high thing that opposes God and His kingdom. The last, ultimate, supreme high thing that opposes God is Satan's kingdom in the heavenlies. To us are committed the weapons that will enable us to defeat it: the blood of Jesus and the word of our testimony.

Thank You, Lord, for the blood of the Lamb. I take it up as a spiritual weapon, along with my testimony, proclaiming that I overcome Satan by the blood of the Lamb and the word of my testimony, and I do not love my life to the death. Amen.

Praying to Change History: God's Atomic Weapon—The Blood of Jesus (audio)

Confessing Faith

I overcome Satan by the blood of the Lamb and the word of my testimony, and I do not love my life to the death.

The Lord has showed me that many Christians, if they looked back on their pasts, would admit to having made a series of negative confessions. You may have talked about what you couldn't do or discussed your failures and disappointments. But, you see, our confessions determine where we go.

There is a vivid example of this truth in the story of the twelve spies Moses sent into the Promised Land. Two came back with positive confessions, ten with negative ones. The majority of the Israelites believed the negative confession, "We cannot." The positive confession was, "We are well able." All the Israelites settled their destinies by their confession. Those who said, "We cannot" could not. And those who said, "We are well able" were well able.

You may have uttered some negative words, spoken statements that did not glorify Jesus, or dwelled on disappointments that only tied you to impotence or failure. If we confess failure, failure will be our portion. If we confess faith, God will be our portion. Just confess to God, "Lord, I'm sorry. I've tied Your hands; because of my unbelief and negative thinking, I have limited what You could do in my life." Scripture says, *"If we confess our sins, He is faithful and just to forgive us our sins and to cleanse us from all unrighteousness"* (1 John 1:9).

When you've rejected negative confessions, thank God that you've come out of that dark, lonely valley. Say, "I can do all things through Christ who empowers me within," which is the literal translation of Philippians 4:13.

Thank You, Lord, for the blood of the Lamb. I proclaim that *"I can do all things through Christ who empowers me within,"* and that I overcome Satan by the blood of the Lamb and by the word of my testimony, and I do not love my life to the death. Amen.

What Is Holiness?, Vol. 2: Treat Your Body as God's Temple (audio)

WEEK 12:

My body is for the Lord, and the Lord is for my body.

Foods for the stomach and the stomach for foods, but God will destroy both it and them. Now the body is not for sexual immorality but for the Lord, and the Lord for the body.

—1 Corinthians 6:13

A Personal God

My body is for the Lord, and the Lord is for my body.

I was once a professor at Britain's largest university, and I held various degrees and academic distinctions. In many ways, I was quite sophisticated—intellectually. But I do not feel in any way intellectually inferior to say I believe the Bible's record of creation. Prior to believing the Bible, I studied many other sources that attempted to explain man's origin, but I found them unsatisfying. In many cases, they contradicted one another. I then turned to study the Bible—not as a believer but as a professional philosopher. I thought to myself, *At least it can't be any sillier than some of the other things I've heard!* To my astonishment, I discovered that the Bible had the answer.

In Genesis, we read a short, simple statement. It begins, *"The* LORD *God"*—that is, "Jehovah God"—God's personal name. This term tells us that a personal God formed a personal man for personal fellowship.

> *The* LORD *God formed* [molded] *man of the dust of the ground, and breathed into his nostrils the breath of life; and man became a living being* [soul]. (Genesis 2:7)

Here we see the union of God's divine, eternal breath from above with the body of clay from beneath, molded by the hands of the Creator. The union of spirit from above and clay from beneath produced a living human personality—one that can have fellowship with the living, personal God.

Thank You, Lord, for Your provision for my body. I proclaim that a
personal God created me for personal fellowship—and that my body
is for the Lord, and the Lord is for my body. Amen.

Bible Psychology: What God's Mirror Reveals: God's Provision for the Believer's Body (audio)

A Miraculous Creation

My body is for the Lord, and the Lord is for my body.

We know about the inner personality of man—his spirit and soul—but let us not be blind to the fact that man's body is also a miraculous and marvelous creation of God. Many believers do not sufficiently value or care for their own bodies. Until the breath of God entered that clay form, it was just clay—nothing more. It became a living, functioning physical body with all its organisms, parts, and members through the miraculous operation of the Spirit of God.

Consider the human eye. On one particular telecast, the American Society of Ophthalmologists presented some fascinating information. If I remember correctly, they said one human eye contains more than three million working parts. What brought that into being? The breath of God. All our muscles, nerves, and glands—all the functions of our physical bodies—owe their origin to the inbreathed breath of God. That is what transformed the clay into a marvelous physical organism. When you grasp that truth, the miracles of divine healing become logical. Who can better repair, restore, and, if need be, recreate the body than the same Agent who initially formed it? The Spirit of God is the Creator and Healer.

I have been privileged to witness creative miracles of God whereby missing bones were restored. I once asked for prayer on behalf of a little girl in San Jose, California, whose elder sister was born with a bone missing from the upper part of both legs. As a result of prayer, God created the bones. I don't claim that it's simple, but it is fathomable when you understand the origin of the human body. It was just a clay form until the Spirit of God moved upon it and produced a complex organism that its Creator can heal.

Thank You, Lord, for Your provision for my body. I am a miraculous and marvelous creation of God, and I proclaim that my body is for the Lord, and the Lord is for my body. Amen.

Bible Psychology: What God's Mirror Reveals: God's Provision for the Believer's Body (audio)

MARCH 21

An Intricate Unity

My body is for the Lord, and the Lord is for my body.

Looking at the book of Job, we see some tremendous revelations about the body. In many ways, there's a wonderful interrelationship between the books of Genesis and Job. Job 10:8–12 is a beautiful summation of God's creative work in our bodies. Verse 8 reads, *"Your hands have made me and fashioned me, an intricate unity."*

As in Genesis 2:7, where the word *"formed"* indicates a skillful work that results from great care, so the book of Job emphasizes the immeasurable skill and care that God devoted to forming the human body:

> *Your hands have made me and fashioned me, an intricate unity; yet You would destroy me. Remember, I pray, that You have made me like clay. And will You turn me into dust again? Did You not pour me out like milk, and curdle me like cheese, clothe me with skin and flesh, and knit me together with bones and sinews?*
> (Job 10:8–11)

What a vivid expression! What a beautiful picture of the interrelationship of the various primary parts of the body. We read on in verse 12, *"You have granted me life and favor, and Your care ["visitation" KJV] has preserved my spirit."*

Later on in Job, we have the other aspect—the spiritual part—of man's nature: *"But there is a spirit in man, and the breath ["inspiration" KJV] of the Almighty gives him understanding"* (Job 32:8).

These words from Job are in perfect accord with those from Genesis. It is the union of the breath of God from above with the clay from beneath that brings into being a total human personality.

Thank You, Lord, for Your provision for my body. I am the union of the breath of God from above with the clay from beneath—and I proclaim that my body is for the Lord, and the Lord is for my body. Amen.

Bible Psychology: What God's Mirror Reveals: God's Provision for the Believer's Body (audio)

God's Blueprint

My body is for the Lord, and the Lord is for my body.

For You formed my inward parts; You covered me in my mother's womb. I will praise You, for I am fearfully and wonderfully made; marvelous are Your works, and that my soul knows very well. My frame was not hidden from You, when I was made in secret, and skillfully wrought in the lowest parts of the earth.

(Psalm 139:13–15)

When I consider the physical body, I am filled with a sense of awe. The substance that eventually became my body was planned and formed by God in the earth long before it ever entered my body. God had appointed the substance that would one day constitute my body.

Your eyes saw my substance, being yet unformed. And in Your book they ["my members" KJV] all were written, the days fashioned for me, when as yet there were none of them. (verse 16)

God had a blueprint for our bodies before they ever came into being. Compare this verse to what Jesus said in Luke 12:7: *"But the very hairs of your head are all numbered. Do not fear therefore; you are of more value than many sparrows."* This statement shows the depth of God's concern for our physical bodies—He has even numbered the hairs on our heads. When we realize this, we must acknowledge that God also has a purpose for this marvelous workmanship, which is revealed in 1 Corinthians 6:19–20: *"Or do you not know that your body is the temple of the Holy Spirit who is in you, whom you have from God, and you are not your own? For you were bought at a price; therefore glorify God in your body and in your spirit, which are God's."*

Thank You, Lord, for Your provision for my body. I will glorify God in my body, and I proclaim that my body is for the Lord, and the Lord is for my body. Amen.

Bible Psychology: What God's Mirror Reveals: God's Provision for the Believer's Body (audio)

MARCH 23

A Living Sacrifice

My body is for the Lord, and the Lord is for my body.

I urge you therefore, brethren, by the mercies of God, to present your bodies a living and holy sacrifice, acceptable to God, which is your spiritual service of worship. (Romans 12:1 NASB)

In the early chapters of Romans, we are confronted with tremendous theology. The application starts with our bodies: we are to present our bodies to God as a living sacrifice.

We might think, *The body isn't so important; it's really the soul that is important.* But let's use a practical analogy: If I asked for a glass of water, I would get both the vessel and its contents. I could not get the water without the glass. That is what God is saying. He wants the vessel, the body—and its contents, the soul. We cannot give the contents without the vessel.

What does it mean to make our bodies *"a living...sacrifice"*? The sacrifices of the Old Testament were animals that were killed, then placed on the altar. God says, "I want *your* body just as completely as the Old Testament sacrifices, but with one difference. I don't want your body dead but living. When I have your body, I have you."

In Matthew 23, Jesus was talking to the Pharisees, explaining what things really mattered in their service to God. They said the offering was more important than the altar. Jesus said, *"You blind men, which is more important, the offering or the altar that sanctifies the offering?"* (Matthew 23:19 NASB). The altar sanctifies the offering that is placed upon it. The offering is made holy by being placed upon God's altar. That is how it is with our bodies. When we place our bodies on God's altar, they become holy. They are sanctified, set apart to God. It is an act each of us has to make.

Thank You, Lord, for Your provision for my body. I present myself to God as a living sacrifice, and I proclaim that my body is for the Lord, and the Lord is for my body. Amen.

How to Find God's Plan for Your Life (audio)

DECLARING GOD'S WORD

A Body of Humiliation

My body is for the Lord, and the Lord is for my body.

When man rebelled against God, his whole personality was affected. The word used in Scripture to describe this condition is *corrupt*. Every area of human personality is affected—spiritual, moral, and physical. Death is at the end of physical corruption. Paul said, *"Through one man sin entered the world, and death through sin, and thus death spread to all men, because all sinned"* (Romans 5:12). Through sin, the poison of corruption entered us. First Corinthians 15:56 tells us, *"The sting of death is sin."* Just as a bee or a wasp introduces its poison into a body with its sting, so Satan introduced the poison of corruption and death through the sting of sin.

We have all become corrupt creatures. In Philippians 3:21, Paul called our present physical state *"the body of our humiliation"* (AMP). We are humiliated because we have rebelled against our Creator. No matter how elegant, healthy, strong, wealthy, or famous we are, we live in bodies of humiliation. We may eat the finest meals and drink the tastiest beverages, but we will still have to use the toilet. We may be strong and healthy, but when we get really warmed up, we start to sweat. Whether wealthy or poor, we all sweat. These built-in bodily functions remind us that we are all rebels and transgressors whose bodies are consequently subject to corruption.

I spent five years training African teachers, and I was interested in their athletic abilities. I would tell these strong young men, "Just bear in mind, one little anopheles mosquito can come along and insert his proboscis into you, and you will be a shivering, fever-wracked mess." That is our body of humiliation. The good news is that Jesus died to redeem us—and not just our souls. He redeemed the whole man—body, soul, and spirit.

Thank You, Lord, for Your provision for my body. I proclaim that Jesus died to redeem me in totality. Therefore, my body is for the Lord, and the Lord is for my body. Amen.

God's Plan for Your Body (audio)

Healing for the Body

My body is for the Lord, and the Lord is for my body.

Scripture says that Jesus *"Himself bore our sins in His own body on the tree, that we, having died to sins, might live for righteousness; by whose stripes you were healed"* (1 Peter 2:24).

On the cross, Jesus took our sins in His own body, which became the sin offering. He took the curse that we deserved upon Himself in His body on the cross that we might be released from sin. The Scripture also says, *"He Himself took our infirmities and bore our sicknesses"* (Matthew 8:17) in His own body, that by His wounds we might be healed. (See 1 Peter 2:24 NASB, NIV.) As far as God is concerned, our release from sin is already accomplished. As far as God is concerned, it is already done.

It is interesting to note that the New Testament does not put healing in the future, but in the past. We have been healed ever since the death of Jesus, *"by whose stripes you **were** healed"* (emphasis added). Healing has already been provided. Christians sometimes ask me, "How can I know if it's God's will for me to be healed?" I usually answer, "If you are a committed Christian, redeemed by the blood of Jesus, I think you're asking the wrong question. The question is not, 'How can I know if it's God's will for me to be healed?' The question is, 'How can I appropriate the healing that God has already provided for me?'" God's purpose is to preserve the whole of us: spirit, soul, and body, as Paul said, *"Now may the God of peace Himself sanctify you completely* [make you completely holy]; *and may your whole spirit, soul, and body be preserved blameless at the coming of our Lord Jesus Christ"* (1 Thessalonians 5:23).

Thank You, Lord, for Your provision for my body. I proclaim that by the death of Jesus on the cross, I was forgiven and healed, and God's purpose is to preserve the whole of me—spirit, soul, and body. My body is for the Lord, and the Lord is for my body. Amen.

God's Plan for Your Body (audio)

The Lord will not forsake His people.

The LORD will not forsake His people, for His great name's sake, because it has pleased the LORD to make you His people.

—1 Samuel 12:22

God Is Present

The Lord will not forsake His people.

God promised Abraham and Jacob that their descendants would be like the sand on the seashore. That is such a vivid picture of Israel throughout the last two thousand years of history. The waves have continually beaten upon them. The rage of men and demons—and Satan himself—has unleashed countless onslaughts against the Jewish people in many different areas at many different times. The sea has been stirred up; it has roared, it has tossed to and fro, it has beaten on the sand. And do you know what happens? The sand always wins. Why? Because God said it would. It is God's Word being worked out.

It is so important to understand that the Jews did not choose to be God's people. It was the Lord who chose them. I believe that every choice God makes is a right choice. No matter how contrary things may appear, the Lord did the right thing. He will not forsake His people—not because they deserve His faithfulness, but for His great name's sake. God's name is committed to Israel; His honor is at stake.

In the New Testament, Jesus Himself gives us the same assurance: *"I will never leave you nor forsake you"* (Hebrews 13:5). At times, we may not be in any way conscious of His presence, but by His Holy Spirit, He is with us. No matter where we go, God is present by His Spirit—invisible, often imperceptible, yet inescapable. For the unbeliever, this may be a terrifying thought; but for the believer, it is a comforting, strengthening assurance.

Thank You, Lord, that You are committed to Israel. I intercede for that nation now. I proclaim that just as the Lord is with Israel, He is with me, for the Lord will not forsake His people. Amen.

Update 78: January 1996 (audio)

MARCH 27

God Will Protect

The Lord will not forsake His people.

I was living in Jerusalem when the State of Israel was born. I remember seeing the Israeli flag go up over the center of Jerusalem. I said to myself, *Surely this must be significant!*

> *Hear the word of the LORD, O nations, and declare it in the isles afar off, and say, "He who scattered Israel will gather him, and keep him as a shepherd does his flock."* (Jeremiah 31:10)

Twenty-five hundred years ago, God ordained that this particular message should be proclaimed in every nation of the earth. It is being fulfilled before your eyes and in your ears today. Now we can say, "He who scattered Israel **is** gathering him and **will** keep him as a shepherd does his flock."

These are days when absolutely no one knows, in the natural, what will happen tomorrow in Israel. A war could break out there within twenty-four hours without any warning. But in the midst of it all, God will protect Israel as a shepherd protects his flock. There is a guarantee that no matter the political pressures and the violence that erupt, God will protect regathered Israel.

The Lord gives us the same promise in Psalm 121:7–8: *"The LORD will protect you from all evil; He will keep your soul. The LORD will guard your going out and your coming in from this time forth and forever"* (NASB). It is so good to know that God is with you, not only when you begin the journey, but also when you come to the end; not just when you go to work in the morning, but also when you come home again in the evening. God is still with you, and He will protect you and keep you—from this time forth and forever. The Creator is our keeper.

Thank You, Lord, that You are committed to Israel. I intercede for that nation now. I proclaim that just as God is the Protector of Israel, He is my Protector and Keeper, for the Lord will not forsake His people. Amen.

Update 98: November 2002 (audio); WFTW15/7 (transcript)

Healer of the Brokenhearted

The Lord will not forsake His people.

In Psalm 147:2–3, we read, *"The LORD builds up Jerusalem; he gathers the exiles of Israel. He heals the brokenhearted and binds up their wounds"* (NIV). Those are beautiful words, but the most exciting thing about them is that they are being fulfilled in this generation, in our lifetime.

I have seen the outworking of those words. Again, I had the privilege to be living in Jewish Jerusalem in May 1948, when the State of Israel was reborn after two thousand years. Today, the Lord is building up Jerusalem. He is gathering the exiles of Israel. He is healing the brokenhearted and binding up their wounds.

That is good news for all who will turn to God. It is good news for God's people, Israel. It is also good news for the church of Jesus Christ because the same God who is gathering Israel is gathering the church back to Himself, bringing us into our inheritance, healing our wounds, and binding up our broken hearts.

There is an ongoing ministry of the Holy Spirit that is very special—a ministry to the brokenhearted. It is a ministry to those whose hearts are wounded. If you carry a wound inside you, turn to God and say, "God, this is a time of restoration. It is a time of regathering. You are healing the brokenhearted. You are binding up their wounds. Lord, You know the wound I have carried so long in my heart. Will You heal me?"

And the invisible finger of God, the Holy Spirit, will reach down where no surgeon can reach and touch that wounded place in your life to bring you healing and restoration.

Thank You, Lord, that You are committed to Israel. I intercede
for that nation now. I proclaim that just as God is healing the
brokenhearted and binding up wounds for Israel, He is bringing
healing and restoration to my life, for the Lord will not forsake His
people. Amen.

WFW-21/2 (transcript)

Showing Mercy to Israel

The Lord will not forsake His people.

It is important for us all to acknowledge the truth of what Jesus said to the Samaritan woman at the well: *"Salvation is of the Jews"* (John 4:22). Without the Jews, we would have no patriarchs, no prophets, no apostles, no Bible—and no Savior! Without all these, how much salvation would we receive? None! The Bible makes it clear that God requires the Christians of all other nations to acknowledge their debt to the Jews and to do what they can to repay it. In Romans 11:30–31, Paul summed up what he had been saying about the debt and the responsibility of the Gentile Christians toward Israel.

> *For as you* [Gentiles] *were once disobedient to God, yet have now obtained mercy through their* [Israel's] *disobedience, even so these* [Israelites] *also have now been disobedient, that through the mercy shown you* [Gentiles] *they* [Israel] *also may obtain mercy.*

In other words, because of God's mercy that has come to us Gentile Christians through Israel, God requires us in our turn to show mercy to Israel. How shall we fulfill this obligation? The following are four practical ways that we may do so.

First, we can cultivate and express an attitude of sincere love for Jewish people.

Second, we can enjoy and demonstrate the abundance of God's blessings in Christ in such a way that the Jews may be made jealous and desire what they see us enjoying.

Third, we can seek the good of Israel through our prayers and petitions, as the Bible exhorts us to do. (See Romans 10:1.)

Fourth, we can seek to repay our debt to Israel by performing practical acts of kindness and mercy.

Thank You, Lord, that You are committed to Israel. I intercede for that nation now. I acknowledge my debt to the Jews, and I proclaim that I will repay it in practical ways, as well as by showing mercy—for the Lord will not forsake His people. Amen.

Our Debt to Israel (booklet)

Favor for Zion

The Lord will not forsake His people.

The Lord says that the regathering of Israel in our day is a banner raised by Him for the nations. Events in Israel and the Middle East today are at the center of world attention and media coverage. This period of Israel's regathering at the end of the age was marked out clearly on God's great prophetic calendar three thousand years ago. Here is one of the passages that make this clear:

> You will arise and have compassion on Zion, for it is time to show favor to her; the appointed time has come. For her stones are dear to your servants; her very dust moves them to pity. The nations will fear the name of the LORD, all the kings of the earth will revere your glory. For the LORD will rebuild Zion and appear in his glory....Let this be written for a future generation, that a people not yet created may praise the LORD.
> (Psalm 102:13–16, 18 NIV)

Now is God's appointed time to have mercy on Zion and to show favor to her. This is not something that Zion or the Jewish people have earned, but something that comes out of God's sovereign grace and mercy. One of the main purposes of what God is doing is to bring glory to His own name in the sight of all the nations by fulfilling His promises to Israel. The rebuilding of Zion is one of the great biblical signs that the time is at hand for the Lord to appear in His glory. We have the great privilege of living in the time that the psalmist here foresaw. I believe we are the ones being created as a people in response to what God is doing for one supreme purpose: to bring praise to the Lord.

Thank You, Lord, that You are committed to Israel. I intercede for that nation now. I proclaim that God is bringing glory to His own name by fulfilling His promises to Israel, for the Lord will not forsake His people. Amen.

The Drama of the Middle East, Part 1 (audio)

DECLARING GOD'S WORD

God of Covenant

The Lord will not forsake His people.

In Psalm 89:34, God said, *"My covenant I will not violate, nor will I alter the utterance of My lips"* (NASB). It is of tremendous importance that we grasp the fact that when God makes a covenant, He will never break it. We need to know that.

Our Bible consists of two covenants: the old and the new. Therefore, the essence of divine revelation is centered in covenant. If God were to break His covenant, we would have no hope. It is my personal conviction that if God were to break His covenant with Israel, we would have no reason to believe that He would not break His covenant with the church. You may say, "Well, Israel failed God." Undoubtedly. But can you honestly say that the church has not also failed God?

I am not capable of presenting God's point of view, but in my limited understanding, I see Israel receiving a covenant and failing dismally. I see the church receiving a covenant and failing even worse than Israel. What is God saying to us about the restoration of Israel? I suggest that God is saying at least four things, all of them extremely topical, relevant, and important for the church of Jesus Christ.

First, God is saying that the Bible is a true, relevant, up-to-date book.

Second, God is saying that He keeps His covenant.

Third, God is saying to us that He is sovereign.

The fourth thing the Lord is saying is that in restoring the Israelites to their land, God has set the stage for the last act of the drama of this age. Every prophecy that relates to the close of this age is predicated on one important factor—the presence of Israel as a sovereign nation within its own borders.

Thank You, Lord, that You are committed to Israel. I intercede for that nation now. I proclaim that God keeps His covenants, for the Lord will not forsake His people. Amen.

"Perspective for a Decade: Israel, God's Banner to the Nations" (*New Wine* article)

God Demands a Response

The Lord will not forsake His people.

I believe that God requires a response from His believing people regarding what He is doing in Israel and the Middle East. We are not permitted to remain neutral, apathetic, or indifferent. God demands a response. In the book of Jeremiah, the prophet told us what the Lord commands us to do:

> *Sing with joy for Jacob; shout for the foremost [or chief] of the nations. Make your praises heard, and say, "O LORD, save your people, the remnant of Israel."* (Jeremiah 31:7–8 NIV)

The *New American Standard Bible* reads, *"Proclaim, give praise, and say"* (verse 7). Combining these two versions, I find there are five responses that God requires. In a sense, they are all vocal: sing, shout, praise, proclaim, and say (or pray).

What are we responding to? The regathering of the remnant of Jacob. To whom is this command addressed? The church, we who believe that the Bible is the Word of God and that we ought to obey it.

God is asking us to intercede for Israel. He is saying, "I am restoring My people. I am regathering them, and I am asking you to unite with Me and My purposes through prayer." I think we must all face this as one of the mysterious facts about God: when He intends to do something, He will say to His people, "Pray that I will do it." In other words, He says, "This is My intention, but it will not happen until you pray."

As Christians, we have a tremendous responsibility to be totally committed to the outworking of God's purposes in history.

Thank You, Lord, that You are committed to Israel. I intercede for that nation now. I proclaim that the Lord is restoring and regathering His people, and I join my prayers with other believers' prayers. The Lord will not forsake His people. Amen.

"Perspective for a Decade: Israel, God's Banner to the Nations" (*New Wine* article)

Jesus was punished
that we might be forgiven.

*Surely He has borne our griefs and carried our
sorrows; yet we esteemed Him stricken, smitten
by God, and afflicted. But He was wounded for our
transgressions, He was bruised for our iniquities; the
chastisement for our peace was upon Him, and by
His stripes we are healed.*

—Isaiah 53:4–5

Punished for Our Peace

Jesus was punished that we might be forgiven.

I remember once talking to a Jewish man who told me why he didn't believe that Jesus was the Messiah: "He couldn't have been a good man; God would never have let Him suffer like that." And that is exactly what the prophet Isaiah said: *"We esteemed Him stricken, smitten by God, and afflicted"* (Isaiah 53:4). But verse 5 says, *"He was wounded for our transgressions, He was bruised ["crushed" NIV] for our iniquities; the chastisement ["punishment" NIV] for our peace was upon Him, and by His stripes ["wounds" NIV] we are healed."*

Two major transactions are mentioned in those verses. The punishment due to our wrongdoing came upon Jesus so that we might be forgiven and have peace. Until the punishment for sin had been inflicted, there was no possibility of peace. Let's look at another passage in Ephesians where Paul was speaking about what took place on the cross:

> **He Himself is our peace**, who has made both [Jew and Gentile] one, and has broken down the middle wall of separation, having abolished in His flesh the enmity, that is, the law of commandments contained in ordinances, so as to create in Himself one new man from the two, thus making peace, and that He might reconcile them both to God in one body through the cross, thereby putting to death the enmity. And He came and preached peace to you who were afar off and to those who were near.
> (Ephesians 2:14–17, emphasis added)

Notice the emphasis on the word *"peace."* There can be no peace for the sinner until he knows that his sins have been forgiven. Jesus was punished so that we might have peace with God through forgiveness. (See also Colossians 1:19–20.)

Thank You, Jesus, for dying on the cross for me. I proclaim that Jesus was punished that we might be forgiven, so I might have peace with God through being forgiven. Amen.

The Fullness of the Cross, Vol. 1: The Exchange Introduced (audio)

DECLARING GOD'S WORD

APRIL 3

Redeemed!

Jesus was punished that we might be forgiven.

O n the cross, Jesus was identified with everything evil that we
have ever done. In return, we were totally forgiven and delivered
from the power of evil.

"*In Him* [Jesus] *we have redemption through His blood, the forgiveness of sins, according to the riches of His grace*" (Ephesians 1:7). When
we have forgiveness of sins, we have redemption; we have been
redeemed. *Redeem* means "to buy back," or "to ransom." Through the
payment of His blood, given as a sacrifice on our behalf, Jesus bought
us back from Satan for God.

In Romans 7, Paul said something that is not always clear to
people who are not familiar with the cultural context of his day: "*I
am carnal, sold under sin*" (verse 14). Remember that the phrase "*sold
under sin*" relates to the Roman slave market. Someone being sold as
a slave had to stand on a block, and from a post behind him, a spear
was extended over his head. So, Paul said, "I am carnal, sold under the
spear of my sin, which is extended over my head. I have no options.
I'm for sale."

When a person is a slave, he has no choices. Again, two women
may be sold in the same market; the owner makes one a cook, the
other a prostitute. The same is true with us as sinners. We may be
good, respectable sinners and look down on prostitutes and addicts.
But it is the slave owner who determines the slave's service.

The good news is that Jesus walked into the slave market and
said, "I'll buy her; I'll buy him. Satan, I've paid the price. These are
now My son and daughter." That is redemption, and it comes only
through the forgiveness of sins.

Thank You, Jesus, for dying on the cross for me. I proclaim that Jesus
bought me back from Satan to God. He was punished that I might be
forgiven. Amen.

Atonement, Vol. 1: A Divinely Ordained Exchange (audio)

Our Need for Forgiveness

Jesus was punished that we might be forgiven.

What makes the word *forgiveness* so special and beautiful? Well, consider some of the results that flow from forgiveness: reconciliation, peace, harmony, understanding, fellowship. Or consider some of the consequences that flow from our failure to forgive and be forgiven: bitterness, strife, disharmony, hatred, war. At times, it seems as if the human race is in danger of being overwhelmed by these evil, negative forces. We can escape this terrible fate only as we learn and apply the principles of forgiveness.

Let us remember that two directions of forgiveness are represented in the Bible. They are well portrayed by the symbol of our Christian faith, the cross, which has two beams—one vertical and one horizontal. These beams represent the two directions of forgiveness: the vertical beam represents the forgiveness we need to receive from God; the horizontal beam represents the forgiveness we need to receive from others, as well as the forgiveness we must extend. The grace for this kind of forgiveness comes only through the cross.

The kind of forgiveness we need and can receive from God is set forth most beautifully in Psalm 32:1–2, where David said, *"Blessed is he whose transgressions are forgiven, whose sins are covered. Blessed is the man whose sin the LORD does not count against him and in whose spirit is no deceit"* (NIV).

Again, the Bible does not talk about a man who does not need forgiveness. It clearly indicates that all of us need forgiveness from God. There are no exceptions. Other psalms tell us there is no man who does not sin. (See, for example, Psalm 14:1–3; 53:1–3.) We have all sinned. Therefore, we all need forgiveness.

Thank You, Jesus, for dying on the cross for me. I admit my own need for forgiveness, and I proclaim that Jesus was punished that I might be forgiven. Amen.

Forgiveness (audio)

Declaring God's Word

Healing through Forgiveness

Jesus was punished that we might be forgiven.

Blessed is the man whose sin the LORD does not count against him and in whose spirit is no deceit. / (Psalm 32:2 NIV)

To receive forgiveness, we must be absolutely honest with God—not covering up or excusing our sins or holding anything back. Referring to when he was found guilty of committing adultery and murder in the matter of Bathsheba, David continued in his psalm,

When I kept silent, my bones wasted away through my groaning all day long. For day and night your hand was heavy upon me; my strength was sapped as in the heat of summer. Then I acknowledged my sin to you and did not cover up my iniquity. I said, "I will confess my transgressions to the LORD"—and you forgave the guilt of my sin. (verses 3–5 NIV)

Like many people, David refused to admit his sin and tried to pretend it never happened, covering it up. But all the time he was like a man with a burning fever. His *"strength was sapped"* and his *"bones wasted away."* Unforgiven sin can produce physical results.

A psychiatrist related this story to me. While visiting a hospital, he met a woman who was in a hopeless condition. Her kidneys had ceased to function, her skin was discolored, and she was in a coma, simply waiting to die. One day, he was prompted by the Holy Spirit to say, "In the name of the Lord Jesus Christ, I remit your sins," later wondering if he had done something foolish. About a week later, he was amazed to see the woman walking down the street—completely healed. Unforgiven sin had caused her physical condition. When her sins were forgiven through this man's intercession, her spirit was clear with God and the way was open for her to be healed.

Thank You, Jesus, for dying on the cross for me. I ask for the physical healing that comes from being forgiven, and I proclaim that Jesus was punished that I might be forgiven. Amen.

Forgiveness (audio)

Forgiven as We Forgive

Jesus was punished that we might be forgiven.

In the Sermon on the Mount, Jesus taught us to pray, *"Forgive us our debts* [trespasses], *as we forgive our debtors* [those who trespass against us]" (Matthew 6:12). This petition says, in other words, "Forgive us as we forgive." Remember that in the same proportion that you forgive others, God will forgive you. If you totally forgive others, God will totally forgive you. But if you only partly forgive others, God will only partly forgive you.

One major reason that many Christians do not receive answers to prayer is their failure to forgive others, usually one specific person. In my experiences with counseling people, I have found unforgiveness to be a common source of blockage in their spiritual lives. I once asked a woman whom I was counseling, "Is there anybody you haven't forgiven?" She said, "Yes," and went on to specify a distinguished person in the United States Department of Justice. I said, "If you want release, you will have to forgive him. There is no alternative. If you don't forgive him, God does not forgive you."

Are we willing to forgive? We may think, *I don't know if I can.* God may also say, "I don't know if I can." We had better make up our minds. Forgiveness is not an emotion; it is a decision. I call this "tearing up the IOU." Somebody might owe us thirty thousand dollars, but we could owe God six million dollars. If we want Him to tear up His IOU, we must first tear up ours.

That is God's unvarying law. It is built into the Lord's Prayer. And the last petition in the Lord's Prayer is a petition for deliverance from the evil one, Satan. We have no right to pray for deliverance until we have forgiven others as we would have God forgive us.

Thank You, Jesus, for dying on the cross for me. I declare my
willingness to forgive others, and I proclaim that Jesus was punished
that I might be forgiven. Amen.

Praying to Change History: Seven Basic Conditions for Answered Prayer (audio)

Declaring God's Word

Remembering His Benefits

Jesus was punished that we might be forgiven.

Bless the LORD, O my soul; and all that is within me, bless His holy name! Bless the LORD, O my soul, and forget not all His benefits. (Psalm 103:1–2)

Here we observe David's spirit telling his soul what to do. David's spirit knew what ought to be done, but it could not happen until David's soul cooperated with his spirit and responded to the challenge.

Let's briefly enumerate the benefits that we are cautioned not to forget. Many Christians do not enjoy these benefits because they fail to remember them. Six specific benefits of God are listed in the next three verses:

Who forgives all your iniquities, who heals all your diseases, who redeems your life from destruction, who crowns you with loving-kindness and tender mercies, who satisfies your mouth with good things, so that your youth is renewed like the eagle's. (verses 3–5)

God forgives all our iniquities, heals all our diseases, redeems our lives from destruction, crowns us with lovingkindness and tender mercies, satisfies our mouths with good things, and renews our youth like the eagle's. I believe there is a close connection between having your mouth filled with good things and having your youth renewed like the eagle's.

I am convinced that it is not the will of God for His people to grow old the way the world grows old. I do not mean that there will not be any change produced by advancing in age, but that aging does not need to be a time of failure, misery, and sickness.

Thank You, Jesus, for dying on the cross for me. I will remember all Your benefits, and I proclaim that Jesus was punished that I might be forgiven. Amen.

Decision, Not Emotion (audio)

Escaping from the Curse

Jesus was punished that we might be forgiven.

In seeking the release from a curse, one main requirement is to confess any known sins committed by yourself or your ancestors, for it may be that it was the sin of your ancestors that exposed you, as one of their descendants, to the curse. Even though you do not bear the *guilt* of their sin, you do *suffer the consequences* of their sin. To escape from the curse, you need to deal with the sin that exposed you or your ancestors to the curse. You do this by confessing the sin and asking God to forgive and blot it out. Proverbs 28:13 says, *"He who covers his sins will not prosper, but whoever confesses and forsakes them will have mercy."* If you cover sin, you will not prosper or be blessed. However, if you confess your sin and forsake it, then you will have God's mercy and redemption from the curse. Again, you must also forgive all other persons. Jesus said,

> And whenever you stand praying, forgive, if you have anything against anyone; so that your Father also who is in heaven may forgive you your transgressions.   (Mark 11:25 NASB)

This is very important. Jesus makes it clear that if we hold unforgiveness, bitterness, or resentment in our hearts when we pray, we erect barriers to the answer to our prayers. It will keep us under the curse. By a decision of our wills, when we pray, we must lay down any kind of resentment, bitterness, or unforgiveness against any person. In the measure in which we forgive others, God forgives us. If we want total forgiveness from God, we must offer total forgiveness to others. This is not being super-spiritual; forgiving other people means that you're exercising what I call "enlightened self-interest."

Thank You, Jesus, for dying on the cross for me. I proclaim that by taking these steps, I am released from any curse, because Jesus was punished that I might be forgiven. Amen.

From Curse to Blessing (booklet)

Week 15:

Jesus was wounded that we might be healed.

He was wounded for our transgressions,
He was bruised for our iniquities;
the chastisement for our peace was upon Him,
and by His stripes we are healed.

—Isaiah 53:5

Total Salvation

Jesus was wounded that we might be healed.

Being born again is an experience of unique importance. Unless you are born again, you cannot see or enter the kingdom of God. (See John 3:3–5.) But it is not a one-time experience; rather, salvation is an ongoing process. Part of salvation is being baptized. I don't want to stir up controversy, but you can be born again without being baptized. If you want to be *saved*, however, baptism is a key part of the process, for *"He who believes and is baptized will be saved"* (Mark 16:16).

Being saved means much more than just getting your soul ready for heaven. Someone once said, "The evangelical concept of salvation is to get souls prepackaged for heaven." That may be so, to a degree, but salvation includes a lot more than being prepackaged for heaven.

I want to examine a passage from the New Testament in which the writer used the Greek word for "to save," which is *sozo*. If we look at where this word appears in the Scriptures, it will give us an idea of what is included in salvation.

The book of Matthew speaks about Jesus' ministry to the sick, saying, *"They...brought to Him all who were sick....And as many as touched it* [His garment] *were made perfectly well* [*"whole"* KJV]*"* (Matthew 14:35–36). The verb used for "well" or "whole" is *sozo*, but it is preceded by a Greek preposition that means "thoroughly." To be "thoroughly saved" is to be perfectly healed. This passage is not talking solely about the condition of the soul; it is also talking about those who are sick. And as many as touched Jesus were totally saved. How total is our salvation?

Thank You, Jesus, for Your work on the cross. I proclaim that for me to be thoroughly saved is to be perfectly healed and that Jesus was wounded that I might be healed. Amen.

The Fullness of the Cross, Vol. 1: Salvation Is All-inclusive (audio)

Healing and Salvation

Jesus was wounded that we might be healed.

Let's look at some places in Scripture where the Greek word *sozo*—meaning "salvation"—is used. In the gospel of Mark, Jesus met a blind man named Bartimaeus on the road to Jericho. (See Mark 10:46–52.) *"Jesus answered and said to him, 'What do you want Me to do for you?' The blind man said to Him, 'Rabboni, that I may receive my sight'"* (Mark 10:51).

The blind beggar, Bartimaeus, had a one-track mind. All he wanted was to get his sight, and get it he did. *"Then, Jesus said to him, 'Go your way; your faith has made you well.' And immediately he received his sight and followed Jesus on the road"* (verse 52). The literal Greek translation of Jesus' words reads, "Your faith has saved you." That's salvation.

In Luke 8:43–48, we read about the woman with the issue of blood who came behind Jesus and touched Him. She did not want to be recognized, however, because according to Jewish law, anyone with an issue of blood was unclean and was not free to touch anybody. This woman was embarrassed, but she was so desperate for healing that she defied the Law.

> Now when the woman saw that she was not hidden, she came trembling; and falling down before Him, she declared to Him in the presence of all the people the reason she had touched Him and how she was healed immediately. And He [Jesus] said to her, "Daughter, be of good cheer; your faith has made you well [*sozo*]. Go in peace."   (verses 47–48)

How wonderful! Being healed from blindness and from an issue of blood are both parts of salvation.

Thank You, Jesus, for Your work on the cross and that my healing is a part of salvation. I proclaim that Jesus was wounded that I might be healed. Amen.

The Fullness of the Cross, Vol. 1: Salvation Is All-inclusive (audio)

APRIL 11

Giving Thanks

Jesus was wounded that we might be healed.

There is tremendous potential in giving thanks. Not only does it release the miracle-working power of God, but also after God's miracle-working power has been set in operation, giving thanks sets the seal on the blessings received.

> As he [Jesus] was going into a village, ten men who had leprosy met him. They stood at a distance and called out in a loud voice, "Jesus, Master, have pity on us!" When he saw them, he said, "Go, show yourselves to the priests." And as they went, they were cleansed. One of them, when he saw he was healed, came back, praising God in a loud voice. He threw himself at Jesus' feet and thanked him— and he was a Samaritan. Jesus asked, "Were not all ten cleansed? Where are the other nine? Was no one found to return and give praise to God except this foreigner?" Then he said to him, "Rise and go; your faith has made you well." (Luke 17:12–19 NIV)

All ten lepers were healed physically. But something extra happened to the one who returned to give thanks. Jesus said, *"Rise and go; your faith has made you well."* The word for *"well"* in Greek is *sozo,* meaning "to save." Again, it nearly always indicates something more than mere physical or temporary provision from God. It is the all-inclusive word for salvation.

There was one important difference between the lepers. Nine were healed in an exclusively physical sense. The tenth, who came back to give thanks to God, was healed not only physically, but also spiritually—his soul was saved. He was brought into a right, eternal relationship with God. The nine others received a partial, temporary blessing; the tenth received total, permanent blessing. The difference was the giving of thanks.

Thank You, Jesus, for Your work on the cross. I proclaim that giving thanks brings total, permanent blessing and that Jesus was wounded that I might be healed. Amen.

Thanksgiving (audio)

He Bore Our Sicknesses

Jesus was wounded that we might be healed.

Surely He has borne our griefs and carried our sorrows; yet we esteemed Him stricken, smitten by God, and afflicted. But He was wounded for our transgressions, He was bruised for our iniquities; the chastisement for our peace was upon Him, and by His stripes we are healed. (Isaiah 53:4–5)

This translation is not literal, and it has consequently deprived millions of English-speaking believers of their physical rights in Christ. Still, there is no doubt as to the correct meaning of these words. *"Griefs"* should be "sicknesses"; *"sorrows"* should be "pains." They are basic Hebrew root words, used with these meanings in the days of Moses and having the same meanings today. This is stated clearly in Scripture:

[Jesus] cast out the spirits with a word, and healed all who were sick, that it might be fulfilled which was spoken by Isaiah the prophet, saying: "He Himself took our infirmities and bore our sicknesses." (Matthew 8:16–17)

[He] Himself bore our sins in His own body on the tree, that we, having died to sins, might live for righteousness; by whose stripes you were healed. (1 Peter 2:24)

We see that Matthew and Peter, Jews alike who knew Hebrew and were inspired by the Holy Spirit, gave the correct meanings to those words of Isaiah. If you combine these passages from Matthew and Peter, you get three statements taken from Isaiah 53:4–5 about the physical and spiritual realms. Physical realm: He took our infirmities; He bore our sicknesses; we are healed. Spiritual realm: He was wounded for our transgressions; He was bruised for our iniquities; the punishment that procured our peace was upon Him.

Thank You, Jesus, for Your work on the cross. Jesus took my infirmities—my sicknesses—and healed me. Jesus was wounded that I might be healed. Amen.

Full Salvation and How to Enter In, Part 1 (audio)

Removing Barriers to Healing

Jesus was wounded that we might be healed.

Often, issues within the hearts and lives of God's people act as barriers to healing. Seven common such barriers are: (1) ignorance of God's Word (see Isaiah 5:13; Hosea 4:6); (2) unbelief (see Hebrews 3:12–13); (3) unconfessed sin (see Proverbs 28:13); (4) resentment and unforgiveness toward others (see Mark 11:25–26); (5) occult involvement (see Exodus 23:24–26); (6) unscriptural covenants, i.e., Freemasonry (see Exodus 23:31–33); and (7) the effects of a curse (see Deuteronomy 28:15–68). Sometimes sicknesses are caused by, or associated with, the presence of evil spirits. Let's look at just one example from the gospel of Luke.

> When the sun was setting, all those who had any that were sick with various diseases brought them to Him; and He laid His hands on every one of them and healed them. And demons [evil spirits] *also came out of many, crying out.* (Luke 4:40–41)

When the supernatural power of God comes into operation, evil spirits cannot stand it any longer; they have to come out.

There are different ways in which evil spirits are associated with sickness. There are spirits of infirmity, pain, crippling, and death, to name only four. Jesus encountered a woman who was bent double and could not stand up straight. Rather than treat her condition as a physical ailment, He said that she had been bound by a spirit of infirmity for eighteen years. Then, He loosed her from the spirit, and she immediately straightened up. (See Luke 13:11–13.)

Thank You, Jesus, for Your work on the cross. I proclaim that when God's supernatural power comes into operation, all barriers to healing fall because Jesus was wounded that I might be healed. Amen.

Invisible Barriers to Healing (audio)

Healing for All

Jesus was wounded that we might be healed.

> *When evening had come, they brought to Him many who were demon-possessed. And He cast out the spirits with a word, and healed all who were sick, that it might be fulfilled which was spoken by Isaiah the prophet, saying: "He Himself took our infirmities and bore our sicknesses."* (Matthew 8:16–17)

Matthew used two words for physical problems: *"infirmities"* and *"sicknesses."* To distinguish between them, we could define *infirmities* as weaknesses—the things we are liable to, such as allergic reactions and bee stings; *sicknesses* we could define as actual diseases, such as cholera or influenza.

Matthew wrote that the healing ministry of Jesus was the fulfillment of Isaiah 53, emphasizing that Jesus *"healed all."* Why? Because in the eternal counsel of God, He had already taken our sicknesses and borne our pains. That is good news! If the church really believed that, evangelism would be pretty simple.

Going to Pakistan was a revealing experience for me because the population is 98 percent Muslim. We had as many as 16,000 people in our meetings without much advertising. Why? Because we prayed for the sick—and they were healed. Not all of them, more like just a few of them. The blind saw, the deaf heard, the lame walked. Believe me, there is no problem getting a crowd when healings occur. It is the number one method in the New Testament to attract people.

Thank You, Jesus, for Your work on the cross. I proclaim that by Jesus' sacrifice, God's healing is available to all, myself included, because Jesus was wounded that I might be healed. Amen.

The Fullness of the Cross, Vol. 1: The Exchange Introduced (audio)

APRIL 15

Appropriating Healing

Jesus was wounded that we might be healed.

In 1943, I was sick and spent many months in the hospital. A woman from the Salvation Army came to visit and pray for me. At that time, I received this word from God: "Consider the work of Calvary; a perfect work—perfect in every respect, perfect in every aspect." I have been considering this statement ever since, and I have only touched the fringe of what took place at the cross. It is a perfect work. From whatever aspect we view the cross, it is finished. Whatever type of help we need, it is settled forever at the cross.

"That sounds easy," you may say, "but how can we appropriate it?" On the subject of healing, many people wonder, *How can I know whether it's God's will to heal?*

If we are children of God, we are asking the wrong question. Healing is the children's bread. Jesus said, *"It is not good to take the children's bread and throw it to the little dogs* [unbelievers]" (Matthew 15:26). The Syro-Phoenician woman had the right answer: "Lord, I don't need a loaf. Just give me a crumb and it'll get the demon out of my daughter." That woman really had faith—a lot more than the children who had the whole loaf offered them and were still sick! A father may not be able to give his family ice cream or T-bone steaks, but every father has an obligation to provide bread. God the Father has put the children's bread on the table—yours and mine.

I rephrase the question in this way: How may I appropriate the healing that is already provided? For the believer, healing and the atonement are never in the future. It is now up to us to appropriate our inheritance. All is provided for us in the testament—the will sealed by the death of Jesus.

Thank You, Jesus, for Your work on the cross. I proclaim that I am now appropriating the perfect work of Jesus on Calvary—for Jesus was wounded that I might be healed. Amen.

Full Salvation and How to Enter In, Part 2 (audio)

WEEK 16:

Jesus was made sin with our sinfulness
that we might be made righteous
with His righteousness.

He made Him who knew no sin to be sin for us, that
we might become the righteousness of God in Him.

—2 Corinthians 5:21

A Clear Exchange

*Jesus was made sin with our sinfulness
that we might be made righteous with His righteousness.*

*He [God] made Him [Jesus] who knew no sin to be sin for us,
that we might become the righteousness of God in Him.*
                                            (2 Corinthians 5:21)

God made Jesus, who knew no sin, to be sin for us, that we might be made the righteousness of God in Jesus. The exchange there is very clear: Jesus was made sin so that we might become righteousness. Notice that it is not by our own righteousness that we are made righteous, but by the righteousness of God. In Matthew 6:33, Jesus said, *"But seek first the kingdom of God and His righteousness, and all these things shall be added to you."*

The only righteousness acceptable in heaven is the righteousness of God received through faith in Jesus Christ. Isaiah 64:6 reads, *"We are all like an unclean thing, and all our righteousnesses are like filthy rags."* This verse does not say that all our *sins* are like filthy rags, but that all our *righteousnesses* are like filthy rags. Even the best efforts we make to be religious—to please God and serve Him in our own strength—are but filthy rags. These filthy rags do not fit us for the courts of heaven. God requires that we put away those filthy rags of our own righteousness. We must cease from relying on our own good works and religious activities, acknowledging that we are sinful. We must believe that Jesus was made sin with our sinfulness on the cross so that we, in turn, might be made righteous with *His* righteousness.

Thank You, Jesus, for Your work on the cross. I proclaim that I put away my own righteousness and seek God's righteousness instead, because Jesus was made sin with my sinfulness that I might be made righteous with His righteousness. Amen.

Atonement (audio)

The Lord's Decision

*Jesus was made sin with our sinfulness
that we might be made righteous with His righteousness.*

Yet it pleased the LORD to bruise Him [Jesus]; He has put Him to
grief.   (Isaiah 53:10)

There is nothing wrong with the translation of this verse, but the word *"pleased"* does not accurately represent our modern usage of the term. It means it was the Lord's decision, or purpose. For instance, a criminal in Britain is sentenced by the judge to be detained "for the queen's pleasure." It's not that the queen takes pleasure in the detention of the criminal, but that she considers it necessary. Historically, this phrase goes back to the Elizabethan period in England. So, when Scripture says *"it pleased the LORD,"* it does not mean the Lord took pleasure in bruising His Son, but rather that it was the Lord's decision, it was His purpose. He saw fit to do it; He saw that it was necessary.

The Hebrew language is so condensed that it is almost impossible to translate it completely and accurately into another language. There are only about four Hebrew words in the first two lines of that verse. Where it says *"It pleased the LORD to bruise Him; He has put Him to grief,"* the best translation I can find is "unto sickness" or "to make Him sickness by bruising Him." The word translated "put Him to grief" (*chalah*) occurs also in Micah 6:13. God was speaking to rebellious, stubborn Israel, saying, *"Therefore also I will make you sick [chalah] by striking you."* There, the New King James Version has translated it by the correct, literal word.

Thank You, Jesus, for Your work on the cross. I proclaim that the
Lord made Jesus sickness by smiting Him and that Jesus was made
sin with my sinfulness that I might be made righteous with His
righteousness. Amen.

Full Salvation and How to Enter In, Part 1 (audio)

The Perfect Offering

Jesus was made sin with our sinfulness
that we might be made righteous with His righteousness.

It was the Lord's "pleasure" to make Jesus sick, or "to make Him sickness by bruising Him." Jesus was bruised unto sickness, physically. His body was crushed, marred, mutilated—whatever word you want to use. He became total sickness on the cross.

> *When You* [God] *make His* [Jesus'] *soul an offering for sin, He shall see His seed.*   (Isaiah 53:10)

Where the English says *"an offering for sin,"* the Hebrew uses only one word, *asham*, which means "guilt," "sin," or "sin offering." In the language of the Old Testament, the same word was used for both guilt and guilt offering. Why? Because under the Levitical law, when the sacrificial animal was brought as a sin offering, the man whose sin was being atoned for laid his hands on the head of the animal and confessed his sin over that animal, thereby symbolically transferring his sin to the animal. In that way, the sin offering became sin with the man's sin. Then, the animal was dealt with; instead of the man being killed, the animal was.

All this, of course, is representative of the death of Christ. The writer of Hebrews said it was not possible for the blood of bulls or goats to take away sins. (See Hebrews 10:4.) The sacrificial system was just a picture leading up to the transaction that was fulfilled on the cross. But here, speaking about the actual event, the Scripture says that God made the soul of Jesus to *be* sin. That is the real meaning of *"make His soul an offering for sin."* The apostle Paul confirmed this point when he quoted Isaiah 53:10 in this passage: *"For He made Him who knew no sin to be sin for us, that we might become the righteousness of God in Him"* (2 Corinthians 5:21).

Thank You, Jesus, for Your work on the cross. I proclaim that Jesus was made sin with my sinfulness that I might be made righteous with His righteousness. Amen.

Full Salvation and How to Enter In, Part 1 (audio)

Complete Provision

*Jesus was made sin with our sinfulness
that we might be made righteous with His righteousness.*

G od, through the cross, has dealt with the problem of guilt. He has made complete provision for the past; *"He forgave us all our sins"* (Colossians 2:13 NIV). Through the death of Jesus Christ on our behalf—through our Representative, who carried our guilt and paid our penalty—God is able to forgive every one of our sinful acts without compromising His own justice, because His justice has been satisfied by the death of Christ. We need to understand that all our past sinful acts, no matter how numerous or how serious, have been forgiven when we put our faith in Jesus.

God not only has made complete provision for the past, but also has made complete provision for the future, *"having canceled the written code, with its regulations, that was against us and that stood opposed to us; he took it away, nailing it to the cross"* (verse 14 NIV).

The written code is the law of Moses. On the cross, Jesus did away with the law of Moses as a means of obtaining righteousness with God. As long as the law was the requirement for righteousness, every time we broke even one of the most minor requirements, we were guilty before God. But when the law was taken out of the way, provision was made for us to live free from guilt because our faith is now reckoned to us as righteousness. As Paul wrote, *"For Christ is the end of the law for righteousness to everyone who believes"* (Romans 10:4 NASB). Christ is the end of the law for righteousness for everyone who believes—Jew or Gentile, Catholic or Protestant, it makes no difference. He is the end of the law as a means to achieve righteousness with God. We are not required to keep the law in order to be righteous.

Thank You, Jesus, for Your work on the cross. I proclaim that God has made complete provision for past, present, and future sins, because Jesus was made sin with my sinfulness that I might be made righteous with His righteousness. Amen.

Spiritual Warfare: The Nature of War (audio)

The "Romans Recipe"

*Jesus was made sin with our sinfulness
that we might be made righteous with His righteousness.*

L et's now look at the "Romans Recipe" of Romans 6. The word *recipe* evokes the image of a cookbook. If we Christians used the Bible in the same simple, practical way that chefs use cookbooks, we would find that God's recipes always work. The Romans Recipe is God's way of making the truths of the gospel work in our lives.

> *What shall we say, then? Shall we go on sinning so that grace may increase? By no means! We died to sin; how can we live in it any longer? Or don't you know that all of us who were baptized into Christ Jesus were baptized into his death? We were therefore buried with him through baptism into death in order that, just as Christ was raised from the dead through the glory of the Father, we too may live a new life. If we have been united with him like this in his death, we will certainly also be united with him in his resurrection. For we know that our old self was crucified with him so that the body of sin might be done away with, that we should no longer be slaves to sin—because anyone who has died has been freed from sin. Now if we died with Christ, we believe that we will also live with him. For we know that since Christ was raised from the dead, he cannot die again; death no longer has mastery over him. The death he died, he died to sin once for all; but the life he lives, he lives to God.*
> (Romans 6:1–10 NIV)

The outcome of this "recipe" is tremendous: *"sin shall not be your master"*—sin will no longer dominate or control you. Deliverance from sin and all its evil consequences comes through our identification with Jesus Christ in His death, burial, resurrection, and ascension.

**Thank You, Jesus, for Your work on the cross. I proclaim that sin shall
not be my master—because Jesus was made sin with my sinfulness
that I might be made righteous with His righteousness. Amen.**

Identification, Part 4 (audio)

DECLARING GOD'S WORD

Entering into Life

*Jesus was made sin with our sinfulness
that we might be made righteous with His righteousness.*

Today, we will look more closely at the ingredients of the "Romans Recipe." Romans 6 (NIV) presents successive points of identification. First, *"we died to sin"* (verse 1) when Jesus died, and we identify ourselves with His death. When Jesus was crucified, our *"old self"* (verse 6), the rebel nature we inherited from Adam, was also crucified. Second, *"we were...buried with him"* (verse 4). By baptism into His death, we died and were buried with Him. Third, we are *"united with him in his resurrection"* (verse 5). Following Him through death and burial, we move out into His resurrection life, sharing His life with Him. The practical, successive consequences of this identification with Jesus in His death, burial, and resurrection are as follows:

1. *"The body of sin* [is] *done away with"* (verse 6). The corrupt, evil nature that enslaved us and made us do wrong even when we desired to do right is rendered powerless. It has been put to death.
2. Consequently, we are *"no longer...slaves to sin"* (verse 6). Sin no longer compels us to do harmful, destructive things that will ultimately bring disaster upon us, on earth and in eternity.
3. Then, we are *"freed from sin"* (verse 7). We are literally justified, or acquitted. Jesus paid the final penalty for our sin; there is no more to pay. Having been released from the power and guilt of sin, we now have good consciences and can stand before the throne of almighty God without fear.
4. Finally, *"we will also live with him* [Christ]" (verse 8). What a tremendous promise! We will share His eternal resurrection life. He died once to sin; He cannot die again. He lives forever to God, and we enter into that eternal life.

Thank You, Jesus, for Your work on the cross. I proclaim that by my identification with Jesus, I am no longer a slave to sin. Jesus was made sin with my sinfulness that I might be made righteous with His righteousness. Amen.

Identification, Part 4 (audio)

We Will Be Delivered

*Jesus was made sin with our sinfulness
that we might be made righteous with His righteousness.*

The next part of the Romans Recipe, the practical how-to, is found in Romans 6:11–13.

First, *"count yourselves dead"* (verse 11). The Bible says we are dead—believe it! Paul said, *"I have been crucified with Christ; it is no longer I who live, but Christ lives in me"* (Galatians 2:20). Paul saw Christ's crucifixion and death as his own. He thought that way and talked that way, reckoning it true. We must do the same.

Steps two and three are negative admonitions: *"Do not let sin reign in your mortal body"* (verse 12) and *"Do not offer the parts of your body to sin"* (verse 13). Before, we could not help yielding to sin; now, we have a choice. There is a power in us greater than sin. We have been liberated, justified. However, we must exercise our wills. When temptation comes, we must firmly and finally say, "No! I will not yield my body or my members! I do not yield to you, Satan; I belong to Jesus."

Step four is positive: *"Offer yourselves to God"* (verse 13). We cannot be independent agents and remain free from sin. We must choose to serve God rather than Satan, offering ourselves as sacrifices to God, giving all we are and all we have—holding nothing back. Next, Paul said, *"Offer the parts of your body to him* [God]" (verse 13). Yield every part of your body to God for Him to use as He wants for His glory.

The result is that *"sin shall not be your master"* (verse 14). We are set free from shame, degradation, agony—all the evils sin brings. If we follow the Romans Recipe—working through our identification with Jesus in death, burial, and resurrection—we will be delivered.

Thank You, Jesus, for Your work on the cross. I proclaim that through identification with Jesus, I will be delivered—because Jesus was made sin with my sinfulness that I might be made righteous with His righteousness. Amen.

Identification, Part 4 (audio)

Jesus died our death that we might receive His life.

But we see Jesus, who was made a little lower than the angels, for the suffering of death crowned with glory and honor, that He, by the grace of God, might taste death for everyone.

—Hebrews 2:9

Atonement: The Hub

Jesus died our death that we might receive His life.

To illustrate the role of the atonement in the total message of the gospel, consider the structure of a wheel, which has three basic sections: the outer circle, the spokes, and the hub. In this picture, the outer circle represents God's complete provision for every area of our lives—spiritual, physical, and financial, for time and through eternity. The spokes that support the outermost circle of the wheel are ways in which God makes provision. For instance, He makes provision through forgiveness (peace), healing (health), deliverance (liberty), sanctification (holiness), and so forth. Now, without the central hub, the spokes have nothing to support them. Also, through the hub comes the driving power to turn the wheel. In God's provision, the atonement is the center hub, supplying the power for the Christian life.

From Hebrews 2:9, we learn that by the grace of God, Jesus tasted death for everyone. He took our place; that which was due to us came upon Him. Isaiah 53:6 says, *"All we like sheep have gone astray; we have turned, every one, to his own way; and the LORD has laid on Him the iniquity of us all"* (Isaiah 53:6).

"Iniquity" also means "rebellion." The rebellion of the entire human race is summed up in that phrase. We have turned our backs on God and gone our own ways—set our own standards, pleased ourselves, lived for ourselves. We have been rebellious, but the Lord placed on Jesus the rebellion of us all; all of our rebellion was concentrated on Him. As He hung on the cross, all the evil consequences of our rebellion came upon Him: sickness, rejection, pain, agony, and, finally, death. But He did not die for Himself. He died our deaths. He tasted death in our place.

Thank You, Jesus, for Your work on the cross. I proclaim that I turn from my rebellion, and that Jesus tasted death in my place—because Jesus died my death that I might receive His life. Amen.

Victory over Death, Part 1 (audio)

His Suffering for Us

Jesus died our death that we might receive His life.

Isaiah 53 gives us a detailed prophetic description of the suffering of Jesus, written more than seven hundred years before it took place.

> He was oppressed and He was afflicted, yet He did not open His mouth; like a lamb that is led to slaughter, and like a sheep that is silent before its shearers, so He did not open His mouth. By oppression and judgment He was taken away; and as for His generation, who considered that He was cut off out of the land of the living, for the transgression of my people to whom the stroke was due? His grave was assigned with wicked men, yet He was with a rich man in His death, because He had done no violence, nor was there any deceit in His mouth.　(Isaiah 53:7–9 NASB)

These details were accurately fulfilled in the sufferings and death of Jesus. First, the Gospels emphasized several times that Jesus made no attempt to answer His accusers, justify Himself, or plead His own cause. (See, for example, Mark 15:3–5.) Unjust accusation and an unfair trial led to His death, and *"He was cut off out of the land of the living."*

The details of His burial are also amazingly accurate: *"His grave was assigned with wicked men, yet He was with a rich man in His death."* We move from the plural *"with wicked men"* to the singular *"a rich man."* Historically, we find that Jesus was taken down for burial with two thieves who were hung on either side of Him, but then He was buried in the tomb of a rich man, Joseph of Arimathea.

Isaiah emphasizes that it was not for His own sin or guilt that Jesus died. He was totally innocent, yet He died the death of a criminal.

Thank You, Jesus, for Your work on the cross. I proclaim that You suffered and died for me—that Jesus died my death that I might receive His life. Amen.

Victory over Death, Part 1 (audio)

Our Amazing Representative

Jesus died our death that we might receive His life.

Let's look at some Scriptures that speak about how Christ identified Himself with the human race and expiated its guilt.

> *Since the children have flesh and blood, he too shared in their humanity so that by his death he might destroy him who holds the power of death—that is, the devil—and free those who all their lives were held in slavery by their fear of death.*
>
> (Hebrews 2:14–15 NIV)

When Adam rebelled, instead of being a king, he became a slave—bound by Satan, death, and corruption. He was no longer free. But in order to deliver human beings from that slavery, Jesus took upon Himself the form of humanity, the Adamic nature. He took upon Himself the same flesh and blood that you and I have so that by His death, He might destroy the one who holds the power of death—that is, the devil—and free all those of us who all our lives were held in slavery by the fear of death. On the cross, Jesus took upon Himself the fallen nature of human beings and their sins. This is also stated in 1 Peter 2:24: *"He himself [Jesus] bore our sins in his body on the tree, so that we might die to sins and live for righteousness; by his wounds you have been healed"* (NIV).

On the cross, Jesus became completely identified with our sin and our guilt. He became the last great guilt offering that took away the sin and guilt of the human race. He bore our sin and our punishment. Our wounds became His wounds, and He died our deaths. He expiated that guilt of rebellion as our representative, the last Adam, hanging on the cross, shedding His lifeblood, giving Himself totally to redeem us.

Thank You, Jesus, for Your work on the cross. I proclaim that You gave Yourself totally to redeem me, and that Jesus died my death that I might receive His life. Amen.

Pride vs. Humility, Part 1 (audio)

APRIL 26

Identifying with Jesus

Jesus died our death that we might receive His life.

Looking beyond Christ's identification with us, we find that, in turn, through faith and repentance, we can be identified with Christ—not only in His death, but also in His subsequent exaltation.

> *But because of his great love for us, God, who is rich in mercy, made us alive with Christ even when we were dead in transgressions—it is by grace you have been saved. And God raised us up with Christ and seated us with him in the heavenly realms in Christ Jesus.* (Ephesians 2:4–6 NIV)

This is the opposite side of identification. First, Jesus identified Himself with us, the fallen race. He took our place, paid our penalty, and died our death. He expiated our guilt. Then, as we identify ourselves with Him and His death in faith, we are also identified with Him in all that follows His death. Three great steps of our identification with Jesus are stated in Ephesians 2:4–6. First, *"God...made us alive with Christ."* Second, *"God raised us up with Christ."* He resurrected us with Christ. But it doesn't stop there. Third, *"God...seated us with Him in the heavenly realms."* God seated us with Christ on His throne. He enthroned us in Christ.

Notice those three upward steps of identification with Jesus: we are made alive with Him, resurrected with Him, and enthroned with Him. The way up is down; from the lowest, we go to the highest. God exalts the lowest to the highest, and this principle runs all through Scripture. It is not just a matter of history but the outworking of a universal law: Whoever humbles himself will be exalted. Whoever exalts himself will be humbled. (See Matthew 23:12 NIV.)

Thank You, Jesus, for Your work on the cross. I proclaim that I humble myself before God, identifying myself with Jesus to be made alive with Him, resurrected with Him and enthroned with Him—because Jesus died my death that I might receive His life. Amen.

Pride vs. Humility, Part 1 (audio)

APRIL 27

Hidden with Christ

Jesus died our death that we might receive His life.

When we are first confronted with the cross, we tend to recoil. But the cross of Jesus is the door to a secret place that no animal can find, no bird can see, and all the rest of creation does not know. (See Job 28:7–8.) It is in the spiritual realm. Paul said,

> Since, then, you have been raised with Christ, set your hearts on things above, where Christ is seated at the right hand of God. Set your minds on things above, not on earthly things. For you died, and your life is now hidden with Christ in God. When Christ, who is your life, appears, then you also will appear with him in glory.
> (Colossians 3:1–4 NIV)

The key phrase, *"your life is now hidden with Christ in God,"* is not talking about the next world, but the here and now. Being hidden with Christ in God means being in the secret place. The secret is that when Jesus died, He did not die for Himself; He died for us as our representative, taking our guilt and condemnation on Himself.

Based on our understanding by faith in Scripture, we know that when Jesus died and was raised, we died and were raised. We passed through death into a realm the senses cannot discern and creatures do not perceive. We are in Christ, and we are in God; nothing can reach us unless it comes through God and through Christ. We are here in the flesh, but our lives are not in this visible world. We may go through many difficulties and pressures in these clay vessels, but we have a life that is eternal, incorruptible, and indestructible. This is total security. No matter what comes, in Christ we are in the secret place of the Most High, protected from all harm and all danger. (See Psalm 91:1–2.) And the door to the secret place is the cross.

Thank You, Jesus, for Your work on the cross. I proclaim that by the cross, I have entered into the secret place of the Most High. I am protected from all harm and danger, because Jesus died my death that I might receive His life. Amen.

Where to Find Security, Part 2 (audio)

DECLARING GOD'S WORD

Abundant, Eternal Life

Jesus died our death that we might receive His life.

J esus called Himself the *"good shepherd"* (John 10:11, 14). The shepherd's provision, as illustrated in Psalm 23, can be summed up in one tremendous phrase: total security. But remember that all provision is measured by our commitment. When our commitment is total, our security is total. If there are limits to our commitment, then we do not enjoy the total security Jesus offers.

We can reinforce this Old Testament illustration by looking at the words of Jesus in the New Testament: *"The thief comes only to steal, and kill, and destroy; I came that they might have life, and might have it abundantly"* (John 10:10 NASB). Jesus was telling us the reason that He came to earth. He summed it up in a simple phrase: that we *"might have life."* Not life in a small or limited way, but life *"abundantly."* Life overflowing. Life for every area of our being. Life more than sufficient for every challenge and every pressure that comes against us.

Then, a little further on, Jesus used the phrase, *"eternal life"*:

> *My sheep hear My voice, and I know them, and they follow Me; and I give eternal life to them, and they shall never perish; and no one shall snatch them out of My hand.* (John 10:27–28 NASB)

Notice the central phrases: *"I give eternal life to them, and they shall never perish."* By this passage, we see that Jesus came so that we might have eternal life, a life that stretches beyond this world. A life that goes beyond the grave. A life that lasts for eternity. I once heard somebody make this insightful comment: "I believe that I shall live as long as God lives because God has become my life." That is the kind of life that Jesus came to offer us. His life—eternally.

Thank You, Jesus, for Your work on the cross. By Your death, I have abundant, eternal life, because Jesus died my death that I might receive His life. Amen.

The Sheepfold (audio)

The Total Exchange

Jesus died our death that we might receive His life.

We all like sheep have gone astray; we have turned, every one, to his own way. (Isaiah 53:6)

This passage can be summarized in one word: *rebellion*. It is the common sin of all humanity. The prophet continued, *"And the LORD has laid on Him [Jesus] the iniquity of us all"* (verse 6). The word *iniquity* (Hebrew, *avon*) means "rebellion," "the punishment for rebellion," and "all the evil consequences of rebellion." On the cross, Jesus—our substitute, the last Adam—became the rebel with our rebellion and endured all the evil consequences of rebellion.

This is the door to God's treasure house, if we can grasp it. This is the exchange: All the evil our rebellion deserved came upon Jesus so that all the good He deserved—because of His perfect obedience—might be offered to us. In whatever way we look at that exchange, it was total. Jesus was punished so that we might be forgiven. He was wounded so that we might be healed. He bore our sin so that we might share His righteousness. He died our death so that we might share His life. He was made a curse so that we might receive the blessing. He endured our poverty so that we might share His abundance. He bore our shame so that we might have His glory. He endured our rejection so that we might have His acceptance.

Just picture the rebel on the cross and know that you are that rebel—indeed, you should be hanging there. But Jesus took your place. He not only bore your rebellion, but also bore all its evil consequences so that you might enter into all the blessings of His perfect obedience. That is grace at work. You cannot earn it, you did not deserve it, and you had no claim upon it. There is only one way to receive it, and that is by faith. Just believe.

Thank You, Jesus, for Your work on the cross. I proclaim that Jesus died my death that I might receive His life. Amen.

The Roman Pilgrimage, Vol. 2: Romans 6:1–6:23 (audio, video)

Jesus was made a curse that we might enter into the blessing.

Christ has redeemed us from the curse of the law, having become a curse for us (for it is written, "Cursed is everyone who hangs on a tree").

—Galatians 3:13

APRIL 30

The Reality of Blessings and Curses

Jesus was made a curse that we might enter into the blessing.

Christ was made a curse on the cross so that we might qualify for and receive the blessing. In order to receive this provision God has made for us, it is necessary that we understand the nature of blessings and curses. If we do not understand these two concepts, we will not be able to avail ourselves of God's provision.

Both blessings and curses are major themes of Scripture. The word *"bless"* or *"blessing"* occurs more than 410 times in the Bible; the word *curse* occurs nearly 160 times. In other words, the Bible has a great deal to say about both. Both are absolutely real—so real that Jesus had to be made a curse so that we might be redeemed from the curse and receive the blessing.

Some people are inclined to think that blessings are real but curses are imaginary, or hypothetical. That is an illogical idea. If we consider any pair of opposites, it stands to reason that if one is real, the other must be real. Take day and night, for example. If day is real, then night is also real. Heat and cold—if heat is real, then cold is real. Good and evil—if good is real, then evil is real. We cannot accept one and ignore the other. So it is with blessings and curses. Blessings are real, and so are curses.

The Bible has much to teach us about the nature of blessings and curses, how they operate, how to recognize a curse at work in your life, and how to be delivered. If we remain ignorant, it will be to our own cost. We will miss much of the total provision that God has made for us through the sacrificial death of Jesus on the cross if we fail to understand His exchange of blessing for curse.

Thank You, Jesus, for Your work on the cross. I proclaim my belief
that blessings are real, and so are curses—so real that Jesus was made
a curse that I might enter into the blessing. Amen.

From Curse to Blessing, Part 1 (audio)

Redeemed from the Curse

Jesus was made a curse that we might enter into the blessing.

Let's consider the nature and scope of our redemption through Christ. Our Scripture for today is Galatians 3:13–14:

> *Christ redeemed us from the curse of the Law, having become a curse for us—for it is written, "CURSED IS EVERYONE WHO HANGS ON A TREE"—in order that in Christ Jesus the blessing of Abraham might come to the Gentiles, so that we might receive the promise of the Spirit through faith.* (NASB)

Paul was referring here to the law of Moses, detailed in the book of Deuteronomy, where God said that everyone who is put to death by hanging on a tree is under a curse. (The word *tree* also signifies a piece of wood that makes a cross.) The evidence that such a person is under the curse is that he is hanging visibly on a piece of wood.

In order to redeem us from the curse of the law, Christ became a curse for us. This was demonstrated visibly when He hung on the cross. It was necessary for Him to become a curse because the curse of God follows all sin and disobedience against God.

The secret of what took place on the cross is that there was a divinely ordained exchange—something that could not be seen by the natural eye, but could be perceived only through the revelation of God through the Holy Spirit and the Scriptures. Christ became a curse—He took the curse due to our sin and disobedience—so that we, in return, through faith in Him, might have access to the blessing that was due to His sinless obedience.

Thank You, Jesus, for Your work on the cross. I proclaim that to redeem me from the curse of the law, Christ became a curse for me. Jesus was made a curse that I might enter into the blessing. Amen.

Claiming Our Inheritance, Part 1 (audio)

Common Indications of a Curse

Jesus was made a curse that we might enter into the blessing.

I have compiled a list of seven common manifestations of a curse. Most curses do not concern one individual exclusively; rather, they usually concern families or larger communities. The essential feature of curses and blessings alike in the Bible is that they are passed down from generation to generation unless something happens to cut them off. I have dealt with people whose problems went back hundreds of years in family history.

On the basis of my personal observation, here are seven indications that usually signify the presence of a curse over your life or your family. If you experience only one of these, I would not say for sure there is a curse. But if several of them show up in your family, in different areas and in multiple generations, you can be almost sure that a curse is in place. These indications are the following: (1) mental and emotional breakdown; (2) repeated or chronic sicknesses, especially if they are hereditary; (3) repeated miscarriages or related female problems; (4) breakdown of marriage and family alienation, especially a family history of them; (5) financial insufficiency, if it is ongoing; (6)being known as "accident-prone"; and (7) having a family a history of suicides or unnatural deaths.

We will not dwell on the problem, but we will affirm the solution. *Jesus was made a curse that we might enter into the blessing.*

Thank You, Jesus, for Your work on the cross. I proclaim that for every indication of a curse in my life, Jesus' death was the solution, for Jesus was made a curse that I might enter into the blessing. Amen.

The Exchange at the Cross (audio, video)

MAY 3

Blessing in All Areas

Jesus was made a curse that we might enter into the blessing.

I want to revisit Galatians 3:13–14 because I want you to absorb it.

> *Christ has redeemed us from the curse of the law...that the blessing of Abraham might come upon the Gentiles in Christ Jesus, that we might receive the promise of the Spirit through faith.*

But what was the *"blessing of Abraham"*? We do not need to speculate about that, because it is specifically revealed in Scripture.

> *Now Abraham was old, well advanced in age; and the LORD had blessed Abraham in all things.* (Genesis 24:1)

This verse might give you the impression that Abraham was hobbling around with a cane, but it just says that he was *"well advanced in age."* It is pretty obvious that he was not hobbling around with a cane because, quite a number of years later, he made a long journey to Mount Moriah and came back again.

What is *"the blessing of Abraham"*? Abraham was blessed *"in all things,"* so the blessing covers *all things*. In this connection, Paul said that we must receive the promise of the Spirit through faith. I believe this means that we can receive the blessing only through receiving the Holy Spirit. The Holy Spirit is the administrator of all our blessed inheritance.

Thank You, Jesus, for Your work on the cross. I proclaim that I receive by faith the promise of the Holy Spirit—*"the blessing of Abraham,"* covering all areas of my life—because Jesus was made a curse that I might enter into the blessing. Amen.

Keys to God's Abundance: The Conditions (audio)

MAY 4

The Administrator of the Blessing

Jesus was made a curse that we might enter into the blessing.

The Holy Spirit is the administrator of all the inheritance of *"the blessing of Abraham"* (Galatians 3:14). In Genesis 24, we find a beautiful story to illustrate this truth. The story tells how Abraham obtained a bride for his son Isaac. It is a very simple but beautiful parable with four main characters, three of whom are the following: Abraham, who represents God the Father; Isaac, Abraham's son, who represents God's only begotten Son, Jesus; and Rebekah, the bride, who represents the church (the bride of Christ). There is one other individual, and he is, in a sense, the main character. That character is the nameless servant, who represents the Holy Spirit. If we read the chapter with those personalities in mind, it will reveal almost limitless truths to us.

Notice that at the beginning of the chapter, it says that everything that Abraham owned was under the control of the servant. He was the administrator of the entire estate of Abraham the father and Isaac the son. That is true of the Holy Spirit, too; He is the administrator of the entire wealth of the Godhead. We are heirs of God and joint heirs with Jesus Christ. But the administrator of our inheritance is the Holy Spirit. Apart from the Holy Spirit, we cannot receive or enjoy our inheritance.

When the Bible speaks about our inheritance as the children of Abraham, it refers specifically to receiving the promise of the Spirit, who alone can bring us into all the blessings that are our inheritance. The blessing of Abraham is *"in all things"* (Genesis 24:1), but the administrator of the blessing is the Holy Spirit. Hence Paul's specific mention in Galatians of receiving the promise of the Spirit.

Thank You, Jesus, for Your work on the cross. I proclaim that the administrator of my inheritance is the Holy Spirit, and I receive the promise of the Spirit by faith—*"the blessing of Abraham"* in all things—because Jesus was made a curse that I might enter into the blessing. Amen.

Keys to God's Abundance: The Conditions (audio)

"The Promise of My Father"

Jesus was made a curse that we might enter into the blessing.

The believer's receiving of the gift of the Holy Spirit does not depend in any way upon his own merits; it depends solely upon the all-sufficiency of Christ's atonement. It is through faith, not by works, *"that we might receive the promise of the Spirit through faith"* (Galatians 3:14).

This idea agrees with Jesus' final charge to His disciples just before His ascension: *"Behold, I send the Promise of My Father upon you; but tarry in the city of Jerusalem until you are endued with power from on high"* (Luke 24:49). Jesus was speaking about the baptism in the Holy Spirit that the disciples would receive at Pentecost.

The phrase *"the Promise of My Father"* gives us wonderful insight into the mind and purpose of God the Father concerning the gift of the Holy Spirit. Someone conservatively estimated that the Bible contains seven thousand distinct promises given by God to His believing people. But among these, Jesus singled out just one from all the rest as being unique: the promise of the Spirit.

Paul called this *"the blessing of Abraham"* (Galatians 3:14), thus linking it with the supreme purpose of God in choosing Abraham for Himself. When God first called Abraham out of Ur, He said, *"I will bless you...; and you shall be a blessing....And in you all the families of the earth shall be blessed"* (Genesis 12:2–3). In subsequent dealings with Abraham, God reaffirmed His purpose many times. *"I will bless you....In your seed all the nations of the earth shall be blessed"* (Genesis 22:17–18). All these promises of God looked forward to Paul's words: *"the promise of the Spirit"* (Galatians 3:14). Jesus shed His blood on the cross to purchase this blessing, promised to the seed of Abraham.

Thank You, Jesus, for Your work on the cross. I proclaim that Jesus shed His blood on the cross to purchase the blessing of Abraham— what He called *"the Promise of My Father"*—and I receive the blessed promise of the Holy Spirit, because Jesus was made a curse that I might enter into the blessing. Amen.

Foundational Truths for Christian Living (book)

Overtaken by Blessings

Jesus was made a curse that we might enter into the blessing.

Once when I was in Ireland, there was a six-year-old boy whose parents gave him some potatoes to plant. He planted his potatoes, and a week later, he went outside to see if they were growing. There was no sign of growth. Two weeks later, he still saw nothing, so he dug them up to see if they were sprouting at all. In the end, he dug them up three or four times, and they never grew!

Some Christians are like that little boy. They plant their potatoes of faith, then dig them up to see if they are growing. The essence of faith is to let God grow us. We meet the conditions, but God fulfills the promise and blesses us. Deuteronomy 28:2 says to those who meet God's conditions, *"All these blessings shall come upon you and overtake you, because you obey the voice of the LORD your God."* I love the word *"overtake."* It is not for us to run after the blessings; they run after us. We can go to bed at night and ponder what blessings will have caught up with us by the time we wake up in the morning!

In the same way, Matthew 6:33 tells us, *"But seek first the kingdom of God and His righteousness, and all these things shall be added to you."* We do not seek the "things"; we seek the kingdom. Then, God adds all the things we need.

These, then, are the conditions for receiving God's abundance: first, our motives and attitudes must be right; second, we must exercise faith; third, we must honor God, our parents, and God's ministers by giving; fourth, we must practice right thinking, speaking, and acting; and fifth, we must let God add in His way and His time. If we meet these conditions, we can be certain that God's abundant blessings will overtake us. This is one way that we enter into God's blessing.

Thank You, Jesus, for Your work on the cross. I proclaim that I will seek first the kingdom of God, and, as I do, that His blessings will overtake me—because Jesus was made a curse that I might enter into the blessing. Amen.

"Victory in Praise" (*New Wine* article)

WEEK 19:

Jesus endured our poverty that we might share His abundance.

For you know the grace of our Lord Jesus Christ, that though He was rich, yet for your sakes He became poor, that you through His poverty might become rich.

—2 Corinthians 8:9

MAY 7

Exhausting the Curse

Jesus endured our poverty that we might share His abundance.

Jesus bore the poverty curse, which is presented in its most absolute form in Deuteronomy 28:48: *"Therefore you shall serve your enemies, whom the LORD will send against you, in hunger, in thirst, in nakedness, and in need of everything."*

Some years ago, while I was preaching on the theme of God's financial provision, I received a revelation from the Holy Spirit that went beyond anything in the sermon outline I had prepared. While I continued to stand before the people and speak to them, I was having an inner mental vision of Jesus on the cross. I saw Him there in all the stark reality Scripture describes. The Holy Spirit went over the four aspects of the poverty curse for me, one by one, showing me that Jesus totally exhausted the curse in all its aspects.

First, He was hungry—when He was taken to be crucified, He had not eaten for nearly twenty-four hours. Second, He was thirsty—"I thirst" was one of His last utterances. Third, He was naked—the Roman soldiers had stripped Him of all His clothing and divided it among themselves. Fourth, He was in want of all things—He had no robe to wear while He died, nor did He own a tomb to be buried in afterward.

Jesus had nothing. Why? Because in the divine purpose of God, He exhausted the poverty curse on our behalf. At first, I did not realize the full implication of what the Holy Spirit was showing me. Looking back, however, I would have to say that this revelation has given me the basis for my faith for prosperity. In the absolute finality of the exchange, Jesus took the poverty curse so that we might receive the blessing of Abraham, whom God blessed *"in all things"* (Genesis 24:1), which is administered by the Holy Spirit.

Thank You, Jesus, for Your work on the cross. I proclaim that You totally exhausted the poverty curse for me in all its aspects because Jesus endured my poverty that I might share His abundance. Amen.

"God's Abundance, Part 3" (*New Wine* article)

His Abundance

Jesus endured our poverty that we might share His abundance.

Many passages of Scripture support the fact that Jesus bore the poverty curse. Let us look at two in particular, starting with 2 Corinthians 8:9: *"For ye know the grace of our Lord Jesus Christ, that, though he was rich, yet for your sakes he became poor, that ye through his poverty might be rich"* (KJV). I used to quote the end of that verse as "might *become* rich"! But the Holy Spirit showed me that it means "might *be* rich." We can become rich and then become poor again, but to "be" rich has a sense of permanence. Jesus took the evil—poverty—so that we might have the good—riches. Jesus took our poverty so that we might have His wealth.

Some people suggest that Jesus was poor throughout His earthly ministry, but I cannot accept this idea as accurate. We need to keep in mind the distinction between *riches* and *abundance*. Jesus was not rich in the sense of having a large bank account or great material possessions, but He certainly had abundance. Any man who can provide food for a crowd of five thousand men (along with women and children) is no pauper! Actually, Jesus had much more left over after feeding about twelve thousand people than He had when He started. (See Matthew 14:15–21.) What a beautiful picture of abundance!

Furthermore, Jesus transmitted this abundance to His disciples. When He sent them out to spread the gospel message, He told them to take nothing extra with them. Yet their testimony afterwards was that they had lacked nothing. (See Luke 22:35.) That is not poverty!

Jesus was never worried or perplexed. He was calmly and completely in control of every situation. He never doubted that His Father's goodness would provide everything He needed. And the Father never failed Him.

Thank You, Jesus, for Your work on the cross. I proclaim that You bore the poverty curse for me that I might have Your wealth because Jesus endured my poverty that I might share His abundance. Amen.

"God's Abundance, Part 3" (*New Wine* article)

All Grace: Enough and More

Jesus endured our poverty that we might share His abundance.

Having poverty means having *"hunger,...thirst,...nakedness,...and [being] in need of everything"* (Deuteronomy 28:48). When exactly did Jesus become poor? He began to become poor the moment He was identified with our sins. From that moment onward, He went deeper and deeper into poverty until, on the cross, He represented the absolute poverty described above.

Understand that at the cross, His poverty was not merely spiritual. He was also physically and materially poor. Therefore, by all the laws of logic, our wealth will not be merely spiritual, either. Jesus became absolutely poor in the physical, material sense so that we might become rich, having every physical and material need met—and having something left over to share with other people.

Second Corinthians 9:8 is the second particular verse we will study that supports the fact that Jesus bore the poverty curse: *"God is able to make all grace abound toward you, that you, always having all sufficiency in all things, may have an abundance for every* [all] *good work."* God is not stingy. He does not give just enough; He gives enough and more. That is abundance. In the verse above, there are two instances of the word *abound* and four instances of the word *all*. I don't know if this language could be any clearer. What does it describe? God's grace.

Interestingly enough, in 2 Corinthians 8 and 9, two chapters that deal with money, the key word is *grace*. It occurs seven times in chapter 8 and twice in chapter 9. It is a grace that operates in the realm of money. However, few professing Christians understand the nature of God's grace. I have sometimes observed that those who speak the most about "grace" often understand it the least.

Thank You, Jesus, for Your work on the cross. I proclaim that Jesus became absolutely poor so that God's grace could abound for me— even in the realm of money—because Jesus endured my poverty that I might share His abundance. Amen.

"God's Abundance, Part 3" (*New Wine* article)

MAY 10

God's Grace in Finances

Jesus endured our poverty that we might share His abundance.

There are three basic principles that govern the operation of God's grace. First, grace can never be earned; conversely, anything that can be earned is not grace:

> And if by grace, then it is no longer of works [what we earn]; otherwise grace is no longer grace. But if it is of works, it is no longer grace; otherwise work is no longer work.   (Romans 11:6)

This principle excludes most "religious" people from the grace of God, because they think they can earn it.

Second, there is only one channel of grace. *"For the law was given through Moses, but grace and truth came through Jesus Christ"* (John 1:17). Any form of grace that comes to us comes solely through Jesus Christ.

Third, there is only one means by which we can appropriate God's grace, and that is faith. This truth is summed up in three successive phrases in Ephesians 2:8–9: *"For by grace you have been saved through faith,...not of works* [what we earn]*."*

Few Christians realize that this principle applies just as much in the realm of financial and material provision as it does in any other area of our lives. Scripture warns us specifically against irresponsibility (Proverbs 10:4), laziness (Proverbs 24:30–34), and dishonesty (Ephesians 4:28). As long as we are guilty of any of these sinful behaviors, we have no right to expect God's grace to work in the financial aspect of our lives. Therefore, as Christians, we are obligated to be honest, hard working, and responsible.

Thank You, Jesus, for Your work on the cross. I proclaim that on the cross, Jesus took my poverty and released God's grace to me in the realm of financial and material provision because Jesus endured my poverty that I might share His abundance. Amen.

"God's Abundance, Part 3" (*New Wine* article)

Meeting God's Conditions

Jesus endured our poverty that we might share His abundance.

We must make an important, logical distinction between *earning God's grace,* which is impossible, and *meeting God's conditions,* which is obligatory. We cannot *earn* God's abundance, which comes only through grace; however, we are required to *meet the conditions* God has laid down for receiving His abundance through faith. If we do not meet these conditions, our faith has no scriptural foundation. In fact, it is merely presumption.

To meet God's conditions, our motives and attitudes must be right. We would all do well to examine our motives very carefully, especially concerning monetary gain. Impure motives concerning money include: (1) idolizing wealth (*"Covetousness...is idolatry"* [Colossians 3:5]; *"The love of money is a root of all kinds of evil"* [1 Timothy 6:10]); (2) pursuing wealth by sinful methods (*"Like a partridge that hatches eggs it did not lay is the man who gains riches by unjust means"* [Jeremiah 17:11 NIV]; [see also Proverbs 28:8]); (3) trusting ultimately in wealth for security and well-being (*"He who trusts in his riches will fall"* [Proverbs 11:28]; *"Let not...the rich man glory in his riches"* [Jeremiah 9:23]); (4) using wealth for selfish gain and self-serving interests (*"There is one who withholds more than is right, but it leads to poverty"* [Proverbs 11:24].)

In Luke 12:16–21, Jesus related the parable of the rich man who built bigger barns and filled them with his produce. But the Lord said to him, *"Fool! This night your soul will be required of you"* (verse 20). Jesus then added, *"So is he who lays up treasure for himself, and is not rich toward God"* (verse 21). The first direction in which we need to be rich is toward God.

Thank You, Jesus, for Your work on the cross. I proclaim that I receive God's abundance for me through faith as I meet His conditions because Jesus endured my poverty that I might share His abundance. Amen.

"God's Abundance, Part 3" (*New Wine* article)

Caring for the Poor

Jesus endured our poverty that we might share His abundance.

Yesterday, we considered four wrong attitudes in relation to money. There is yet another attitude that we must be careful to avoid, and that is a wrong attitude toward the poor. The Bible consistently warns us against despising or exploiting the poor.

There are a multitude of Scripture verses on this subject, but we will look at several verses from Proverbs:

> *He who despises his neighbor sins; but he who has mercy on the poor, happy is he.* (Proverbs 14:21)

> *He who has pity on the poor lends to the LORD, and He will pay back what he has given.* (Proverbs 19:17)

> *Whoever shuts his ears to the cry of the poor will also cry himself and not be heard.* (Proverbs 21:13)

> *He who gives to the poor will not lack, but he who hides his eyes will have many curses.* (Proverbs 28:27)

> *The righteous considers the cause of the poor, but the wicked does not understand such knowledge.* (Proverbs 29:7)

These verses—and others like them—place a tremendous responsibility upon us to have concern for the needs of the poor. One mark of righteousness is considering the cause of the poor. Conversely, a mark of wickedness is simply averting one's eyes from the plight of the poor. Furthermore, a reward is promised in relation to caring for the poor. When we give to the poor, Solomon told us, we are lending to the Lord. When the Lord repays our loans, He does not forget the interest!

Thank You, Jesus, for Your work on the cross. I proclaim that I will have concern for the needs of the poor, and that I will care for them, because Jesus endured my poverty that I might share His abundance. Amen.

"God's Abundance, Part 3" (*New Wine* article)

Enjoying the Blessing

Jesus endured our poverty that we might share His abundance.

L et's look at the list of curses in Deuteronomy 28. Read this entire chapter for yourself, considering whether you are enjoying a blessing or enduring a curse. If we are redeemed children of God, the curses do not belong to us, but the blessings do. Let us focus particularly on those blessings and curses related to wealth and poverty:

> *If you do not obey the voice of the LORD your God, to observe carefully all His commandments and His statutes which I command you today, that all these curses will come upon you and overtake you:....Cursed shall be your basket and your kneading bowl....You shall grope at noonday, as a blind man gropes in darkness; you shall not prosper in your ways....Because you did not serve the LORD your God with joy and gladness of heart, for the abundance of everything, therefore you shall serve your enemies, whom the LORD will send against you, in hunger, in thirst, in nakedness, and in need of everything; and He will put a yoke of iron on your neck until He has destroyed you.*
> (Deuteronomy 28:15, 17, 29, 47–48)

The will of God is expressed in verse 47—that we should serve the Lord our God with joy and gladness of heart for the abundance of all things. *Abundance* is a beautiful word that occurs many times in the Bible. In essence, it means you have all you need, and then some— you have blessings left over for others. The will of God is that we, as His people, should serve Him with joy and gladness for the abundance of all things He gives to us.

Thank You, Jesus, for Your work on the cross. I proclaim that I will serve You with joy and gladness for the abundance of all things, because Jesus endured my poverty that I might share His abundance. Amen.

Identification, Part 2 (audio)

WEEK 20:

Jesus bore our shame that we might share His glory.

Looking unto Jesus, the author and finisher of our faith, who for the joy that was set before Him endured the cross, despising the shame, and has sat down at the right hand of the throne of God.

—Hebrews 12:2

Freed from Shame

Jesus bore our shame that we might share His glory.

S hame is a cruel and ugly emotion, and it is found even among Christians. It is often the result of sexual abuse or emotional abuse, such as being ridiculed at school. I once read a story about a headmaster who singled out one boy and told him to stand up, then said to the whole class, "All of you have passed your exams except him." How could this young man feel anything but shame? Many experiences of childhood can cause shame. Those that happened longest ago are sometimes the hardest to uproot. First in is often last out.

Perhaps the most common source of shame in our Western civilization is sexual abuse (even by professing Christians). I have dealt with countless victims in this regard. Only when they come to the cross will they be set free from that shame.

This prophetic utterance describes what Jesus did for us:

The Lord GOD has opened My ear; and I [Jesus] was not rebellious, nor did I turn away. I gave My back to those who struck Me, and My cheeks to those who plucked out the beard; I did not hide My face from shame and spitting. (Isaiah 50:5–6)

Jesus said, "I *gave* My back." He could have saved Himself; He could have called for twelve legions of angels to rescue Him. (See Matthew 26:53.) But He did not. He gave His back. The depictions we see of the scourging of Jesus have very little to do with our own familiar reality. It was a horrible scene because the scourge had little pieces of metal or bone embedded in the thongs. When they fell on a man's body, they tore away the skin and exposed the raw flesh. That is what Jesus endured for our sake. And He did not hide His face from shame and spitting. On the cross, Jesus bore our shame.

Thank You, Jesus, for Your work on the cross. I proclaim that on the cross, Jesus freed me from shame—because He bore my shame that I might share His glory. Amen.

Overcoming Guilt, Shame and Rejection (audio, video)

MAY 15

"Despising the Shame"

Jesus bore our shame that we might share His glory.

Here is a brief account of what happened after Jesus' arrest in the garden of Gethsemane. Pontius Pilate had handed Jesus over to the soldiers to take Him out to be executed.

> Then the soldiers of the governor took Jesus into the Praetorium and gathered the whole garrison around Him. And they stripped Him and put a scarlet robe on Him. When they had twisted a crown of thorns, they put it on His head, and a reed in His right hand. And they bowed the knee before Him and mocked Him, saying, "Hail, King of the Jews!" Then they spat on Him, and took the reed and struck Him on the head. [Remember, every blow of that reed pressed the crown of thorns deeper into His skull.] And when they had mocked Him, they took the robe off Him, put His own clothes on Him, and led Him away to be crucified.... Then they crucified Him, and divided His garments, casting lots, that it might be fulfilled which was spoken by the prophet: "They divided My garments among them, and for My clothing they cast lots." Sitting down, they kept watch over Him there.
> (Matthew 27:27–31, 35–36)

Jesus was actually exposed naked two times in that scene. And they sat and watched Him on the cross for three hours. Most depictions of Jesus on the cross show Him wearing a little loincloth. But there was no loincloth; He was exposed naked. His shame was exposed to everybody who passed by, mocking Him.

The epistle to the Hebrews emphasizes this truth: *"Jesus, the author and finisher of our faith,...for the joy that was set before Him endured the cross, despising the shame"* (Hebrews 12:2).

Thank You, Jesus, for Your work on the cross. I proclaim that Jesus was exposed to shame on my behalf, enduring the cross and *"despising the shame"*—because He bore my shame that I might share His glory. Amen.

Overcoming Guilt, Shame and Rejection (audio, video)

Sharing His Glory

Jesus bore our shame that we might share His glory.

What is the opposite of shame? I think that what is closest to being antithetical to shame is glory.

For it was fitting for Him, for whom are all things and by whom are all things, in bringing many sons to glory, to make the captain of their salvation perfect through sufferings. (Hebrews 2:10)

Notice, Jesus was bringing many sons to *glory*. He bore our shame so that we might share His glory. Some of us have backgrounds of which we are ashamed—filled with things we have never fully gotten over, events that haunt and disturb us. These negative thoughts and painful memories hinder those moments when we want to worship and praise God. Just remember that Jesus, naked for three hours on the cross, bore our shame completely so that we might share His glory.

I once spoke in Holland about Jesus bearing our shame, and a Dutch woman sent me her testimony as a response. As a young girl, she had been sexually abused—gang raped by a group of young boys—and also suffered further sexual molestation. Later, she married, but her marriage was not happy because of the deep bitterness in her heart against men. She could not escape the shame of what she had endured. Then, the Lord did something wonderful.

Sitting alone in her bedroom, she had a vision of Jesus on the cross, absolutely naked. She realized two things: first, that He had borne her shame; and second, that He was a man. Though she was so bitter against men, she realized it was a Man who paid the penalty of her shame. Isn't that beautiful? Bear in mind that Jesus, naked on the cross, was exposed to the jeers and taunts of passersby. It was the primary object of crucifixion, and Jesus endured it all.

Thank You, Jesus, for Your work on the cross. I proclaim that Jesus paid the penalty of our shame, for He bore my shame that I might share His glory. Amen.

Overcoming Guilt, Shame and Rejection (audio, video)

The Joy Set before Him

Jesus bore our shame that we might share His glory.

Hebrews 12:2 calls Jesus the *"author and finisher of our faith."* The same verse in *The New Testament: An Expanded Translation* by Kenneth S. Wuest refers to Jesus as the *"originator and perfecter"* of our faith.

Let me encourage you with those words. Whatever Jesus begins, He is going to complete. If He has started something in you, He will complete it. That is His faithfulness—not our cleverness.

Hebrews 12:2 continues, saying that Jesus, *"for the joy that was set before Him endured the cross, despising the shame, and has sat down at the right hand of the throne of God."* On the cross, Jesus endured shame, but He did not let it deter Him. For the joy that was set before Him, He did not consider shame a worthy reason to turn away from His purpose. What was *"the joy that was set before Him"*? The joy of bringing many sons to glory. In order to bring you and me—and millions and millions of others like us—to glory, Jesus Christ endured the shame of the cross.

There is no form of death more shameful than crucifixion. It is shameful because it is the lowest form of punishment reserved for the most debased of criminals. It is shameful because of the very way in which the death occurs. The Scriptures state clearly that the Roman soldiers took all of Jesus' clothing away from Him. Jesus hung naked on the cross before the eyes of the people for three hours or more. People walked past and made fun of Him. How would you feel in that situation? In a single word: shameful. Jesus endured the shame because He saw that through it, He could bring us to glory.

Thank You, Jesus, for Your work on the cross. I proclaim that Jesus endured the shame to bring many sons to glory. For the joy set before Him, Jesus bore my shame that I might share His glory. Amen.

Atonement, Vol. 2: Shame vs. Glory (audio)

Helping God's Chosen Ones

Jesus bore our shame that we might share His glory.

My wife and I were once involved in helping two Jewish women who had escaped from Soviet Russia. In a sense, these women had cast themselves on our mercy. We went to a lot of pain and trouble to help them, and, by the grace of God, we ultimately succeeded in doing so. One day, I was complaining to myself as I toiled up a steep hill in Haifa for them. It was a hot day, and, though these women were always very grateful, I was thinking that this was an awful lot to go through for them. And God gave me this verse; I did not know where to find it in the Bible, but the words just came to me:

> *Therefore I endure all things for the sake of the elect* [God's chosen ones], *that they also may obtain the salvation which is in Christ Jesus with eternal glory.* (2 Timothy 2:10)

From that experience, I saw that my position was far from that of Jesus on the cross. The inconvenience I was enduring was so miniscule in comparison. But the purpose was to help God's chosen ones enter into salvation with eternal glory.

We all need to devote more time to thinking about that word *glory*, because it is our destination. If there is a price to pay for glory, believe me, it is worth it. We may be called upon sometime to give up those two idols of convenience and comfort. If we could just get a vision of all that can come out of our personal inconvenience and sacrifice, we would one day see people in glory who are there because of what we did.

That was the motivation of Jesus. He did not do it for Himself but to bring many sons to glory.

Thank You, Jesus, for Your work on the cross. I proclaim that I will give up those two idols of convenience and comfort, as Jesus did, to help bring salvation to God's chosen ones. Jesus bore my shame that I might share His glory. Amen.

Atonement, Vol. 2: Shame vs. Glory (audio)

Boasting in the Cross

Jesus bore our shame that we might share His glory.

One day, the Holy Spirit spoke to me through tongues and inter-pretation: "Consider the work of Calvary, a perfect work; perfect in every respect, perfect in every aspect." God showed me that if I could understand fully what Jesus did on the cross at Calvary, I would find it was perfect, complete. There was nothing that needed to be added, nothing that could ever be taken from it. Every need had been supplied. It made me want to know more about the cross. Gradually, over the years, the Holy Spirit has opened up the Scriptures to me more and more.

> *But God forbid that I should glory* [boast], *save in the cross of our Lord Jesus Christ, by whom the world is crucified unto me, and I unto the world.* (Galatians 6:14 KJV)

Paul had only one thing to boast about—the cross of our Lord Jesus Christ. That is an amazing statement when you consider that in Paul's day, the cross was the absolute embodiment of all that was shameful and revolting.

In his book *A Doctor at Calvary*, Pierre Barbet, a Catholic surgeon, tried to pinpoint and describe the physical experience of a person being crucified. The problem was that there was no standard of refer-ence because no one in the past two centuries has ever seen a person crucified on a cross. It brought home to me how remote the cross can be to us as an instrument of shame and torture.

Paul did not boast about his Jewish ancestry or the churches he founded or the miracles he had seen. He boasted only about the cross. May that same spirit be in each one of us—a spirit willing to be emp-tied of carnal boastfulness, pride, and self-sufficiency—so that we can humbly acknowledge the cross of Jesus Christ.

Thank You, Jesus, for Your work on the cross. I proclaim that I will boast in the cross of Jesus Christ, for Jesus bore my shame that I might share His glory. Amen.

The Work of the Cross (audio)

Ordained for Glory

Jesus bore our shame that we might share His glory.

Those God foreknew he also predestined to be conformed to the likeness of his Son, that he might be the firstborn among many brothers. And those he predestined, he also called; those he called, he also justified; those he justified, he also glorified. What, then, shall we say in response to this? If God is for us, who can be against us? He who did not spare his own Son, but gave him up for us all—how will he not also, along with him, graciously give us all things? (Romans 8:29–32 NIV)

When we are identified with Jesus in His death, we enter into His abundant inheritance. We become heirs of God and joint heirs with Jesus Christ. But there is a process. Five stages were outlined by Paul, all of which are in the past tense. The first two steps took place in eternity before time began: God *foreknew* us and *predestined* us. Then, God *called* us through the preaching of the gospel. When we responded to the call, He then *justified* us. But He didn't stop there; He also *glorified* us. He brought us up to share glory with Jesus in heaven as kings and priests. Not in the future, but in the past.

Since, then, you have been raised with Christ, set your hearts on things above, where Christ is seated at the right hand of God. Set your minds on things above, not on earthly things. For you died, and your life is now hidden with Christ in God. When Christ, who is your life, appears, then you also will appear with him in glory. (Colossians 3:1–4 NIV)

We already share Christ's glory, but it is in the unseen, invisible world. Where Jesus is, we are.

Thank You, Jesus, for Your work on the cross. I proclaim that God foreknew me, predestined me, called me, justified me, and glorified me. Jesus bore my shame that I might share His glory. Amen.

Identification, Part 3 (audio)

Jesus endured our rejection that we might have His acceptance with the Father.

Having predestined us to adoption as sons by Jesus Christ to Himself, according to the good pleasure of His will, to the praise of the glory of His grace, by which He made us accepted in the Beloved.

—Ephesians 1:5–6

MAY 21

We Are Accepted!

Jesus endured our rejection
that we might have His acceptance with the Father.

Rejection, simply defined, is the sense of being unwanted or the sense that, although you want people to love you, no one does. Or it can be the desire to belong to a group from which you feel excluded—it seems you're always on the outside looking in. One reason that so many people today suffer from the problem of rejection is the form of our society and its pressures, particularly those causing the breakup of family life.

What is the opposite of rejection? It is acceptance. I love the last part of Ephesians 1:6, which says, *"He [God] has made us accepted in the Beloved."* Jesus, God's true and only begotten Son, was rejected so that we, who were unworthy rebels, might have His acceptance with the Father. The surest remedy for our problems is to believe that Jesus bore our rejection that we might have His acceptance with the Father.

God's family is the best family. There is none equal to it. Even if your own family did not care for you—perhaps your father rejected you or your mother never had time for you—God still wants you. You are accepted. You are the object of His special care and affection. Everything He does in the universe revolves around you.

When God says that we are accepted, He does not mean that we are merely tolerated. We never take too much of His time. The only thing that upsets Him is when we stay away too long. He does not push us off into a corner and say, "Wait. I'm too busy. I don't have time for you." Rather, He says, "I'm interested in you. I want you. You're welcome. Come in. I've been waiting a long time for you."

Thank You, Jesus, for Your work on the cross. I proclaim that *"God has made me accepted in the Beloved,"* and He welcomes me. Jesus endured my rejection that I might have His acceptance with the Father. Amen.

"From Rejection to Acceptance" (*New Wine* article)

DECLARING GOD'S WORD

MAY 22

Remedy for Rejection

*Jesus endured our rejection
that we might have His acceptance with the Father.*

I believe the primary result of rejection is the inability to receive or communicate love. None of us can communicate love unless we have first received love. This point was made by John in the New Testament, when he wrote, *"We love Him [God] because He first loved us"* (1 John 4:19). I do not believe anyone can love unless he has first been loved. Thus, a person who has never been loved cannot transmit love.

The secondary results of rejection are the three main ways in which people commonly react to rejection: first, there is the person who gives in; second, there is the person who holds out; and, third, there is the person who fights back. These three ways of reacting to rejection have one thing in common. Each is essentially defensive, offering a method of covering up the hurt. None of them is a positive solution. God, however, has a positive solution.

In Isaiah 61:1, we find a promise that was fulfilled through the coming of Jesus the Messiah: *"The Spirit of the Lord GOD is upon me, because the LORD has anointed me to bring good news to the afflicted; He has sent me to bind up the brokenhearted, to proclaim liberty to captives, and freedom to prisoners"* (NASB).

In fulfillment of this promise, God has provided a remedy for rejection. It comes to us through Jesus and the cross. God's eternal purpose, even before creation, was that we might become His children—His sons and His daughters. When Jesus bore our sin and suffered our rejection, He opened the way for our acceptance by the One whose acceptance truly matters.

Thank You, Jesus, for Your work on the cross. I proclaim that I step out of the results of rejection, receiving instead the remedy God has provided for me in Jesus Christ the Messiah. I proclaim that Jesus endured my rejection that I might have His acceptance with the Father. Amen.

Rejection: Cause and Cure (audio)

The Holy Spirit's Probe

Jesus endured our rejection
that we might have His acceptance with the Father.

The first step in overcoming rejection is to recognize the problem. Once you recognize it, you can deal with it. You are not alone in this; God will help you recognize it. Let me give you a practical illustration.

During World War II, when I was serving as a medical orderly in the desert in North Africa, I was working with a man who was a brilliant doctor. One of our soldiers was struck with a piece of shrapnel. He came into the medical station with this tiny, black puncture mark in his shoulder. I set to work attending to him, and I asked the doctor, "Shall I get out a dressing to dress the wound?"

The doctor said, "No, give me the probe." So, I handed him the little silver stick, and he put it in the wound and moved it around. Nothing happened for a few moments. Suddenly, the probe touched the little piece of shrapnel inside, and the patient let out a yelp. The doctor knew he had found the problem.

When I again asked if I should bring the dressing, the doctor replied, "No, bring me the forceps." He put the forceps in and removed the piece of shrapnel. Only then did he want to apply the dressing.

You may be putting a little dressing of religion over a wound that cannot heal because there is something inside that is causing it to fester. However, if you will open your heart to the Holy Spirit, He will reveal the source of the problem. If the Holy Spirit's probe touches a piece of shrapnel, yelp if you must, but don't resist! Ask Him to use His forceps to remove the problem. Then, God can apply something that will truly heal the wound rather than patch it up temporarily.

Thank You, Jesus, for Your work on the cross. I proclaim that I am opening my heart to the Holy Spirit's probe to reveal the source of my problem. Jesus endured my rejection that I might have His acceptance with the Father. Amen.

God's Remedy for Rejection (book)

Experiencing His Acceptance

*Jesus endured our rejection
that we might have His acceptance with the Father.*

To receive God's provision for rejection, you must grasp two basic facts. First, God did not make a lot of different provisions for each of the various needs of humanity. Instead, He made just one, all-inclusive provision that covers all the needs of all people. This cover-all provision was the sacrificial death of Jesus on the cross.

Second, what took place on the cross was an exchange that God Himself had planned. All the evil consequences of our sins came upon Jesus so that, in return, all the benefits of Jesus' sinless obedience might be made available to us. For our part, we have done nothing to deserve this, and we have no merits or rights by which to claim it. It proceeded solely out of the unfathomable love of God.

Therefore, it is futile to approach God on the basis of some merit or virtue that we imagine we possess. Nothing we have to offer of ourselves can be compared with the merit of the sacrifice that Jesus offered on our behalf.

Christ bore our rejection on the cross, along with all of the shame and betrayal, agony and heartache. In fact, a broken heart was the cause of His death. We are accepted because of His rejection. We are accepted in the Beloved. It was an exchange. Jesus bore the evil so that we might receive the good. He carried our sorrows so we might have His joy. The way is opened for man to come to God without shame, without guilt, without fear. Jesus bore our rejection so that we might experience His acceptance.

Thank You, Jesus, for Your work on the cross. I proclaim the truth of the exchange Jesus made for me: I am accepted because of His rejection. I receive the good because He bore the evil. I have His joy because He carried my sorrows. I proclaim that Jesus endured my rejection that I might have His acceptance with the Father. Amen.

God's Remedy for Rejection (book)

Steps to Acceptance

*Jesus endured our rejection
that we might have His acceptance with the Father.*

There are four steps you must take to experience acceptance with God. The first thing is to forgive every person who has rejected you or harmed you in any way. As Jesus instructed us, *"When you stand praying, if you hold anything against anyone, forgive him, so that your Father in heaven may forgive you your sins"* (Mark 11:25 NIV).

This statement is all-inclusive: if you hold anything against anyone, forgive, and then God will forgive you. But if you do not forgive others, God does not forgive you. This truth applies especially in our attitudes toward our parents, who most commonly cause the problem of rejection. Lives have changed when people have realized they have a scriptural obligation to honor their parents. Ephesians 6:2 says, *"'Honor your father and mother,' which is the first commandment with a promise."* That does not mean that you ignore their faults completely, but you must forgive them and determine to honor them to the greatest extent that you are able. I have never known anyone who had a wrong relation to his parents who was really blessed and prosperous. Second, you must lay down the negative results of rejection: bitterness, resentment, hatred, rebellion. These attitudes are poisonous; they will infect your entire life. They will cause deep emotional problems and, quite likely, physical problems, as well. You cannot afford to entertain these thoughts.

By a resolute decision of your will, push them from you. Say with conviction, "I lay down bitterness, resentment, hatred, and rebellion." People who have recovered from alcoholism are often told, "Resentment is a luxury you can no longer afford." That is true. None of us can afford resentment. Its effects are toxic.

Thank You, Jesus, for Your work on the cross. I forgive every person who has rejected me, and I lay down bitterness, resentment, hatred, and rebellion. I proclaim that Jesus endured my rejection that I might have His acceptance with the Father. Amen.

Rejection: Cause and Cure (audio)

DECLARING GOD'S WORD

Accepting Ourselves

*Jesus endured our rejection
that we might have His acceptance with the Father.*

By an act of faith, you must believe what God says in the Bible: that you are accepted in Christ. Scripture tells us that God's purpose from eternity was to make us His children, and He accomplished this purpose, He made it possible, through Jesus' death on the cross on our behalf. (See Ephesians 1:4–6.) When you come to God through Jesus, God accepts you. He will not turn you away.

To make this step toward acceptance, you must accept yourself. Many times, this is the hardest thing for us to do. We look back over a record of failures and false starts, maybe the ways in which we have failed others. You may label yourself "failure," but God labels you "My son" or "My daughter." We must accept ourselves because God has accepted us.

When you come to God through Jesus, you are a new creation: *"If anyone is in Christ, he is a new creation; old things have passed away; behold, all things have become new. Now all things are of God, who has reconciled us to Himself through Jesus Christ"* (2 Corinthians 5:17–18). That is the new creation. Do not think about yourself in terms of what you were before you came to Christ, for you have become a new creation.

Let us pray together: "God, I thank You that You love me, that You gave Jesus, Your Son, to die on my behalf. I thank You that He bore my sins, took my rejection, and paid my penalty. And because I come to You through Him, I am not rejected, I am not unwanted, I am not excluded. You really love me. I really am Your child. You really are my Father. I belong to Your family. Heaven is my home. Thank You, God. Amen."

Thank You, Jesus, for Your work on the cross. I believe what God says—that I am accepted in Christ—and I accept myself, as well. I proclaim that Jesus endured my rejection that I might have His acceptance with the Father. Amen.

Rejection: Cause and Cure (audio)

Finding Your Place

*Jesus endured our rejection
that we might have His acceptance with the Father.*

There is another important stage in achieving acceptance, and that is receiving acceptance from God's people. This means finding your place in the body of Christ.

You see, as Christians, we are never isolated individuals. We are brought into a relationship with our fellow believers. That relationship is one of the ways in which our acceptance is worked out in our day-to-day living. It is not enough to be accepted by the Father in heaven. That is the first step, and indeed the most important one. However, after that, acceptance has to find expression in our relationships with our fellow believers.

Collectively, Christians constitute one body, with each Christian being a member of that body. None of us can say to our fellow believers, "I don't need you." We all need one another. God has created the body in such a way that the members are interdependent. None of them can function effectively on its own. That principle applies to each one of us. It applies to you. You have to find your place in the body of Christ. You need the other members, and they need you. Finding your place in the body makes your acceptance a real, day-to-day experience.

If you are crying out in your heart for this kind of involvement, I suggest that you pray this prayer: "Lord, I long to dwell in Your house, to be part of a spiritual family of committed believers. If there are any barriers in me, I ask You to remove them. Guide me to a group where this longing of mine can be fulfilled, and help me to make the needed commitment to them. In the name of Jesus, amen."

Thank You, Jesus, for Your work on the cross. I proclaim that I am open to finding my place in the body of Christ, as I just prayed. I proclaim that Jesus endured my rejection that I might have His acceptance with the Father. Amen.

Rejection: Cause and Cure (audio)

Jesus was cut off by death that we might be joined to God eternally.

For He was cut off from the land of the living; for the transgressions of My people He was stricken.

—Isaiah 53:8

But he who is joined to the Lord is one spirit with Him.

—1 Corinthians 6:17

Spiritual Life: Fellowship with God

Jesus was cut off by death that we might be joined to God eternally.

After Peter drew his sword in Jesus' defense, so that He would not be arrested in the garden of Gethsemane, Jesus said to him, *"Put your sword into the sheath. Shall I not drink the cup which My Father has given Me?"* (John 18:11). Jesus drank the cup to the very dregs. You see, Jesus' work was not completed on the cross. In fact, the bitterest dregs came after physical death. In every sense, Jesus exhausted the cup. First, there was spiritual death; second, physical death; and third, spiritual banishment from God.

Jesus tasted death for every person so that we might have life. And we have life in the three aspects of life that Jesus forfeited. The parallel is exact.

First of all, we have spiritual life—we are brought into union and fellowship with God here in this life, right now, through faith in Jesus Christ. Jesus was joined to the Lord; He lived by the life of the Father. He said, *"I and My Father are one"* (John 10:30). This was the case until He took our iniquity upon Himself and was separated from the Father. He was cut off that we might be united. Through faith in Jesus, you and I can be joined to the Lord in the Spirit and walk this life in union with God, just as Jesus walked His life in union with the Father by the Spirit. This is the end purpose of the gospel.

First John 1:3 states, *"That which we have seen and heard we declare to you, that you also may have fellowship with us; and truly our fellowship is with the Father and with His Son Jesus Christ."* Jesus forfeited the fellowship so that we might enter into the fellowship.

Thank You, Jesus, for Your work on the cross. I proclaim that Jesus tasted death that I might have life; that He was cut off that I might be united; that He forfeited the fellowship that I might enter into it. I proclaim that Jesus was cut off by death that I might be joined to God eternally. Amen.

Spiritual Conflict, Vol. 2: God's Secret Plan Unfolds: Jesus Tasted Death in All Its Phases (audio)

Physical Life: Resurrection Life

Jesus was cut off by death that we might be joined to God eternally.

Jesus tasted death in every aspect for every person so that we might have life in every aspect. Yesterday, we talked about the first aspect, which is spiritual life. Today, we will look at the second aspect, which is physical life. This life comes in two successive phases. First, we have life in our physical bodies now. But our bodies are mortal; thus, second, at the resurrection, our bodies will be changed into immortal bodies.

> But if the Spirit of Him who raised Jesus from the dead dwells in you [that means "dwells in you right now," not after the resurrection], He who raised Christ from the dead will also give life to your mortal bodies through His Spirit who dwells in you.
> (Romans 8:11)

We each have a mortal body with resurrection life. Mortal flesh, a mortal body, but resurrection life made manifest in it. Not just operating in it, but made manifest in it. If this verse does not refer to divine healing and divine physical strength and vitality, then I do not understand these words! But that is not the conclusion. The conclusion is a changed body. Concerning this changed body, Paul wrote,

> Behold, I tell you a mystery: We shall not all sleep, but we shall all be changed; in a moment, in the twinkling of an eye, at the last trumpet. For the trumpet will sound, and the dead will be raised incorruptible, and we shall be changed. For this corruptible must put on incorruption, and this mortal must put on immortality.
> (1 Corinthians 15:51–54)

Thank You, Jesus, for Your work on the cross. I proclaim that because Jesus tasted death for me, I have life—resurrection life now and life eternal. I proclaim that Jesus was cut off by death that I might be joined to God eternally. Amen.

Spiritual Conflict, Vol. 2: God's Secret Plan Unfolds: Jesus Tasted Death in All Its Phases (audio)

May 30

Eternity with God

Jesus was cut off by death that we might be joined to God eternally.

The third aspect of the life we have in Christ is the consummation of the work of Jesus in eternity—an eternity spent in the presence of God rather than being eternally banished to hell.

> *For the Lord Himself will descend from heaven with a shout, with the voice of an archangel, and with the trumpet of God. And the dead in Christ will rise first. Then we who are alive and remain shall be caught up together with them in the clouds to meet the Lord in the air. And thus we shall always be with the Lord.*
>
> (1 Thessalonians 4:16–17)

The consummation of redemption is eternity in the presence of God. The last two chapters of Revelation describe our eternity in the presence of God:

> *Now I saw a new heaven and a new earth, for the first heaven and the first earth had passed away. Also there was no more sea [no more separation, no more bitterness]. Then I, John, saw the holy city, New Jerusalem, coming down out of heaven from God, prepared as a bride adorned for her husband.* (Revelation 21:1–2)

I believe the New Jerusalem is the church coming down out of heaven. And it is God's permanent dwelling place. One of the supreme purposes of God in the church is to have a dwelling place where He can live permanently. Verse 3 says, *"And I heard a loud voice from heaven saying, 'Behold, the tabernacle of God is with men, and He will dwell with them, and they shall be His people. God Himself will be with them and be their God.'"*

Thank You, Jesus, for Your work on the cross. I proclaim that I will have eternity in the presence of God instead of banishment, because Jesus was cut off by death that I might be joined to God eternally. Amen.

Spiritual Conflict, Vol. 2: God's Secret Plan Unfolds: Jesus Tasted Death in All Its Phases (audio)

Union with Christ

Jesus was cut off by death that we might be joined to God eternally.

> *But he who is joined to the Lord is one spirit with Him.*
>
> (1 Corinthians 6:17)

The word *"joined"* is not in the past tense but the ongoing present tense. In other words, "He who is cleaving continually to the Lord is one with Him." There is a spiritual union with God that is parallel to the physical union between a man and a woman. That is what the Scripture says. It is so real, so intimate, that the believer can cleave to God so that he is one with Him.

Just as Jesus is one with the Father, so believers can be one with the Son. *"He who is joined to the Lord is one spirit."* I want to emphasize again that it is not a single event in the past tense. It is a continuing present: "He who is cleaving continually to the Lord." Jesus lived by continual union with the Father. If the union had ever been broken, which it never was until the cross, He would have forfeited life. And you and I, as believers, live only insofar as we live in continual union with the Son, Jesus Christ. Living in union with Him, we are one spirit.

The primary activity of the human spirit is union with God. It is the only part of man that can be united directly with God. The great privilege we have with our spirits is union and communion with God.

The believer has to live by his union with Christ, just as Christ lived by His union with the Father. We are dependent for life, moment by moment, upon our union with Christ. Don't ever trust in yesterday's experience for today.

Thank You, Jesus, for Your work on the cross. I proclaim that I am living in union with Christ—and that we are one spirit. Jesus was cut off by death that I might be joined to God eternally. Amen.

Spiritual Conflict, Vol. 2: God's Secret Plan Unfolds: God's Purpose for the New Race (audio)

Communion with the Creator

Jesus was cut off by death that we might be joined to God eternally.

In 1 Thessalonians 5:23, Paul prayed, *"Now may the God of peace Himself sanctify you completely; and may your whole spirit, soul, and body be preserved blameless."* Paul here put together the three elements that make up a complete human personality, listing them in descending order from the highest to the lowest: first, *spirit*; second, *soul*; third, *body*.

The spirit is the part of the human personality that was directly breathed into man by God at creation. It is therefore capable of direct union and communion with the Creator. In 1 Corinthians 6:17, Paul said, *"He who is joined to the Lord is one spirit with Him."* It would not be correct to say "one *soul* with Him." Only man's spirit is capable of direct union with God. In the original pattern of creation, man's spirit related upward to God, his Creator, and downward to his own soul. God communicated directly with man's spirit and, through man's spirit, with his soul. Together, man's spirit and soul expressed themselves through his body.

Let me give you three definitions of the functions of spirit, soul, and body—definitions that are simple but no less helpful. The spirit is God-conscious. The soul is self-conscious. The body is world-conscious. Through the spirit, we are conscious of God. In our souls, we are conscious of ourselves. And through our bodies and their senses, we relate to the world around us.

When the spirit of man is brought back into union with God, it is rekindled to become a lamp. The Holy Spirit comes in and fills up that lamp, shedding light on man's whole inner being. (See Proverbs 20:27.)

Thank You, Jesus, for Your work on the cross. I proclaim that I am in direct union and communion with my Creator, because Jesus was cut off by death that I might be joined to God eternally. Amen.

Blessing or Curse: You Can Choose (book)
What Is Man?, Part 2 (audio)

Marriage Relationship with the Lord

Jesus was cut off by death that we might be joined to God eternally.

In Romans 7, Paul said that through the law, we were married. The law was like a marriage covenant, and it was for life. To whom—or to what—were we married? We were married to our fleshly nature. The whole essence of the law is that we are required to keep it in our own ability. Doing this is dependent on our fleshly nature, which explains why it never works.

Coming under the law is like participating in a marriage ceremony in which you are married to your fleshly nature. As long as your fleshly nature remains alive, you must remain married to it; you cannot divorce it and marry somebody else. The good news is that your first spouse died. When did that first spouse die? When Jesus died on the cross. Our old man was crucified with Him. When you grasp that fact, you say, "Praise God. I'm free. I don't have to go on with this awful spouse of mine who gave me an awful life and gave me no blessings, peace, or righteousness. I'm not tied to that vile spouse any longer. I can be married to another."

The alternative is to be married to the One who rose from the dead—the risen, glorified Christ. He can become your husband whether you are man or woman. What we are talking about is a relationship in the Spirit. In 1 Corinthians 6:15–16, Paul provided a picture of sexual union between a man and a prostitute. He used that picture of union to help people envision another kind of union that they can have—a union with the Lord. It is not sexual; it is spiritual—that is, a marriage relationship with the Lord. *"He who is joined to the Lord is one"* (1 Corinthians 6:17)—not in soul or in body, but in spirit.

Thank You, Jesus, for Your work on the cross. I proclaim that I am married in the Spirit to the One who rose from the dead—the risen, glorified Christ. I proclaim that Jesus was cut off by death that I might be joined to God eternally. Amen.

The Roman Pilgrimage, Vol. 2: Romans 6:23–7:16 (audio, video)

Worship: The Consummation

Jesus was cut off by death that we might be joined to God eternally.

In John 4:23–24, Jesus said that the Father is looking for those who will worship Him in spirit and in truth. Worship is a function of the spirit. What is the act by which we are joined to the Lord as one spirit? Worship. That is why worship is the highest activity of human beings.

When we are joined to the Lord in worship, we begin to bring forth or birth the things that God wants brought forth. Worship is not a sort of appendix to the Christian life. It is not an afterthought, a mere addition to our services. Worship is the culmination—it is the confirmation. If I may say this without offending anybody, worship is the consummation of our marriage to the Lord. It unites us with Him as one spirit. When we have that marriage union, it is always for the sake of procreation. That is when we procreate; that is when we bring forth spiritual fruit. By "spiritual fruit," I mean the fruit of the Spirit, which is listed in Galatians 5:22–23: *"love, joy, peace, longsuffering, kindness, goodness, faithfulness, gentleness, self-control."*

The people who bring forth the kinds of fruit specified in this passage do not need to be governed by the law. They are not under the law. They have escaped from their marriage to the flesh under the law, and they are free to be married by the Holy Spirit to the resurrected Christ and bring forth the kind of fruit that is appropriate to that union. The key to the Christian life is not effort. It is union.

Thank You, Jesus, for Your work on the cross. I proclaim that as I worship the Lord, I am united to Him in one spirit. I proclaim that Jesus was cut off by death that I might be joined to God eternally. Amen.

The Roman Pilgrimage, Vol. 2: Romans 6:23–7:16 (audio, video)

WEEK 23:

I have been forgiven and set free from my sins.

In [Jesus Christ] *we have redemption through His blood, the forgiveness of sins.*

—Colossians 1:14

A Clean Record

I have been forgiven and set free from my sins.

O ne of the most wondrous aspects of God's nature is that when He forgives, He does not partially forgive. He totally forgives. Micah stated this beautifully:

> *Who is a God like you, who pardons sin and forgives the transgression of the remnant of his inheritance? You do not stay angry forever but delight to show mercy. You will again have compassion on us; you will tread our sins underfoot and hurl all our iniquities into the depths of the sea.* (Micah 7:18–19 NIV)

Isn't that beautiful? Everything that we have ever done wrong— everything that could ever make us feel guilty, every accusation that the enemy could ever bring against us—God treads underfoot and hurls into the depths of the sea.

Someone remarked once that when God casts your sins into the sea, He puts up a notice that says, "No Fishing!" Don't ever try to go back and resurrect something that God has buried. If God has forgiven you, you are forgiven. There are no questions. God's forgiveness is total. In Isaiah God speaks to His people, saying:

> *I, even I, am he who blots out your transgressions, for my own sake, and remembers your sins no more.* (Isaiah 43:25)

When God forgives us, He blots out the record. It is clean. It is just as though that which was forgiven had never taken place. Not only does He blot out the record, but He blots it out from His own memory. He says that He will remember our sins no more.

God does not have a bad memory, but He does have the ability to forget. And when He forgives, He forgets!

Thank You, Lord, for Your forgiveness. I proclaim that God's forgiveness for me is total: He has blotted out my record and it is clean. I have been forgiven and set free from my sins. Amen.

The Three Most Important Words (booklet)

Nothing Shall Hurt Us

I have been forgiven and set free from my sins.

For He [God] delivered us from the domain of darkness, and transferred us to the kingdom of His beloved Son, in whom we have redemption, the forgiveness of sins.

(Colossians 1:13–14 NASB)

Through our faith in Jesus and His sacrificial death, God has delivered us from the domain of darkness. Notice that word *domain*. In the original Greek, it is *authority*. Satan has authority over the disobedient, the unbelieving, and the unsaved. But through Jesus, God has delivered us from that domain of darkness and transferred us into the kingdom of the Son of His love, in whom we have redemption.

Note the key word *redemption*. We have been bought back. We are no longer under the power of the curse, because of the redeeming death and shed blood of Jesus Christ.

For this purpose the Son of God was manifested, that He might destroy the works of the devil. (1 John 3:8)

Why did Jesus come? To destroy the works of the devil. That includes the curse!

Behold, I give you the authority to trample on serpents and scorpions, and over all the power of the enemy, and nothing shall by any means hurt you. (Luke 10:19)

Satan may have power, but Jesus has given us power over the power of Satan, so that *"nothing shall by any means hurt [us]."*

Thank You, Lord, for Your forgiveness. I proclaim that Jesus has delivered me from the domain of darkness, and that He has given me power over all the power of Satan, so that *"nothing shall by any means"* hurt me. I have been forgiven and set free from my sins.
Amen.

Transformed for Life (book)

JUNE 6

Replacing the Old Sinful Man

I have been forgiven and set free from my sins.

Providing complete deliverance from the tyranny of sin required a threefold provision of God. First of all, He had to deal with our sins—the sinful acts we have all committed. Because Jesus paid the full penalty for our sins on the cross, God can forgive us without compromising His own justice. His first provision, therefore, is forgiveness.

Then, God also had to deal with the corrupt nature within us that caused us to go on committing those sinful acts. His provision was execution—to put that sinful nature to death. The good news is that the execution took place more than nineteen centuries ago, when Jesus died on the cross.

That's not the end, however. God's purpose is to replace the old, sinful man with a new man of His own creating. Paul explained this provision in the book of Ephesians, saying,

> Put off, concerning your former conduct, the old man...and be renewed in the spirit of your mind, and...put on the new man which was created according to God, in true righteousness and holiness. (Ephesians 4:22–24)

We should not assume, however, that the old man will passively accept his sentence of execution. On the contrary, he will struggle—fiercely, at times—to regain his control over us. This explains Paul's words of warning in Colossians 3:3, where he said, *"For you died."* Then, in verse 5, he said, *"Therefore put to death your members which are on the earth."* We must stand in faith that the death of our old man is an accomplished fact, and we must actively resist his attempts to regain control over us.

Thank You, Lord, for Your forgiveness. I proclaim that on the cross, Jesus put my sinful nature to death, replacing it with a new nature. I actively resist my old man's attempts to regain control over me, proclaiming that I have been forgiven and set free from my sins. Amen.

Rules of Engagement (book)

Total, Permanent Victory

I have been forgiven and set free from my sins.

T he sacrificial death of Jesus on the cross is the only basis of God's provision for every need of the whole human race. Instead of God doing a lot of different actions at different times, Scripture says, *"By one offering* [sacrifice] *He has perfected forever those who are being sanctified"* (Hebrews 10:14).

The writer of Hebrews explained that after Jesus had offered that one sacrifice, He *"sat down at the right hand of God"* (verse 12). Why did He sit down? Because He was never going to have to do it again.

Through His work on the cross, Jesus administered to Satan and his kingdom a total, permanent, irreversible defeat. Jesus will never have to do that work again. Satan has already been defeated. You and I do not have to defeat Satan. But we must apply the victory that Jesus has already won and walk in that victory.

We read in Colossians 1:12, *"Giving thanks to the Father who has qualified us to be partakers of the inheritance of the saints in the light."* Our inheritance is in the light, and there is no darkness whatsoever in it. It is totally in the light. How has He done it?

> *He has delivered us from the power* [I prefer to say *"domain"*] *of darkness and conveyed* [translated] *us into the kingdom of the Son of His love, in whom we have redemption through His blood, the forgiveness of sins.*   (verses 13–14)

By redemption through the blood of Jesus, we have been delivered from the domain of darkness and translated, or carried over, into the kingdom of the Son of God's love.

Thank You, Lord, for Your forgiveness. I proclaim that through the cross, Jesus administered to Satan and his kingdom a total, permanent, irreversible defeat. I apply the victory Jesus has won, and I walk in that victory, for I have been forgiven and set free from my sins. Amen.

Lucifer Exposed (book)

Freedom from Legalism

I have been forgiven and set free from my sins.

In Romans 8:15, Paul was speaking to Christians baptized in the Holy Spirit, and he said, *"For you did not receive the spirit of bondage again to fear."*

Bondage means enslavement. Paul was warning Christians not to let the devil get them back into slavery. And the suggestion is very clear that the form of slavery to which they would be enticed to return would be that of religious slavery—subservience to the law from which they had been delivered when Jesus died on the cross.

The whole of the book of Galatians deals with this very issue of not being enslaved by religious legalism after having been set free by the gospel and the power of the Holy Spirit. As a matter of fact, Paul treated that issue as something much more severe and dangerous than even sexual sins, such as fornication or adultery. It is quite remarkable, but the epistle to the Galatians is the only one of Paul's epistles that he does not open by giving thanks to God for the people to whom he was writing. So upset was he by what the Galatians were doing that he launched straight into his subject. *"I marvel that you are turning away so soon from Him who called you in the grace of Christ"* (Galatians 1:6).

This is a clear example of religious demons bringing people back into the slavery of legalism. Let us heed Paul's emphatic warning: *"Be not entangled again with the yoke of bondage* [slavery]*"* (Galatians 5:1 KJV).

Thank You, Lord, for Your forgiveness. I proclaim that I will not be enslaved by religious legalism after having been set free by the gospel and by the power of the Holy Spirit. I have been forgiven and set free from my sins. Amen.

Deliverance and Demonology: Nature and Activity of Demons (audio)

190   *DECLARING GOD'S WORD*

"No Condemnation"

I have been forgiven and set free from my sins.

There is therefore now no condemnation to those who are in Christ Jesus....For what the law could not do in that it was weak through the flesh, God did by sending His own Son in the likeness of sinful flesh. (Romans 8:1, 3)

There are two kinds of coffee: percolated and instant. Percolated coffee takes longer to make because it has to go through the brewing process. The book of Romans is like percolated coffee. We cannot get instant coffee out of Romans chapter 8. We must go through the preceding seven chapters. Those are the percolator. But the result is that much richer. Only when we have been through those chapters do we get to the *"therefore."* The preceding chapters deal with the total sinfulness of all humanity, as well as with the failure of religion to change man's sinful nature. Using the examples of Abraham and David (see chapter 4), with a comparison between Adam and Christ (see chapter 5), Paul moves on in chapter 6 to reveal God's remedy for the old man: execution. God doesn't patch up the old man. He doesn't reform him. He executes him! The good news is that this execution took place when Jesus died on the cross.

Romans 7 deals with our relationship to the Law. I always used to think, *Why come to the law after all that?* But I have learned that the ultimate hurdle we have to get over, the last stage of this percolator, is how we relate to the Law. Without the percolator, we cannot live in Romans 8, because the essential condition is *"no condemnation."* The moment in which we come under condemnation is the moment when we are out of the Spirit-controlled life of Romans 8. The devil's main objective is to bring us under condemnation. The objective of God's Word, especially in Romans, is to deliver us from condemnation.

Thank You, Lord, for Your forgiveness. I am free from the devil's efforts to bring me under condemnation, and there is no condemnation for me because I am in Christ Jesus. I have been forgiven and set free from my sins. Amen.

Lucifer Exposed (book)

Fully His

I have been forgiven and set free from my sins.

There was a boy who lived in a town on the seaside. He was a skilled and clever carver, and he carved himself a little wooden boat. When he put sails on it, it really sailed. One day, he took it down to the shore and was sailing it at the edge of the sea, but the tide changed and carried his boat out to sea, and he could not recover it. So, he went home without his boat.

With the next change of the wind and tide, the boat came back again. A man walking along the seashore found the boat, picked it up, and saw it was a beautiful piece of work. He took it to a local shop and sold it. The shop owner cleaned it up and put it on display in his shop window with a price of thirty-five dollars.

Some while later, the boy walked past the shop, looked in the window, and saw his boat with a price of thirty-five dollars. He knew, however, that he had no way to prove that it was his boat. If he wanted his boat, there was only one thing he could do: buy it back.

He set to work, taking any job he could to earn the money to buy his boat. Once he earned the money, he walked into the shop and said, "I want to buy that boat." He paid the money, and, when he got the boat in his hands, he walked outside and stopped on the sidewalk. He held the boat to his chest and said, "Now you're mine. I made you and I bought you." That is redemption. First, the Lord made us, but we were in Satan's slave market. Then, He bought us. We are doubly His. Can you see how valuable you are to the Lord? Think of yourself as that boat for a moment. You may feel so inadequate, so worthless. You wonder whether God ever really cares. Just try to believe that you are that boat in the Lord's arms and He is saying to you, "Now you're Mine. I made you and I bought you. I own you; you're fully Mine."

Thank You, Lord, for Your forgiveness. I proclaim that I am in the Lord's arms, and He has declared that I am His. He made me and bought me; He loves me; I am fully His. I have been forgiven and set free from my sins. Amen.

The Good News of the Kingdom, Vol. 1: The Kingdom for All Nations (audio)

WEEK 24:

I am a child of God.

But as many as received Him, to them He gave the right to become children of God, to those who believe in His name.

—John 1:12

True Identity

I am a child of God.

The reason that Jesus Christ came to earth was—and is—to bring us to God. If we stop short of this revelation of God, we have stopped short of the full and final outworking of redemption's purpose. When we come into the fullness of this revelation and into that direct relationship with God as Father, it supplies certain factors that are conspicuously lacking in the emotional experience of many people in our culture. The three things that come out of this revelation and relationship are identity, self-worth, and security.

Identity is a real problem for people today. An interesting clue to this problem was the success of the book and TV miniseries *Roots*. The essence of that story was a man's search for his roots, or origins, in order to gain a stronger sense of identity. All humanity is busy with the same search. Men and women want to know where they came from, who is behind them, how it started, and who they are. Scripture and psychology agree that a person really does not answer the question, "Who am I?" until he or she knows who his or her father is.

Today, human relationships between parents and children increasingly have become broken and fragmented, and the result has been a widespread identity crisis. Christianity's answer to that identity crisis is to bring men and women into a direct, personal relationship with God the Father through Jesus Christ the Son. People who truly know God as Father no longer have an identity problem. They know who they are—they are children of God. Their Father created the universe, their Father loves them, and their Father cares for them.

Thank You, Jesus, that You have redeemed me. I proclaim that because of my relationship with God the Father, through Jesus, I know who I am. I proclaim that I am a child of God. Amen.

Fatherhood (audio)

True Self-worth

I am a child of God.

I cannot begin to count the number of people I have ministered to whose greatest problem was a failure to appreciate themselves sufficiently. They had too low an esteem of themselves, which caused them many spiritual and emotional agonies.

First John 3:1 says, *"See how great a love the Father has bestowed upon us, that we should be called children of God; and such we are"* (NASB). Once we really comprehend that we are children of God, whom He loves intimately and personally; that God is interested in us, is never too busy for us, and desires a direct and personal relationship with each of us, we gain a tremendous increase in self-worth.

Once when I was on my way to a meeting, I literally ran into a woman. We were going in opposite directions at considerable speed. After our collision, she picked herself up and said, "Mr. Prince, I've been praying that if God wanted you to speak to me, we'd meet."

"Well," I said, "we've met. But I can only give you about two minutes. I'm very busy." She began to tell me what her problem was, and after a while, I interrupted her, saying, "I'm sorry, I've only got one minute left...but I think I know your problem. Will you follow me in this prayer?" I led her in a prayer in which she just thanked God because He was her Father and she was His child, that He loved her, that He cared for her, that she was special, and that she belonged to the best family in the universe. Then, we parted ways.

About a month later, I received a letter from the same woman, in which she wrote, "I just want to tell you that being together with you and praying that prayer has completely changed my attitude toward life. For the first time, I really have a sense of my own worth."

Thank You, Jesus, that You have redeemed me. I proclaim that it is
my direct and personal relationship with the Lord that gives me
self-worth. I proclaim that I am a child of God. Amen.

Fatherhood (audio)

Coming to the Father

I am a child of God.

When Jesus came to earth, His ultimate purpose was to bring to the Father those who would turn to Him. Scripture states this truth in many places, such as the following:

> *For Christ also died for sins once for all, the just for the unjust, in order that He might bring us to God.* (1 Peter 3:18 NASB)

Why did Jesus die? *"That He might bring us to God."* Jesus was not the end; He was the way. He said that Himself, quite emphatically, in John 14:6:

> *Jesus said to him, "I am the way, and the truth, and the life; no one comes to the Father, but through Me."* (NASB)

Jesus is the way, but the Father is the destination. I think that, many times in our Christian faith, we really miss the purpose of God. We talk a great deal about the Lord Jesus Christ as our Savior, our Intercessor, our Mediator, and so on. All of these terms are wonderful and true, but they stop short of God's purpose. God's purpose is not merely that we should come to the Son, but also that, through the Son, we should come to the Father.

Thank You, Jesus, that You have redeemed me. I proclaim that through the Son, I come to the Father. I proclaim that I am a child of God. Amen.

Fatherhood (audio)

Accepted!

I am a child of God.

I like the way the King James Version translates Ephesians 1:6, because of one word in particular: *"accepted." "To the praise of the glory of his grace, wherein he hath made us accepted in the beloved"* (KJV).

Again, when God says we are accepted, it does not mean we are just tolerated. It means we are much favored. We are the objects of His particular, loving care and attention. We are number one on His list of things to take care of in the universe. He does not push us off in a corner and say, "Wait, I'm busy," or "I don't have time for you now," or "Don't make a noise; Daddy is sleeping." He says, "I'm interested in you. I want you. You're welcome. Come in; I've been waiting a long time for you."

It is like the father in the story of the prodigal son. He was out there looking for the boy to come home. Others did not have to say, "You know, your son is coming home." The first one to know it was the father. He knew it before all the rest of the family. God's attitude to us in Christ is like that. We are not rejects. We are not second-class citizens. And we are not servants.

When the prodigal came back, he was willing to be a servant. He said, "Father, just make me one of your hired servants." But if you read the story carefully, you will notice that when the son confessed his sins, his father interrupted him—he didn't allow him to finish speaking. He never allowed him to say, "Make me as one of your hired servants." On the contrary, he said, *"Bring out the best robe and put it on him, and put a ring on his hand and sandals on his feet. And bring the fatted calf here and kill it, and let us eat and be merry; for this my son was dead and is alive again; he was lost and is found"* (Luke 15:22–24). Praise God!

Thank You, Jesus, that You have redeemed me. I proclaim that by the grace of God, I am *"accepted in the beloved."* I proclaim that I am a child of God. Amen.

From Rejection to Acceptance (audio)

In the Father's Arms

I am a child of God.

Picture a little child held securely by his father's arm, with his face pressed against the father's shoulder. There may be great confusion and distress all around. The world may seem to be falling apart. But the little child is totally at peace, not at all concerned by the events taking place around him. He is secure in his father's arms.

We, too, are held securely by our Father. Jesus has assured us that our Father is greater than all who may surround us and that no one is able to snatch us out of His hand.

Jesus also gave this assurance to His disciples: *"Do not fear, little flock, for it is your Father's good pleasure to give you the kingdom"* (Luke 12:32). We may be just a little flock, surrounded by wild beasts of all kinds. But if our Father has committed Himself to giving us the kingdom, no power in the universe can withhold it from us.

Thank You, Jesus, that You have redeemed me. I proclaim that I am secure in the Father's arms. I am a child of God. Amen.

To Please My Father (Teaching Legacy Letter)

Pleasing the Father

I am a child of God.

In Philippians 2:3, Paul warned us servants of the Lord, *"Let nothing be done through selfish ambition or conceit."*

Over the years, I have observed that one persistent, pervasive problem in the church is personal ambition and competition among leaders, specifically ministers. Lest I sound judgmental, let me add that I observed this tendency first and foremost in my own life.

We often make the mistake of equating security with success. We think, *If I build the biggest church or hold the largest meeting or amass the most names on my mailing list, I will be secure.* But this is a delusion. In actual fact, the more we aim at personal success, the less secure we become. We are continually threatened by the possibility that someone else might build a bigger church or hold a larger meeting or amass more names on his mailing list.

As for me, I have found my perfect pattern in Jesus, who said, *"The Father has not left Me alone, for I always do those things that please Him"* (John 8:29). I am no longer motivated by personal ambition. I have discovered a sweeter, purer motive: simply to please my Father.

I am training myself to approach every situation and decision with a single, simple question: *How can I please my Father?* In times of frustration or apparent failure, I seek to turn my focus from trying to solve the problem to maintaining an attitude that is pleasing to my Father. As servants of Christ, there will be no competition among us if we are motivated by the simple desire to please our Father. Harmony and mutual concern take the place of striving and self-seeking.

Thank You, Jesus, that You have redeemed me. I proclaim that my motive in life is to please my Father—because I am a child of God. Amen.

To Please My Father (Teaching Legacy Letter)

Our True Home

I am a child of God.

Once when I was really concerned about my own spiritual condition, I asked God to make heaven more real to me. I believe heaven is the home of every child of God.

I have never met a child who did not have a rather clear idea about his own home. A child might not know the street outside, but he knows his own home. I think one of the marks of us, as God's children, is that we feel at home in relationship to heaven. This earth is beautiful; this life is exciting. But this world is not our final resting place.

The great saints of God were looking ahead, out of time and into eternity, and they had some glimpses of what was to come. Physical death was not going to be a jump into the unknown. They had some clear revelation of what they could expect. I am looking forward to the temple. I am looking forward to the angels. And I am looking forward to the four living creatures. There is so much that I am looking forward to. I think that the sea of glass mingled with crystal is going to be very exciting. (See, for example, Revelation 3:5; 4:6–8; 7:15.) There will be no dull moments in heaven.

Thank You, Jesus, that You have redeemed us. I proclaim that heaven is the home of every child of God—and that includes me, because I am a child of God. Amen.

God's Last Word, Vol. 2: Review/Hebrews 8:1–8:7 (audio)

WEEK 25:

I am a friend of Christ.

No longer do I call you servants, for a servant does not know what his master is doing; but I have called you friends, for all things that I heard from My Father I have made known to you.

—John 15:15

God's Standard of Friendship

I am a friend of Christ.

Alas, in the world today, the word *friend* has been watered down. It has become a cheap word, and friendship can be a cheap thing. But I want you to know that God's standard of friendship has not changed. For God, friendship is based on covenant commitment. Through covenant commitment, Abraham became a friend of God. Under the new covenant, Jesus wants to bring us into the same relationship with Him—as His friends—that Abraham entered into under the old covenant.

In John 15:15, Jesus said to His disciples,

No longer do I call you slaves,…but I have called you friends.

(NASB)

That is a promotion, from being a slave to being a friend. But we need to understand that, for us just as much as it was for Abraham, friendship is not cheap. It costs something to be a friend of Jesus. For us, the basis of friendship with Jesus is the same as it was for Abraham. It is covenant commitment. Jesus was about to lay down His life for us when He said, *"Greater love has no one than this, that one lay down his life for his friends"* (John 15:13 NASB). But remember, if we are to be Jesus' friends, we have to lay down our lives for Him. It is a two-way commitment.

Thank You, Jesus, that You have redeemed me. I proclaim that because Jesus laid down His life for me, I will lay down my life for Him, for I am a friend of Christ. Amen.

Relationship with God (audio)

Perfect Fellowship

I am a friend of Christ.

In his first epistle, John said,

> What we have seen and heard we proclaim to you also, that you also may have fellowship with us; and indeed our fellowship is with the Father, and with His Son Jesus Christ.
>
> (1 John 1:3 NASB)

In other words, the gospel is an invitation from the Godhead for us to share the fellowship that the Father and Son share with one another. The Greek word for *fellowship* is *koinonia*. It is an important word in New Testament Greek that literally means, "sharing in common." So, fellowship is sharing in common. We are invited to share the same relationship that God the Father and God the Son have together. One thing is clear about this relationship: God the Father and God the Son have everything in common. Neither withholds anything from the other.

In John 17:10, Jesus said to His Father,

> *And all* [things that are] *mine are thine, and thine are mine.*
>
> (KJV)

That's perfect *koinonia*, perfect fellowship—the perfect sharing of all things. It is the perfect pattern of relationship into which God wants to bring us.

Thank You, Jesus, that You have redeemed me. I proclaim that I have been invited to share the same relationship that the Father and Son have together. I enter into that perfect fellowship, because I am a friend of Christ. Amen.

Relationship with God (audio)

The Price of Friendship

I am a friend of Christ.

Often, the measure of God's commitment to you is determined by the measure of your commitment to Him. God never makes partial commitments, and He does not want any partial commitments. God has established the price of a relationship with Him. It is *everything you have.* "*He...that forsaketh not all that he hath, he cannot be my disciple*" (Luke 14:33 KJV).

You may say, "That sounds hard." But it is realistic. Let me tell you two facts about God's kingdom. First of all, God never has a sale. He never reduces the price on any item. If you want the relationship that Peter, Paul, and John had with the Lord, you must pay what they paid. God has not offered a discount.

The second fact is good news: in God's kingdom, there is no inflation. The price has never gone up, and it has never gone down. It is always the same.

The outcome of a commitment to God is peace, security, and joy. Do you want it? You have to make the decision. Jesus said,

> *Behold, I stand at the door, and knock: if any man hear my voice, and open the door, I will come in to him, and will sup with him, and he with me.*   (Revelation 3:20 KJV)

Notice the order Jesus established in this verse. First, you give Jesus your supper, and then He gives you His. As Jesus said to His Father, "*All Mine are Yours, and Yours are Mine*" (John 17:10). Are you willing to make that kind of commitment to God?

Thank You, Jesus, that You have redeemed me. I proclaim that I am willing to pay the price of total commitment to that relationship, for I am a friend of Christ. Amen.

Relationship with God (audio)

Enjoying God

I am a friend of Christ.

Right at the beginning of human history, when man first related to God, their relationship was so simple. There were not a lot of religious rituals and paraphernalia. Enoch just *"walked with God"* (see Genesis 5:22, 24). As we go on further in the Bible, we meet the great father of the faith, Abraham, with his most honorable title, which was *"friend of God"* (James 2:23). He and God simply enjoyed one another's company.

I sometimes long to get away from all the theology and all the religious formalities and just have a relationship of being God's friend—walking with Him and enjoying His company. I really believe God loves to be enjoyed by His people.

Sometimes, we get so preoccupied with methodology and theology and doctrine that we lose sight of God in the midst of it all. We get into the middle of the forest, where all we can see are trees. We no longer can see the whole picture. Then, we have to back out of the forest, take a fresh look around, and consider adjusting our priorities.

Thank You, Jesus, that You have redeemed me. I proclaim my desire to walk with God and enjoy His company, for I am a friend of Christ. Amen.

Relationship with God (audio)

The Measure of Commitment

I am a friend of Christ.

God entered into covenant with Abraham, as recorded in Genesis 15. Each person involved—God and Abraham—made a total commitment. There came a time when God called on Abraham to fulfill his commitment and offer his son, Isaac, as a sacrifice. But God's commitment was just as total as Abraham's. So, two thousand years later, the other side of the covenant came to the fore: God gave up His only Son, the Lord Jesus Christ.

Remember that the commitment you make to God usually determines the measure of God's commitment to you. Total commitment to God calls for total commitment from God. That is the very essence of a covenant relationship. However, Abraham's covenant with God had a further practical effect on his personal relationship with God. In his epistle, James spoke about what Abraham did when he offered up Isaac, and the result of his willingness to do so.

> Was not Abraham our father justified by works, when he offered up Isaac his son on the altar? You see that faith was working with his works, and as a result of the works, faith was perfected; and the Scripture was fulfilled which says, "And Abraham believed God, and it was reckoned to him as righteousness," and he was called the friend of God. (James 2:21–23 NASB)

Through that covenant commitment and through its outworking in the offering up of Isaac, Abraham was reckoned as God's friend. That is a very significant and honorable title. The lesson is this: covenant is the door to true friendship. When two individuals make a covenant with one another and live out the terms of their covenant, that is true friendship at work.

Thank You, Jesus, that You have redeemed me. I proclaim my total commitment to God, and His to me—our covenant is the door to true friendship. I proclaim that I am a friend of Christ. Amen.

Relationship with God (audio)

206   *DECLARING GOD'S WORD*

Submitting to God's Instruction

I am a friend of Christ.

When God sets out to teach, He chooses His students on the basis of their character—not on their intellectual abilities, academic degrees, or social standing. He looks for an inner attitude of the heart toward Himself, an attitude of reverent submission and respect. Furthermore, God sets the curriculum. He teaches such individuals *"in the way that he [God] shall choose"* (Psalm 25:12 KJV). Often, the way God chooses is not the way that we would choose for ourselves. We might incline toward themes of prophecy or revelation that seem profound, whereas God's curriculum might focus on what is humble and down-to-earth: service, sacrifice, and faithfulness.

For those who submit to God's instruction, there is a wonderful reward: *"The secret of the LORD is with them that fear him"* (Psalm 25:14 KJV). In human relationships, we share our secrets only with those whom we trust. Likewise, when God shares His secrets with us, it is proof that we have earned His trust. It is our certificate of graduation from His school.

This truth is illustrated beautifully in the relationship of Jesus to His disciples. After He had put them through three years of rigorous discipline, He told them, *"I no longer call you servants, because a servant does not know his master's business. Instead, I have called you friends, for everything that I learned from my Father I have made known to you"* (John 15:15 NIV). First, Jesus Himself learned from the Father through perfect submission to Him. Then, Jesus, in turn, passed on all He had learned from the Father to those who submitted in like manner to Him.

God still chooses His students on this basis. Neither His requirements nor His curriculum have changed.

Thank You, Jesus, that You have redeemed me. I proclaim my desire to submit completely to the Lord's instruction and thereby to become His friend, for I am a friend of Christ. Amen.

Through the Psalms with Derek Prince (book)

Intelligent Partners with God

I am a friend of Christ.

The first man, Adam, was not a slave, for God called him to intelligent partnership. When God wanted the animals to be named, He said, "Adam, come here and look at these animals. Tell Me what you think they should be named." In Hebrew, a name is always indicative of one's nature. So, in naming the animals, Adam had to understand their natures and their relationships to one another. Whatever Adam called an animal, that was its name. God did not name the animals; He told Adam to do that. But God gave Adam the insight and the wisdom that he needed to complete the assignment. Likewise, in our new relationship with God in Jesus Christ, we are not slaves; rather, we are intelligent partners with God.

John 15:15 is an astonishing statement:

I no longer call you servants, because a servant does not know his master's business. Instead, I have called you friends, for everything that I learned from my Father I have made known to you. (NIV)

Jesus held nothing back. If there is something we do not know, it is because we have not availed ourselves of what is revealed. But the real problem comes in doing what we already *know*. Jesus acted on everything the Father showed Him; if we would do the same, the same revelation would be made available to us.

Thank You, Jesus, that You have redeemed me. I proclaim that I want to avail myself of all that the Lord reveals, and to follow through on what I already know. I proclaim that I am a friend of Christ. Amen.

Spiritual Conflict, Vol. 2: God's Secret Plan Unfolds: God's Purpose for the New Race (audio)

Declaring God's Word

Week 26:

I have been made righteous through faith.

Therefore, having been justified by faith, we have peace with God through our Lord Jesus Christ.

—Romans 5:1

JUNE 25

Made Righteous

I have been made righteous through faith.

We are justified through faith in the blood of Jesus. Let's read what Paul wrote about this in Romans:

> *Now to him* [the religious person] *that worketh is the reward not reckoned of grace, but of debt. But to him that worketh not, but believeth on him that justifieth the ungodly, his faith is counted for righteousness.* (Romans 4:4–5 KJV)

Notice verse 5. The first thing you have to do is to stop trying to make yourself righteous. Stop trying to be a little better. Call a halt to all that. *"To him that worketh not."* What should we do? Let's look again at the end of that passage: *"But to him that worketh not, but believeth on him that justifieth the ungodly, his faith is counted for righteousness"* (verse 5 KJV). Just believe. Is it that simple? If it is not that simple, we will never make it. God makes unrighteous people righteous—that is what the Scripture says, and I believe it.

> *For he hath made him to be sin for us, who knew no sin; that we might be made the righteousness of God in him.*
> (2 Corinthians 5:21 KJV)

I like to change the order of the words in that verse, substituting specific names for the pronouns. "For God has made Jesus, who knew no sin, to be sin for us, that we might be made the righteousness of God in Jesus." There is the complete exchange. *Jesus was made sin with our sinfulness so that we might be made righteous with His righteousness.* This righteousness is available through faith in His blood. We are made righteous through faith in the blood of Jesus Christ.

Thank You, Jesus, for Your sacrifice. I proclaim that righteousness is available through faith in Your blood. I have been made righteous through faith. Amen.

Spiritual Conflict Series, Vol. 3: God's People Triumphant: Spiritual Weapons—The Blood, The Word, Our Testimony (audio)

One Act of Obedience

I have been made righteous through faith.

For as through the one man's disobedience the many were made sinners, even so through the obedience of the One the many will be made righteous. (Romans 5:19 NASB)

By Adam's one act of disobedience, many—that is, all—of his descendants were made sinners. But by Jesus' one act of obedience, all who believe in Him are made righteous.

The parallel is important because the people who became sinners as a result of Adam's sin, including you and me, were not just sinners by label; they were sinners by nature and by act.

Correspondingly, when we are made righteous through faith in Jesus, it is not that God just puts a new label on us by taking away the label "sinner" and applying the label "righteous." Rather, we are actually *made* righteous, by nature and by act.

Just as surely as Adam's disobedience made us all sinners, in exactly the same way, Christ's obedience can make us all righteous. Not just in theory, not just in theology, but in the way we live—in the very nature that is in us.

Thank You, Jesus, for Your sacrifice. I proclaim that by one single act of obedience on Your part, I have been made righteous through faith. Amen.

The Roman Pilgrimage, Vol. 1: Romans 5:1–5:21 (audio, video)

Products of Righteousness

I have been made righteous through faith.

Righteousness produces certain immediate and definite observable results. The whole of our lives, including our attitudes, our relationships, and the effectiveness of our acts of Christian service, will depend on how far we realize that we have been made righteous. We read in Proverbs 28:1, *"The wicked flee when no man pursueth: but the righteous are bold as a lion"* (KJV). Few Christians today are bold. Most are timid, apologetic; they back down when confronted with evil. The root cause is a failure to realize that they are righteous in God's sight—as righteous as Jesus Christ Himself. When we acknowledge and appreciate that fact, it makes us bold.

Let's look at some other results of righteousness. Isaiah 32:17 says, *"And the work of righteousness shall be peace; and the effect of righteousness quietness and assurance for ever"* (KJV). This passage speaks of three products of righteousness: peace, quietness, and assurance, which come when we realize that we have been made righteous with Jesus Christ's righteousness. Romans 14:17 tells us, *"For the kingdom of God is not meat and drink; but righteousness, and peace, and joy in the Holy Ghost"* (KJV). Peace, quietness, joy, and assurance are products of righteousness. If we do not receive righteousness by faith, we may struggle to achieve these results, but in vain. It is pathetic to see Christians trying to be joyful, have peace, relax, and have assurance—just because somebody told them they ought to. My experience is that when Christians really receive the assurance of the forgiveness of sin and of righteousness by faith, the results of righteousness follow automatically. The key is getting people to realize that they have been made righteous with the righteousness of Jesus Christ.

Thank You, Jesus, for Your sacrifice. I proclaim that the righteousness of Jesus brings boldness, peace, quietness, and assurance, which I receive because I have been made righteous through faith. Amen.

Spiritual Conflict Series, Vol. 3: God's People Triumphant: Spiritual Weapons—The Blood, The Word, Our Testimony (audio)

The Gift of Righteousness

I have been made righteous through faith.

Jesus said in Matthew 6:33, *"Seek ye first the kingdom of God, and his righteousness"* (KJV). Any other righteousness we might endeavor to seek is on too low a level. The only righteousness that will admit us into heaven is the righteousness of God, which comes only by faith in Jesus Christ. It is received by faith as a gift. Here is the first specific manifestation of God's grace in the lives of those who come to Him through Jesus Christ: righteousness. God cannot do anything for us until He has made us righteous; it is the first thing He does when we approach Him.

You would probably agree that the majority of Christians have never grasped this truth. In fact, I think you will find that much of the church's liturgy—including our music and our hymns—are designed to leave us sin-conscious. In many cases, we almost feel that it's presumptuous to consider ourselves anything but sinful. This is a remarkable fact.

There is one thing the devil fights against as powerfully as anything else, and that is any person who begins to realize what it is to be made righteous by faith. Satan will keep you, by any means that he can, under some measure of condemnation and guilt, and he'll keep you feeling very religious about it, too.

Many people would feel embarrassed or presumptuous to call themselves "righteous," for they think that they have to earn righteousness. Scripture, however, emphasizes that, rather than being something we can merit, righteousness is a gift no one deserves. It is a free, unmerited gift. You either receive it as a gift, or you live without it. The choice is yours.

Thank You, Jesus, for Your sacrifice. I proclaim that I receive the righteousness of God by faith in Jesus Christ as a free and unmerited gift. I proclaim that I have been made righteous through faith. Amen.

The Nine Gifts of the Holy Spirit, Vol. 1: Gifts of Revelation and Power: Explanation of the Greek Word "Charisma" (audio)

Life in the Son

I have been made righteous through faith.

By putting our faith in Jesus Christ's sacrificial death on our behalf, by letting Him bear the guilt of our sin, and by receiving, by faith, His righteousness, which is imputed to us, we are justified. In that righteousness, I can face God, death, and eternity without a tremor, without fear.

The apostle John wrote in his first epistle,

> *And the witness is this, that God has given us eternal life, and this life is in His Son. He who has the Son has the life; he who does not have the Son of God does not have the life. These things I have written to you who believe in the name of the Son of God, in order that you may know that you have eternal life.*
>
> (1 John 5:11–13 NASB)

God has given a testimony to the whole human race that He has offered to us eternal life. This life is in the person of His Son, Jesus Christ. If we receive Jesus Christ, in Him we have received eternal life.

Notice, this is stated in the present tense: *"He who has the Son **has** the life."* It is not something that is going to happen after death. It is something that happens now, in this time-space world. If you wait until after death to accept His life, you will have waited too long; it will be too late. Settle that issue now! He who has the Son has life. Make sure that you, too, have life!

Thank You, Jesus, for Your sacrifice. I proclaim that I have life now, because I have the Son. I proclaim that I have been made righteous through faith. Amen.

Victory over Death, Part 3 (audio)

The Life of the Vine

I have been made righteous through faith.

To explain to people the importance of having Him in their lives, Jesus used an analogy about the vine and the branches. (See John 15:1–8.) Jesus said, *"I am the vine, you are the branches"* (verse 5). He was very specific. He has given us a point of orientation in interpreting the whole picture. Jesus Himself is the vine.

For a vine to live and bear fruit, there must be sap—a source of nutrients that flows up from the roots, through the trunk, and into the branches. If the sap does not reach the branches, however, they will wither and fail to bear fruit. The key to the life of the vine is the sap, which represents the Holy Spirit. In Romans 8:10, Paul said,

> *If Christ be in you, the body is dead because of sin; but the Spirit is life because of righteousness.* (KJV)

We experienced Christ's death because of our sins. But, having experienced His death, we enter into His life because of His righteousness imputed to us through faith. (See Romans 6:6–8.) And, having His righteousness, we partake of His life. We partake of the life that flows from the roots, through the trunk of the vine, and into the branches. Paul told us in Romans 8:10 that the life is the Holy Spirit. The Spirit is life.

Thank You, Jesus, for Your sacrifice. I proclaim that the life of the vine, which is the Holy Spirit, flows in me. I have been made righteous through faith. Amen.

The Vine and the Branches (audio)

Imputed and Outworked Righteousness

I have been made righteous through faith.

Let us be glad and rejoice, and give honour to him: for the marriage of the Lamb is come, and his wife hath made herself ready. And to her was granted that she should be arrayed in fine linen, clean and white: for the fine linen is the righteousness of saints.
(Revelation 19:7–8 KJV)

There are two Greek words that mean "righteousness." One is *dikaiosune*, the other is *dikaioma*. *Dikaiosune* is righteousness as an abstract concept. *Dikaioma* is righteousness manifested in act, or an act of righteousness. When you and I believe in Jesus Christ, His righteousness—*dikaiosune*—is imputed to us. We are made righteous with His righteousness. When we live out our faith, we express that imputed righteousness in *dikaioma*, which is outworked righteousness, or an act of righteousness.

It is interesting to note that the word used here in Revelation is the plural form of *dikaioma*, *dikaiomata*. The fine linen is the righteous acts of the saints. It is a very searching statement. *"His wife hath made herself ready."* She has done this by her acts of righteousness.

Every culture that I have encountered has embraced one common rule regarding marriage ceremonies. The bridegroom never prepares the bride; rather, the bride always prepares herself. The responsibility is placed on her alone. The Scripture says that the wife of Christ, the church, has made herself ready by her outworked righteous acts. The imputed righteousness of Christ will not avail for the bridal feast. It must be the outworked righteousness—acts that we believers perform because of Christ's gift of righteousness, given freely to us.

Thank You, Jesus, for Your sacrifice. I proclaim that I am living out my faith, expressing imputed righteousness, and acting out my faith, expressing outworked righteousness. I proclaim that I have been made righteous through faith. Amen.

The Vine and the Branches (audio)

I have been united with God
and have become one in spirit with Him.

He who is joined to the Lord is one spirit with Him.

—1 Corinthians 6:17

United with God

I have been united with God
and have become one in spirit with Him.

It is so important to understand the distinction between the human spirit and the soul. It is not the soul that is united with God, but the spirit—for the spirit was created for union with God; indeed, it cannot live out of union with God. As a result of regeneration, the spirit of the born-again believer is able to unite with God.

Let us review three simple descriptions of the orientations of spirit, soul, and body. The spirit is God-conscious. The soul is self-conscious. The body is world-conscious.

Through our spirits, we are conscious of God. In our souls, we are conscious of ourselves. And through our bodies and their senses, we relate to the world around us.

When man's spirit is reunited with God, the rekindled spirit becomes a lamp. Filled with the Holy Spirit, it illuminates the inward nature of man which was dark and alienated from God up to that time. We need to remember that when the Bible was written, the fuel for every lamp was olive oil, and olive oil is always a type, or symbol, of the Holy Spirit.

> *The spirit of man is the lamp of the LORD, searching all the innermost parts of his being.* (Proverbs 20:27 NASB)

When the spirit of man is brought back into union with God and the Holy Spirit comes in and fills up that lamp, then the lamp inside man—his spirit—is illuminated, shedding light on his entire inner being. He is no longer in darkness.

Thank You, Lord, for joining me to You. I proclaim that in union with the Lord, by the illumination of the Holy Spirit, I am no longer in darkness. I proclaim that I have been united with God and have become one in spirit with Him. Amen.

What Is Man?, Part 2 (audio)

Joined to the Lord

*I have been united with God
and have become one in spirit with Him.*

If you have never been shocked by the Bible, you have probably never really read it, because the Bible says some extremely shocking things. Take 1 Corinthians 6:16, for example: *"Or do you not know that he who is joined to a harlot [prostitute] is one body with her? For 'the two,' He [God] says, 'shall become one flesh.'"* We all understand what this verse is talking about—sexual immorality, fornication, and being physically united with a prostitute. With that context in mind, look at what Paul said next: *"But he who is joined to the Lord is one spirit with Him"* (verse 17). This verse cannot be taken out of context. As we have seen, in verse 17, Paul was talking about a union that is just as real as the sexual union—not a physical union, but a spiritual union. That is what it means to be married to the One who is risen from the dead. It is not our souls that are united to the Lord; rather, it is our spirits, for *"he who is joined to the Lord is one spirit."*

Your soul is capable of theology, and it is probably overburdened with it, but your spirit knows God. The spirit is the God-inbreathed part of man. That is what brought man into being in the first place in the garden of Eden. The Lord breathed into Adam's nostrils the spirit of life. (See Genesis 2:7.) And that part of man never finds rest until it is reunited with God. You can chase after all the pleasures and philosophies of the world, but your spirit is not interested in them. Your spirit just wants God, and it is your spirit that can be united with God just as truly as a body of a man can be united with the body of a prostitute. Never separate those two verses. They are totally different, but their analogy is exact and helps us to understand their relationship.

Thank You, Lord, for joining me to You. I proclaim that *"he who is joined to the Lord is one spirit with Him"*—and that this truth applies to me. I have been united with God and have become one in spirit with Him. Amen.

Who Has Bewitched You?: The Only Basis for Righteousness (audio)

Spirit to Spirit

I have been united with God
and have become one in spirit with Him.

There are many facets of the truths about the Old Testament tabernacle of God. One essential, basic fact is that it was a triune building. In other words, it was three in one. It was one single place, but there were three areas: the Outer Court, the Holy Place, and the Holy of Holies.

In this trinity, we find many references to eternal truth. For instance, God is three in one—Father, Son, and Spirit—three persons in one God. Man is likewise triune; one man is made up of spirit, soul, and body. I believe that heaven is triune, as well. There are three heavens—the visible heaven, which we see; an intermediate heaven, which is the headquarters of Satan's kingdom; and a third heaven, which is where God dwells; this is the current location of paradise.

I also believe that the three areas of the tabernacle correspond to the three areas of human personality. The Outer Court, with its natural light of sun, moon, and stars, corresponds to the physical body with the physical senses, which are the source of understanding or perception. The Holy Place corresponds to man's soul, and it speaks about revealed truth. And the Holy of Holies corresponds to man's spirit and speaks about directly apprehended truth. This is truth that is apprehended only by direct, personal contact with God, for it is the spirit of man alone that is united with God. *"He who is joined to the Lord is one spirit"* (1 Corinthians 6:17)—not one soul or one body, but one spirit.

Direct contact with God is spirit to Spirit, and that is where direct revelation comes.

Thank You, Lord, for joining me to You. I proclaim that my direct, personal contact with God is spirit to Spirit. I proclaim that I have been united with God and have become one in spirit with Him.
Amen.

Reigning Now with Christ: We Are a Kingdom of Priests (audio)

Communion with God

*I have been united with God
and have become one in spirit with Him.*

Let's look at some of the functions of the spirit as it relates to the soul and the body. We have seen that the spirit is God-conscious, the soul is self-conscious, and the body is world-conscious. It is very important to understand that the soul is self-conscious. Whenever people are focused on themselves—their own problems and needs— they are operating in the realm of the soul.

The primary activity of the spirit is union with God. It is the only part of man that can be directly united with God. In 1 Corinthians 6:17, Paul said, *"He who is joined to the Lord is one spirit with Him"*—not one soul, not one body, but one spirit. The great privilege we have with our spirits is union and communion with God. The highest activity of man's spirit is worship.

Man's soul contains these three elements: will, intellect, and emotions. The will is the part of me that says, "I want"; the intellect is the part that says, "I think"; and the emotions are the part of me that says, "I feel." Together, these three components make up the soul.

The body is world-conscious; through the senses, the body contacts the surrounding time-space world. God's original purpose was that man's spirit should direct his soul, and that his soul should direct his body. The spirit can direct the body only through the soul. There is one exception to this, and that is speaking in tongues. That is why speaking in tongues is such a unique experience. When we speak in tongues, our spirits control the physical member, the tongue, without the soul's involvement. That is why it is such a tremendously important experience.

Thank You, Lord, for joining me to You. I proclaim that I have been united with God and have become one in spirit with Him. Amen.

Who Am I?: Why You Have a Body (audio)

Worship in the Spirit

I have been united with God
and have become one in spirit with Him.

As we fulfill the Lord's requirement for our bodies and our souls, our spirits are liberated to enter into a fellowship with God—a fellowship even more wonderful than that which was lost through the fall. Paul said in 1 Corinthians 6:17, *"But he who is joined to the Lord is one spirit with Him."* The implication is clear. The redeemed spirit can now enjoy a union with God that is close and intimate. It is the spirit alone, however—not the soul or the body—that can experience this direct, intimate union with God.

It is primarily through the act of worship that our spirits enter into this union with God. In John 4:23–24, Jesus said, *"The true worshipers will worship the Father in spirit and truth....God is Spirit, and those who worship Him must worship in spirit and truth."* Jesus made it clear that true worship must be an activity of our spirits.

In the contemporary church, there is little understanding of the nature of worship, mainly because we do not discern the difference between the spirit and the soul. Worship is not entertainment—that belongs in the theater, not the church. Nor is worship the same as praise. We praise God with our souls, and it is right to do so. Through our praise we have access to God's presence. But once we are in His presence, it is through worship that we enjoy true spiritual union with Him. To be able to worship God in this way is the goal of salvation—first on earth, then later in heaven. It is the highest and holiest activity of which a human being is capable. Worship, however, is possible only when the soul and the body come into submission to the spirit and in harmony with it. Such worship is often too profound for words. It becomes an intense and silent union with God.

Thank You, Lord, for joining me to You. I proclaim that my highest activity is union with God, to worship in spirit and truth. I have been united with God and have become one in spirit with Him. Amen.

Spirit, Soul and Body (Teaching Legacy Letter)

Spiritual Fruit

*I have been united with God
and have become one in spirit with Him.*

Worship is the act by which we are joined to the Lord as one spirit. That is why worship is the highest activity of human beings. Again, when we are joined to the Lord in worship, we begin to bring forth (or birth) the things that God wants brought forth.

Worship is not an appendix to the Christian life; it is not a little addition to services. It is the culmination. It is the confirmation. Once more, if I may put it in this way without offending anyone, it is the consummation of our marriage to the Lord. We are united with Him as one spirit, and when we have that marriage union, it is always for the sake of procreation. That is when spiritual fruit comes out of our lives.

You need to know the identity of the husband with whom you are united. Paul wrote in Galatians 5:19–21, *"Now the deeds of the flesh are evident, which are: immorality, impurity, sensuality, idolatry, sorcery, enmities, strife, jealousy, outbursts of anger, disputes, dissensions, factions, envying, drunkenness, carousing, and things like these"* (NASB). The deeds of the flesh are all too evident. You can tell people that you are spiritual, but if you are truly fleshly, it will show. Let me ask you this: Do you want your children to act like what is described in the passage from Galatians? Because that is what the flesh brings forth. You cannot find one good thing in that entire list. The flesh cannot produce anything acceptable to God. It is corrupt. Jesus said that a corrupt tree cannot bring forth good fruit. (See Matthew 7:18.) It is impossible.

Thank You, Lord, for joining me to You. I proclaim that my goal of being united with God is to bring forth spiritual fruit. I proclaim that I have been united with God and have become one in spirit with Him. Amen.

The Roman Pilgrimage, Vol. 2: Romans 6:23–7:16 (audio, video)

JULY 8

Channels of Spiritual Life

*I have been united with God
and have become one in spirit with Him.*

*The spirit of man is the lamp of the LORD, searching all the inner-
most parts of his being.* (Proverbs 20:27 NASB)

Let us recall that when the spirit of man is brought back into union
with God, and the Holy Spirit comes in and fills up that lamp, then
that lamp inside man is illuminated and sheds light on his whole
inner being. He is no longer in darkness. Furthermore, the reborn
spirit becomes a channel through which the Holy Spirit can flow out
into this world. Jesus said,

*"He who believes in Me, as the Scripture said, 'From his inner-
most being shall flow rivers of living water.'" But this He spoke
of the Spirit* [the Holy Spirit], *whom those who believed in Him
were to receive; for the Spirit was not yet given, because Jesus
was not yet glorified.* (John 7:38–39 NASB)

After the Holy Spirit was given on the day of Pentecost, the regen-
erated spirit of man became a channel or riverbed through which rivers of spiritual life could flow out into this world. That is a marvelous
transformation, because just before saying the above, Jesus said, *"If
any man is thirsty, let him come to Me and drink"* (verse 37). So, this
transformation of regeneration and the infilling of the Holy Spirit
produces a marvelous change—a man who was thirsty, who did not
even have enough for himself, now becomes a channel through which
waters of spiritual life can flow out to the needy world around him.

Thank You, Lord, for joining me to You. I proclaim that I will be a
channel through which the Holy Spirit and waters of spiritual life can
flow out to reach a needy world. I proclaim that I have been united
with God and have become one in spirit with Him. Amen.

What Is Man?, Part 2 (audio)

I have been bought at a price; I belong to God.

Do you not know that your body is the temple of the Holy Spirit who is in you, whom you have from God, and you are not your own? For you were bought at a price; therefore glorify God in your body and in your spirit, which are God's.

—1 Corinthians 6:19–20

Belonging to Jesus

I have been bought at a price; I belong to God.

Do you not know that your body is a temple of the Holy Spirit who is in you, whom you have from God, and that you are not your own? (1 Corinthians 6:19 NASB)

Why are you not your own? Because somebody else has bought you. When you have been bought by somebody else, then you no longer belong to yourself.

Who bought you? Jesus. With what method of payment? His blood. So, if you have been bought by Jesus, remember, you do not belong to yourself. If you belong to yourself, then you are not bought with the blood of Jesus. Again, you cannot belong to yourself and to the Lord. The Lord wants you for Himself. He has paid the price of His precious blood. If you want to hold on to your own life, then, remember, you have not been bought with a price. You cannot have it both ways. If you belong to God, you do not belong to yourself. If you belong to yourself, you do not belong to God.

For you have been bought with a price [the precious blood of Jesus]: *therefore* [because of the price that has been paid for you] *glorify* [honor] *God in your body.* (verse 20)

When Jesus died on the cross, He paid a total price for a total redemption. He did not redeem just a part of you. He redeemed the whole of you—spirit, soul, and body. Jesus died to redeem you. If you have accepted redemption through His blood, then you are not your own; you now belong to Him. Both your spirit and your body are God's, because Jesus paid the price of His blood to possess you.

Thank You, Lord, that You have purchased me. I proclaim that Jesus paid the total price for my redemption. I have been bought at a price; I belong to God. Amen.

Praying to Change History: God's Atomic Weapon: The Blood of Jesus (audio)

Instruments God Uses

I have been bought at a price; I belong to God.

The Bible teaches that the physical body is the temple of the Holy Spirit, and that when Jesus died on the cross and shed His blood, He redeemed our bodies in addition to our spirits and souls. We belong to Him entirely—spirit, soul, and body.

God has a sincere interest in, and a specific purpose for, our bodies. The body is to be the temple of the Holy Spirit. (See 1 Corinthians 6:19.) It is to be the place in man where the Holy Spirit dwells. The Bible tells us that God does not dwell in temples made by hands. (See Acts 7:48.) We can build Him as many churches, synagogues, or tabernacles as we like, but God will not dwell there. God has chosen to dwell in the physical bodies of those who believe in Him. Thus, the believer's body has an important function as a residence of the Holy Spirit.

Furthermore, Paul explained this about our physical members: *"Neither yield ye your members as instruments of unrighteousness unto sin: but yield yourselves unto God, as those that are alive from the dead, and your members as instruments of righteousness unto God"* (Romans 6:13 KJV). The various members of the physical body are intended to be instruments (or weapons) that God can use. They do not belong to us; they belong to God. We are to yield them to God.

It is logical and obvious that God wants His "weapons" in good condition, not feeble or broken-down. He wants our bodies to be healthy and our members to be strong, effective, and active, because they are the members of Christ. In a certain sense, Christ has no body on the earth except ours. Our bodies are the instruments God uses to enact His will on the earth. I have become convinced that God expects us to keep our bodies as strong and as healthy as we can.

Thank You, Lord, that You have purchased me. I proclaim that the members of my physical body are instruments God can use, and I yield them to Him. I have been bought at a price; I belong to God.
Amen.

How to Fast Successfully (book)

The Pearl of Great Price

I have been bought at a price; I belong to God.

In Matthew 13:45–46, Jesus told a parable that, in my opinion, most beautifully describes the wonder of our redemption:

> *Again, the kingdom of heaven is like a merchant seeking beautiful pearls, who, when he had found one pearl of great price, went and sold all that he had and bought it.*

For me, this parable depicts the redemption of a human soul. Jesus is the merchant—not a tourist or a sightseer, but a man who has dealt in pearls all His life—and He knows the exact value of every pearl. The pearl that He has purchased is just one human soul—yours or mine. It cost Him all He had, everything He owned.

Updated to our contemporary culture, I can picture the scene when that merchant broke the news to his wife.

"Honey, I've sold our car."

"You sold our car! Well, at least we still have a roof over our heads."

"No, I sold our house, too!"

"Whatever made you do all that?"

"I found the most beautiful pearl I've ever seen. I've been looking all my life for such a pearl. It cost me everything I had. Wait till you see it!"

What does this mean to you and me? Each of us may picture ourselves as that one priceless pearl worth everything Jesus had—even His own blood.

Thank You, Lord, that You have purchased me. I proclaim that I am that priceless pearl purchased by God. I have been bought at a price; I belong to God. Amen.

Do You Realize How Valuable You Are? (Teaching Legacy Letter)

JULY 12

His Forever!

I have been bought at a price; I belong to God.

Remember, it cost Jesus everything He had to buy you back to Himself. Though He was Lord of the entire universe, He laid aside all His authority and power to die in absolute poverty. He owned nothing. The burial clothes and the tomb in which He was buried were both borrowed.

> *Though He was rich, yet for your sakes He became poor, that you through His poverty might become rich.* (2 Corinthians 8:9)

Perhaps you have never seen yourself as important. Maybe you have a poor self-image or low sense of self-esteem. You may look back on a life of pain and disappointment—a deprived and unhappy childhood, a marriage that ended in divorce, a career that never materialized, or years wasted on drugs and alcohol. Your past and your future both convey the same message: FAILURE!

Not so to Jesus! He loved you so much that He gave up everything to redeem you for Himself. Repeat the beautiful words of the apostle Paul, making them your own: *"The Son of God...loved me and gave Himself for me"* (Galatians 2:20). Say it again: "God loved me and gave Himself for me." And again, "The Son of God loved me and gave Himself for me."

See yourself as that pearl held in the nail-scarred hand of Jesus. Hear Him saying to you, "You're so beautiful! You cost Me everything I had, but I don't regret it. Now you're Mine forever!"

You cannot do anything to earn this. You can never change yourself or make yourself good. All that you can do is to accept what Jesus has done for you and thank Him for it! You belong to Him forever!

Thank You, Lord, that You have purchased me. I proclaim that Jesus loved me and gave Himself for me, and I belong to Him forever! I have been bought at a price; I belong to God. Amen.

Do You Realize How Valuable You Are? (Teaching Legacy Letter)

The Purchase Price

I have been bought at a price; I belong to God.

Consider the price that Jesus paid. The price is stated very clearly in various parts of the New Testament. In Acts 20:28, Paul addressed the elders of the church at Ephesus, saying, *"Therefore take heed to yourselves and to all the flock, among which the Holy Spirit has made you overseers, to shepherd the church of God which He purchased with His own blood."*

Notice that Paul gave to Jesus the specific title of "God." He said, ***"God**...purchased* [the church] *with **His** own blood."* The purchase price was the blood of Jesus. Then, in 1 Peter 1:17, we read, *"And if you call on the Father, who without partiality judges according to each one's work, conduct yourselves throughout the time of your stay here in fear."* He was not talking about a slavish fear, but rather about a deep sense of responsibility that comes due to the price that Jesus paid to redeem us. We must never treat ourselves as cheap. When we realize we have been redeemed by the blood of Jesus, we cannot afford to make ourselves cheap.

> *You were not redeemed with corruptible* [perishable] *things, like silver or gold, from your aimless conduct received by tradition from your fathers, but with the precious blood of Christ, as of a lamb without blemish and without spot.*   (verses 18–19)

The price Jesus paid to redeem us was His precious blood. He is called the Lamb of God, without blemish and without spot. A blemish is something a creature is born with. A spot is something that would mar or stain it afterward. Jesus is without blemish, meaning He is without original sin, and He is without spot, meaning He is without personal sin. It is His perfect blood that has redeemed us.

Thank You, Lord, that You have purchased me. I proclaim that I have been redeemed by the precious blood of Jesus. I have been bought at a price; I belong to God. Amen.

The Fullness of the Cross, Vol. 4: The Cost of Redemption (audio)

JULY 14

Presenting Our Bodies

I have been bought at a price; I belong to God.

It is important to truly understand that Jesus redeemed the whole person: spirit, soul, and body. One reason for the redemption of the body was so that it might become the temple of the Lord. The Lord is not going to dwell in a temple that has not been redeemed, one that still belongs to Satan. He will not dwell there. Our bodies have been redeemed so that God may dwell in them by His Holy Spirit. They were redeemed by the blood of Jesus.

What is the response that God requires from us? This is where it becomes extremely practical and is very important for all of us to understand. Paul said,

> *I beseech you therefore, brethren, by the mercies of God, that you present your bodies a living sacrifice, holy, acceptable to God, which is your reasonable service.* (Romans 12:1)

Given all that God has done for us through Jesus' death on the cross, how are we expected to respond? We are to present our bodies as living sacrifices. Why "living sacrifices"? Paul was contrasting living sacrifices with the sacrifices of the Old Testament, which involved the bodies of animals being killed and then placed on God's altar as an offering to wipe away sin and guilt. Paul was saying, "Place your body on God's altar, but don't kill it. Place it on the altar as a *living* sacrifice." Once you have placed your body on God's altar, it no longer belongs to you. It belongs to God. Everything that was offered as a sacrifice on God's altar became His.

That is exactly what God asks us to do, to present our bodies to Him as living sacrifices, to give up the ownership of our bodies and to put them in God's hands.

Thank You, Lord, that You have purchased me. I proclaim that I am presenting my body to You as a living sacrifice. I have been bought at a price; I belong to God. Amen.

God's Plan for Your Body (audio)

Sanctified, Set Apart, Translated

I have been bought at a price; I belong to God.

Wherefore Jesus also, that he might sanctify the people with his own blood, suffered without the gate. (Hebrews 13:12 KJV)

The blood of Jesus sanctifies each believer. Again, *sanctify* is a religious word, and many people are confused about its meaning. The word *sanctify* is related to the word *saint* and is directly related in the original biblical languages to the word for "holy." So, *to sanctify* means "to make saintly," or "to make holy." Holiness includes the aspect of being set apart to God. The one who is sanctified finds himself in an area where God has access to him but the devil does not. To be sanctified is to be removed from the area of Satan's reach and placed in an area where we are available to God. That is what it is to be sanctified: set apart to God, made holy. Just like righteousness, sanctification does not come by works, by effort, or by religion. It comes only by faith in the blood of Jesus. You belong to God, you are under God's control, and you are available to God. Anything that is not of God has no right of approach to you; it is kept away by the blood.

In Colossians 1:12–13, Paul wrote, *"Giving thanks to the Father, who has qualified you to share in the inheritance of the saints in the kingdom of light. For he has rescued us from the dominion of darkness and brought us into the kingdom of the Son he loves"* (NIV). Through faith in the blood of Jesus, we have been removed from the area of Satan's authority and translated into the kingdom of God. We have been totally translated. We are not *going to be* translated; we have *already been* translated—spirit, soul, and body. We are not in the devil's territory. We are not under the devil's laws. We are in the territory of the Son of God, and we are under His laws.

Thank You, Lord, that You have purchased me. I proclaim that I have been sanctified, set apart to God, and translated into the kingdom of God. I have been bought at a price; I belong to God. Amen.

Spiritual Conflict, Vol. 3: God's People Triumphant: Spiritual Weapons—The Blood, The Word, Our Testimony (audio)

WEEK 29:

I am a member of the body of Christ.

Now you are the body of Christ, and members individually.

—1 Corinthians 12:27

Finding Our Place

I am a member of the body of Christ.

Proverbs 27:8 says, *"Like a bird that wanders from its nest is a man who wanders from his place."* Have you ever seen a bird that got out of its nest and could not get back in again? Nothing is more weak and pitiful than that. This image aptly illustrates what it is to be out of your place. I have counseled many people whom I simply had to tell, "One of your problems is that you are not in your right geographical place. This is not the place where you ought to be. You will never really flourish until you find your place."

However, "your place" is not primarily a geographical location; rather, it is a place in God, a place in the body of Christ. Scripture says that every one of us should be a member of the body. As a member, each one of us has to fit into the right place for that member. A hand looks ridiculous at the end of a leg. A foot looks ridiculous at the end of an arm. You have to find out what kind of a member you are so that you will fit into the place that is appropriate for you.

> *God...has saved us and called us with a holy calling, not according to our works, but according to His own purpose and grace which was given to us in Christ Jesus before time began.*
>
> (2 Timothy 1:8–9)

That is a tremendous passage, almost unsearchable in its depth. It says that God *"has saved us,"* but it does not stop there. There is no punctuation; he continued immediately, *"and called us."* To be saved is to be called. There is no one who is saved but not called.

There are multitudes of Christians who are saved and do not know their callings. But it is not because they are not called. When you are saved, you are saved to a calling. You will be frustrated and unfulfilled until you find and fulfill your calling.

Thank You, Jesus, for making me a part of Your body. I proclaim that I find my place and my calling in You. I am a member of the body of Christ. Amen.

Finding Your Place: Your Calling Is Holy (audio)

We Need One Another

I am a member of the body of Christ.

In Ephesians 1:22–23, Paul provided a picture of God's people here on earth. He said, *"The church...is His [Christ's] body."* Paul developed this theme in 1 Corinthians, saying, *"Now you are the body of Christ, and members individually"* (1 Corinthians 12:27). He used various examples from the physical body to emphasize the fact that, as Christians, we are all interdependent; we all need one another.

The most complete and authoritative picture of the church as the body of Christ is given in Ephesians. It is most significant, therefore, that throughout this epistle, Paul spoke consistently of Christians in the plural. He had virtually nothing to say to or about individual Christians. (See Ephesians 1:3–12.) A careful reading of the rest of Ephesians will confirm that this is the book's message from beginning to end. There are no promises and no prayers for any individual. Only in the last six verses is there one brief exception: Paul closed by asking for special prayer for himself.

This focus on the collective body of Christ comes to its climax in Ephesians 6:10–18, where Paul spoke about our spiritual warfare. In verse 12, all the key words are in the plural—both those that refer to God's people and those that refer to the opposing forces: *we* wrestle against *principalities, powers, rulers,* and *hosts.*

Depicted thusly, spiritual warfare is not a conflict between individuals, but a vast war between opposing armies. There is no room here for "lone rangers" pursuing their individual goals. Victory will require controlled and concerted action by God's people, working together as members of one body. This will demand discipline and a readiness to submit to scriptural authority.

Thank You, Jesus, for making me a part of Your body. I proclaim that I am not alone, but I take my stand with the rest of the body of Christ, for I am a member of the body of Christ. Amen.

Because of the Angels, Part 3: Principles of Spiritual Protection (Teaching Legacy Letter)

My Specific Place

I am a member of the body of Christ.

Jesus said that if we have *"faith as a mustard seed,"* we can move a mountain. (See Matthew 17:20.) It is not the quantity of your faith, but rather the quality, that matters. Faith is given to those who are realistic and humble.

Why does God give you a specific measure of faith? (See Romans 12:3.) Because He has a specific place for you in the body of Christ. He has ordained you to serve a specific function as a specific member of the body of Christ. The faith He has given you is designed for your position in the body. If God wants you to be a hand, He will give you "hand" faith. If He wants you to be an ear, He will give you "ear" faith. If He wants you to be a toe, He will give you "toe" faith. But if you are a toe and you are trying to be a nose, there will be a complete imbalance between what you are trying to do and the faith that you have. The reason is not that you do not have enough faith, but that you are trying to use your faith for something for which it was not meant to be used. It was given for the specific job and place you have in the body of believers.

My hand does a wonderful job as a hand. It opens my Bible, turning the pages. It does most everything I ask of it. But if should I try to do those jobs with my foot, I would be in trouble.

If you are always struggling for faith, you are probably trying to do the wrong job. You are a hand trying to be a foot, or a foot trying to be a hand. This is God's way of guiding you into your place.

Thank You, Jesus, for making me a part of Your body. I proclaim that God is guiding me into my specific place, for I am a member of the body of Christ. Amen.

Finding Your Place: Your Calling Is Holy (audio)

Knit Together

I am a member of the body of Christ.

Paul pointed out in 1 Corinthians 12 that each member depends on the other. No member is independent of the others. The eye cannot say to the hand, "I don't need you." The head cannot say to the foot, "I don't need you." Even the weakest members can be the ones that are actually the most important.

No member of the human body is more vulnerable or sensitive than the eye. Yet few, if any, are more valuable. Notice how carefully nature has protected the eye all around. The primary function of several other areas of the face is to protect the eye. But the eye gets all that protection and honor not because it is strong, but because it is weak. This is the way the body has been knit together. The strong must protect the weak. We cannot ignore or despise any member of the body of Christ, big or small, strong or weak.

This principle is true of the members of Christ's body. We need one another; we depend on one another. We must honor one another. When one member suffers, the others suffer with it. When one member is honored, the others are honored with it. (See 1 Corinthians 12:26.) That is the nature of the universal body of Jesus Christ, the church.

Thank You, Jesus, for making me a part of Your body. I proclaim that I am knit together with other members—and I honor them—for I am a member of the body of Christ. Amen.

The Church, Vol. 1: Universal and Local: The Universal Church (audio)

JULY 20

Working Together

I am a member of the body of Christ.

For through the grace given to me I say to every man among you not to think more highly of himself than he ought to think; but to think so as to have sound judgment, as God has allotted to each a measure of faith. For just as we have many members in one body and all the members do not have the same function, so we, who are many, are one body in Christ, and individually members one of another. (Romans 12:3–5 NASB)

The renewed mind directs us to our proper place in the body. We come to realize that each of us is just one member, incomplete on our own, incapable of functioning on our own as God intends us to function. In order to be complete and to function in accordance with God's purpose and plan, each of us has to become a member in the body. We have to be joined to other members by a kind of commitment that enables us to work together, and not just as isolated individuals.

When traveling on airplanes, I have often marveled as the plane's navigation system zeroed in on the particular airport and the two locked on to one another. The plane came down in exactly the right place at exactly the right speed to make a safe and smooth landing. I suggest thinking of your renewed mind like the navigation system of an airplane. When you synchronize yourself with the Spirit of God, then your renewed mind brings you down into exactly the right place in the body—you become a member of God's body, the body of Christ, the church.

Thank You, Jesus, for making me a part of Your body. I proclaim that the Lord is bringing me into exactly the right place in His body, because I am a member of the body of Christ. Amen.

How to Find God's Plan for Your Life (audio)

Treating One Another Right

I am a member of the body of Christ.

The world is full of all kinds of people. Just looking at someone's exterior, you might say, "I don't see much to get excited about." You could look in the mirror and perhaps say the same thing about yourself. But we need to look below the surface and see our brothers and sisters as members of the body of Christ—people for whom Jesus shed His blood and died.

If we fail to appreciate and honor other people, we are grieving the heart of the Lord, because the Lord loves everyone enough to die for them. It grieves the Lord bitterly if we have a wrong attitude toward a member of His body, if we look down on others and discount their value.

I believe that was the problem of the people of Corinth, whom Paul addressed in two epistles. There were many wrong relationships between them. They did not discern the Lord's body in one another (see 1 Corinthians 11:29), and Paul said, *"For this reason many are weak and sick among you, and many sleep* [have died]" (verse 30). I suppose this reason could well be the major cause of sickness among Christians today. I have to say, with deep regret, that many Christians do not treat one another at all like fellow members of Christ's body.

Thank You, Jesus, for making me a part of Your body. I proclaim that I will, by Your grace, honor other members, seeing them as individuals for whom Jesus died, for I am a member of the body of Christ.
Amen.

Communion in Its Fullness (audio)

God Has Placed Us

I am a member of the body of Christ.

For even as the body is one and yet has many members, and all the members of the body, though they are many, are one body, so also is Christ....For the body is not one member, but many. If the foot should say, "Because I am not a hand, I am not a part of the body," it is not for this reason any the less a part of the body. And if the ear should say, "Because I am not an eye, I am not a part of the body," it is not for this reason any the less a part of the body. If the whole body were an eye, where would the hearing be? If the whole were hearing, where would the sense of smell be? But now God has placed the members, each one of them, in the body, just as He desired. (1 Corinthians 12:12, 14–18 NASB)

There are three things we need to see in this statement of Paul. First, the choice of where and what we are to be in the body is not ours, but God's. God has arranged the members of His body and assigned their functions. It is not for us to decide; rather, God decides and reveals His decisions to us.

Second, as this comes to pass in our lives, we merge our lives in a larger entity, the body—yet we still retain our individuality. It is like a little finger that finds its place on a hand, side-by-side with four other fingers, and is thus connected to the total life and purpose of a complete body. As Christians, we never lose our individual identities, but we do become a part of a larger, corporate group, all the while being the particular members that God ordained us to be.

Third, as a corporate body, we are able to represent Christ in His fullness to the world. None of us can adequately represent Christ on our own; but when we are united to a body, that body can totally, corporately, and fully represent Jesus Christ to our world.

Thank You, Jesus, for making me a part of Your body. I proclaim that God has placed me, with an individual identity, as part of the whole, representing Christ in His fullness to the world. I am a member of the body of Christ. Amen.

How to Find God's Plan for Your Life (audio)

DECLARING GOD'S WORD

WEEK 30:

I am holy.

He chose us in Him before the foundation of the world, that we should be holy and without blame before Him in love.

—Ephesians 1:4

What Is Holiness?

I am holy.

T here is tremendous misunderstanding about holiness. Many Christians try to achieve holiness by abstaining from things. They think, *If I do not do this or that, then I am holy.* But that has nothing to do with being holy. There are things you cannot do if you are holy, but to suggest that holiness means cutting down on the number of things you are involved in is not correct. Holiness is not negative. Paul wrote in Colossians 2:20, *"Therefore, if you died with Christ from the basic principles of the world, why, as though living in the world, do you subject yourselves to regulations...?"* This is most people's view of holiness—subjecting oneself to regulations. Paul went on to provide a list of regulations some people follow in an attempt to achieve holiness:

> *"Do not touch, do not taste, do not handle," which all concern things which perish with the using; according to the commandments and doctrines of men....These things indeed have an appearance of wisdom in self-imposed religion, false humility, and neglect of the body, but are of no value against the indulgence of the flesh.* (verses 21–23)

In other words, abstaining from certain things does not make you holy; it is not God's holiness. In Matthew 5:16, Jesus explained the relationship between holiness and our actions: *"Let your light so shine before men, that they may see your good works and glorify your Father in heaven."* Letting *"your light...shine"* means doing good works so that other people are able to see God. It does not mean observing a set of negative rules. It is a positive, powerful force. In fact, I believe that holiness is the most powerful force at work in our universe. To retreat into a negative lifestyle and call it "holiness" is self-deception. It is not what God means by holiness at all.

Thank You, Lord, that You have called me. I proclaim that I will "let my light shine" as a positive, powerful force, for I am holy. Amen.

Update 94, March 2001 (audio)

Called Holy Ones

I am holy.

Paul described the Roman believers as *"beloved of God, called to be saints"* (Romans 1:7). The word *"saints"* simply means "holy." The words *"to be"* were actually added by the translators. In Greek, this literally says, "called holy ones."

Remember that holiness is not some kind of extra qualification that a few believers may acquire; rather, it is something that is expected of all believers. Paul did not conceive of some special "super class" of believers who go on to a higher plane inaccessible to the rest of us. Paul assumed that all believers were going to be holy.

When you accept the gospel invitation of faith in Jesus Christ, God calls you a holy one. You are one who is set apart, ready to yield to the Holy Spirit and to righteousness. You may look at yourself and say, "Well, I really don't seem to be very holy," but recall what Paul said: that God *"calls those things which do not exist as though they did"* (Romans 4:17). God called Abraham *"a father of many nations"* before he had even one son. (See Genesis 17:4–5.)

When God calls you something, it is because He is going to make you something. When God calls you holy, you are holy, because He has called you holy. It may take some time to work out holiness in your life, but that is His decree for you.

Thank You, Lord, that You have called me. I proclaim that You are working out Your calling in my life, for I am holy. Amen.

You Shall Receive Power (book)

His Will for Us

I am holy.

Furthermore, we have had human fathers who corrected us, and we paid them respect. Shall we not much more readily be in subjection to the Father of spirits and live? For they indeed for a few days chastened us as seemed best to them, but He [God] for our profit, that we may be partakers of His holiness. (Hebrews 12:9–10)

It is God's desire that we might partake of His holiness. The author of Hebrews continued, *"Pursue peace with all people, and holiness, without which no one will see the Lord"* (verse 14). First, we are to pursue holiness. Second, in order to achieve holiness, I believe we must pursue peace with all people. We are to attempt to live peaceably, avoiding quarrels or disagreements, if we are able. The writer of Hebrews also issued a solemn warning. He said that we will not see the Lord unless we become partakers of His holiness.

Another Scripture passage that expresses God's desire for holiness in His people says, *"For this is the will of God, your sanctification"* (1 Thessalonians 4:3). What exactly is *"sanctification"*? To an extent, the English language obscures the words' true meaning. An English word ending in the suffix "-ify" means to make something correspond to the quality indicated by whatever precedes the "-ify." For example, *purify* means "to make pure"; *clarify* means "to make clear"; *rectify* means "to make right." By extension, *sanctify* means "to make sanct." But what is *sanct*? By derivation, it is the same as *saint*; and *saint*, in turn, is the same as *holy*. All three words—*sanctify, saint,* and *holy*—are derived from one basic Greek word, *hagios,* the root word for "holy." Very simply, then, sanctification is the process of making something—or someone—holy.

Thus, we can accurately translate 1 Thessalonians 4:3 in this way: "For this is the will of God, that you be made holy."

Thank You, Lord, that You have called me. I will pursue holiness, as well as pursue peace with all people to partake of Your holiness, for I am holy. Amen.

"Partakers of His Holiness" (*New Wine* article)

DECLARING GOD'S WORD

God's Initiative

I am holy.

In the process of sanctification, as in every redemptive process, the initiative is with God, not with man. It begins with God's choice of us, made in eternity. Thereafter, the sequence of events in time is as follows: (1) the Holy Spirit begins to influence us; (2) He draws us aside from the broad way to destruction (see Matthew 7:13) that we would have followed (see Matthew 7:13); (3) He brings us face-to-face with the truth, which is Jesus Himself (see John 14:6); (4) He imparts to us faith to believe the truth; and (5) through believing the truth, we enter into salvation.

In Ephesians 2:8, Paul wrote that we are saved by faith. He then reminded us that this faith does not come from ourselves; rather, it is a gift from the Holy Spirit. In this sense, we could define *sanctify* as "to set apart to God." In many cases, the process of sanctification begins long before we come to know God personally. Both the apostle Paul and the prophet Jeremiah were sanctified in their mothers' wombs. (See Galatians 1:15; Jeremiah 1:5.) God begins to set us apart to Himself long before we have any knowledge of it.

[We are] *elect* [chosen] *according to the foreknowledge of God the Father, in sanctification of the Spirit, for obedience and sprinkling of the blood of Jesus Christ.* (1 Peter 1:2)

God's choice, made in eternity, is based on His foreknowledge—it is never arbitrary, never random. The Holy Spirit draws us aside to a place of confrontation with the claims of Christ, then gives us grace to obey the gospel. When we obey, the blood of Jesus is sprinkled upon us. In this passage from 1 Peter, we see that the initiative in the process of sanctification is with God, not man, and that the first agent acting in the process is the Holy Spirit.

Thank You, Lord, that You have called me. I proclaim that it is God's initiative, His choice, made in eternity—and that it was not arbitrary. I am holy. Amen.

"Partakers of His Holiness" (*New Wine* article)

Washed by His Word

I am holy.

In the Old Testament, after the blood of an animal sacrifice had been shed, the sacrifice had to be washed in pure water. First John 5:6 says that Jesus came *"by water and blood."* The blood is the redeeming blood of Christ, shed on the cross, and the water is the pure water of the Word. Christ redeems us by His blood, then sanctifies and cleanses us by the washing of water by the Word. (See Ephesians 5:25–26.)

Praying to the Father for His disciples, Jesus said, *"Sanctify them by Your truth. Your word is truth"* (John 17:17). One primary way in which the Word of God sanctifies us is by changing how we think. Sanctification proceeds from the inside out, not from the outside in. Again, the "religious" way to sanctification is to lengthen the dress, cut the hair, wipe off the lipstick, and so forth. Yet in Romans 12:2, Paul said, *"Be transformed by the renewing of your mind, that you may prove what is that good and acceptable and perfect will of God."* In Ephesians 4:23, he said, *"Be renewed in the spirit of your mind."* The Holy Spirit renews our minds through the truth—God's Word.

In English, we have the term *brainwash*, which usually has a negative connotation. The word would be appropriate, however, to describe in a positive light the way in which the Holy Spirit renews our minds, washing them clean with the pure water of God's Word. This must happen by our faith, an indispensable element in our sanctification. God's Spirit and God's Word never vary; our faith enables us to receive what God offers through these agents. Furthermore, there is a direct connection between the Word of God and our faith, for *"faith comes by hearing, and hearing by the word of God"* (Romans 10:17). The more we give heed to God's Word, the more our faith expands, enabling us to appropriate the total provision God has made for our holiness.

Thank You, Lord, that You have called me. I proclaim that I am being washed and renewed by the pure water of God's Word. I appropriate the total provision God has made, for I am holy. Amen.

"Partakers of His Holiness" (*New Wine* article)

Set Apart by the Blood

I am holy.

Jesus shed His blood to redeem us, to sanctify us, or set us apart to God, and to make us holy. It is possible to live in a place where sin and Satan cannot touch us, a place where we are protected and sanctified by the blood of Jesus.

In 1 John 1:7, we read, *"But if we walk in the light as He is in the light, we have fellowship with one another, and the blood of Jesus Christ His Son cleanses us from all sin."* The present tense in this passage indicates a continual action. If we walk continually in the light, we have continual fellowship, and the blood of Jesus keeps us continually clean. We are kept pure and undefiled; we do not live in the vile contamination of this evil world. We are separated unto God, sanctified, and set apart by the blood of Jesus.

The practical key is the place of sanctification—the altar. In the Old Testament, until the sacrifice was placed on the altar, it was just the dead body of a beast. But when the sacrifice was placed on the altar and bound to it, the sacrifice became holy, set apart to God. This is just as true for the New Testament believer. Paul said, *"I beseech you therefore, brethren, by the mercies of God, that you present your bodies a living sacrifice, holy, acceptable to God, which is your reasonable service"* (Romans 12:1). The only difference between sacrifices in the Old and New Testaments is that our bodies remain alive—living sacrifices—when we place them on the altar. The principle of sanctification remains the same. It is the altar that sanctifies the gift placed upon it. The inward change in our thoughts and motives cannot be achieved until we have renounced all rights over our own bodies and placed them, without reservation, upon God's altar, to be used as God desires.

Thank You, Lord, that You have called me. I proclaim that I am protected and set apart, sanctified, by the blood of Jesus. I present my body as a living sacrifice, for I am holy. Amen.

"Partakers of His Holiness" (*New Wine* article)

Obeying God under Grace

I am holy.

What is the difference between obeying God under the law and obeying God under grace? The ultimate purpose of both is obedience to God, but this obedience is accomplished in different ways. To illustrate this point, let's look at a simple commandment given in both the Old Testament, under the law of Moses, and the New Testament, in one of the epistles. The exact words are used, and they apply whether we are under the law or under grace.

In the Old Testament, God was speaking through Moses to Israel, and He said, *"For I am the LORD who brings you up out of the land of Egypt, to be your God. You shall therefore be holy, for I am holy"* (Leviticus 11:45). In context, "being holy" means that you have to keep a set of extremely complicated rules, which are delineated in great detail throughout the remainder of the book of Leviticus. In this case, holiness is attained by the methods of legalism: "Do this. Don't do that."

The New Testament passage is addressed to Christians who have accepted Jesus' redemption on their behalf: *"As obedient children, not conforming yourselves to the former lusts, as in your ignorance; but as He who called you is holy, you also be holy in all your conduct, because it is written, 'Be holy, for I am holy'"* (1 Peter 1:14–16). The quotation is taken from Leviticus, so does that mean Peter was telling us that we must observe all the Old Testament rules about animal sacrifices and mildews and bodily fluids? Obviously not. So, he must expect something different. The holiness of the law says, "I have to keep all these rules." The alternative response of faith is, "I don't follow a set of rules. I let Jesus be holy, in me and through me."

Thank You, Lord, that You have called me. I proclaim that holiness doesn't come by obeying all the rules but by Jesus' redemption on my behalf. Jesus in me is my holiness, and I am holy. Amen.

The Roman Pilgrimage, Vol. 2: Romans 7:25–8:4 (audio, video)

I have been adopted as a child of God.

Having predestined us to adoption as sons by Jesus Christ to Himself, according to the good pleasure of His will.

—Ephesians 1:5

His Sons and His Daughters

I have been adopted as a child of God.

Praise be to the God and Father of our Lord Jesus Christ, who has blessed us in the heavenly realms with every spiritual blessing in Christ. For he chose us in him before the creation of the world to be holy and blameless in his sight. In love he predestined us to be adopted as his sons through Jesus Christ, in accordance with his pleasure and will—to the praise of his glorious grace, which he has freely given us in the One he loves. (Ephesians 1:3–6 NIV)

Paul here explained what was God's eternal purpose even before creation: that we might become His children—His sons and His daughters. The only way that this could be achieved was through the substitutionary death of Jesus on the cross. When Jesus bore our sin and suffered our rejection, He opened the way for our acceptance. For that period alone, He lost His status as God's Son so that we might gain that same status—as God's sons and daughters.

I love the sixth verse, *"To the praise of his glorious grace, which he has freely given us in the One he loves."* The word that is translated *"freely given us"* is a very powerful word. It is the same word used by the angel in saluting the Virgin Mary, *"You who are highly favored"* (Luke 1:28 NIV). It means that we have become the objects of God's special favor. The *New King James Version* says that God *"has made us accepted in the Beloved"* (Ephesians 1:6).

You must realize that Jesus bore your sin and rejection so that you might have His acceptance as one of His children.

Thank You, Lord, that You chose me in love. I proclaim that Jesus bore my rejection that I might have His acceptance. I have been adopted as a child of God. Amen.

Rejection: Cause and Cure (audio)

God's Irresistible Love

I have been adopted as a child of God.

For he [God] chose us in him [Christ] before the creation of the world to be holy and blameless in his sight. In love he predestined us to be adopted as his sons through Jesus Christ.

(Ephesians 1:4–5 NIV)

There are two possible ways of punctuating the above verse: "to be holy and blameless in his sight in love..." or "to be holy and blameless in his sight. In love...." Whichever period placement you use, the fact remains that God's love precedes time. Before the creation of the world, God loved us, chose us, and predestined us. He arranged the course of His life so that we would encounter Him and experience His love.

There is a very simple statement in the Song of Solomon that says, *"Love is as strong as death"* (8:6). Death is inevitable. When death comes, nobody can turn it away. Nobody can say, "I'm not ready. I won't accept you." No man has the power to resist death.

But the New Testament takes us one step further. When Jesus died and rose again from the dead, He proved that love is stronger than death. The most irresistible, negative force in the universe was conquered by the most irresistible, positive force in the universe— the love of God. Love always achieves its objectives; it is invincible. It accepts no barriers. It will get past every obstacle in order to get to where it wants to go.

God's love is individual and everlasting. It precedes time; it is irresistible. Then, picture yourself as the pearl in the hand of Jesus. Say to yourself, "His love for me is individual and everlasting. It precedes time. It is irresistible." Then, remember what it cost Him—all He had. Stop to tell Him, "Thank You."

Thank You, Lord, that You chose me in love. I proclaim that before the creation of the world, God loved me, chose me, and predestined me by His irresistible love. I have been adopted as a child of God. Amen.

Extravagant Love (booklet)

The Weapon of the Word

I have been adopted as a child of God.

The temptations Satan brings against us follow a pattern. First, he tempts us to doubt what God has said—that our sins have been forgiven, that God really loves us, that we have been accepted into God's family as His children, that we have been released from the curse, and that we have entered into the blessing. But the final thrust of Satan's tactics is to tempt us to direct disobedience.

Jesus used only one weapon to defeat Satan: the *rhema*, or the spoken Word of God. He countered each temptation with the same phrase: *"It is written."* (See, for example, Matthew 4:4, 7, 10.) Each was a direct quotation from the Old Testament. Satan has no defense against the Word of God thus quoted directly at him. He has no choice but to withdraw in defeat.

In all of this, Jesus is our perfect example. He did not rely on any wisdom or arguments of His own; rather, He used precisely the same weapon God has given to us: the Word of God. Our security depends on following the example of Jesus. Satan is a thousand times wiser and stronger than we are. He can point to a thousand flaws in our own righteousness. But there is one weapon against which he has no defense: the Word of God, spoken in faith.

Such, then, is the path that leads us out of the territory overshadowed by curses and into the territory that enjoys the sunlight of God's blessings. Its first requirement is unswerving faith, based on the exchange that took place on the cross. Faith of this kind reckons God's promises as effective from the moment they are apprehended. By prompt, unquestioning obedience and patient endurance, we move from our legal rights in Christ into the full, experiential enjoyment of them. We meet all satanic opposition with "the sword of the Spirit": the spoken Word of God. (See Ephesians 6:17.)

Thank You, Lord, that You chose me in love. I proclaim that I will meet all satanic temptations and opposition with the Word of God. I proclaim that I have been adopted as a child of God. Amen.

Blessing or Curse: You Can Choose (book)

Children and Coheirs

I have been adopted as a child of God.

In Romans 8:15–17, Paul was writing to Christians about what was available to them through their faith in Christ.

> *For you did not receive a spirit that makes you a slave again to fear, but you received the Spirit of sonship. And by him* [the Holy Spirit] *we cry, "Abba, Father." The Spirit himself testifies with our spirit that we are God's children. Now if we are children, then we are heirs—heirs of God and co-heirs with Christ, if indeed we share in his sufferings in order that we may also share in his glory.* (NIV)

The word *Abba* is the Aramaic or Hebrew equivalent of the English word "Daddy." Thus, we see here a relationship of intimacy with God the Father, whom we address as *Daddy.* The Spirit of God Himself gives us the assurance and confidence to do so.

The Bible tells us that we are God's children, but the Spirit of God reinforces that truth personally to each of us, in our hearts. We are God's children. And when we become children, we become heirs. We are made heirs of God and coheirs with Christ. Of course, one condition is stated: if we are willing to share His sufferings. If we share in the inheritance, we also share in the sufferings. Remember, the pearl is a product of pressure and stress.

It is important to understand what it means to be coheirs. It does not mean that we each get a little fraction of the total inheritance. Rather, it means that Jesus, as the first Son of God, has the whole inheritance, and we share the whole inheritance with Him. Each one of us has a right to the entire inheritance, which is the inheritance of Jesus. The law of God's kingdom is sharing. We do not each grab our own portions, but we all share together everything that God the Father has and everything that Christ the Son has.

Thank You, Lord, that You chose me in love. I proclaim that I am a child of God and a coheir with Christ. I have been adopted as a child of God. Amen.

Extravagant Love (booklet)

A Father's Love

I have been adopted as a child of God.

God's family is the best family. Again, even if your own family did not care for you, bear in mind that God wants you. You are accepted; you are highly favored; you are the object of His special care and affection. Everything He does revolves around you.

Paul said to the Corinthians, who were not exactly top-notch Christians, *"All this is for your benefit"* (2 Corinthians 4:15 NIV). Everything God does, He does for us. You do not get conceited when you realize this fact. Instead, you become humble. There is no room left for arrogance when you see the grace of God. It is significant that, before His crucifixion, Jesus' last prayer with His disciples was for those who were His followers, as well as for those who would follow afterward. (See John 17:20.) That prayer concerned our relationship with God as our Father, and it concluded, *"Righteous Father, though the world does not know you, I know you, and they know that you have sent me. I have made you known to them"* (John 17:25–26 NIV).

Jesus makes God known to us as Father. The Jews had known God as Yahweh for fourteen centuries, but the only Person who could introduce Him as Father was His Son. Six times in this prayer for His disciples, Jesus addressed God as Father (see verses 1, 5, 11, 21, 24, 25).

When Jesus prayed, *"And [I] will continue to make you known"* (verse 26), He was saying that He would continue to reveal God as Father. Then, we come to the purpose of this revelation: *"In order that the love you have for me may be in them and that I myself may be in them"* (John 17:26 NIV). God has exactly the same love for us as He has for Jesus. We are as dear to God as Jesus Himself is. However, there is another aspect to this. Because Jesus is in us, we can love God in the same way that Jesus loves Him.

Thank You, Lord, that You chose me in love. I proclaim that God, my Father, has exactly the same love for me as He has for Jesus, and I love God the same way Jesus loves Him. I have been adopted as a child of God. Amen.

God's Remedy for Rejection (book)

AUGUST 4

The Place of Maturity

I have been adopted as a child of God.

It is not God's purpose for us to remain permanently as children. God has a plan for us to grow up into mature sons. But this is where we are again dependent on the Holy Spirit. Apart from the Holy Spirit, we cannot grow up, we cannot mature. As Paul said in Romans 8:14, *"For all who are being led by the Spirit of God, these are sons of God"* (NASB).

The word for *"sons,"* in this verse, is not the same as the word for *"children"* in the other passages. This means a mature son—one who is responsible, who is in control of his life, who knows how to act, and who has authority.

How do we come to that place of maturity? Paul said, *"All who are being led by the Spirit of God, these are sons of God."* That is the second great ministry of the Spirit in our lives as members of God's family: to mature us. But this comes by one process alone: being led by the Spirit of God. There is no other way to reach maturity. And "being led" is a continual action. We have to be led continually—every day, every hour, in every situation—by the Spirit of God. That is the only way that we can live as mature sons of God.

The tragedy in the church today is that countless numbers of people who have been born again of the Spirit of God have never learned to be led by the Spirit of God. Consequently, they never achieve maturity. They always remain, in some sense, spiritually childish. This result is not because the provision for the maturation process is not there, but it is because they have not understood how to avail themselves of that provision. The provision is to be led by the Holy Spirit.

Thank You, Lord, that You chose me in love. I proclaim that I will move into maturity through the process of being led by the Spirit of God. I have been adopted as a child of God. Amen.

How to Be Led by the Holy Spirit, Part 1 (audio)

Relationship with Our Father

I have been adopted as a child of God.

In the last two verses of John 17, we find the final utterance of Jesus to His disciples before He suffered and died on the cross. I believe that these two verses are the climax of the entire purpose of the gospel. Here is part of the prayer that Jesus prayed.

> *O righteous Father! The world has not known You, but I have known You; and these [disciples] have known that You sent Me. And I have declared to them Your name.* (John 17:25–26)

The name Jesus came to reveal was *Father.* You find very few uses of the word *Father* as a title of God in the Old Testament. The only person who could fully reveal the Father was the Son. Then, Jesus said,

> *I have declared to them Your name, and will declare it, that the love with which You loved Me may be in them, and I in them.*
> (verse 26)

The ultimate purpose of the gospel is this love relationship with God by which God loves us in exactly the same way that He loved—and still loves—Jesus, and that we love God in exactly the same way that Jesus loves Him. That is the purpose—to bring us into the family of God, to bring us into a relationship with God as Father that is the same relationship that Jesus has. It enables us to love God with the same love with which Jesus loves Him. You cannot ask for more. It is unimaginable. It is past our human minds to conceive what it entails. But it is the goal, the ultimate purpose. Everything else is secondary.

Thank You, Lord, that You chose me in love. I proclaim that my ultimate goal and purpose is to come into a love relationship with God as my Father, for I have been adopted as a child of God.
Amen.

Guilt, Shame, Rejection (audio)

DECLARING GOD'S WORD

I have access to God through the Holy Spirit.

For through Him we both have access by one Spirit to the Father.

—Ephesians 2:18

Our Dependence upon the Holy Spirit

I have access to God through the Holy Spirit.

In our fleshly nature, all of us have certain weaknesses. These weaknesses are not of the body but of the mind—of our understanding. They manifest themselves in two related ways. First, we often do not know what we should pray for. Second, even when we do know what to pray for, we do not know *how* to pray for it. We therefore have no other recourse except total dependence on the Holy Spirit. He alone can show us both the *what* and the *how* of prayer. (See Romans 8:26–27.)

In the book of Ephesians, Paul emphasized our dependence upon the Holy Spirit to give us prayers that are acceptable to God. He stressed that it is only Jesus and the Holy Spirit who can give us access to God:

> *For through Him* [Jesus Christ] *we both* [Jews and Gentiles] *have access by one Spirit* [the Holy Spirit] *to the Father.*
> (Ephesians 2:18)

Two conditions for acceptable prayers are here combined: *through Jesus* and *by the Holy Spirit*. Each is essential. There is no natural force that can carry our puny human voices from earth to the very ears of God on His throne in heaven. Only the supernatural power of the Holy Spirit can do that. Without Him, we have no access to God.

Thank You, Lord, that I can come to You. I proclaim my total
dependence upon the Holy Spirit, who can give me access through
Jesus to the Father. I have access to God through the Holy Spirit.
Amen.

Blessing or Curse: You Can Choose (book)

The Way to the Father

I have access to God through the Holy Spirit.

There is no other way to God the Father but through Jesus Christ—and Him crucified. We have access to God through Jesus alone and by only one Spirit. There is only one Spirit who gives humans access to God the Father—the Holy Spirit. He operates only through the Lord Jesus Christ. If you come by any door other than Jesus, or if you come through any other spirit, you do not have access to God; you have access to the realm of Satan. Instead of going into the realm of light, you will go into the realm of darkness.

Remember, Satan transforms himself into an angel of light, and his ministers transform themselves as ministers of righteousness. (See 2 Corinthians 11:14–15.) They often use beautiful, sweet, loving words and long, eloquent phrases—even quoting Scripture—in order to get you into the realm of darkness. They do this under the guise of being angels of light. If you do not come by Jesus Christ crucified on the cross, and if you do not come by the Holy Spirit of God, you can get into the occult, supernatural realm. I have been there, and I know what it is like. Before I found Jesus, I was a practicing yogi. There was a time when I got out of the natural, but what I got into scared me, even then. I didn't like it. I decided that once was enough.

Some years later, when I was confronted with the gospel and the power of the Holy Spirit, the great barrier between me and Christ was Yoga. I could not break through that mental barrier. God had to perform a miracle of deliverance. I didn't know about demons, but I wanted to come to Jesus. I could not reach Him until that Yoga demon had lost its power over my mind. You can theorize, but I know what it is like. It is one of a thousand different ways of being deceived into the territory of Satan and becoming enslaved.

Thank You, Lord, that I can come to You. I proclaim that I will come to the Father through Jesus Christ crucified on the cross and by the Holy Spirit of God. I have access to God through the Holy Spirit. Amen.

Demons and Demonology: Cult and Occult—Satan's Snares Disclosed (audio)

The Door and the Shepherd

I have access to God through the Holy Spirit.

Jesus said, *"I am the door"* (John 10:9). Two verses later, He said, *"I am the good shepherd"* (verse 11). Have you ever stopped to consider how Jesus can be both the door and the shepherd? It's so simple, and yet so profound. Jesus crucified is the door. Jesus resurrected is the shepherd. But if you want the resurrected Christ as your shepherd, you have to come by the crucified Christ, who is the door. Only those who come by the crucified Christ have the resurrected Christ as their shepherd.

> *For through Him* [Jesus Christ] *we both* [Jews and Gentiles] *have access by one Spirit to the Father.* (Ephesians 2:18)

There are one way—Jesus—and one Spirit—the Holy Spirit—that lead us to the Father. If you do not come by Jesus, you do not have the Holy Spirit to lead you to the Father. The Holy Spirit will not honor any other approach to God than through Jesus Christ, and Him crucified.

When you come through Jesus, the door, you have the supernatural testimony of the Holy Spirit. All true, God-centered religion always receives the supernatural testimony of divine approval. If it is lacking, we had better ask why, because God has promised to honor the truth with supernatural attestation, and He always has, all through the history of Scripture.

Thank You, Lord, that I can come to You. I proclaim that there is one way—Jesus—and there is one Spirit—the Holy Spirit—that lead us to the Father. I have access to God through the Holy Spirit. Amen.

Bible Psychology, Vol. 2: Achieving Inner Harmony: Relationship Between Believer's Spirit and Soul (audio)

We Are Family

I have access to God through the Holy Spirit.

In the New Testament, God's people are very seldom referred to by the title *Christians,* or even *believers.* The most common title used is *brothers,* emphasizing membership in one spiritual family. As Paul wrote in Ephesians 2:18, *"For through Him* [Jesus Christ] *we both* [Jews and Gentiles] *have access by one Spirit to the Father."* Notice that all three persons of the Godhead are represented here. Through Jesus the Son, we have access to the Father by one Spirit.

The next verse reveals the wondrous result: *"Now, therefore* [because we have access to the Father], *you are no longer strangers and foreigners, but fellow citizens with the saints and members of the household of God"* (verse 19). The word *"household"* would be best represented in contemporary English by the word *family.* Because Christ has gained us access to the Father, we have become members of God's family.

The composition of God's family is determined by each member's relationship with the Father. In New Testament Greek, there is a very close similarity between the words *father* and *family.* The word for "father" is *pater;* the word for "family" is *patria,* which is derived from *pater.* This relationship is brought out clearly in Paul's prayer:

> *For this reason I bow my knees to the Father of our Lord Jesus Christ, from whom the whole family in heaven and earth is named.* (Ephesians 3:14–15)

There is a direct play here on the words *"Father"* and *"family."* From God the Father *(pater),* the whole family *(patria)* in heaven and earth is named. Family comes from fatherhood. Having God as our Father makes us members of His family.

Thank You, Lord, that I can come to You. I proclaim that I have become a member of God's family. I have access to God through the Holy Spirit. Amen.

Rediscovering God's Church (book)

Bringing Us to the Father

I have access to God through the Holy Spirit.

Jesus said, *"I am the way, the truth, and the life"* (John 14:6). We often quote that Scripture; it is a favorite evangelistic text. However, we rarely stop to consider its full implication. A *way* is meaningless unless it takes us somewhere. A way is not an end in itself. So, when Jesus said, *"I am the way,"* He was implying that He had come to take us somewhere.

Where is He taking us? He explained, *"No one comes to the Father except through Me"* (verse 6). In other words, He was saying, "I am the way to the Father. I am the revelation of the Father. If you have seen Me, you have seen the Father." (See verses 7–9.)

> *And He* [Jesus] *came and preached peace to you who were afar off* [the Gentiles] *and to those who were near* [the Jews]. *For through Him we both* [Jew and Gentile] *have access by one Spirit to the Father.* (Ephesians 2:17–18)

Again, all three persons of the Godhead are included in that one verse: through the Son, by the Spirit, to the Father. But the Father is the destination. The verse is meaningless if you leave out the Father. The ultimate objective is to reveal the Father and to bring us to Him. If we stop short of the fulfillment of that objective, we have missed the purpose for which Jesus came.

> *For Christ also died for sins once for all, the just for the unjust, in order that He might bring us to God.* (1 Peter 3:18 NASB)

Why did Jesus die? That our sins might be forgiven, yes. But that was only one stage in the process. The ultimate purpose was that He might bring us to God.

Thank You, Lord, that I can come to You. I proclaim that Jesus died for the ultimate purpose of bringing us to God. I have access to God through the Holy Spirit. Amen.

Knowing God as Father: The Fatherhood of God (audio)

One Way for Liberty

I have access to God through the Holy Spirit.

It is a vital fact that the Holy Spirit is a person. Not only is He a person, but He is Lord, just as much as God the Father is Lord and God the Son is Lord. He is coequal with the other two members of the Godhead. This means that we must have the same attitude of reverence toward the Holy Spirit that we have toward the Father and the Son.

In 2 Corinthians 3:17, Paul made this simple statement: *"Now the Lord is the Spirit; and where the Spirit of the Lord is, there is liberty."*

In this passage, we see the contrast between bondage to the law, or a legal system, and liberty. There is only one way to have liberty. Where the Holy Spirit is, there is liberty.

Many Christians have the strangest ideas about liberty. They say, "If we aren't dancing on the platform by 6:45 p.m. on Sunday evening, we are not having liberty." Or, "If we don't all clap our hands, we don't have liberty." Some preachers think that if they don't stomp on the platform and shout, they don't have liberty.

Liberty is not following a certain program in church. It is not going through certain motions, such as lifting up your hands. That can be liberty, but it can just as easily be bondage. It depends on whether the Holy Spirit is prompting it, or if you are doing it out of a religious tradition. Religious tradition produces bondage; the Holy Spirit produces liberty.

Thank You, Lord, that I can come to You. I proclaim that where the Holy Spirit is, there is liberty. I have access to God through the Holy Spirit. Amen.

Make Your Calling Sure: Continually Led by the Spirit (audio)

Access by the Spirit

I have access to God through the Holy Spirit.

We have no more access to God than we have by the Holy Spirit because there is a principle in the Godhead. The One who is sent as the representative must be honored if one is to have access to the Godhead. So, when the Father sent the Son, He said, "From now on, no one comes to Me except through the Son. You cannot bypass My representative and come to Me because, in every situation and circumstance, I uphold the One whom I have sent."

When Jesus had finished His task on earth and had returned to the Father, the Father and the Son sent the Holy Spirit. The same principle applies again. We have no access to the Father and the Son except by the Spirit. We cannot bypass the Spirit and come to the Father or to the Son.

> *For through Him* [Jesus Christ] *we both* [Jews and Gentiles] *have access by one Spirit to the Father.* (Ephesians 2:18)

We cannot leave out the Holy Spirit and still have access. Many Christians focus on the fact that we have access to God through His Son, Jesus. That is perfectly true, but it is not the whole truth. It is through the Son, by the Spirit, to the Father. Likewise, the Father indwells us when we are in the Son, through His Spirit. In each direction, whether we are going to God or whether God is coming to us, the Spirit is an essential part of the equation. We have access in the Son through the Spirit to the Father. The Father indwells us when we are in the Son through the Spirit.

If we leave the Holy Spirit out of that equation, we have no access to God, and God has no access to us. We are totally dependent on the Holy Spirit.

Thank You, Lord, that I can come to You. I proclaim that I am totally dependent on the Holy Spirit for access to the Son and to the Father. I have access to God through the Holy Spirit. Amen.

Make Your Calling Sure: Continually Led by the Spirit (audio)

WEEK **33:**

I have been made perfect in Christ.

You are complete in Him, who is the head of all principality and power.
—Colossians 2:10

The Meaning of Perfect

I have been made perfect in Christ.

The word *perfect* frightens some people. They have the impression that being perfect means that you never do anything wrong, you never say anything wrong, you never make any mistakes. These people say, "If that is the objective, I give up now, because it is unattainable." But the word *perfect* is found in Scripture, and we cannot get away from it. Sooner or later, we have to face it.

Perfect has three main meanings in Scripture. The first is "mature," or "fully grown up." We all see that as a reasonable objective—one that gives us nothing to fear. Another related meaning is "complete," having nothing deficient or defective. Keep in mind that these two meanings do not necessarily go together. A person may be fully grown up and still have defects in some areas of his body. He may even be missing part of his body, such as a limb, a digit, or an organ. In this case, he is mature yet incomplete. Another person might have all of his members intact and functioning, but he might not be fully grown up or mature. We have to combine the ideas of maturity and completeness in this picture of perfection.

In Ephesians 4, in the phrase *"the perfecting of the saints"* (verse 12 KJV), the Greek verb for *perfect* means "to articulate," or "to fit together." A related word is used in Hebrews 11:3, where it says that by the Word of God, *"the worlds were framed,"* or "fitted together." So, the word *perfect* also has to do with putting something together in such a way that every part works harmoniously with the others and fulfills its proper function. We have three distinct ideas—maturity, completeness, and proper integration—fit together in such a way that the whole functions harmoniously. That is the objective that Scripture sets before us as believers.

Thank You, Lord, for Your work in me. I proclaim that God is *"perfecting"* me—He is maturing me, completing me, and fitting me into the place He has for me. I have been made perfect in Christ.
Amen.

Perfecting the Saints (audio)

Doing the Will of God

I have been made perfect in Christ.

Why are we here on earth? It is not to do our own will, but rather to do the will of Christ, who commissioned us. Paul wrote in Colossians 1:9, *"For this reason we also, since the day we heard it, do not cease to pray for you, and to ask that you may be filled with the knowledge of His will in all wisdom and spiritual understanding."* We are to be filled with the knowledge of God's will. In other words, the knowledge of Christ's will is to take over the whole of our minds. It is to completely control our thinking. Every motive and every intention is to be controlled by the knowledge of the will of Christ.

Paul continued in Colossians 4:12, *"Epaphras, who is one of you, a bondservant of Christ, greets you, always laboring fervently for you in prayers, that you may stand perfect and complete in all the will of God."*

The believer becomes perfect and complete only insofar as he fulfills the whole will of God. Hebrews 13 states this truth beautifully:

> Now the God of peace, that brought again from the dead our Lord Jesus, that great shepherd of the sheep, through the blood of the everlasting covenant, make you perfect in every good work to do his will. (Hebrews 13:20–21 KJV)

We are made perfect and complete, we come to fulfillment, only insofar as we do the will of God, just as Jesus found fulfillment during His earthly life only in doing the will of God.

If there is disharmony, frustration, or emotional tumult in your life, consider checking your relationship to the will of God, for you can be made perfect only insofar as you know and do the will of God. Anything else will bring only incompleteness and frustration.

Thank You, Lord, for Your work in me. I proclaim my hope to stand perfect and complete in all the will of God, finding fulfillment only in doing His will. I have been made perfect in Christ. Amen.

Spiritual Conflict, Vol. 2: God's Secret Plan Unfolds: God's Purpose for the New Race (audio)

Accessing God's Total Provision

I have been made perfect in Christ.

In order to stand perfect and complete in the fullness of God's will, a Christian must avail himself of all that God has provided for him through Christ. He cannot omit any part of God's total provision and expect that some other part will serve as a substitute for that which has been omitted.

Yet, it is at this point precisely that so many Christians go astray in their thinking. Consciously or unconsciously, they reason that because they know they have availed themselves of some part, or parts, of God's provision for them, they do not need to concern themselves about other parts that they have omitted.

For instance, some Christians put a significant emphasis upon witnessing by word of mouth but are negligent about the practical aspects of daily Christian living. Conversely, other Christians are careful about their conduct but fail to witness openly to their friends and neighbors. Each of these types of Christians tends to criticize or despise the other, yet both are equally at fault. Good Christian living is no substitute for witnessing by word of mouth. On the other hand, witnessing by word of mouth is no substitute for good Christian living. God requires both. The believer who omits one or the other does not stand perfect and complete in the will of God.

Thank You, Lord, for Your work in me. I proclaim my desire to avail myself of all that God has provided for me through Christ, so that I may stand perfect and complete in the will of God, for I have been made perfect in Christ. Amen.

Foundational Truths for Christian Living (book)

DECLARING GOD'S WORD

Complete in Christ

I have been made perfect in Christ.

I was once a professional philosopher. As such, I looked here, there, and everywhere for the answer to life's problems. I looked in Christianity, as it was then presented to me, and concluded that Christianity did not have the answer. I was perfectly right—it didn't. I turned to Greek philosophy, I turned to Yoga, I turned to all sorts of ridiculous things. Then, in 1941, in an army barrack room one evening around midnight, when no one else was awake, I had a personal encounter with the Lord Jesus Christ. And in that encounter, I discovered that I had met the answer.

Sometime later, I read something Paul wrote concerning Jesus Christ: *"In [Him] are hid all the treasures of wisdom and knowledge"* (Colossians 2:3 KJV). I said to myself, *Why should I grub around any longer in the rubbish bins of human wisdom when all the treasures are hidden in Jesus Christ?* And I made a decision that the Bible is the book with the answers, and I resolved to find in it what God has hidden in Jesus Christ.

Sometimes I have strayed; sometimes I have become deflected and diverted. But Jesus is *"the Alpha and the Omega, the Beginning and the End, the First and the Last"* (Revelation 22:13) and *"the author and finisher of our faith"* (Hebrews 12:2). We are complete in Him. If you ever start to look outside Christ, you will find all sorts of interesting theories and stimulating presentations, but you will be feeding on the husks when you could be living on the Father's bread.

Thank You, Lord, for Your work in me. I proclaim that Jesus is the answer—the Alpha and Omega, the Beginning and the End, the First and the Last, the author and finisher of faith. I am complete in Him, for I have been made perfect in Christ. Amen.

Strength through Knowing God: The Source of Strength (audio)

AUGUST 17

The Fullness of Christ: God Himself

I have been made perfect in Christ.

*See to it that no one takes you captive through hollow and decep-
tive philosophy, which depends on human tradition and the basic
principles of this world rather than on Christ. For in Christ all
the fullness of the Deity lives in bodily form, and you have been
given fullness in Christ.* (Colossians 2:8–10 NIV)

That is my aim—to enter into the fullness that has been given to
us in Jesus Christ, who is to be our ultimate goal and satisfaction.
We can illustrate this with a parallel to the tabernacle of Moses, as
described in the Old Testament. Its structure was in three sections:
first, the Outer Court; then, inside the first curtain, the Holy Place;
and inside the second curtain, the Holy of Holies. Again, one simple
way to distinguish between these is by the light available in each section.

In the Outer Court, the light is natural, provided by the sun,
moon, and stars. In the Holy Place, there is no natural light. The light
is provided by the seven-branched candlestick, where oil is ignited in
the bowls to provide light. Once inside the Holy Place, you are no longer living by your senses, but by faith. Remarkably, beyond the second
curtain, there was no light at all. There was only one reason to enter:
to meet with God. When a man with a true heart went in beyond that
second veil, it became gloriously illuminated with the supernatural
presence of God, called the *shekinah*. That is the ultimate goal. There
is nothing to entice us beyond that second veil except God. He provides no alternative attractions—it is God or nothing. If God does
not come, you are left in total darkness. Living with God as our goal
means pursuing no alternative attractions. It is God Himself, God
alone. The light that I seek is neither natural nor artificial; it is supernatural—the presence of God Himself.

Thank You, Lord, for Your work in me. I proclaim that it is God
Himself and God alone whom I seek—the fullness of Christ—for I
have been made perfect in Christ. Amen.

Learning by Living, Part 2 (audio)

AUGUST 18

By One Sacrifice

I have been made perfect in Christ.

For by one offering [sacrifice] *He has perfected forever those who are being sanctified.* (Hebrews 10:14)

In this verse, we have two tenses, and both are significant. The first one is called the perfect tense: *"for by one offering* [sacrifice] *He has perfected forever...."* You can say the sacrifice is perfectly perfect. It is completely complete. Just before this phrase, the writer of Hebrews said that the Old Testament priests always stood, offering again and again the same sacrifices that could never take away sin. Then, the writer said about Jesus, *"But this Man, after He had offered one sacrifice for sins forever, sat down at the right hand of God"* (Hebrews 10:12). Notice the contrast between the Old Testament priests, who stood, and Jesus, who offered His sacrifice and sat down. Why did Jesus sit down? Because He had nothing left to do. He had done it all. Whereas the job of the Old Testament priests was never finished because their sacrifices were not adequate to deal with the real problem, Jesus' death on the cross was a complete and final act.

As far as what Jesus has done, it is complete and perfect. Nothing must be added to it, and nothing can ever be taken away from it. Jesus' sacrifice is valid forever. That is the perfect tense.

Then, speaking about those of us who are appropriating Jesus' sacrifice, the author of Hebrews wrote, *"He has perfected forever those who are being sanctified"* (Hebrews 10:14). *"Are being sanctified"* is in the present progressive tense. What Jesus has done is perfect, and our appropriation of it is continual, ongoing. As we are sanctified, as we are set apart to God more and more, and as we draw closer to God and appropriate more of God's provision and promises, we are entering more and more into the provision of the sacrifice.

Thank You, Lord, for Your work in me. I proclaim that by one sacrifice, Jesus has perfected those who are being sanctified—and that includes me. I have been made perfect in Christ. Amen.

Complete Salvation and How to Receive It, Part 1 (audio)

Perfect Circles

I have been made perfect in Christ.

As I have said before, the term *perfect* often frightens people. To make this word less frightening, I would like to use a simple example from mathematics.

Let's take the use of the word *round*. There is only one standard for round. Something is either round or not round. If something is round, it is a circle. There is just one kind of circle; there are not three or four different kinds of circles. However, there are many different sizes of circles.

God the Father is the great circle, the measureless round ring that encompasses the whole universe. Jesus does not expect us to have the same magnitude as God, but He does expect us to have the same character as God. You and I may be very tiny circles—operating in some small areas where God has placed us with apparently trivial, humdrum duties. But, for each of us in our own little area, God wants us to be a perfect circle. Perfectly round. Just as round as that "great circle," God the Father, who encompasses the whole universe.

So, when you read Jesus' command to *"be perfect"* (Matthew 5:48), think of it in terms of being "round." Don't be lopsided, having little bulges. Don't have deficiencies. You may not be very big, but you can be a perfect circle.

Thank You, Lord, for Your work in me. I proclaim that God wants me to be a "perfect circle"—and, by His grace, I will be, for I have been made perfect in Christ. Amen.

Progress to Perfection, Part 1 (audio)

Our old man was put to death in Christ that the new man might come to life in us.

Do not lie to one another, since you have put off the old man with his deeds, and have put on the new man who is renewed in knowledge according to the image of Him who created him.

—Colossians 3:9–10

New Man Living

Our old man was put to death in Christ
that the new man might come to life in us.

The exchange that we are dealing with here is between the old man and the new man. The old man died in Christ on the cross, so that, by exchange, the new man might live in us now. This is a theme that runs through the New Testament, but it is dealt with very infrequently in many sections of the church today. The contrast between the old man, who died on the cross, and the new man, who has been resurrected with Christ, is brought forth through the resurrection of Jesus.

Our old man being crucified in Christ is a historical event that actually took place at a specific moment in time. I think it tremendously strengthens our faith when we view it in this way. It is something that actually did happen. It is true, whether we believe it or not; it is true, whether we know it or not. But when we know it and believe it, it has a tremendous effect on our lives. In Romans 6:6, Paul stated that *"our old man was crucified with Him, that the body of sin might be done away with, that we should no longer be slaves of sin."* A more modern translation could say "annulled," but I prefer to say "rendered ineffective; put out of action."

The slavery of having sin as our master is terminated in our lives when we realize that the old man died and that a new man now lives in us. But if we do not realize this, believe it, and act upon it, there is no full escape from the slavery of sin. This is the only way out of the bondage or slavery of sin.

Thank You, Jesus, for the exchange at the cross. I proclaim that my slavery to sin is terminated, because my old man was put to death in Christ that the new man might come to life in me. Amen.

Spiritual Conflict, Vol. 2: God's Secret Plan Unfolds: The Cross Canceled Satan's Claims (audio)

The Product of Truth

Our old man was put to death in Christ
that the new man might come to life in us.

Let's look a little more fully at the exchange that takes place between the old man and the new man. The old man was the product of the devil's lie. He was the product of deception. His whole nature is deception and corruption. He is the product of the serpent. The old man is just as crooked as the snake that brought him into being. There is no truth in him—he is crooked to the core. The more he tries to be straight, the more crooked he becomes.

What is the solution? The old man was crucified so that the new man might be brought forth. Ephesians 4:22 instructs us to *"put off... the old man"*; then, in verse 24, we are exhorted to *"put on...the new man."* This is the exchange. The old set of clothing goes; the new set of clothing is put on.

Ephesians 4:24 goes on to describe the new man as having *"true righteousness and holiness."* I would like to restate the verse in this way: "Who, after God, is created in righteousness and true holiness." More literally, "Who, in accordance with God's plan [God's standards, God's thinking, or God's purpose, however you would like to understand it], was created in righteousness and holiness of truth." The new man is the product of the truth of God's Word concerning Jesus Christ. The truth, received into our hearts by faith, brings forth a new man, which brings forth righteousness and holiness. The new man was created in accordance with God's standards, or purpose, in righteousness and holiness, which are products of the truth.

Thank You, Jesus, for the exchange at the cross. I proclaim that my
"old man" was crucified with Christ that my *"new man"* might be
brought forth. I receive this truth by faith in my heart: that my old man
was put to death in Christ that the new man might come to life in me.
Amen.

Spiritual Conflict, Vol. 2: God's Secret Plan Unfolds: The Cross Canceled Satan's Claims (audio)

Incorruptible Seed

Our old man was put to death in Christ
that the new man might come to life in us.

Whoever has been born of God does not sin, for His [God's] seed remains in him; and he cannot sin, because he has been born of God. (1 John 3:9)

Does this verse tell us that a born-again believer never sins? If so, a lot of us would be left out, myself included! Is there any one of us who is truly born of God of whom it could be said, "He cannot commit sin"? I do not believe so. What, then, is the meaning of this verse?

My understanding is that it is talking about the new nature that has been born in us. This is a nature that cannot sin—the Jesus nature. It is the new man. This is very important to realize because only as we cultivate and yield to that nature do we come into a life of victory over sin.

In 1 John 5:4, we read, *"For whatever is born of God overcomes the world."* Notice that John specified *"**whatever** is born of God,"* not *whoever.* He was referring to a person, but also to a nature. That is my understanding. It is the nature of the new man. This new nature cannot sin; it is incorruptible. Do you know why it is incorruptible? God's seed remains in the new man. What is the seed? We find out in 1 Peter 1:23, *"Having been born again, not of corruptible seed but incorruptible, through the word of God which lives and abides forever."*

What is the nature of the seed of God's Word? It is incorruptible. Its exact opposite is the nature of the old man, which is corruptible (and is indeed already corrupt).

Thank You, Jesus, for the exchange at the cross. I proclaim that a new creation has been born in me—a nature that cannot sin, the Jesus nature. I proclaim that my old man was put to death in Christ that the new man might come to life in me. Amen.

The Fullness of the Cross, Vol. 1: Salvation Is All-inclusive (audio)

Being Renewed

Our old man was put to death in Christ
that the new man might come to life in us.

Jesus was God veiled in flesh. When the flesh of Jesus was pierced and torn on the cross, the veil was parted.

In this present age, Christ is revealed in the believer; He lives in the believer but He is still veiled by the flesh. The book of Colossians gives us another aspect of this truth. In speaking about the new man—that is, who we are in Christ, members of the new race—Paul said to the believers,

> *You have put off the old man with his deeds, and have put on the new man who is renewed in knowledge according to the image of Him who created him.* (Colossians 3:9–10)

I prefer to make it more literal: "who is *being* renewed." Renewal is a continuous process that takes place in the present. We are going through a process in order to be renewed.

Then, it says, literally, "into the acknowledgment of the Creator." It is not just knowing Jesus intellectually, but also acknowledging Him in every area of our lives, that brings His image into us.

The end purpose of the process of renewal is for us to reproduce His image. I believe this is a perfectly justifiable paraphrase. Let's repeat it: "Being renewed into the acknowledgment of the Creator so as to reproduce His image." In other words, the end purpose is to restore the image that was marred by the fall. Of course, the consummation of this purpose will come at the resurrection, when even the physical body of the believer will be transformed into the likeness of Christ's resurrection body.

Thank You, Jesus, for the exchange at the cross. I proclaim that I am being renewed into the image of Him who created me. I proclaim that my old man was put to death in Christ that the new man might come to life in me. Amen.

Spiritual Conflict, Vol. 2: God's Secret Plan Unfolds: God's Purpose for the New Race (audio)

Spiritual Nourishment

Our old man was put to death in Christ
that the new man might come to life in us.

We have said that the new birth, through God's Word, produces within the spirit a completely new nature—a new kind of life. This leads us to consider the next major effect that God's Word produces.

In every realm of life, there is one unchanging law: as soon as a new life is born, the first and greatest need of that new life is nourishment to sustain it. For example, when a human baby is born, that baby may be sound and healthy in every respect, but unless he quickly receives nourishment, he will languish and die.

The same law is true in the spiritual realm. When a person is born again, the new spiritual nature produced within that person immediately requires spiritual nourishment, both to maintain life and to promote growth. The spiritual nourishment God has provided for all His born-again children is found in His own Word. God's Word is so rich and varied that it contains nourishment adapted to every stage of spiritual development. God's provision for the first stages of spiritual growth is described in the first epistle of Peter. Immediately after Peter wrote in chapter 1 about being born again of the incorruptible seed of God's Word, he went on to say, *"Therefore, laying aside all malice, all deceit, hypocrisy, envy, and all evil speaking, as newborn babes, desire the pure milk of the word, that you may grow thereby"* (1 Peter 2:1–2). For newborn spiritual babes in Christ, God's appointed nourishment is the pure milk of His own Word. This milk is a necessary fuel for continued life and growth.

Thank You, Jesus, for the exchange at the cross. I proclaim my commitment to God's Word as my source of spiritual nourishment for continued life and growth, and I proclaim that my old man was put to death in Christ that the new man might come to life in me. Amen.

Foundational Truths for Christian Living (book)

Putting on the New

Our old man was put to death in Christ
that the new man might come to life in us.

R eligion always tries to change man from the outside in: make the skirts longer, make the dresses looser, add something to the border, put something on your head, take off the makeup, lengthen the sleeves, cut the hair, or whatever it is. God always operates in the opposite way. He changes man from the inside out. God begins with what we think. He says, "If there is going to be any effective change, you have to think in another way. Another Spirit has to have access to your mind. You have been under the deception of Satan; now, you must open up to the Spirit of truth, the Holy Spirit." As a result of doing that, we are able to put on the new man—the opposite of the old man.

Ephesians 4:24 says, *"Put on the new man which was created according to God, in true righteousness and holiness."* This new man was created according to God, in righteousness and true holiness. He was created according to God's plan; he is the product of God's purpose, God's standard, God's pattern. The old man is the product of Satan's deception; the new man is the product of God's truth.

It is significant that Satan came to the human race in the form of a serpent. By its very nature, a snake is a crooked animal, and I think that is a vivid picture of the devil—he is a very crooked being. He never comes out with full truth. The distinctive word that describes the old man is *corrupt*.

We have to put off the old man and put on the new. The distinctive words that describe the new man are *righteous* and *holy*.

Thank You, Jesus, for the exchange at the cross. I proclaim that I am putting off the *"old man"* and putting on the *"new man,"* for my old man was put to death in Christ that the new man might come to life in me. Amen.

Release from the Tyranny of Self (audio)

Corresponding Fruit

*Our old man was put to death in Christ
that the new man might come to life in us.*

James spoke about the inconsistencies of religious people:

> With the tongue we praise our Lord and Father, and with it we
> curse men, who have been made in God's likeness. Out of the
> same mouth come praise [or blessing] and cursing. My broth-
> ers, this should not be. Can both fresh water and salt water flow
> from the same spring? My brothers, can a fig tree bear olives, or
> a grapevine bear figs? Neither can a salt spring produce fresh
> water. (James 3:9–12 NIV)

James combined two pictures there. One is of a tree. He said that
a fig tree will never bear another kind of fruit, such as olives. The
kind of tree indicates the kind of fruit that it will bear. The tree, in
that picture, is the heart; the fruit is the words that come out of the
mouth. The second picture James used is that of a spring of water. He
said that if brackish, salty water comes out of a spring, you know the
water in the spring is salty.

The two trees represent two natures. A tree that produces fruit
different from what it should produce is corrupt; that tree represents
the old man. A good tree is the new man in Jesus Christ. The old man
cannot bring forth good fruit. Jesus said that clearly many times.
(See, for instance, John 15:1–8.) Out of that old, carnal nature will
always come fruit that corresponds to that nature.

The fountain, or spring, represents something spiritual. A pure
spring is the Holy Spirit. A corrupt, salty, impure spring is another
spirit.

Thank You, Jesus, for the exchange at the cross. I proclaim that out of
my new nature will come good fruit, for my old man was put to death
in Christ that the new man might come to life in me. Amen.

Derek Prince on Experiencing God's Power (book)

In love, my Father has predestined me to be adopted as His son or daughter.

Having predestined us to adoption as sons by Jesus Christ to Himself, according to the good pleasure of His will.

—Ephesians 1:5

Favored and Accepted

In love, my Father has predestined me
to be adopted as His son or daughter.

He [God] chose us..., having predestined us to adoption as sons
by Jesus Christ to Himself, according to the good pleasure of His
will, to the praise of the glory of His grace, by which He made us
accepted in the Beloved. (Ephesians 1:4–6)

Who is *"the Beloved"*? Jesus. Notice the order there. We are chosen, predestined, adopted, and accepted. Say these steps aloud: "I am chosen, predestined, adopted, accepted." I am aware that some of the modern translations do not use the word *accepted*. The Greek phrase translated as *"He made us accepted"* means, "God has bestowed His favor upon us totally." Again, when the angel Gabriel saluted the Virgin Mary, he said, *"Rejoice, highly favored one"* (Luke 1:28). *Favored* is the same Greek word as in Ephesians, and "accepted" is a good way to translate it. We are not merely tolerated by God. We are not just standing on the sidelines. Rather, we are the objects of His highest favor. Can you believe that? It is incredible.

In my opinion, feelings of insecurity are linked directly to the problem of rejection. The solution is to become part of God's family. God has not changed. God is love. God loves every one of His children. There are no second-class children of God. If you are a child of God, you do not have to tiptoe down the corridor and knock at His door, hoping that He will deign to let you in. He is waiting for you with open arms.

Thank You, Father, that I am Your child. I proclaim that I am chosen, predestined, adopted, accepted. God has bestowed His favor upon me completely. In love, my Father has predestined me to be adopted as His son or daughter. Amen.

Total Security (audio)

The Antidote to Loneliness

In love, my Father has predestined me
to be adopted as His son or daughter.

When I ask myself how many lonely Christians are in the world today, the probable answer overwhelms me. I believe there should be no such thing as a lonely Christian. One of the greatest single changes we need to make is rethinking our picture of what it means to be a Christian. It means to be a member of God's family. Not just in some nice theological phrase, but in the membership of a real family.

To be lonely is a very unhappy condition. Yet, in today's world, there are millions and millions of lonely people. Even though the population of the earth is increasing rapidly, and even though many people live in large cities, these large cities and this highly populated earth of ours are filled with lonely people.

It is possible to be lonely even in the midst of a crowd. It is possible to be lonely in a big city. In fact, that is the worst form of loneliness—to be surrounded by people, and, at the same time, to feel cut off from them by an invisible barrier that you have no idea how to break through.

Loneliness is not God's plan for the life of any individual. From eternity, God is a Father. The source of all fatherhood—of every family, in heaven and on earth—is God. As Paul wrote in Ephesians 3:15, *"From [God] the whole family in heaven and earth is named."* Right at the beginning of human history, God provided a mate for the first man because He decided, *"It is not good that man should be alone"* (Genesis 2:18). That is God's attitude. He wants to take us out of our loneliness and to set us in the family of God. He wants to give us brothers and sisters with whom to share His love.

Thank You, Father, that I am Your child. I proclaim that loneliness is not God's plan for my life. He has set me in the family of God. In love, my Father has predestined me to be adopted as His son or daughter. Amen.

Update 94, March 2001 (audio)

Family: A Shared Life Source

In love, my Father has predestined me
to be adopted as His son or daughter.

We are all members of God's family because we all have one Father. Jesus is our elder brother, and we are all members of the same family.

Let me relate a little incident that comes to mind when I think about the family of God. It happened in the days when some of the Scottish Christians up in the Highlands were being severely persecuted by the English army. On her way to a secret meeting of believers, a Scottish lass was arrested by an English policeman, who asked her where she was going. She did not want to lie, but she also did not want to betray her fellow believers, so she lifted her heart to the Lord in prayer and asked Him for an answer. This is how she responded to the policeman: "My elder brother died, and I am on my way to my father's house to hear the will read."

That was a good answer. Jesus is the elder brother, God is our Father, and it is our Father's house.

What is the essential feature of the family? I believe it is a shared life source. God the Father is the life source of us all, and we are together in His family. It is not an institution, not an organization, but a life source that we all share.

What is required of us, as members of God's family? I suggest that it is mutual acceptance. Jesus calls us His brothers because God calls us His sons. If God calls our fellow believers His sons, we have to call them our brothers. That is not always easy. You may choose your friends, but you do not choose your family. Even so, we must accept one another.

Thank You, Father, that I am Your child. I proclaim that I am a
member of God's family, with God as my Father and Jesus as my
elder brother. In love, my Father has predestined me to be adopted
as His son or daughter. Amen.

Seven Pictures of God's People, Part 2 (audio)

DECLARING GOD'S WORD

The Best Family in the Universe

In love, my Father has predestined me
to be adopted as His son or daughter.

Sometimes there are problems with earthly parents that can never be resolved. But, friends, it does not matter if nobody wanted you, nobody loved you, or your parents were not even married. When you come to God through Jesus Christ, you become a member of the best family in the universe, and God has no second-class children.

God's family is the best family. There is no family quite equal to it. Again, even if your own family did not care for you—perhaps your father rejected you, your mother never had time for you, or your husband never showed you affection—God wants you. You are accepted. You are the object of His special care and affection. Remember, everything He does in the universe revolves around you.

As I wrote earlier, when God says that we are accepted, He does not mean *tolerated*. We never bother Him. We do not upset Him or disturb Him. We never take too much of His time. The only thing that upsets Him is when we stay away too long.

He does not push us off into a corner and say, "Wait. I'm too busy. I don't have time for you." Rather, He welcomes us eagerly and lovingly.

Thank You, Father, that I am Your child. I proclaim that by coming to Jesus Christ, I have become a member of the best family in the universe. God welcomes me, because in love, my Father predestined me to be adopted as His son or daughter. Amen.

How to Overcome Rejection and Betrayal (audio)

Welcoming the Prodigal

*In love, my Father has predestined me
to be adopted as His son or daughter.*

Let us review a central truth illustrated in the parable of the prodigal son, which Jesus related to His disciples in Luke 15:11–32. The father was out there looking for his boy to bring him back home. Other people did not have to come and say, "Your son's come home!" because the first one to know it was the father. He knew it before the rest of the family found out.

God's attitude toward us in Christ is like that. We are not rejects. We are not second-class citizens. We are not just servants. When the prodigal came back, he was willing to be a servant. But his father would not hear of it. On the contrary, he said,

> Bring out the best robe and put it on him, and put a ring on his hand and sandals on his feet. And bring the fatted calf here and kill it, and let us eat and be merry; for this my son was dead and is alive again; he was lost and is found.   (verses 22–24)

The whole household was turned upside down to welcome the prodigal.

Likewise, Jesus said, *"There will be more rejoicing in heaven over one sinner who repents than over ninety-nine righteous persons who do not need to repent"* (verse 7 NIV). That's how God welcomes us in Christ.

Thank You, Father, that I am Your child. I proclaim that God
welcomes me in Christ, rejoicing that I am alive. In love, my Father
predestined me to be adopted as His son or daughter. Amen.

"From Rejection to Acceptance" (*New Wine* article)

God Chose in Advance

In love, my Father has predestined me
to be adopted as His son or daughter.

Blessed be the God and Father of our Lord Jesus Christ, who has blessed us with every spiritual blessing in the heavenly places in Christ, just as He chose us in Him before the foundation of the world. (Ephesians 1:3–4)

God foreknew us, and, on the basis of His foreknowledge, He chose us. You are not where you are because *you* made the choice; you are where you are and who you are because *God* made the choice. That truth makes a world of difference to your attitude toward yourself and your situation, both of which were initiated by God. You did not set your life in motion; God did.

God not only foreknew us, but He also predestined us. Some people are afraid of the word *predestined* and what it implies. I want to suggest to you that it merely means that God arranged, in advance, the courses that our lives would follow. As Paul stated in Romans 8:29, *"For whom He foreknew, He also predestined."* He worked it all out in advance.

Then, in Ephesians 1:11, Paul wrote, *"We have obtained an inheritance* [in Christ], *being predestined according to the purpose of Him who works all things according to the counsel of His will."*

This assurance should give you security. You have been predestined; the course of your life has been arranged in advance by the One who works out everything in the way He plans it. He works all things according to the counsel of His own will.

Thank You, Father, that I am Your child. I proclaim that the course of my life has been arranged in advance by the One who works everything the way He wants it. In love, my Father predestined me to be adopted as His son or daughter. Amen.

The Roman Pilgrimage, Vol. 2: Romans 8:26–8:39 (audio)

What God Has Done!

*In love, my Father has predestined me
to be adopted as His son or daughter.*

When Jesus died on the cross, the veil in the temple separating a holy God from sinful man was torn in two, a declaration that we can have His acceptance. (See, for example, Matthew 27:51.) It was torn from top to bottom so that nobody could ever say that a man was responsible. This act was done by God. The torn veil is the Father's invitation to every person who believes in Jesus, "Come in; you are welcome. My Son has endured your rejection so that I may offer you My acceptance."

> *Blessed be the God and Father of our Lord Jesus Christ, who has blessed us with every spiritual blessing in the heavenly places in Christ, just as He chose us in Him before the foundation of the world.* (Ephesians 1:3–4)

Notice that this ultimate choice is not ours, but God's. Do not imagine that you are saved because you chose to be saved! You are saved because God chose you, and you responded to His choice. You might change your mind, but God does not change His.

There is a great deal of misplaced emphasis in many contemporary presentations of the gospel that seems to indicate that everything depends on what we do. It is true that we have to choose, but we would never be able to choose if God had not chosen us in the first place. You will find you are much more secure as a Christian when you are basing your relationship with God not on what you do but on what God has done. God is more dependable than you and I!

Thank You, Father, that I am Your child. I proclaim that I am a child
of God, based not on what I do, but on what God has done. In love,
my Father has predestined me to be adopted as His son or daughter.
Amen.

Atonement, Vol. 2: Rejection vs. Acceptance (audio)

WEEK 36:

My Father knows what I need, even before I ask Him.

For your Father knows the things you have need of before you ask Him.

—Matthew 6:8

God Knows Me Completely

My Father knows what I need, even before I ask Him.

God knows each of us totally, even beyond knowing how many hairs are on our heads. (See Matthew 10:30.) In this beautiful passage from Psalms, David began with what seems like a gasp of astonishment:

> O LORD, Thou hast searched me and known me. Thou dost know when I sit down and when I rise up; Thou dost understand my thought from afar. Thou dost scrutinize my path and my lying down, and art intimately acquainted with all my ways. Even before there is a word on my tongue, behold, O LORD, Thou dost know it all. Thou hast enclosed me behind and before, and laid Thy hand upon me. Such knowledge is too wonderful for me; it is too high, I cannot attain to it. Where can I go from Thy Spirit? Or where can I flee from Thy presence? (Psalm 139:1–7 NASB)

Think about what David said: God knows our thoughts from a distance. A man who once had a revelation of God related that the angel who brought the revelation told him, "Men's thoughts sound as loud in heaven as their voices do on earth." That was a shock to me. But that is essentially what David said here.

Surely, when we consider all of that, we must echo these words of David: *"Such knowledge is too wonderful for me; it is too high, I cannot attain to it."* David asked, *"Where can I go from Thy Spirit?"* That is the key that explains how God knows everything in the whole universe—through His Spirit. The Spirit of God permeates the entire universe; there is no place where the Spirit of God is not present. Through His Spirit, God knows everything that we know, and more—He knows things we can never know, such as the number of hairs on our heads.

Thank You, Father, that You know me completely. I proclaim that through His Spirit, God knows everything that I know about myself and more. My Father knows what I need, even before I ask Him. Amen.

Secure in God's Choice, Part 1 (audio)

God Knows All

My Father knows what I need, even before I ask Him.

Closely related to the eternal nature of God is His omniscience. In 1 John 3:20, we are confronted with a profound yet simple revelation: *"God...knows all things."* There is nothing that God does not know. From the tiniest insect in the earth to the most distant star in the galaxy, there is nothing that God does not know completely.

God knows things about us that we do not know about ourselves. As I wrote yesterday, He knows the number of hairs on each of our heads. (See Matthew 10:30.)

God knew the number of inhabitants in the city of Nineveh. (See Jonah 4:11.)

He knew—and controlled—the growth of the plant that shaded Jonah. He also knew—and controlled—the action of the worm that caused the plant to wither. (See Jonah 4:6–7.)

The apostle Paul wrote about the things that *"eye has not seen, nor ear heard, nor have entered into the heart of man"* (1 Corinthians 2:9). He continued, *"But God has revealed them to us through His Spirit. For the Spirit searches all things, yes, the deep things of God"* (verse 10).

The Holy Spirit both plumbs the deepest depths and scales the highest heights of all that was, is, and is to come. His knowledge is infinite. It is in the light of this infinite knowledge that we must each be prepared to give an account of ourselves to God. *"And there is no creature hidden from His sight, but all things are naked and open to the eyes of Him to whom we must give account"* (Hebrews 4:13).

Thank You, Father, that You know me completely. I proclaim that God's knowledge is infinite—there is nothing He does not know. My Father knows what I need, even before I ask Him. Amen.

The Holy Spirit: Eternal, Omniscient, Omnipresent (Teaching Legacy Letter)

Jesus' Supernatural Knowledge and Wisdom

My Father knows what I need, even before I ask Him.

The supernatural knowledge and wisdom of God was manifested throughout the earthly ministry of Jesus, but perhaps never more clearly than through His dealings with Judas Iscariot. When the disciples told Jesus, *"We have come to believe and know that You are the Christ* [Messiah], *the Son of the living God"* (John 6:69), Jesus gave them an answer in which He revealed that being the Messiah would entail being betrayed by one of His own followers: *"'Did I not choose you, the twelve, and one of you is a devil?' He spoke of Judas Iscariot, the son of Simon, for it was he who would betray Him, being one of the twelve"* (John 6:70–71). Jesus knew, by the Holy Spirit, that Judas would betray Him, even before Judas knew it himself.

Even so, Judas could not carry out his plan until Jesus spoke a word that released him to do so. At the Last Supper, Jesus warned His disciples, *"One of you will betray Me"* (John 13:21). When questioned about who it would be, Jesus replied,

> *"It is he to whom I shall give a piece of bread when I have dipped it." And having dipped the bread, He gave it to Judas Iscariot, the son of Simon. Now after the piece of bread, Satan entered him. Then Jesus said to him, "What you do, do quickly."...Having received the piece of bread, he then went out immediately.* (John 13:26–27, 30)

I am awed by the realization that Judas could not carry out his plan to betray Jesus until Jesus Himself spoke the word that released him to do it. Throughout this whole scene, it was the Betrayed, not the betrayer, who was in control.

Thank You, Father, that You know me completely. I proclaim that Jesus manifested the supernatural knowledge and wisdom of God, who knows all. My Father knows what I need, even before I ask Him. Amen.

The Holy Spirit: Eternal, Omniscient, Omnipresent (Teaching Legacy Letter)

SEPTEMBER 6

God Is in Control

My Father knows what I need, even before I ask Him.

When we comprehend the completeness of God's knowledge—His foreknowledge, in particular—it gives us the assurance that no matter what happens, God is never taken by surprise. There is no such thing as an emergency in the kingdom of heaven. Not only does God know the end from the beginning, but He Himself is both *"the Beginning and the End"* (Revelation 21:6). And He is always in total control.

God specifically knows those whom He has chosen to be with Him in eternity. *"For whom He foreknew, He also predestined to be conformed to the image of His Son, that He might be the firstborn among many brethren"* (Romans 8:29).

If, by the mercy and grace of God, we make it through to that glorious, eternal destination, Jesus will never greet any one of us with the words, "I never expected to see *you* here!" Rather, He will say, "My child, I've been waiting for you. We couldn't sit down to the marriage feast until you came." At that glorious banquet, I believe that every place setting will carry the name of the person for whom it is prepared.

Until the number of the redeemed is complete, God waits with amazing patience, *"not willing that any should perish but that all should come to repentance"* (2 Peter 3:9).

Thank You, Father, that You know me completely. I proclaim that God is always in total control; He is never taken by surprise. My Father knows what I need, even before I ask Him. Amen.

The Holy Spirit: Eternal, Omniscient, Omnipresent (Teaching Legacy Letter)

SEPTEMBER 7

Praying in the Will of God

My Father knows what I need, even before I ask Him.

The prayer of petition is a prayer that we use to make requests of God. It has a legitimate, albeit small, place in prayer, for God knows what we need before we even ask Him. Many people think that praying means going to God with your shopping list. But that is not what He needs or requires.

We all have needs, from time to time, but if we can learn to pray, that is the greatest answer. As my friend Bob Mumford used to say, "What should I do? Give people just one nugget out of the mine or show them the way to the mine itself?" I might pray for you, and you might be healed—that is a gold nugget. But I could also show you the way to the mine. Then, you could get as many gold nuggets as you wanted.

> Now this is the confidence that we have in Him, that if we ask anything according to His will, He hears us. And if we know that He hears us, whatever we ask, we know that we have the petitions that we have asked of Him. (1 John 5:14–15)

So, if we have a petition, and we are praying in the will of God, we should end that petition knowing that we have what we asked for. If we pray according to the will of God, then we know He hears us. If we know He hears us, we know we have that for which we have asked.

Thank You, Father, that You know me completely. I proclaim that when I pray according to the will of God, I know that He hears me. And if I know that He hears me, I know I have that for which I ask. My Father knows what I need, even before I ask Him. Amen.

The Prayer Orchestra (audio)

DECLARING GOD'S WORD

Receiving When We Ask

My Father knows what I need, even before I ask Him.

One of the great secrets of getting things from God is receiving. There are many people who ask but never receive. There is a Scripture verse that is very emphatic about this principle of receiving. Jesus was speaking about petitioning God, and He said,

> *Therefore I say to you, whatever things you ask when you pray, believe that you receive them, and you will have them.*
>
> (Mark 11:24)

The *New International Version* says, *"Believe that you have received it,"* which is a more literal translation. We receive the things we ask for *when we pray.* If you pray in that way—believing that when you pray, you receive—you will have what you ask for.

Notice that receiving is not the same as having. Receiving is settling it; having is the experience that follows. Let's say you have a financial need. You pray. You are in touch with God. You say, "God, we need fifteen hundred dollars by Thursday." Then, you say, "Thank You, God." You have received it. Nothing has changed in your circumstances, but you have received it nevertheless. You will have it.

Thank You, Father, that You know me completely. I proclaim that I receive what I request when I pray, because receiving is settling it. My Father knows what I need, even before I ask Him. Amen.

The Prayer Orchestra (audio)

SEPTEMBER 9

My Exceedingly Great Reward

My Father knows what I need, even before I ask Him.

For the love of money is a root of all sorts of evil, and some by longing for it have wandered away from the faith, and pierced themselves with many a pang. (1 Timothy 6:10 NASB)

The love of money is a root of all kinds of evil. Once we allow the love of money into our lives, out of it will come all sorts of evils and temptations and pain. The remedy is to *"seek first the kingdom of God and His righteousness, and all these things shall be added to you"* (Matthew 6:33). Get your priorities right. God knows we need certain things; it is just a question of priorities.

Let's look now at some of the assurances found in the Bible of the presence and provision of the Lord.

The word of the LORD came to Abram in a vision, saying, "Do not be afraid, Abram. I am your shield, your exceedingly great reward." (Genesis 15:1)

No man shall be able to stand before you all the days of your life; as I was with Moses, so I will be with you. I will not leave you nor forsake you. (Joshua 1:5)

The LORD is my shepherd; I shall not want [lack]. (Psalm 23:1)

The LORD is for me; I will not fear; what can man do to me? (Psalm 118:6 NASB)

The Lord is for us. There is no reason to fear. What can man do to us if God is for us? In Romans 8:31, Paul said, *"If God is for us, who can be against us?"*

Thank You, Father, that You know me completely. I proclaim that the Lord is my exceedingly great reward; the Lord is with me and for me. He is my Shepherd; I shall not lack. My Father knows what I need, even before I ask Him. Amen.

God's Last Word, Vol. 4: Hebrews 12:25–13:6 (audio)

DECLARING GOD'S WORD

Week 37:

As a father has compassion on his children, so God has compassion on me.

As a father has compassion on his children, so the
LORD has compassion on those who fear him.

—Psalm 103:13 (NIV)

Freedom to Love

*As a father has compassion on his children,
so God has compassion on me.*

*But he who looks into the perfect law of liberty and continues in
it, and is not a forgetful hearer but a doer of the work, this one
will be blessed in what he does.*   (James 1:25)

*If you really fulfill the royal law according to the Scripture, "You
shall love your neighbor as yourself," you do well.*   (James 2:8)

The law *"You shall love your neighbor as yourself"* is called two things:
the *"perfect law of liberty"* and the *"royal law."* It is the perfect law
in that it encompasses every other law. When you really love your
neighbor, fervently and with a pure heart, you cannot but keep all the
other commandments. By keeping that one law, you are obeying all
the laws. It is also the royal, or kingly, law.

It is the perfect law of liberty, or freedom, because nobody can
stop you from loving. Once you have made up your mind to love, people can say all sorts of mean things about you and treat you miserably,
but they cannot stop you from loving. The only person who is totally
free is the person who loves.

Jesus was the perfect example of freedom in love. The authorities
did everything to Him: they beat Him, they pierced His hands and
His feet, they put a crown of thorns on His head, they gave Him vin-
egar to drink, they abused Him, they reviled Him. But the one thing
they could not do was to stop Him from loving. He loved them to the
end. (See Luke 23:34.)

If you love with that kind of love, nobody can stop you from
doing exactly what you want to do—love. That is why love is called
the *"perfect law of liberty."*

Thank You, Lord, that You care so much. I proclaim that I have made
up my mind to love in obedience to God's perfect law of liberty. As
a father has compassion on his children, so God has compassion on
me. Amen.

Commanded to Love (audio, video)

Moved with Compassion

As a father has compassion on his children,
so God has compassion on me.

How is compassion portrayed in Scripture? Let's look at an incident from the first chapter of Mark.

> *Now a leper came to Him [Jesus], imploring Him, kneeling down to Him and saying to Him, "If You are willing, You can make me clean." Then Jesus, moved with compassion, stretched out His hand and touched him, and said to him, "I am willing; be cleansed." As soon as He had spoken, immediately the leprosy left him, and he was cleansed.*   (Mark 1:40–42)

It says that Jesus was *"moved with compassion."* This response refers to the bowels—compassion is a gut feeling. The King James Version refers to the *"bowels of compassion"* (1 John 3:17). The "bowels of compassion" are where our deepest feelings lie—not in the physical heart, but in the gut. This is where it all begins. This is the source of everything.

When my first wife, Lydia, was writing her autobiography, she used the phrase, "My bowels were moved." The editors of the book had to explain that this was not the right way to express that feeling in English. But in every other language I know—Latin, Greek, Hebrew—the deepest, innermost part of you is not referred to as the heart but the bowels. Whether it is love, fear, hatred, or another emotion, its place of origin is the bowels, which are at your very depth.

Thank You, Lord, that You care so much. I proclaim that just as Jesus was moved with compassion, I want to respond in the same way in the deepest, innermost part of me. As a father has compassion on his children, so God has compassion on me. Amen.

Commanded to Love (audio, video)

What Moves Us?

As a father has compassion on his children,
so God has compassion on me.

One of the greatest problems in the church today is personal ambition on the part of ministers. The apostle Paul addressed this issue with the church at Philippi, saying,

> *Therefore if there is any consolation in Christ, if any comfort of love, if any fellowship of the Spirit, if any affection and mercy, fulfill my joy by being like-minded, having the same love, being of one accord, of one mind. Let nothing be done through selfish ambition or conceit, but in lowliness of mind let each esteem others better than himself.* (Philippians 2:1–3)

Those are very powerful words. Paul was not talking about superficial feelings. They go deep.

I have met many wonderful ministers, but the primary driving force of today's church, as I see it, is ambition: ambition to build a bigger church, to hold a larger meeting, to put more names on the mailing list, or to make oneself known. Maybe I am being cynical, but, nevertheless, ambition seems to be a primary force in contemporary Christianity. However, Paul said, *"Let nothing be done through selfish ambition."*

I have a question for those of you in the Lord's service. It is, by extension, a question for everyone, for all believers are to be in the Lord's service. By what are you moved? What prompts you to do the things you do? To speak the words you speak? To relate to people the way you do? Are you motivated by the love of God and by compassion? First John 4:7–8 exhorts us, *"Beloved, let us love one another, for love is of God; and everyone who loves is born of God and knows God."*

Thank You, Lord, that You care so much. I proclaim my desire to be motivated by the love of God and by compassion. As a father has compassion on his children, so God has compassion on me. Amen.

Commanded to Love (audio, video)

The Fountain of Compassion

As a father has compassion on his children,
so God has compassion on me.

In Psalm 84:6, we read, *"As they pass through the Valley of Baca, they make it a spring* [or a fountain]." After nearly sixty years as a Christian—walking in the way of the Lord, speaking in tongues—I experienced a transformation. Something entirely new happened within me—a spring was opened inside me that was a fountain of compassion. I had known the love of God for a long time, and I had always loved my family, but this spring was unlike anything I had ever experienced.

This spring had another source apart from Derek Prince. I began to understand what the Bible means when it says that Jesus was *"moved with compassion."* (See, for example, Matthew 9:36; Mark 1:41.) I realized God was sharing His compassion with me, and I prayed, "Lord, let this fountain never become defiled or contaminated, and let it never become stopped up." God alone determined when it would spring up. And when the fountain of compassion is flowing within me, it attracts people to me. They do not know why they are drawn to me, but they sense something for which they have been longing. I believe that God is waiting for us to love one another with His divine love.

God has done something else in me, too. He has given me a supernatural concern for orphans, widows, the poor, and the oppressed. We can talk about faith and righteousness, but if we do nothing for the people who really need us, these words are empty and meaningless. There is no shortage of people who need us. They are all around us—people who need to be loved are everywhere. They are lonely; no one cares for them; they lack answers and are desperate. You don't have to go far from home to find people like that. Compassion is the purpose of God. It is what He's waiting to see manifest in us.

Thank You, Lord, that You care so much. I proclaim my desire for
the fountain of God's compassion to flow in me and through me, out
to those around me who are needy and desperate. As a father has
compassion on his children, so God has compassion on me. Amen.

Commanded to Love (audio, video)

SEPTEMBER 14

Caring for the Uncared For

As a father has compassion on his children,
so God has compassion on me.

I have written a little booklet entitled *Orphans, Widows, the Poor and Oppressed*. This booklet astonishes me. As I wrote yesterday, even after I had been preaching for well over fifty years, and when I had the impression that I would be preaching for the rest of my life, God gave me a new kind of compassion I never expected to receive. My rendering of Psalm 84:6 is, "When you pass through the Valley of Baca [weeping], God will open a fountain."

I have passed through the valley of weeping, and God has opened that fountain for me. It is something sovereign that only God could do. It is compassion. I have become deeply concerned—almost passionately—about the people our society neglects and treads underfoot: the orphans, the widows, the poor, and the oppressed. I am amazed by how much the Bible has to say about our responsibility to care for them. From cover to cover of the Bible, it is a major theme of God's righteousness—whether it is in the Patriarchs, under the Law of Moses, in the Prophets, or in the New Testament.

Generally speaking, we, as Christians, have completely missed a vital area of our faith and our profession, which is to care for those whom no one else cares for.

Thank You, Lord, that You care so much. I proclaim the truth of Psalm 84:6: *"When you pass through the Valley of Baca [weeping], God will open a fountain."* I proclaim that I will walk in this vital area of faith and profession, caring for those for whom no one else cares. As a father has compassion on his children, so God has compassion on me. Amen.

Update 90: January 2000 (audio)

A Measure of Righteousness

As a father has compassion on his children,
so God has compassion on me.

The words of Job are remarkable. He is here listing sins he did *not* commit, of which he was not guilty. Many professing Christians, however, could be guilty of these sins. *"If I have kept the poor from their desire, or caused the eyes of the widow to fail, or eaten my morsel by myself, so that the fatherless could not eat of it..."* (Job 31:16–17).

Notice the three groups that Job listed: the poor, the widows, and the fatherless (or orphans). Job said, in essence, "If I have not done what I ought to have done for them, I am a sinner, and I have failed my basic obligations." He went on,

> *(But from my youth I reared him as a father, and from my mother's womb I guided the widow); if I have seen anyone perish for lack of clothing, or any poor man without covering; if his heart has not blessed me, and if he was not warmed with the fleece of my sheep; if I have raised my hand against the fatherless, when I saw I had help in the gate; then let my arm fall from my shoulder, let my arm be torn from the socket.* (verses 18–22)

Job did not fail to care for the people who had no food, clothing, or families to care for them. Then, he said that if his arm were not engaged continually in these acts of mercy and generosity, it had no place in his body at all. His viewpoint is totally different from the viewpoint most people have today. This was the standard of righteousness of the patriarchs, too, even before the law of Moses and even before the gospel. God requires us to restore this kind of righteousness in the church by going out of our way to care for widows, orphans, and those with no food, clothing, or shelter.

Thank You, Lord, that You care so much. I proclaim that God requires me to restore this kind of righteousness—caring for the needy—in the church. As a father has compassion on his children, so God has compassion on me. Amen.

Update 90: January 2000 (audio)

SEPTEMBER 16

Clothed with Righteousness

As a father has compassion on his children,
so God has compassion on me.

B elow, we will read Job's testimony of the way he lived. God Himself bore testimony to Job that he was a righteous man. These words have gripped me so much that I can hardly get beyond them.

> *When the ear heard, then it blessed me, and when the eye saw,*
> *then it approved me; because I delivered the poor who cried out,*
> *the fatherless and the one who had no helper. The blessing of a*
> *perishing man came upon me, and I caused the widow's heart to*
> *sing for joy. I put on righteousness, and it clothed me; my justice*
> *was like a robe and a turban. I was eyes to the blind, and I was*
> *feet to the lame. I was a father to the poor, and I searched out the*
> *case that I did not know.* (Job 29:11–16)

Isn't it remarkable that Job's righteousness was not his own? There is no self-righteousness anywhere in the Bible. Job said, *"I put on righteousness, and it clothed me."* He was clothed with a righteousness that he had received from God by faith. This was the outworking of his righteousness.

The poor, the widows, and the fatherless are the objects of God's compassion. These are the people whom God has in mind when He speaks about righteousness—the widows, the fatherless, the poor, the blind, and the lame. We can measure how much of God's righteousness we have by looking at the way we relate to these types of people.

Thank You, Lord, that You care so much. I proclaim that the poor, the widow, and the fatherless are the objects of God's compassion—and they must be recipients of my compassion, as well. As a father has compassion on his children, so God has compassion on me. Amen.

Orphans, Widows, the Poor and Oppressed (audio, booklet)

WEEK 38:

I have received the Spirit of sonship, and by Him, I cry, "*Abba*, Father."

For you did not receive a spirit that makes you a slave again to fear, but you received the Spirit of sonship. And by him we cry, "Abba, Father."

—Romans 8:15 (NIV)

The Spirit of Adoption

I have received the Spirit of sonship,
and by Him, I cry, "Abba, Father."

For as many as are led by the Spirit of God, these are sons of God.
For you did not receive the spirit of bondage [slavery] *again to*
fear, but you received the Spirit of adoption by whom we cry out,
"Abba, Father."   (Romans 8:14–15)

Abba is the Aramaic or Hebrew word commonly used for "daddy."
In Israel, a little child will call his father, "Abba." And because we
have received the Spirit of adoption, we have the right to address God
as *Abba*. Father. Daddy.

Paul told us that we have two options. We can be led by the Spirit
of God, or we can be under the spirit of slavery. The spirit of slavery
makes us fearful of punishment; the Spirit of adoption leads us as
God's children.

The Greek word that is translated as *sons* indicates a "mature son."
When you are first born again of God's Spirit, you become a child. But
as you are led, you become a mature son or daughter of God. The pathway to maturity is being led by the Holy Spirit, no longer bound under
a spirit of slavery. As Paul wrote in Galatians 5:18, *"But if you are led by*
the Spirit, you are not under the law."

In order to become a mature son or daughter of God, you must
be led by the Spirit. But remember, if you are led by the Holy Spirit,
you are not under the law. That is our freedom—not a freedom to do
evil, but a freedom to love. Our motivation to do service for Jesus is
love, the most powerful motivator in the world. It works even when
fear does not. That's what God is bringing us to. That's what makes us
mature sons and daughters of God. That's the result of being delivered from the law.

Thank You, Father, that I am Your child. I proclaim that I am no
longer bound under a spirit of slavery. I have received the Spirit of
adoption. I have received the Spirit of sonship, and by Him, I cry,
"Abba, Father." Amen.

The Fullness of the Cross, Vol. 2: Deliverance from the Law (audio)

Birth and Adoption

I have received the Spirit of sonship,
and by Him, I cry, "Abba, Father."

When you receive Jesus Christ, you become a child of God, and you also receive the "Jesus nature," a nature that knows to call God the Father "Daddy." This is a very natural relationship.

In Romans 8, Paul addressed two major subjects—birth and adoption. Do not confuse them; they are distinctly different. Birth produces a nature; adoption gives a legal standing.

God is so good to us that we get it both ways—birth and adoption—but they don't give us the same thing. We receive something distinct by each process.

This is perfectly understandable in the light of the customs of the Roman Empire. In Paul's day, it was not uncommon for the Roman emperor to have many sons, but when he chose one particular son to succeed him as emperor, he would also adopt that son. Then, all the legal rights of the empire would go to that adopted son. The purpose of adoption was legal—it assured the son's inheritance.

We are born again at regeneration, and we receive the "Jesus nature." But, at the baptism in the Holy Spirit, we receive adoption. Heaven's best Lawyer comes in and assures us that we are the children of God. This is what assures us of the inheritance we receive. Do you see the implication?

It is just like the Roman emperor. If he has a son by natural birth, his son gets his nature. But in order to receive the inheritance, that son needs to be adopted; this gives him a legal standing and rightful inheritance.

Thank You, Father, that I am Your child. I proclaim that by birth and adoption, I have received both a natural and legal standing. I have received the Spirit of sonship, and by Him, I cry, "Abba, Father."
Amen.

Way into the Spirit-filled Life: Romans 8: The New Life in the Spirit (audio)

SEPTEMBER 19

Led by the Spirit

I have received the Spirit of sonship,
and by Him, I cry, "Abba, Father."

There is a popular teaching that convinces people that they must be super-spiritual to be considered sons of God. But Paul contradicted this idea in the eighth chapter of Romans, where he wrote that all who are led regularly by the Holy Spirit are indeed sons of God. *"For as many as are led by the Spirit of God, these are sons of God"* (Romans 8:14). In one sense, if you are *already* perfect, you do not need the Holy Spirit. You need the Holy Spirit, though, if you are to *become* perfect.

The way to live as a real son or daughter of God is to be led regularly by the Holy Spirit. As Jesus said, *"My sheep hear My voice,...and they follow Me"* (John 10:27). By *"hear,"* Jesus meant *regularly* hear, *regularly* follow. This is not an up-and-down, once a week process; rather, it is a regular, continuing relationship.

Paul continued in Romans 8:15, *"For you did not receive the spirit of bondage again to fear, but you received the Spirit of adoption by whom we cry out, 'Abba, Father.'"* The *"spirit of bondage,"* very simply, is the law. Instead of being bound by the law, you have received the Spirit of God, who assures you of your identity as a child of God. As a child of God, you have all the rights of the inheritance. Paul assured us, *"The Spirit Himself bears witness with our* [regenerated] *spirit that we are children of God, and if children, then heirs* [inheritance is the subject]; *heirs of God and joint heirs with Christ"* (verses 16–17).

Many people receive assurance of being children of God only when they are baptized in the Holy Spirit. The Holy Spirit comes in to assure you that you are a child of God and that you have a legal right to your inheritance. You are not merely born, but you are also adopted, and this passage clearly connects adoption and inheritance.

Thank You, Father, that I am Your child. I proclaim that I am a child of God, with all the rights of inheritance. I have received the Spirit of sonship, and by Him, I cry, *"Abba, Father."* Amen.

Way into the Spirit-filled Life: Romans 8: The New Life in the Spirit (audio)

Going on to Pentecost

I have received the Spirit of sonship,
and by Him, I cry, "Abba, Father."

The Spirit Himself bears witness with our spirit that we are
children of God.   (Romans 8:16)

Let me point out one simple, historic fact—a conclusion at which most sound Bible scholars have arrived. There is a direct correspondence in time periods between the deliverance of Israel out of Egypt and the experience of the early Christians.

The Passover lamb's execution corresponds to the day on which Jesus died.

The crossing of the Red Sea corresponds to Jesus' resurrection from the grave.

The receiving of the Law at Mount Sinai, fifty days after the Passover, corresponds to the outpouring of the Spirit at Pentecost.

I point this out because when you have been delivered through the blood and through the resurrection of Jesus, you have two choices: you can go to Sinai, or you can go to Pentecost. Quite a lot of people go to Sinai—they go back under the law. They *"receive the spirit of bondage again to fear"* (verse 15). But Paul said, in essence, "You have not received a spirit of bondage to fear; you have received the Spirit of adoption, who tells you that you are a child of God."

Thank You, Father, that I am Your child. I proclaim that I have not received a spirit of bondage again to fear, but a spirit of adoption, which tells me that I am a child of God. I have received the Spirit of sonship, and by Him, I cry, *"Abba, Father."* Amen.

Way into the Spirit-filled Life: Romans 8: The New Life in the Spirit (audio)

Suffering and Reigning

I have received the Spirit of sonship,
and by Him, I cry, "Abba, Father."

Paul wrote in Romans 8:18, *"For I consider that the sufferings of this present time are not worthy to be compared with the glory which shall be revealed in us."* If we wish to reign with Christ, we must be prepared to suffer. We read in 2 Timothy,

> *This is a faithful saying: For if we died with Him, we shall also live with Him. If we endure [suffer], we shall also reign with Him. If we deny Him, He also will deny us. If we are faithless, He remains faithful; He cannot deny Himself.* (2 Timothy 2:11–13)

So, we see that if we suffer, we will reign; but if we deny Jesus Christ, He will deny us. There come times in our lives when we are challenged to either suffer with Him or deny Him, and the issues are put clearly before us. (See, for example, Acts 14:22; Philippians 1:29–30; 2 Thessalonians 1:4–10.)

I have a beautiful picture that I would like to describe to you. It comes from the tabernacle, and it concerns three of the main colors, especially in the high priest's garments: blue, purple, and scarlet. Blue is a type of heavenly color; scarlet is a type of human nature, as well as the blood; and purple is the perfect blending of blue and scarlet, which speaks of Christ as God incarnate. The blue of heaven and the scarlet of earth blend to make purple. This is a beautiful picture of the nature of Jesus Christ—both God and man, perfectly blended in a new color.

The significance of purple in Scripture is twofold: it signifies royalty and suffering. You cannot wear the purple in the kingdom if you do not first wear it on earth by suffering. If we suffer, we will reign.

Thank You, Father, that I am Your child. I proclaim that if I endure suffering, I shall also reign with You. I have received the Spirit of sonship, and by Him, I cry, "Abba, Father." Amen.

Way into the Spirit-filled Life: Romans 8: The New Life in the Spirit (audio)

The Scope of Our Inheritance

I have received the Spirit of sonship,
and by Him, I cry, "Abba, Father."

Let's look at a verse that speaks about the extent of our inheritance in Christ. Romans 8:32 reads, *"He [God] who did not spare His own Son [Jesus], but delivered Him up for us all, how will He not also with Him freely give us all things?"* (NASB). When we receive Christ, God freely gives us *all things*. Apart from Him, we receive nothing. There is a strong emphasis in this verse on the scope of the inheritance and its absolute freedom. We cannot earn it. We receive it as a free gift that includes all things. We are heirs of the total inheritance—all that God the Father has, all that God the Son has—when we receive Christ.

In his first epistle to the Corinthians, Paul tried to show the believers how rich they were. He actually rebuked them a little because they were acting as though they were poor. They were being mean, petty, and envious toward one another. Paul said, in effect, "You people don't realize what you've got."

"So then let no one boast in men. For all things belong to you, whether Paul or Apollos or Cephas or the world or life or death or things present or things to come; all things belong to you, and you belong to Christ; and Christ belongs to God" (1 Corinthians 3:21–23 NASB). What a breathtaking statement. Paul said, in effect, "All things belong to you. Stop acting petty and frivolous. Don't get hung up on preachers, either. Stop being so small-minded. Everything is yours." Remember, the gift of the inheritance is freely given to us; we cannot earn it. But it is important that we ask the Holy Spirit to enlarge our faith and understanding. The Holy Spirit is the administrator, and unless He speaks to us and guides us into the truth, these will just be words, not reality. The Holy Spirit makes the promises a reality.

Thank You, Father, that I am Your child. I proclaim that by receiving Christ, I am an heir of the total inheritance. I have received the Spirit of sonship, and by Him, I cry, "Abba, Father." Amen.

Extravagant Love (booklet)

The Eternal Fatherhood of God

I have received the Spirit of sonship,
and by Him, I cry, "Abba, Father."

Let's take a closer look at the relationship of the Father to His children: *"For this reason I bow my knees to the Father of our Lord Jesus Christ, from whom the whole family in heaven and earth is named"* (Ephesians 3:14–15).

The J. B. Phillips translation of verse 15 reads, *"From whom all fatherhood, earthly or heavenly, derives its name."* This verse contains a tremendous revelation—that the fatherhood of God is eternal, named after the fatherhood of God in heaven and deriving its sanctity and authority from being a projection on earth of the divine, eternal fatherhood of God in heaven.

Before creation ever took place, God was already a Father—the Father of our Lord Jesus Christ. This relationship of fatherhood and sonship within the Godhead is eternal. Before creation was brought into being, God was eternally a Father and Christ was eternally His Son. Every fatherhood in creation is named after the eternal fatherhood of God.

In a familiar verse from the gospel of John, Jesus said, *"In My Father's house are many mansions"* (John 14:2). This verse reveals the fact that God is a Father, and He has a house. In Scripture, however, the word *house* is never used primarily to indicate a physical, material building. Rather, it is always used of a family and the building they occupy. When Jesus said, *"In My Father's house,"* He was talking about God's heavenly family. God is eternally a Father, and family life has its origin in eternity in the father/son relationship within the Godhead.

Thank You, Father, that I am Your child. I proclaim that the
fatherhood of God is eternal, and I am part of God's heavenly family.
I have received the Spirit of sonship, and by Him, I cry,
"Abba, Father." Amen.

Fatherhood (audio)

DECLARING GOD'S WORD

WEEK 39:

My Father has made me.

Do you thus deal with the LORD, O foolish and unwise people? Is He not your Father, who bought you? Has He not made you and established you?

—Deuteronomy 32:6

SEPTEMBER 24

Doubly His

My Father has made me.

Here is a parable I told to a group of Maoris, who are great wood carvers, to illustrate the price Jesus paid to redeem us from our sins.

There was once a boy who carved a beautiful little wooden sailboat. One day he took it down to the ocean to sail, but the wind changed and carried his boat out to sea. Since he could not recover his boat, he went home without it.

The next high tide brought the boat back again, and it was found by a man walking along the seashore. He inspected the boat and saw that it was beautifully made, so he sold it to a shopkeeper who cleaned it up and put it in his window, priced to sell.

Some while later, the boy passed by the shop and saw his boat. He knew immediately that it was his, but he had no way to prove it. So, if he wanted it back, he knew he would have to buy it.

He set to work to earn the money by washing cars, mowing lawns, and other tasks. When he finally raised the necessary funds, he walked into the shop and bought back his boat. He took it in his hands, and, holding it to his breast, said, "Now you're mine! I made you and I bought you."

Picture yourself as that boat. You may feel inadequate or worthless; you may wonder if God really cares. But the Lord is saying to you, "Now you're doubly Mine—I made you and I bought you; you're fully Mine."

Thank You, Lord, for Your work in me. I proclaim that I am doubly the Lord's because He made me and He bought me. My Father has made me. Amen.

The Good News of the Kingdom, Vol. 1: The Kingdom for All Nations (audio)

DECLARING GOD'S WORD

SEPTEMBER 25

The Breath of Life

My Father has made me.

In Genesis 2:7, we read the account of the creation of man. A personal God created a personal man for personal fellowship with Himself. Here, it is Person to person. It is not an abstraction. It is not some mysterious force at work in the universe, but it is a Person creating another person in order to have fellowship with that person. To me, this so vividly brings out the fact that one main reason that God created man was to enjoy fellowship with him.

Picture the scene! The Lord kneeled down, took dust in His hands, mixed it with water, and molded it into the body of a man. But it was lifeless! Then, something marvelous happened. The Creator leaned forward, put His divine lips against the lips of clay, pressed His divine nostrils against the nostrils of clay, and breathed life into them. His breath penetrated the form of clay and transformed it into a living human being with every organ of its body functioning perfectly, and with all the marvelous spiritual, intellectual, and emotional responses of which a human being is capable. No other being has ever been created in such a way.

The words used to describe this miracle are particularly vivid. The Hebrew language is one in which the sounds of certain words relate directly to the action they name. The sound of the Hebrew word translated *"breathed"* can be rendered *yip-pach*. It consists of a tiny, internal "explosion," followed by a forceful, ongoing release of air from the throat. Thus, it vividly represents the action it names.

As the Lord stooped down over those lips and nostrils of clay, He did not let out a languid sigh. He exhaled a forceful breath into that body of clay, which thus received a miraculous impartation of the very life of God.

Thank You, Lord, for Your work in me. I proclaim that the Lord wants to enjoy fellowship with me, and He breathed His life into me. My Father has made me. Amen.

Bible Psychology, Vol. 1: What God's Mirror Reveals: Triune Man at Creation (audio)

Our Priceless Bodies

My Father has made me.

Let's look for a moment at something the Bible says about the material out of which the human body is made. Some of you probably do not know that the Bible has quite a lot to say about that.

It always grieves me when Christians downgrade their own bodies and talk about them as if they were inferior or of little importance. Brothers and sisters, our bodies are miracles. If your car was totaled in a wreck and you had to replace it, all you would need is a certain amount of dollars and you could purchase a new car. But if you injure even one eye, there is no way you can pay for a new eye. It is priceless. So it is with every other major organ of the body. It grieves me when I see Christians taking more care of their cars than they do of their bodies. That is a very foolish scale of values.

Psalm 139 is a psalm that David wrote as a meditation on the marvels of his own body. David said to the Lord,

> *I will praise You, for I am fearfully and wonderfully made; marvelous are Your works, and that my soul knows very well.*
>
> (Psalm 139:14)

David was talking about his physical body. I wonder if you would agree to say those same words about your own body. It would change the attitude of some of you. Some Christians are almost burdened down with their bodies. They seem to wish that they did not have the problem of a body. That is a false viewpoint. Say these words aloud right now: "I will praise You, for I am fearfully and wonderfully made."

Thank You, Lord, for Your work in me. I proclaim that my body is priceless, and I say, "*I will praise You, for I am fearfully and wonderfully made.*" My Father has made me. Amen.

God's Plan for Your Body (audio)

This Marvelous Workmanship

My Father has made me.

In the book of Job, we find a beautiful summation of God's creative work in forming our bodies:

> *Your hands have made me and fashioned me, an intricate unity; yet You would destroy me. Remember, I pray, that You have made me like clay. And will You turn me into dust again? Did You not pour me out like milk, and curdle me like cheese,...?*
>
> (Job 10:8–11)

As in Genesis 2:7, where the word *"formed"* indicates a very careful, skillful work, so, too, Job emphasizes the immense skill and care that God devoted to forming the human body. What vivid expressions! Verses 10–11 say, *"Did You not...clothe me with skin and flesh, and knit me together with bones and sinews?"* What a beautiful picture of the interrelationship of the various main parts of the body. In Psalm 139, David wrote, *"Thine eyes did see my substance, yet being unperfect; and in thy book all my members were written, which in continuance were fashioned, when as yet there was none of them"* (verse 16 KJV).

God brought your body into being on a blueprint, and there is a number for every member. Every member is written up in God's book. Compare that statement with what Jesus said in Luke 12:7: *"But the very hairs of your head are all numbered. Do not fear therefore; you are of more value than many sparrows."* Such is the intensity of God's concern for our physical bodies—He takes an interest in even the smallest details. When we realize this truth, we must also realize that God has a purpose for the marvelous workmanships that are our own bodies.

Thank You, Lord, for Your work in me. I proclaim that God formed me with immense skill and care—and that He has a purpose for this marvelous workmanship that is my body. My Father has made me.
Amen.

Bible Psychology, Vol. 2: Achieving Inner Harmony: God's Plan for the Believer's Body (audio)

SEPTEMBER 28

His Dwelling Place

My Father has made me.

What is the purpose for which our bodies were made? It is an important purpose, and the answer is exciting and simple. In his first epistle to the church at Corinth, Paul wrote,

> *Or do you not know that your body is the temple of the Holy*
> *Spirit who is in you, whom you have from God, and you are not*
> *your own?* (1 Corinthians 6:19)

Why did God design and create a body for man? The answer is amazing. He wanted the body of each redeemed believer to be a temple for Him to dwell in, through His Holy Spirit. Again, if you view your own body from that perspective, it will give you a totally different attitude toward it. Your body was designed to be a temple for God to inhabit.

The Bible tells us that God does not dwell in temples made with hands. (See Acts 7:48; 17:24.) You could build any building—a synagogue, a cathedral, a church, whatever you desire—but God will not live there. When God's people meet in such buildings, God will be there with them, but He doesn't live there. God has designed His own temple. What is it? Our bodies.

It is staggering to think that almighty God, the Creator of heaven and earth, wants to occupy our physical bodies and make them His temple.

When Jesus was speaking about the Holy Spirit in John 7, He said, *"'He that believeth on me, as the scripture hath said, out of his belly shall flow rivers of living water.' (But this spake he of the Spirit...)"* (verse 38 KJV). There is an area in your physical body that God wants to occupy with His Holy Spirit.

Thank You, Lord, for Your work in me. I proclaim that my body is the temple of the Holy Spirit, who is within me. My Father has made me. Amen.

God's Plan for Your Body (audio)

Presenting Our Members

My Father has made me.

Let's continue to consider God's purpose for the human body. Our physical members are to become slaves, or instruments, of righteousness. First, the Holy Spirit takes up His dwelling place; then, our bodies become His instruments.

> *I am speaking in human terms because of the weakness of your flesh. For just as you presented your members* [physical members] *as slaves to impurity and to lawlessness, resulting in further lawlessness, so now present your members as slaves to righteousness, resulting in sanctification* [holiness].
> (Romans 6:19 NASB)

God's program for our physical members is for us to present them to Him as slaves, ready to do His will no matter what. Romans 6:13 tells us to present our physical members *"as instruments of righteousness."* When presented to God without reservation, our bodies become sanctified and worthy temples of the Holy Spirit.

When our members are yielded to Him without reservation, as slaves or instruments to do His will, then God says, "All right, since the body is Mine, I'll accept full responsibility for its maintenance and its well-being, both in this life and in the next."

Thank You, Lord, for Your work in me. I proclaim that I now present my body to God, without reservation, to be a sanctified and worthy temple of the Holy Spirit. My Father has made me. Amen.

What Is Man?, Part 2 (audio)

Placed on the Altar

My Father has made me.

In Romans 12:1, Paul instructed us to sacrifice our bodies while we are still living: *"Therefore, I urge you, brothers, in view of God's mercy, to offer your bodies as living sacrifices, holy and pleasing to God—this is your spiritual act of worship"* (NIV).

If you offer your body as a living sacrifice to God, you no longer claim ownership of your body. You no longer decide where your body will go. You no longer decide what your body will do. You no longer decide what your body will eat or what it will wear. You have given up the right to make those decisions. From now on, your body no longer belongs to you—it belongs to God. You have sacrificed it, living, to Him on His altar.

Whatever is placed on the altar of God belongs to God from that point on. It no longer belongs to the person who gave it. That is what God requires: that we sacrifice our bodies, just as Jesus sacrificed His body. The difference is that Jesus sacrificed His body through death, while we are asked to sacrifice our bodies when still alive—to hand them over to God, to give up our rights and our claims to them.

Now, that concept may sound very frightening. But I want to tell you that it is very exciting. God has all sorts of ideas about what He will do with you and your body. But He is not going to tell you until your body belongs to Him. You must first commit your body to Him, and then you will understand what to do with it.

Thank You, Lord, for Your work in me. I proclaim that I now place my body as a living sacrifice on God's altar. It no longer belongs to me, but to God. My Father has made me. Amen.

Objective for Living: To Do God's Will (audio)

Pray for the peace of Jerusalem:
"May they prosper who love you."

Pray for the peace of Jerusalem:
"May they prosper who love you."

—Psalm 122:6

OCTOBER 1

Praying for the Peace of Jerusalem

Pray for the peace of Jerusalem: "May they prosper who love you."

I n Genesis 12:2–3, we read God's original promise to Abraham when
He told him to leave Ur of the Chaldeans and go to another land:

> *I will make you into a great nation and I will bless you; I will make
> your name great, and you will be a blessing. I will bless those who
> bless you, and whoever curses you I will curse; and all peoples on
> earth will be blessed through you.*   (NIV)

The Jewish people are the touchstone by which all other nations
are going to be judged. Scripture gives us a warning in this regard:
"May all who hate Zion, be put to shame and turned backward" (Psalm
129:5 NASB). Any nation that opposes God's purpose for the restoration of Zion will be put to shame and turned backward. Nations
determine their destinies by how they respond to the restoration of
God's people.

A beautiful and familiar promise of blessing for those who align
themselves with God's purposes for Jerusalem, for Israel, and for
God's people is found in Psalm 122:6: *"Pray for the peace of Jerusalem:
they shall prosper that love thee"* (KJV). We cannot merely take a neutral
attitude and say, "Let's see what happens." We have to actively align
ourselves with what God is saying in His Word and what He is doing
in history.

The primary way in which we can do this is through our prayers.
We can pray for the peace of Jerusalem and for its restoration—for
Jerusalem to become all that God has declared in the Scriptures that
it shall be. To those who pray and are concerned, this is the promise:
"They shall prosper that love thee."

Thank You, Lord, for the blessing You promise to those who love
Israel. I proclaim that those who pray and are concerned about
Jerusalem will prosper. I pray for the peace of Jerusalem: *"May they
prosper who love you."* Amen.

Prophetic Guide to the End Times (book)

Seeking Israel's Good by Prayer

Pray for the peace of Jerusalem: "May they prosper who love you."

The Bible exhorts us to seek the good of Israel through our prayers. To pray effectively in this way, we need to search out from the Scriptures God's purposes for Israel and Jerusalem. Then, we need to set ourselves to pray intelligently and consistently for the outworking and fulfillment of those purposes. As we make this scriptural study, we will discover that, ultimately, righteousness and peace are ordained to flow forth from Jerusalem to all the nations of the earth. Thus, the well-being of every nation is included in this prayer for Jerusalem and depends on its fulfillment.

A challenging scriptural example of this kind of praying was provided by Daniel, who prayed three times daily with his window open toward Jerusalem. Daniel's prayers disturbed Satan and threatened his kingdom such that he used the jealousy of evil men to bring about a change in the laws of the entire Persian Empire so that Daniel's prayers would be rendered illegal. Still, praying for Jerusalem meant so much to Daniel that he preferred to be cast into the lions' den rather than give up his praying. Ultimately, Daniel's faith and courage overcame the satanic opposition. He emerged triumphant from the lions' den—and kept praying for Jerusalem.

From my own experience of many years, I have discovered that making a commitment of this kind to pray for Jerusalem and Israel definitely stirs up a special measure of opposition from satanic forces. On the other hand, I have also discovered that God's promise given to those who pray in this way holds true.

This is a scriptural pathway to prosperity—not merely financial or material prosperity, but also a prosperity that encompasses an abiding assurance of God's favor.

Thank You, Lord, for the blessing You promise to those who love Israel. I proclaim that as I pray for Jerusalem, I receive an abiding assurance of God's favor. I pray for the peace of Jerusalem: *"May they prosper who love you."* Amen.

Our Debt to Israel (booklet)

God's Restoration for His People

Pray for the peace of Jerusalem: "May they prosper who love you."

The call to pray for Jerusalem is directed at everyone who accepts the Bible as God's authoritative Word. God requires all of His people, from every nation and every background, to be concerned about the peace of one particular city: Jerusalem. There is a practical reason for this. God's purpose for this age will climax in the establishment of His kingdom. Each time we pray the familiar words, *"Thy kingdom come,"* we are aligning ourselves with this purpose. (See, for example, Matthew 6:10 KJV.)

We must remember, however, that the prayer continues, *"Thy will be done in earth, as it is in heaven"* (verse 6:10 KJV). It is on earth that God's kingdom is to be established. His kingdom is invisible as yet to human eyes, but it is not vague or amorphous. It will ultimately have a tangible, earthly realization. The capital and center of God's kingdom on earth will be the city of Jerusalem. The administration of righteous government will go forth from Jerusalem to all nations on earth. In response, the gifts and worship of these nations will flow back to Jerusalem. Thus, the peace and prosperity of all nations depend on that of Jerusalem. Until Jerusalem enters into her peace, no nation on earth can know true, lasting peace.

To all who heed God's call to love Jerusalem and pray for her peace, God gives a special, precious promise: *"They shall prosper"* (Psalm 122:6 KJV). The word translated *"prosper"* goes beyond the material realm. It denotes a deep, inner well-being, a freedom from care and anxiety. As we align ourselves with God's plan by praying for Jerusalem, we experience a foretaste of His peace. A sense of inner rest and peace comes to those who, in the midst of all the turmoil of this world, associate themselves actively with God's plans to restore His people.

Thank You, Lord, for the blessing You promise to those who love Israel. An inner peace comes to me as I pray for God's purposes of restoration for His people. I pray for the peace of Jerusalem: *"May they prosper who love you."* Amen.

Through the Psalms with Derek Prince (book)

DECLARING GOD'S WORD

OCTOBER 4

Reminding the Lord

Pray for the peace of Jerusalem: "May they prosper who love you."

In Isaiah 62, God calls us to intense, persistent prayer, especially on behalf of Jerusalem:

> *I have posted watchmen on your walls, O Jerusalem; they will never be silent day or night. You who call on the LORD, give yourselves no rest, and give him no rest till he establishes Jerusalem and makes her the praise of the earth.* (Isaiah 62:6–7 NIV)

In the New Testament, Jesus related the parable of the unjust judge, whom a widow kept beseeching incessantly. Jesus concluded with this question: *"And will not God bring about justice for his chosen ones, who cry out to him day and night?"* (Luke 18:7 NIV). Both these passages indicate that some themes are so important and urgent that they demand our prayers not only in the daytime, but through the night hours, as well. The restoration of Jerusalem is one of these themes.

The prophet Isaiah also described these *"watchmen"* as those *"who call on the LORD."* The literal Hebrew meaning of the word translated *"call"* is interesting. It means "those who *remind* the Lord." In modern Hebrew, it is the word for a secretary. One important task of a secretary is reminding the employer of the appointments recorded on his calendar. This provides practical insight into the way God wants us to pray for Jerusalem. As His "intercessor-secretaries," we have two main responsibilities: first, to be familiar with His prophetic calendar; second, to remind Him of the appointments recorded in it. One such appointment is God's end-time commitment to restore Israel and to rebuild Jerusalem.

Thank You, Lord, for the blessing You promise to those who love Israel. I proclaim that I will remind the Lord *"till He establishes Jerusalem and makes her the praise of the earth."* I pray for the peace of Jerusalem: *"May they prosper who love you."* Amen.

Promised Land (book)

October

Speaking Comfort

Pray for the peace of Jerusalem: "May they prosper who love you."

How do we align ourselves with God's purpose for Israel? I want to suggest one simple way. In Isaiah 40:1–2, God said, *"'Comfort, yes, comfort My people!' says your God. 'Speak comfort to Jerusalem, and cry out to her, that her warfare is ended, that her iniquity is pardoned; for she has received from the LORD's hand double for all her sins.'"*

I have analyzed that verse, and where it says *"comfort My people,"* because of the immediate reference to Jerusalem, I understand it to mean the Jewish people. The Jewish people cannot be comforted apart from Jerusalem. Their hearts are totally bound up with the city of Jerusalem. So, if I am right, and *"My people"* is the Jewish people, to whom are these words spoken? They are spoken in the plural (in Hebrew) to somebody who would say, *"Comfort My people."* They must be spoken to people who accept the God of the Bible and the authority of His Word. Who can that be? You and me. People like us, believing Christians. What does God say? "Comfort My people, Israel." God requires us to comfort Israel.

I have been friends with a number of Jewish believers in Jesus, and one thing that they will point out to me is the fact that the church worldwide spends much more time criticizing Israel than comforting Israel. We were not called to criticize; rather, we have been commanded to comfort. Will you accept that responsibility?

I believe this comforting is one way of preparing the way of the Lord. Centuries of prejudice, alienation, and misunderstanding must be broken down. They must be melted away by the warmth of real Christian love. I believe that is our assignment at this time.

Thank You, Lord, for the blessing You promise to those who love Israel. I proclaim that I will comfort God's people and speak comfort to Jerusalem. I pray for the peace of Jerusalem: *"May they prosper who love you."* Amen.

Where Are We in Bible Prophecy?: Israel in the End Times (audio, video)
The Last Word on the Middle East: Our Response to God's Purpose (audio)

The Lord, Our Healer

Pray for the peace of Jerusalem: "May they prosper who love you."

Right after God first redeemed Israel out of Egypt and the Israelites became His redeemed and covenant people, the first specific revelation of Himself that He gave them was that of healer. This attribute is stated in Exodus 15:26, where the Lord said to Israel, *"For I, the* LORD, *am your healer"* (NASB).

The phrase *"your healer,"* in modern Hebrew, means "your doctor." The word used in Exodus 15:26 is precisely the same word as the modern Hebrew word for *doctor*. It has not changed its meaning in more than three thousand years of the history of the Hebrew language. The Lord said emphatically to Israel, "I am your doctor."

Two things that do not change are the Lord's name and the Lord's covenant. The Lord's position and function as the healer of His people is united with His name and His covenant. In other words, it never changes.

Many centuries later, when Jesus came to Israel as its Savior and Redeemer, thereby fulfilling the promises of the Messiah, He again manifested God as the healer of His people. The healing ministry of Jesus did not proceed from Himself—it did not initiate with Him—but it was the expression of God's healing nature and God's healing covenant with His people. The foundation of God's provision of healing and health for His people is His Word, the Scriptures.

How important it is to see that God's answer to our need is primarily in His Word! If we ignore His Word, then we really do not have any right to expect that He will meet our needs. But if we turn to His Word and seek Him through it, we will find that in His Word, He does meet all our needs—spiritual and physical.

Thank You, Lord, for the blessing You promise to those who love Israel. I proclaim that the Lord's position and function as the Healer of His people is united with His name and His covenant. I pray for the peace of Jerusalem: *"May they prosper who love you."* Amen.

Walking through the Land of God's Promises, Part 3 (audio)

Peace and Prosperity

Pray for the peace of Jerusalem: "May they prosper who love you."

I pray daily for the peace of Jerusalem and Israel. I believe that when the Bible says, *"Pray for the peace of Jerusalem"* (Psalm 122:6), it also means that we are to pray for the peace of Christ's body. We should be concerned not just about our own little area, but for the total needs of the body of Christ. We are not to judge other Christians; we are to pray for them.

Psalm 122:7 says, *"Peace be within your walls, prosperity within your palaces."* I believe that this verse illustrates the divine order: when we have peace, we will have prosperity. When we are at war with one another—criticizing one another, turning against one another, and undermining one another—we will not know prosperity. First, peace; then, prosperity.

Verse 8 reads, *"For the sake of my brethren and companions, I will now say, 'Peace be within you.'"*

I want to add one more basic principle. We need to escape from the tendency to be self-centered. Self-centeredness is the devil's prison. The more the devil gets you centered in yourself, the more he has you at his mercy. I have dealt with hundreds of people in deliverance from evil spirits, and I have found one almost universal feature of people who need deliverance—they are self-centered. By deliberate effort and choice of our own wills, we must break loose from being self-centered.

What I love in verse 8 is the phrase, *"For the sake of my brethren and companions."* It is not enough that things are going well for me. I need to be concerned about the needs of my brothers and companions—Christians from other backgrounds, other denominations, other prayer groups, and so forth.

Thank You, Lord, for the blessing You promise to those who love Israel. I proclaim, *"Peace be within your walls, prosperity within your palaces."* I pray for the peace of Jerusalem: *"May they prosper who love you."* Amen.

"Fitly Joined Together" (*New Wine* article)

WEEK 41:

Let us fear lest we fail to rest in Christ.

Therefore, since a promise remains of entering His rest, let us fear lest any of you seem to have come short of it.

—Hebrews 4:1

God's Command to Rest

Let us fear lest we fail to rest in Christ.

In Deuteronomy 28, we find a list of all the blessings and curses. The blessings begin with these words: *"If you diligently obey* [hearken to] *the voice of the LORD your God,...all these blessings shall come upon you"* (verses 1–2). The curses begin with these words: *"If you do not obey the voice of the LORD your God,...all these curses will come upon you"* (verse 15). They hinge on heeding or ignoring the voice of the Lord.

Obedience in worship is the appointed way to come into that attitude and relationship in which we really hear God's voice. Or, to state it another way, we do not hear God's voice unless we possess an attitude of worship. Then, in hearing God's voice, we enter into His rest. Thus, worship is the way to rest. Only those who really know how to worship can really enjoy rest.

> *There remains, then, a Sabbath-rest for the people of God; for anyone who enters God's rest also rests from his own work, just as God did from his. Let us, therefore, make every effort to enter that rest, so that no one will fall by following their example of disobedience.* (Hebrews 4:9–11 NIV)

Scripture brings out the fact that because of disobedience, the people of God failed to enter into rest. I am not insisting we observe the Sabbath or make Sunday the Sabbath. I am just pointing out that we can miss the fact that God has commanded us to rest.

I have come to believe that if I am busy seven days a week, every week, I am not pleasing God. Moreover, I am sure to endanger my health with this degree of busyness. God is doing something in my heart about Sabbath rest. I believe He can do something in your heart, too, that will cause you naturally to keep His divine, eternal, unchanging laws.

Thank You, Lord, for the promise of entering Your rest. I proclaim that I *"make every effort to enter that rest."* I shall fear lest I fail to rest in Christ. Amen.

Rules of Engagement (book)

An Attitude of Worship

Let us fear lest we fail to rest in Christ.

We can consider these questions as we meditate on this call to enter God's rest: Are we making the best use of our time? Do we really know what it means to rest? Are we capable of disciplining ourselves to stop doing things—even mentally? Can we ever lie down and stop thinking about what we ought to be doing?

God is more concerned with character than with achievements. Achievements are important only in the realm of time, but character is eternal. It determines what we will be throughout eternity.

Isaiah had a vision of heaven with glorious creatures and the throne of the Lord. (See Isaiah 6.) Worship was conducted in heaven by creatures called seraphim (Hebrew, *seraph*), a word that relates directly to the word for *fire*. These are fiery creatures close to the throne of God, and they cried out day and night, *"Holy, holy, holy is the LORD"* (Isaiah 6:3). Each one had six wings, which they used impressively. With two wings, they covered their faces; with two other wings, they covered their feet; and, with the two remaining wings, they flew. (See verse 2.) I interpret covering the face and feet as the humility of worship; I interpret flying as acts of service.

I believe in the importance of thanking God and praising Him out loud—even dancing, clapping, and singing. But there comes a time when I will put my "wings" over my face and over my feet in humble worship and listen to hear what God says.

"Today, if you will hear His voice: do not harden your hearts" (Psalm 95:7–8). Develop an attitude of worship and learn to rest. Remember, the Spirit of the Lord is looking for a certain type of person—one whose heart is perfect toward God. Be that person of character, and God will show Himself strong on your behalf.

Thank You, Lord, for the promise of entering Your rest. I proclaim that I am developing an attitude of worship and am learning to rest. I shall fear lest I fail to rest in Christ. Amen.

Rules of Engagement (book)

Choosing to Worship and Rest

Let us fear lest we fail to rest in Christ.

In Psalm 95:7, we are given two reasons that we should worship the Lord: *"For he is our God and we are the people of his pasture, the flock under his care"* (NIV). The first reason to worship God is because He *is* God—*our* God, the only being in the universe worthy of worship. We can praise other men and women, but we must not worship them. Worship is the most distinctive way for us to relate to God as God.

I am convinced that whatever we worship gains control of us. The more we worship it, the more like it we become—and the more it gains power over us. If we do not worship God, how much is He really our God?

The second reason that we should worship Him is that *"we are the people of His pasture."* Worship is the way in which we recognize Him as our God, and it is the appropriate response to His care for us. This psalm ends with a solemn warning:

> *Today, if you hear his voice, do not harden your hearts as you did at Meribah....For forty years I was angry with that generation; I said, "They are a people whose hearts go astray, and they have not known my ways." So I declared on oath in my anger, "They shall never enter my rest."*   (verses 7–8, 10–11 NIV)

This passage sets before us two options: entering into true worship or refusing to do so. In worship, we hear God's voice. Upon hearing and obeying His voice, we enter into rest. The inescapable conclusion is the importance of hearing God's voice. As we read in Jeremiah 7:23, *"This is what I commanded them, saying, 'Obey My voice, and I will be your God'"* (NASB). This is one of the simplest statements of what God requires: *"Obey My voice, and I will be your God."*

Thank You, Lord, for the promise of entering Your rest. I proclaim that I choose to enter into true worship, hear and obey Your voice, and enter into rest. I shall fear lest I fail to rest in Christ. Amen.

The True Heart of Worship (Teaching Legacy Letter)

Walking in Proper Fear

Let us fear lest we fail to rest in Christ.

The first "let us" statement in the book of Hebrews says, "*Therefore… let us fear*" (Hebrews 4:1). Does that statement surprise or offend you? Most Christians have no room for fear.

The people responsible for bringing me to the Lord were a fine Christian couple who lived in Yorkshire, England. When I visited them after World War II, they were not doing well—spiritually. The man believed that there was no room for fear in the Christian life. I pointed out that it depends on the kind of fear you are talking about. Psalm 19 says, "*The fear of the LORD is clean, enduring forever*" (verse 9). There is never an end to that kind of fear. This man had decided never to use medicine, a position that conveys a sense of arrogance. I linked it with his attitude that rejected fear of any kind. Tragically, he developed diabetes, and his leg had to be amputated. He could hardly get over the shock that his faith had not brought him healing. I think the real problem was a failure to understand that a certain kind of fear is very much a part of the Christian life. The words in Hebrews, "*let us fear,*" are addressed to Christian believers, not unbelievers. Bear in mind that there is always a possibility of not getting what God has appointed for us. The entire verse says, "*Therefore, since a promise remains of entering His rest, let us fear lest any of you seem to have come short of it.*"

Every promise is two-sided. It offers you good, but if you fail to claim the promise, you are deprived of something. So much in the Christian life is the same way. The good is available, but there is always the possibility of missing it. I believe that we have to come with this attitude of fear if we are going to be able to enter into God's rest.

Thank You, Lord, for the promise of entering Your rest. I proclaim that I come to God with the proper attitude of fear to enter into His rest. I shall fear lest I fail to rest in Christ. Amen.

God's Last Word, Vol. 1: Hebrews 4:1–4:16 (audio)

Believing and Entering

Let us fear lest we fail to rest in Christ.

For we who have believed do enter that rest [or are entering into the rest], *as He has said* [quoting from Psalm 95]: *"So I swore in my wrath, 'They shall not enter My rest;'" although* [God's] *works were finished from the foundation of the world. For He has spoken in a certain place of the seventh day in this way: "And God rested on the seventh day from all His works"; and again in this place: "They shall not enter My rest."* (Hebrews 4:3–5)

In that passage, *"believed"* is in the past tense; *"enter"* is in the present tense. Before we can enter into God's rest, we must have already believed. We do not keep believing again; it is something that is done once. We have made the decision, and, on that basis, we can proceed to enter into rest. Those who must continually decide to believe anew do not qualify to enter into the rest. Only we who have believed enter into rest.

Following up on this theme of rest, let's turn to the Old Testament for a moment. Genesis 2:2 reads, *"And on the seventh day God ended His work which He had done, and He rested on the seventh day from all His work which He had done."* God's rest is a ceasing from all the work He did. I believe that God did not rest because He was tired. Instead, He took pleasure in relaxation. He sat back, looked at everything He had made, and took time to enjoy it.

How many of us ever take the time to enjoy the things that we have done or made? Today, by the time they have done something, most people are busy starting the next thing. The pattern that God established, though, is taking time to enjoy whatever you do after you have finished it. Whatever it may be that you have done, it is godly to relax and enjoy it. In fact, the ability to relax is a divine ability.

Thank You, Lord, for the promise of entering Your rest. I proclaim that one of the pleasures God wants to share is His rest—He wants me to enter into the rest that He entered. So, I shall fear lest I fail to rest in Christ. Amen.

God's Last Word, Vol. 1: Hebrews 4:1–4:16 (audio)

Enjoying Creation

Let us fear lest we fail to rest in Christ.

We talk about tithing—what God demands of our resources—but what about God's demands on our time? From the Israelites, God demanded one day out of seven—a higher proportion than that which He demanded of their material possessions. How many people in the church today really give God one day out of seven? That is one reason that there are so many nervous breakdowns—there are frustrated, frantic, busy people who never get the job done.

God was the first One who rested. He worked, then rested. A Palestinian Arab friend of mine who owns many restaurants says, "God did not work because He had a family to support. And God did not rest because He was tired. It was on a much higher level than that. God worked because He is a Creator." God rested, I believe, because He wanted to enjoy what He had created. If we never take time to enjoy what we have created, we are in a miserable condition.

Which takes more faith: to work or to rest? Israel failed to enter into rest because of unbelief. Why can a Christian not rest? Also because of unbelief. That is the diagnosis of the problem.

Relaxation comes in knowing that God initiated it. My wife and I used to go away on "vacation." But *vacation* means you have nothing to do—it is taken from the word *vacant*. Sometimes, though, it is good to have nothing to do. But my wife and I felt that *vacation* was the wrong word to use. Instead, we called these periods *holidays*, which means "holy day." God showed us that it is a sin to never take a holiday. In Israel's calendar, as God ordained it, many holidays were required. There were no options. They are God-ordained holidays—not because someone wants to be lazy, but because God has said to take a holiday.

Thank You, Lord, for the promise of entering Your rest. I proclaim that God rested to enjoy what He created, and I will do the same. I shall fear lest I fail to rest in Christ. Amen.

The Headship of Jesus, Part 1 (audio, video)

Walking...and Resting...in Faith

Let us fear lest we fail to rest in Christ.

The one basic reason that the Israelites did not enter their God-given inheritance was unbelief. The same thing will keep us from our inheritance, too. The writer of Hebrews applied their situation to us, saying, *"The word which they heard did not profit them, not being mixed with faith in those who heard it"* (Hebrews 4:2). God's Word can come to us, but it does us no good, nor does it accomplish God's purposes of blessing, if it is not combined with faith. It takes faith to make the Word of God work in our lives.

The next verse says, *"For we who have believed do enter that rest"* (verse 3). True faith brings us into rest. Do you have that rest of faith? Have you met those conditions, or are you in danger of being like the Israelites, who hardened their hearts? Because of their unbelief, they missed all that God had for them. What a tragedy if that should happen to us today! Yet the writer of Hebrews makes it very clear that it can happen—indeed, that it will happen—if we are not diligent about entering that rest.

A little further on in Hebrews, we have the practical application of this lesson: *"Let us therefore be diligent to enter that rest, lest anyone fall according to the same example of disobedience"* (Hebrews 4:11).

You may have heard me say, "When you find a *therefore* in the Bible, you need to find out what it is 'there for.'" The above verse begins with a "therefore." The point is, let us not go astray in the same way that the Israelites did in the Old Testament. Let's guard ourselves against unbelief. Let's be diligent and apply ourselves to walking in faith, conserving and cultivating our faith, strengthening and encouraging one another's faith. Let's not make the same terrible and tragic error that Israel made through unbelief. Bear in mind that there is a direct, causal connection between unbelief and disobedience.

Thank You, Lord, for the promise of entering Your rest. I proclaim that true faith brings me into rest. I shall fear lest I fail to rest in Christ.
Amen.

Faith, Part 1 (audio)

WEEK 42:

Let us be diligent.

Let us therefore be diligent to enter that rest,
lest anyone fall according to the same example
of disobedience.

—Hebrews 4:11

The Importance of Diligence

Let us be diligent.

Diligence is the second "let us" resolution that occurs in the fourth chapter of Hebrews: *"Let us therefore be diligent to enter that rest, lest anyone fall through following the same example of disobedience"* (Hebrews 4:11 NASB).

I pointed out previously that this warning is based on the experience of the Israelites on their journey from Egypt through the wilderness. Most of them did not make it through to the Promised Land—the destination and rest that God had promised them—because of their misconduct and wrong attitudes. And they fell in the wilderness. Scripture says that their carcasses fell in the wilderness because of unbelief and disobedience. (See Numbers 14:29, 32.) And through unbelief and disobedience, they failed to hear the voice of the Lord. They had the externals, but they did not have the great essential, inner reality of all true religion—hearing the voice of the Lord.

So, that was the mistake of Israel—a tragic mistake. After saying, *"Let us fear"* (Hebrews 4:1), the writer of Hebrews went on—still on the basis of the example of Israel—to say, "Let us be diligent." I believe that is very natural. If we really take to heart the dangers of that spiritual condition and do fear, in that sense, the next thing we will naturally do is become diligent.

Let's consider for a moment what diligence is. One way to find out the meaning of a word is to consider what its opposite is. An obvious opposite of diligence is laziness. The Bible does not have one good word to say about laziness. It is a theme that does not receive enough attention in contemporary Christendom.

Thank You, Lord, for the promise of entering Your rest. I proclaim that the essential, inner reality of all true religion is hearing the voice of the Lord. I shall be diligent. Amen.

Twelve Steps to a Good Year, Part 1 (audio)

Growing and Progressing

Let us be diligent.

Continuing with the theme of diligence, let's consider what the writer of Hebrews said a little further on: *"We want each of you to show this same diligence to the very end, in order to make your hope sure. We do not want you to become lazy, but to imitate those who through faith and patience inherit what has been promised"* (Hebrews 6:11–12 NIV). We not only need to be diligent, but we also need to be diligent to the very end. The opposite of diligence is stated there in plain words: *"to become lazy."* Not physically lazy, but spiritually lazy.

> *For this very reason, make every effort* ["giv[e] *all diligence"* NKJV] *to add to your faith goodness; and to goodness, knowledge; and to knowledge, self-control; and to self-control, perseverance; and to perseverance, godliness; and to godliness, brotherly kindness; and to brotherly kindness, love.*   (2 Peter 1:5–7 NIV)

The Christian life is not static. It is a life of adding, growth, and progress. To be static in the Christian life is to backslide. To do that adding, as described in the passage above, requires diligence. It requires making every effort. Peter then went on with an *if:*

> *For if you possess these qualities in increasing measure, they will keep you from being ineffective and unproductive in your knowledge of our Lord Jesus Christ. But if anyone does not have them, he is nearsighted and blind, and has forgotten that he has been cleansed from his past sins.*   (verses 8–9 NIV)

Would you believe that it is possible for somebody to be cleansed from his past sins and then forget that it even happened? It sounds unrealistic, but Scripture indicates that it *is* possible.

Thank You, Lord, for the promise of entering Your rest. I proclaim my need to imitate those who through faith and patience inherit what has been promised. I shall be diligent. Amen.

Twelve Steps to a Good Year, Part 1 (audio)

OCTOBER 17

Overcoming Laziness

Let us be diligent.

In 2 Peter 1:8–9, Peter set before us an alternative; we have two options. One is to be effective and productive in our knowledge of the Lord Jesus Christ. The other is to be ineffective and unproductive through a condition that he described as being *"nearsighted and blind"* (verse 9 NIV). Those are strong words. In light of this condition, Peter continued with a *therefore*. This therefore relates to the warning that Peter had given:

> *Therefore, my brothers, be all the more eager to make your calling and election sure. For if you do these things, you will never fall, and you will receive a rich welcome into the eternal kingdom of our Lord and Savior Jesus Christ.* (2 Peter 1:10–11 NIV)

That is good news. There are things we can do that will guarantee we never fall, and also that we will have a rich welcome into the kingdom of our Lord.

Basically, the condition about which we are warned is laziness. I am deeply troubled by the lack of concern in Christian circles about laziness. The majority of Christians view drunkenness with horror. They would reject any person who professed to being a Christian if he were drunk. While I agree that drunkenness is a sin, and while I certainly don't condone it, I believe that laziness is much more severely condemned in the Scripture than drunkenness. The problem is that many Christians who would never be found drunk are habitually lazy. So, let's heed that warning to be diligent.

Thank You, Lord, for the promise of entering Your rest. I proclaim that I will combat laziness, being *"all the more eager to make my calling and election sure."* I shall be diligent. Amen.

Twelve Steps to a Good Year, Part 1 (audio)

Adding Personal Diligence

Let us be diligent.

Two beautiful verses in Proverbs have long been a guiding light to me. Together, they sum up the conditions for true riches, or enduring wealth. One condition, the Lord meets; the other, we meet. Both conditions must be fulfilled in order for us to attain the result. The condition the Lord meets is stated in Proverbs 10:22: *"It is the blessing of the LORD that makes rich, and He adds no sorrow to it"* (NASB).

The great, primary condition for true riches—spiritual and otherwise—is the blessing of the Lord. We cannot count on anything being really good apart from the blessing of the Lord. On the other hand, the blessing of the Lord, by itself, is not sufficient. In Proverbs 10:4, we read, *"Poor is he who works with a negligent hand, but the hand of the diligent makes rich"* (NASB). It takes the Lord's blessing plus our own diligence to attain to true wealth. It is not enough to simply expect the blessing of the Lord, or even to receive the blessing of the Lord. It will not accomplish its purpose in your life unless you add to it your own personal diligence. Remember, diligence is the opposite of laziness.

That is a verse I have proved true in my own experience through decades of Christian living. I have been in many different situations, in many different forms of ministry, and in many different lands and continents, and I think I can say that, by the grace of God, I have always displayed diligence in things small and great. In every situation with which I have been involved, I have left it in better condition—spiritually, financially, and in every obvious way—than the condition it was in when I found it. The blessing of the Lord makes rich, but also the hand of the diligent makes rich. Add those two together and you have true spiritual riches.

Thank You, Lord, for the promise of entering Your rest. I proclaim that *"the blessing of the Lord makes rich,"* and *"the hand of the diligent makes rich."* I shall be diligent. Amen.

Twelve Steps to a Good Year, Part 1 (audio)

October 19

Fulfillment of God's Promises

Let us be diligent.

M ost of God's promises are conditional. In other words, when God makes a promise, He says, "If you will do this, then I will do that." We have no right to claim the promise unless we first meet the condition He puts forth.

We need to see that the fulfillment of God's promises does not depend upon our circumstances, but upon our fulfilling God's conditions. We must keep our eyes on the conditions, making sure that we fulfill them instead of being influenced by the circumstances that might prevent us from doing so.

Let's look at the example of Abraham. God had promised Abraham a son who was to be his heir, but he reached the age of ninety-nine, and still no heir had come. (On his own, he produced Ishmael, but he was not to be the heir.) Why did God allow Abraham to reach such an old age before He fulfilled His promise? Why does God often allow us to come to a position of seeming impossibility before He fulfills the promises we are claiming?

First, we are emptied of excessive self-confidence. We realize that if something is going to be done, God will be the only one who can do it. Abraham's own body was worthless in terms of procreation, as was the womb of his wife. There was no natural way that the promise could be fulfilled. Abraham had to focus his eyes exclusively on God, the only one capable of fulfilling the promise.

Second, when the promise is finally fulfilled, all the glory goes to God. Remember, the purpose of the promises is that God may be glorified. When there is a possibility of us doing something on our own, we might be tempted to take the credit. But when we come to the place where we know we cannot do it by our own effort, we are exhausted of self-confidence, and all the glory truly goes to God.

Thank You, Lord, for the promise of entering Your rest. I proclaim that the purpose of the promises is that God may be glorified. I shall be diligent. Amen.

Claiming Our Inheritance, Part 2 (audio)

Declaring God's Word

Cultivating Diligence

Let us be diligent.

Diligence is a fruit that has to be cultivated. Here are some brief directions about how it should be cultivated.

In 2 Timothy 2:6, Paul said, *"The hard-working farmer must be first to partake of the crops* [produce, fruit]." Here, Paul was bringing out a simple, basic fact: cultivating crops takes hard work. It is not done without effort. That fact is equally true of the fruit of the Spirit—to cultivate it requires hard work. I want to suggest two ways in which we can cultivate spiritual fruit in our lives.

First, we need to study God's Word, for it is the basis of all God's provision for us. If we are not familiar with His Word, we almost inevitably forgo many of His provisions. Again, Paul wrote to Timothy, *"Be diligent to present yourself approved to God, a worker who does not need to be ashamed, rightly dividing the word of truth"* (2 Timothy 2:15). In order to divide, or handle, the word of truth—Scripture, the Word of God—accurately, we must be workers. In a certain sense, we have to roll up our sleeves and get to work.

The second direction we must follow is to spend time in prayer. By prayer, I don't mean merely talking to God, but listening—something that is just as important, if not more so, than talking to Him. Here, again, Jesus provided us with the perfect pattern. The whole basis of Jesus' earthly ministry was His relationship with His Father. In order to cultivate and maintain that relationship, Jesus took plenty of time in prayer. Very often, it was early in the morning. It was there that He heard the Father's voice and received direction for His ministry.

Thank You, Lord, for the promise of entering Your rest. I proclaim that I will cultivate diligence in my life by studying God's Word and spending time in prayer. I shall be diligent. Amen.

Fruit of the Spirit, Part 1 (audio)

The Fruit of Diligence

Let us be diligent.

The fruit of diligence may be produced by cultivating fellowship. We must not try to lead the Christian life on our own. Scripture says that we are all members of one body, and we all need one another. (See, for example, Romans 12:4–5.) I often think of David going out to meet Goliath, taking just five smooth stones from the brook as weapons. Why did those stones have to be smooth? They would not have been accurate missiles if they had not been smooth, and inaccuracy might have cost David his life. The stones were smooth because they had been lying in the brook, where water had been passing over them regularly. They had been jostled against one another, and this action rubbed away their sharp edges.

I believe that when the Lord Jesus Christ wants to find Christians He can use, He goes to the brook, where the pure water of God's Word has been flowing over them, washing them, rounding them off. There, they have been in fellowship with one another, rubbing away the rough edges. Cultivating fellowship will make us into smooth stones.

My last recommendation is to submit to discipline. Fruit does not come in a person's life without discipline. I have two main forms of discipline in mind. First, self-discipline—the way in which we organize our lives. This discipline includes even the simplest of things, such as when we get up in the morning, what we eat, what we wear, and personal cleanliness. Managing all these details is essential to cultivating fruit. Beyond that, I believe every Christian in normal situations should be subject to church discipline. He should be a member of a church, under the authority of the church leaders and subject to their discipline.

Thank You, Lord, for the promise of entering Your rest. I proclaim that the fruit of diligence comes by fellowship and discipline, and I welcome both. I shall be diligent. Amen.

Fruit of the Spirit, Part 1 (audio)

Let us hold fast our confession.

Seeing then that we have a great High Priest who has passed through the heavens, Jesus the Son of God, let us hold fast our confession.

—Hebrews 4:14

The High Priest of Our Confession

Let us hold fast our confession.

Jesus' position as High Priest relates to our confession. Let's look at three passages from the book of Hebrews. First, Hebrews 3:1 reads, *"Therefore, holy brethren, partakers of the heavenly calling, consider the Apostle and High Priest of our confession, Christ Jesus."* Jesus was the Apostle sent out by God to provide redemption. Having provided redemption, He returned to God to be our High Priest in the presence of God. He is the High Priest of our confession. That idea is radical: No confession, no High Priest. If we close our lips on earth, we silence our Advocate in heaven. The more we confess, the more we release His high priestly ministry on our behalf.

Next, we'll read Hebrews 4:14: *"Seeing then that we have a great High Priest who has passed through the heavens, Jesus the Son of God, let us hold fast our confession."* To *hold fast* means to say something, then keep on saying it. Don't back off. Don't get discouraged.

Finally, *"Having a High Priest over the house of God,...let us hold fast the confession of our hope without wavering, for He who promised is faithful"* (Hebrews 10:21, 23). Notice the change there. It is not "the confession of our faith" but *"the confession of our hope."* If we confess *faith* long enough, it becomes *hope.* *"Faith is the substance of things hoped for"* (Hebrews 11:1). When we have built a substance of faith, then hope comes. My definition of biblical hope is "a confident expectation of good." But we must hold fast the profession or confession *without wavering.* Why does it say *"without wavering"*? Let me illustrate with the following image. When you are traveling in an airplane and the Fasten Seat Belt sign goes on, it tells you to expect turbulence. In the same way, *"without wavering"* tells you to expect opposition. The battle is fought and won when we maintain our confession.

Thank You, Jesus, that You are the High Priest of our confession.
I proclaim that Jesus is my Advocate in heaven, in the presence of
God, and I hold fast that confession without wavering. I shall hold fast
my confession. Amen.

Complete Salvation and How to Receive It, Part 2 (audio, video)

Making the Right Confession

Let us hold fast our confession.

I can illustrate "confession" from a book entitled *Fear No Evil*, written by Natan Sharansky, a Jewish refusenik. Sharansky was not a Christian, but even so, the KGB (Soviet secret police) arrested him and put him through nine years of misery. As I read his story, I saw in the KGB the most vivid demonstration of Satan and his tactics. In Natan Sharansky, I recognized the way to win. He was a highly qualified chess player, and he decided to deal with the KGB as he would with a chess opponent: by staying one move ahead.

Though he did not have a faith in a personal God, he did have a concept of God through his Jewish roots. Many Jewish prayers begin with "O Lord, our God, king of the universe." In teaching himself Hebrew, he decided to write out a prayer that he could repeat whenever needed. It was a petition for God to be with him, protect his family, and bring him to Israel. Whenever he was under pressure—for instance, awaiting interrogation—he would repeat the prayer several times. He said that prayer about ten times a day for nine years—that amounts to more than thirty thousand times! How many Christians would go on praying the same prayer thirty thousand times?

One aim of the KGB was to get Sharansky to make the wrong confession. If he would just say that he was a traitor, they would release him. But he refused. The battle raged for nine years. By making the right confession and reiterating the right prayer, he won. Being victorious, he later immigrated to Jerusalem.

How that impressed me about Satan's tactics! Satan uses every kind of pressure, every inducement, every lie—all with one aim: to get us to make the wrong confession. We defeat him, however, by maintaining the right confession.

Thank You, Jesus, that You are the High Priest of our confession. I proclaim that we defeat our enemy by maintaining the right confession. I shall hold fast my confession. Amen.

Complete Salvation and How to Receive It, Part 2 (audio, video)

The Words We Speak

Let us hold fast our confession.

Another word for *confession* is *testimony*. We read in the book of Revelation, "*They overcame him* [Satan] *by the blood of the Lamb and by the word of their testimony*" (Revelation 12:11).

We have acknowledged that we overcome Satan when we testify personally to what the Word of God says the blood of Jesus does for us. Testimony is a very simple thing—just saying words that agree with Scripture. Testimony saves us; it is our protection. I cannot over-emphasize its importance.

The writer of Hebrews called Jesus the "*High Priest of our confession*" (Hebrews 3:1). *Confession* literally means "saying the same as." For us, as believers in the Bible and in Jesus Christ, confession means saying with our mouths the same thing that God says in His Word. We make the words of our mouths agree with the Word of God. Jesus can advocate on our behalf only when we make the right confession. Whether we call it "testimony" or "confession," it is indispensable in order for us to receive the salvation of God.

Jesus said, "*For by your words you will be justified, and by your words you will be condemned*" (Matthew 12:37). We settle our destinies by the words that we speak. James said the tongue is like the rudder on a ship; even though it is a small part of the ship, it determines exactly where the ship will go. (See James 3:4.) We determine the course of our lives by the way in which we use our tongues. We can say the right thing and make the words of our mouths agree with the Word of God, or we can say the wrong thing and cause our lives to go off course. We will either come safely to harbor or end in shipwreck according to how we use our tongues.

Thank You, Jesus, that You are the High Priest of our confession. I proclaim that I overcome the enemy by the blood of the Lamb and by the word of my testimony. I shall hold fast my confession. Amen.

How to Apply the Blood (audio)

Our Advocate

Let us hold fast our confession.

Jesus is the *"High Priest of our confession"* (Hebrews 3:1). Our confession enlists Jesus as our High Priest, but the opposite, unfortunately, is also true. If we make no confession, we have no High Priest. It's not that Jesus has ceased to be our High Priest, but that we give Him no opportunity to minister as our High Priest.

He is the High Priest of our *confession*. If we say the right things with our mouths in faith, according to Scripture, then Jesus has eternally obligated Himself to see that we will never be put to shame— that we will always experience what we confess. But if we do not say the right things, then, alas, we silence the lips of our High Priest. He has nothing to say in heaven on our behalf.

Jesus is also called our *"Advocate"* (1 John 2:1). The word *advocate* is similar to the modern word *attorney*. Jesus is the legal expert who is there to plead our case in heaven. He has never lost a case. But if we do not make a confession, He has no case to plead, so the case goes against us by default.

We can see how important confession is; therefore, it is very important that we give heed to this third "Let us" passage in Hebrews: *"Let us hold fast our confession"* (Hebrews 4:14). This principle of right confession has a central place in the gospel, as well as in our experience of salvation. In fact, there is no salvation without right confession.

Thank You, Jesus, that You are the High Priest of our confession. I proclaim that as I speak in faith with my mouth according to Scripture, Jesus has eternally obligated Himself that I will experience what I confess. I shall hold fast my confession. Amen.

Twelve Steps to a Good Year, Part 1 (audio)

The Heart and the Mouth

Let us hold fast our confession.

In the tenth chapter of Romans, Paul explained as clearly as anywhere in the New Testament what is required for salvation. He began,

> *"The word is near you, in your mouth and in your heart" (that is, the word of faith which we preach): that if you confess with your mouth the Lord Jesus and believe in your heart that God has raised Him from the dead, you will be saved.*
>
> (Romans 10:8–9)

The basis for salvation is the Word, and it has to be appropriated by faith. Then, there are two things we must do—one with the heart, one with the mouth. We have to believe with the heart, but we have to confess, or say it out, with the mouth. Paul went on,

> *For with the heart one believes unto righteousness, and with the mouth confession is made unto salvation.* (Romans 10:10)

You see? No confession, no salvation. It is good to believe in the heart, but belief alone is not sufficient. We must not only believe in our hearts, but we must also say it out boldly with our mouths, making the words of our mouths agree with the Word of God. Our initial confession relates us to Jesus as High Priest, but His ongoing ministry on our behalf as High Priest depends on our ongoing confession.

Thank You, Jesus, that You are the High Priest of our confession. I proclaim that I both believe in my heart and confess with my mouth the promises of God for me. I shall hold fast my confession. Amen.

Twelve Steps to a Good Year, Part 1 (audio)

The Fruit of Our Words

Let us hold fast our confession.

The entire Bible shows that our words determine our destinies. As we read in Proverbs 18:21, *"Death and life are in the power of the tongue, and those who love it will eat its fruit"* (NASB). The tongue is either going to produce death in our lives, if we make a wrong confession, or life, if we make a right confession. Whatever we say with our tongues, we are going to eat the resultant fruit. That truth was echoed by the words of Jesus when He said, *"And I say to you, that every careless word that men shall speak, they shall render account for it in the day of judgment. For by your words you shall be justified, and by your words you shall be condemned"* (Matthew 12:36–37 NASB).

Christians often say silly things that are not honoring to God, and then excuse themselves by saying, "I didn't really mean it." But Jesus said, *"Every careless word."* It is not an excuse to say that you didn't really mean something. We must hold fast our confession.

Ultimately, there are only two alternatives in our relationship to Christ and the Scripture: to confess or to deny. Again, Jesus said,

> *Everyone therefore who shall confess Me before men, I will also confess him before My Father who is in heaven. But whoever shall deny Me before men, I will also deny him before My Father who is in heaven.* (Matthew 10:32–33 NASB)

Those are the two alternatives given to us. There is no third alternative. In spiritual things, in the long run, there is no neutrality. Jesus said, *"He who is not with Me is against Me"* (Matthew 12:30). We either we make the right confession to salvation, or we make the wrong confession, which will not produce salvation.

Thank You, Jesus, that You are the High Priest of our confession. I proclaim that I confess before men that Jesus is my Lord, and He confesses me before our Father, who is in heaven. I shall hold fast my confession. Amen.

Twelve Steps to a Good Year, Part 1 (audio)

No Matter What Pressures Come

Let us hold fast our confession.

When the Bible says to hold fast your confession (see Hebrews 4:14), it is really issuing a warning that we will be subjected to pressures that might cause us to back off what we have said. But we should not back off. We should hold fast our confession, what we profess.

First, we make the right confession, making the words of our mouths agree with the words of Scripture. We articulate what Jesus has done for us, exactly as the Word of God says. For instance, *"By His stripes we are healed"* (Isaiah 53:5). *"He became poor, that* [we]...*might become rich"* (2 Corinthians 8:9). "He tasted death that we might have life." (See Hebrews 2:9.) "He took the curse that we might receive the blessing." (See Galatians 3:13–14.) Those are the right confessions. We make them, and then, no matter what pressures come against us, no matter how much things may seem to go the wrong way, we *hold fast* our confession. That is what makes our faith effective, and that is what releases the high priestly ministry of Jesus in heaven on our behalf.

Faith relates us to that which our senses cannot perceive. As long as we are slaves of our senses, we really cannot move in faith. Paul said this clearly in 2 Corinthians 5:7: *"For we walk by faith, not by sight."* In other words, what we do, and the way in which we live as Christians, is based on faith—on what we believe, not on what we see or know from our senses. Our senses may tell us one thing, and our faith another—that is when conflict comes. That is why the writer of Hebrews says to make your confession and then to hold it fast. Even if our senses tell us it is not so, if God's Word says it is so, it is so.

Thank You, Jesus, that You are the High Priest of our confession. I proclaim that I will make right confessions without backing off, no matter what pressures come. I shall hold fast my confession. Amen.

Identification, Part 4 (audio)

DECLARING GOD'S WORD

Let us draw near to the throne of grace.

Let us therefore come boldly to the throne of grace, that we may obtain mercy and find grace to help in time of need.

—Hebrews 4:16

An Invitation from God

Let us draw near to the throne of grace.

This is the fourth "Let us" statement in Hebrews. I believe the fourth step is directly related to the first three steps, and that the sequence is significant. In order to be able to draw near with confidence to the throne of grace, we need to make sure that we have taken the first three steps.

The first step is to fear: *"Let us fear"* (Hebrews 4:1). Fearing means that we come with an attitude of reverence and an awareness of our need of God's grace. Second, *"Let us...be diligent"* (Hebrews 4:11). This is our response to God's grace: we are not slack, lazy, indifferent, or presumptuous. God's grace does not justify our indifference or presumption; rather, it provokes us to be diligent. The third step is: *"Let us hold fast our confession"* (Hebrews 4:14). We must have the right confession; we have to say with our mouths the truth about Jesus and what He has done for us.

In regard to our approaching the throne of grace, we are told to come for two things: mercy and grace. My conviction is that if God invites us to come, and if we meet the conditions I have outlined, then mercy and grace await us. We will never be disappointed. God would never give an invitation that He would not stand behind and fulfill. If we come as God's children, we do not come as beggars. God has no second-class children. He never holds us at a distance if we have met the conditions for approach. It is very important that we come with confidence. That is faith in action. It is faith that will not be denied. It is faith that takes God at His Word and believes that God is as good as His Word. It is faith in God's faithfulness. That is how we are to approach the throne—with confidence.

Thank You, Lord, that I can come boldly to You. I proclaim that because God invites me to come to His throne, and because I meet the required conditions, I come with the confidence that mercy and grace are waiting for me. I shall draw near to the throne of grace.
Amen.

Praying to Change History: Seven Basic Conditions for Answered Prayer (audio)

Throwing Off Condemnation

Let us draw near to the throne of grace.

It is important that we approach God without condemnation; in other words, boldly, because, *"if I regard iniquity in my heart, the Lord will not hear"* (Psalm 66:18).

If I *"regard iniquity in my heart,"* it means that I come to God with a consciousness in my heart of something that condemns me. Every time I try to approach God with faith, Satan reminds me of something that is not right and that has not been dealt with—maybe a sin that has not been confessed, or, if it has been confessed, is still lingering because I have not claimed and received God's forgiveness. I am therefore conscious of this thing in my heart all the time. And if I come with condemnation, I do not receive that for which I pray.

I must remove the consciousness of sin from within my heart. Basically, this is done by faith. *"If we confess our sins,"* the Scripture says, *"He [God] is faithful and just to forgive us our sins and to cleanse us from all unrighteousness"* (1 John 1:9). We cannot do anything about the sin problem except confess, repent, and trust God for the forgiveness and cleansing that He has promised us. After that, we must not go on worrying about our sins, because if we remain conscious of sin as we pray, God will not hear our prayers. As the Scripture says, *"If I regard iniquity in my heart, the Lord will not hear."*

Yet the psalmist went on to say, *"But certainly God has heard me"* (Psalm 66:19). In other words, the psalmist rises above Satan's attempt to condemn him and says, "God has heard me." Why does God hear us? Because we come in the name of Jesus. Because we come with praise and thanksgiving. Therefore, we are not condemned.

Thank You, Lord, that I can come boldly to You. I proclaim that I throw off Satan's attempt to condemn me, declaring that *"God has heard me,"* because I come in the name of Jesus. I shall draw near to the throne of grace. Amen.

Praying to Change History: Seven Basic Conditions for Answered Prayer (audio)

OCTOBER 31

Eliminating Every Hindrance

Let us draw near to the throne of grace.

The Bible says, *"If our heart condemns us, God is greater than our heart, and knows all things"* (1 John 3:20). We need not keep anything from God. We have to be open and honest with Him—sincerely confessing every transgression, sinful thought, and shortcoming. But then, when all has been confessed, we need to accept complete forgiveness and complete cleansing, for we know that God will never remember our sins or hold them against us anymore. Then, we can come to Him without condemnation.

Speaking about prayer, Paul said in 1 Timothy 2:8, *"I desire therefore that the men pray everywhere, lifting up holy hands, without wrath and doubting."* We must get rid of the dark inner emotions and attitudes that hinder our access to God. We must get rid of wrath and doubting. The Bible says that if we doubt, we are condemned. (See Romans 14:23.) You see, we cannot come with condemnation into the presence of God. The Bible says,

> He who doubts is like a wave of the sea driven and tossed by the wind. For let not that man suppose that he will receive anything from the Lord; he is a double-minded man, unstable in all his ways. (James 1:6–8)

We must dismiss the whole question of guilt, along with every negative or wrong attitude concerning ourselves and other people. We must come boldly. As Hebrews 4:16 says, *"Let us therefore come boldly to the throne of grace, that we may obtain mercy and find grace to help in time of need."* Remember, it is a throne of grace that we approach, and grace is enthroned with God. It is not justice we come to God for; rather, it is grace.

Thank You, Lord, that I can come boldly to You. I proclaim that I rid myself of condemnation and of every other hindrance to come boldly to the throne of grace. I shall draw near to the throne of grace. Amen.

Praying to Change History: Seven Basic Conditions for Answered Prayer (audio)

Come Boldly

Let us draw near to the throne of grace.

We come boldly to the throne of God because it is a throne of grace. We do not come on the basis of our merit, but we come in the name of Jesus, with praise and thanksgiving, without condemnation. We come boldly because God has bid us to come. The author of Hebrews wrote, *"We have confidence ["boldness" NKJV] to enter the Most Holy Place by the blood of Jesus"* (Hebrews 10:19 NIV).

When we pray to God, we should never approach Him with condemnation. Condemnation is one of the greatest enemies to answered prayer. And the basic source of condemnation is a search for self-righteousness. If we feel that we must justify ourselves, we will never do it to our own satisfaction. There must come a time when we lay aside every attempt to justify ourselves and simply say, "I receive by faith the righteousness of Jesus Christ, imputed to me by my faith in Him, according to the Word of God. I will neither parade my good works nor blush for my bad deeds. I will come boldly because it is a throne of grace. I will not examine or analyze my own heart all the time to determine if I am good enough. I will trust God that the blood of Jesus has cleansed me from all sin. And I will come boldly to the throne, right into the Holiest of All." That is a glorious way of access.

"Let us draw near with a true heart," the Scripture says, *"in full assurance of faith, having our hearts sprinkled from an evil conscience"* (Hebrews 10:22). An evil conscience will keep us from successful prayer. We must allow the blood of Jesus to be applied to our hearts and receive with complete assurance the fact that we are forgiven—cleansed because of what Jesus has done—and then come boldly into the presence of almighty God.

Thank You, Lord, that I can come boldly to You. I proclaim that the blood of Jesus has cleansed me from all sin, and I come boldly to the throne, right into the holiest of all. I shall draw near to the throne of grace. Amen.

Praying to Change History: Seven Basic Conditions for Answered Prayer (audio)

Watching Our Motives

Let us draw near to the throne of grace.

We come near to the throne of grace to petition God for specific needs. Let us look at an important condition—our motives. God searches every motive; He is very conscious of the reasons for which we pray. James 4:2 says, *"You do not have because you do not ask."* The main reason that Christians do not have is a simple failure to ask. But then, James said in verse 3, *"You ask and do not receive, because you ask amiss, that you may spend it on your pleasures."* In other words, self-centered prayers indicate that our motives are wrong. We are simply aiming to get some creature comfort, personal satisfaction, or indulgence.

What is the correct motive? Jesus has already stated it: *"That the Father may be glorified in the Son. If you ask anything in My name, I will do it"* (John 14:13–14).

That is the motive behind the prayers that God answers. The prayer must be prayed sincerely so that God, in answering that prayer, may be glorified through Jesus Christ. As Paul explained in 2 Corinthians 1:20, *"For all the promises of God in Him* [Jesus Christ] *are Yes, and in Him Amen, to the glory of God through us."*

The whole purpose of coming to God and claiming His promises is so that God may be glorified through us in answering them. As we claim more and more of God's promises, we glorify Him more and more. The more we fail to claim God's promises, however, the less we glorify Him. The person who glorifies God most is the person who claims God's promises in Christ the most.

The motive that is acceptable to God is one that seeks answers to prayer so that He might be glorified. These prayers must be offered in the name of His Son Jesus Christ.

Thank You, Lord, that I can come boldly to You. I proclaim that my motive in praying is that God may be glorified through Jesus Christ in answering my prayers. I shall draw near to the throne of grace. Amen.

Praying to Change History: Seven Basic Conditions for Answered Prayer (audio)

According to His Lovingkindness

Let us draw near to the throne of grace.

P salm 51 is a prayer that David prayed during a time of deep distress, when his soul was hanging in the balance. It was a prayer of repentance after his sins—committing adultery with Bathsheba and arranging the murder of her husband, Uriah—had been uncovered. David wrote, *"Have mercy upon me, O God, according to Your lovingkindness; according to the multitude of Your tender mercies, blot out my transgressions"* (Psalm 51:1).

"According to Your lovingkindness" is another way of saying "Your covenant-keeping faithfulness." David was saying, in effect, "You have committed Yourself to forgive me if I meet the necessary conditions, and I appeal to You on that basis." How important it is to approach God on that basis.

Psalm 106:1 says, *"Praise the LORD! Oh, give thanks to the LORD, for He is good! For His mercy* [lovingkindness, faithfulness to His covenant] *endures forever."* Mercy is an aspect of God's eternal nature. Hebrews 4:16 says, *"Let us therefore come boldly to the throne of grace, that we may obtain mercy and find grace to help in time of need."*

First, we need mercy, but we also need grace. What does the Bible say about grace? Grace cannot be earned. If you can earn it, it is not grace. Religious people often think that they have to earn everything. Consequently, they tend to turn down the grace of God. As Paul wrote, *"If by grace, then it is no longer of works....But if it is of works, it is no longer grace"* (Romans 11:6). Two things are mentioned in Hebrews 4:16 that we cannot earn. We cannot earn mercy, and we cannot earn grace. We need mercy for the past and grace for the future. It is by God's grace alone that we can become the kind of people, and live the kind of lives, that He requires of us.

Thank You, Lord, that I can come boldly to You. I proclaim that I come according to God's lovingkindness to receive mercy for my past and grace for my future. I shall draw near to the throne of grace. Amen.

What Is Holiness?, Vol. 1 – Holiness: The Essence of God (audio)

By His Righteousness

Let us draw near to the throne of grace.

It is important to remember that it is neither our righteousness nor our faithfulness that forms the basis for our confidence in approaching God's throne. Rather, it is God's righteousness and God's faithfulness. The first epistle of John expresses this thought: *"Beloved, if our heart does not condemn us, we have confidence toward God. And whatever we ask we receive from Him"* (1 John 3:21–22).

Any attitude that thinks we have some kind of righteousness or claim in ourselves to approach God results in our approaching Him without full confidence because there is ultimately nothing in ourselves. We have no righteousness of our own. Our confidence cannot be based in ourselves.

We must also come to the place where we do not allow our hearts to condemn us—where we are trusting not in our own righteousness or our own wisdom but in God's faithfulness. And that produces confidence. Paul said, *"There is therefore now no condemnation to those who are in Christ Jesus"* (Romans 8:1). In the remainder of that chapter, Paul painted the most glorious picture of a life that is filled and controlled by the Holy Spirit, enumerating all the blessings, privileges, and benefits of that life. But the entry into that chapter—and into that kind of life—is presented in that first verse above. We must lay aside all condemnation.

One requirement for a right approach to God is coming in the name of Jesus. When we come in Jesus' name, we have assurance that our prayers are heard because of Him. It takes our attention off our own lives and works. When we come in the name of Jesus, we believe that our sins have been forgiven and that we are accepted by God as His children. This pleases God. It is how He wants us to come.

Thank You, Lord, that I can come boldly to You. I come to the throne of God in the name of Jesus, believing that my sins have been forgiven and that I am accepted by God as His child. I shall draw near to the throne of grace. Amen.

How to Pray and Get What You Pray For, Part 2 (audio)

Week 45:

Let us press on to maturity.

Therefore, leaving the discussion of the elementary principles of Christ, let us go on to perfection, not laying again the foundation of repentance from dead works and of faith toward God.

—Hebrews 6:1

An Ongoing Path

Let us press on to maturity.

We have looked so far at four "Let us" statements in the book of Hebrews. Now, we turn to the fifth such statement—one that could be a new resolution for us. Hebrews 6:1 reads, *"Therefore leaving the elementary teaching about the Christ, let us press on to maturity"* (NASB). Many Christians have the impression that in the Christian life, you can somehow "arrive," reaching a point where you can settle down and say, "Now, I'm there." But that is not true. To remain static in the mature spiritual life is almost impossible. As Proverbs 4:18 says, *"The path of the righteous is like the light of dawn, that shines brighter and brighter until the full day"* (NASB). The phrase *"the path of the righteous"* is not speaking about a specific believer or group of believers but about each and every righteous person.

Notice that righteousness is a path. It is not designed for standing still, much less for sitting down. As a path, righteousness implies motion, progress, and development. This path is like the light of dawn when we first come to know the Lord in His glorious fullness as Savior and Lord. It is like the sun rising after the darkness, or like a dawn that comes to our hearts. But dawn is not the end of God's purposes; it is just the beginning.

When we are walking in the path of righteousness, the light should always be getting brighter. With every step, with each new day, the light should be brighter than it was before. *"Until the full day"*: that is our destination, the height of noonday.

God is not content for us to stop at anything less than the full brightness of the noonday sun. Dawn is our beginning point, the path is the way of progress, and the light gets brighter and brighter. But there is no stopping permitted until we reach the full day.

Thank You, Lord, that You are leading me onward. I proclaim that righteousness is a path, and God expects motion, progress, and development on my part. I shall press on to maturity. Amen.

Twelve Steps to a Good Year, Part 2 (audio)

Advancing to Maturity

Let us press on to maturity.

This particular "Let us" is very appropriate to the New Testament Hebrew people because they had failed to live in accordance with it. They had trusted their special privileges and rested in them. They had become, quite frankly, lazy; they simply took things for granted.

> *We have much to say about this, but it is hard to explain because you are slow to learn. In fact, though by this time you ought to be teachers, you need someone to teach you the elementary truths of God's word all over again. You need milk, not solid food! Anyone who lives on milk, being still an infant, is not acquainted with the teaching about righteousness. But solid food is for the mature, who by constant use have trained themselves to distinguish good from evil.* (Hebrews 5:11–14 NIV)

What the writer was saying there—bluntly—is that the Hebrews were mere spiritual infants. They had no right to be infants at that stage in their Christian progress. They had had so many opportunities over many years that by then, they should have advanced to maturity. The writer of Hebrews also explained the only way to advance to maturity. We must train ourselves to distinguish good from evil. Advancing to maturity on the path of righteousness comes in practice by training ourselves constantly. It does not happen automatically; it requires discipline. That is why one of the earlier steps was "Let us be diligent." We must train ourselves to distinguish good from evil.

Many times, even large Christian congregations are unable to distinguish what is spiritual and scriptural from that which is just a fleshly presentation with soulish appeal. The only remedy is to train ourselves by constant use and careful practice.

Thank You, Lord, that You are leading me onward. I proclaim that I do not trust in special privileges or rest in them, but I am training myself to advance to maturity. I shall press on to maturity. Amen.

Twelve Steps to a Good Year, Part 2 (audio)

Being Built Up

Let us press on to maturity.

God has made a special provision for attaining spiritual maturity, which Paul recorded in Ephesians 4:11: *"It was he [the risen Christ] who gave some to be apostles, some to be prophets, some to be evangelists, and some to be pastors and teachers"* (NIV). Five main ministries are mentioned in this verse: apostles, prophets, evangelists, pastors, and teachers. The following verses tell us their purposes:

> *To prepare God's people for works of service, so that the body of Christ may be built up until we all reach unity in the faith and in the knowledge of the Son of God and become mature, attaining to the whole measure of the fullness of Christ.* (verses 12–13 NIV)

This passage spells out two purposes for these various ministries. The first is to prepare us for works of service. We cannot automatically do the work that we are expected to do; we must be prepared, or trained. These five ministries are there to train us.

The second purpose is to build up the body of Christ. These ministries are placed within the body of Christ in order to bring us into a unity of faith and maturity. Jesus Christ, as Head of the church, has provided these ministries, and I believe that God's people will never attain maturity without them. Paul continued, *"From him [Christ] the whole body, joined and held together by every supporting ligament, grows and builds itself up in love, as each part does its work"* (verse 16 NIV).

The ultimate goal is not a lot of separated, isolated individuals, each one doing his own thing. Rather, the goal is a single body, held together by ligaments—strong bands that hold the various parts together, building up the body so that it can grow. It is essential that each part of the body does its work.

Thank You, Lord, that You are leading me onward. I proclaim that God's goal is to prepare His people for works of service as each part of the body does its work. I shall press on to maturity. Amen.

Twelve Steps to a Good Year, Part 2 (audio)

NOVEMBER 8

God's Program for Maturity

Let us press on to maturity.

In God's program, there are two main requirements for coming to maturity. First, we must come under the discipline of the God-given ministries Paul listed in Ephesians 4:11: apostles, prophets, evangelists, pastors, and teachers. Without their discipline, oversight, and instruction, I do not see how God's people can ever attain to maturity. Jesus Christ never made a provision that was not important, and this one is no exception. I believe it is essential. The second condition is that we must not remain isolated individuals; rather, we must be part of a growing body of believers.

Then, in that same passage, Paul stated a sobering alternative. If we do not follow God's program for maturity, this will be the consequence: *"Then we will...be infants, tossed back and forth by the waves, and blown here and there by every wind of teaching and by the cunning and craftiness of men in their deceitful scheming"* (Ephesians 4:14 NIV).

If we do not come under this fivefold ministry—if we do not become part of a body and accept this scriptural discipline—then, according to Paul, we will remain infants. We will be *"tossed back and forth..., and blown here and there by every wind of teaching and by the cunning and craftiness of men in their deceitful scheming."* I know many, many believers who match this description. Every year, they have a new fad, a new doctrine, and often a new teacher to provide and perpetuate the fad. We must come under the discipline of godly, Scripture-based ministries. We also must be part of a body of believers. That is the only way to maturity.

How about you? Are you under discipline? Are you part of a body? Are you advancing to maturity?

Thank You, Lord, that You are leading me onward. I proclaim that I am coming under discipline to be part of a growing body, because I want to advance to maturity. I shall press on to maturity. Amen.

Twelve Steps to a Good Year, Part 2 (audio)

November

Doing the Father's Will

Let us press on to maturity.

In Ephesians 1:5, Paul said of all believers that God has *"predestined us to adoption as sons by Jesus Christ to Himself."* He further described God's purpose for His children in Romans 8:29: *"For whom He [God] foreknew, He also predestined to be conformed to the image of His Son, that He [Jesus] might be the firstborn among many brethren."* Thus, Jesus is the pattern Son, the One to whom we must all conform in coming to maturity. He Himself is the new and living way by which we go on to perfection, enter the holiest, and draw near to God. (See Hebrews 6:1; 10:19–22.) The way that led Jesus to perfection is the same way that each of us must follow.

The path to maturity was no easier for Jesus than it is for us. He *"was in all points tempted as we are, yet without sin"* (Hebrews 4:15). In His human nature, Jesus experienced every form of temptation we experience, and yet He never sinned. It is no sin to be tempted! Sin comes only when we yield to temptation.

What was it that enabled Jesus, in spite of His true humanity, to overcome all temptation? His success lay in His single-hearted, unchanging motivation to do the Father's will. This fact was prophetically foreshown by David in Psalm 40:7–8: *"Then I said, 'Behold, I come; in the scroll of the book it is written of me. I delight to do Your will, O my God.'"*

During His earthly ministry, Jesus repeatedly disclosed this underlying motive for all He did. He could never know final satisfaction until He had finished every task His Father had assigned. Near Jacob's well, He told His disciples, *"My food* [that which upholds and strengthens Me] *is to do the will of Him who sent Me, and to finish His work"* (John 4:34). (See also John 5:30; 6:38.)

Thank You, Lord, that You are leading me onward. I proclaim that I conform to Jesus in coming to maturity, doing the will of God and finishing His work. I shall press on to maturity. Amen.

"Behold the Man" (*New Wine* article)

Denial of Self-will

Let us press on to maturity.

The distinctive function of an Old Testament priest was to offer sacrifice. Thus, being a priest, Jesus had to offer sacrifice. Since He was not a Levite, He could not offer the sacrifices of the law, so He offered His own specific priestly sacrifice, which was prayer.

> He had offered up prayers and supplications, with vehement cries and tears to Him [God the Father] who was able to save Him from death, and was heard because of His godly fear, though He was a Son, yet He learned obedience by the things which He suffered. (Hebrews 5:7–8)

Jesus' reverent obedience caused the Father to hear His prayers. He learned obedience through suffering. Jesus had to learn obedience, and we have to learn obedience in the same way. We find out what obedience is by obeying. We do not find it out by listening to sermons on obedience. Those may help us, but obedience has to be worked out, step-by-step, by obeying. Obedience brings suffering because it demands denial of one's self-will. The key phrase in the obedience of Jesus was, *"Not My will, but Yours, be done"* (Luke 22:42). Every step of obedience in the Christian life is one of self-denial. Jesus said, *"If anyone desires to come after Me, let him deny himself"* (Matthew 16:24). That is painful, for the old ego does not like to be denied. Ego says, "I want," "I'm important," "This suits me," "I feel good," "I don't want," and the like. Following the Lord requires a continual denial of that ego.

In the above passage from Hebrews, God was talking to us about coming into maturity as sons through obedience. Jesus is the pattern. God brought Him to maturity through obedience. This is the pathway for you and me, too. This is the new and living way.

Thank You, Lord, that You are leading me onward. I proclaim that following the Lord requires a continual denial of my ego, and I choose to follow Jesus' pattern in meeting this requirement. I shall press on to maturity. Amen.

Seven Pictures of God's People: The Temple and the Family of God (audio)

Our Spiritual Objective

Let us press on to maturity.

Let us go on to perfection, not laying again the foundation of repentance from dead works and of faith toward God, of the doctrine of baptisms, of laying on of hands, of resurrection of the dead, and of eternal judgment. (Hebrews 6:1–2)

We seek to go on to perfection. Unfortunately, as I previously noted, the word *perfection* has an unattractive sound for most Christians because of some doctrine of sinless perfection that they've been exposed to. In most cases, those who claim to have achieved perfection demonstrate just the opposite by their words, behavior, and lifestyles. This hypocritical attitude has turned people away from the pursuit of perfection.

I would like to remind you of three alternative translations of the word *perfection* that make better sense: "maturity," "fulfillment," and "completion." The Greek word translated *"perfection"* comes from a noun that means "end." Therefore, it suggests a goal or objective toward which we are moving. I think we would all agree that having a spiritual objective is desirable. Having entered into the way of righteousness by faith, we can go on, or we can go back. God will have no pleasure in anyone who turns back, so we belong to those who are moving on into the full salvation of their souls. (See Hebrews 10:38–39.)

There are two things: the actual and the ideal. To be mature is to see the ideal and live with the actual. To fail is to accept the actual and reject the ideal; and to accept only that which is ideal and refuse the actual is to be immature. Do not criticize the actual because you have seen the ideal; Do not reject the ideal because you see the actual. Maturity is to live with the actual but hold on to the ideal.

Thank You, Lord, that You are leading me onward. I proclaim that I belong to those who are moving on into the full salvation of my soul—the goal of maturity, fulfillment, completion. I shall press on to maturity. Amen.

The Way into the Holiest, Vol. 1: A Call to Perfection: Let Us Go On to Perfection (audio)
"The Actual and the Ideal" (*New Wine* article)

WEEK 46:

Let us draw near to the Most Holy Place.

Therefore, brothers, since we have confidence to enter the Most Holy Place by the blood of Jesus... let us draw near to God with a sincere heart in full assurance of faith, having our hearts sprinkled to cleanse us from a guilty conscience and having our bodies washed with pure water.

—Hebrews 10:19, 22 (NIV)

NOVEMBER 12

Taking Our Place with Christ

Let us draw near to the Most Holy Place.

We can contrast this confession with another "Let us" phrase found in the book of Hebrews: *"Let us...come boldly to the throne of grace"* (Hebrews 4:16). This one says, in essence, *"Let us draw near to God."* We need to understand it in its context. It is directly related to the statement in Hebrews 10:

> *Since we have confidence to enter the Most Holy Place..., let us draw near to God.* (Hebrews 10:19, 22 NIV)

To me, this passage clearly says that "drawing near to God" is equivalent to "entering the Most Holy Place."

Let's compare these two statements. "Let us come boldly to the throne" means that we are to come for the help we need—for mercy and grace. But, "Let us draw near to God," I think, takes us much further. The suggestion is not merely that we come to the throne for help, but also that we are invited to take our place with Christ on the throne. That is what it means to enter the Most Holy Place.

There is not enough space to give a detailed exposition of the tabernacle, but there were three main areas. First, there was the Outer Court. Then, beyond the first curtain of the tent was the Holy Place. And finally, beyond the second curtain was the Most Holy Place. The language in Hebrews is based on the pattern of the tabernacle.

Our destination is the Most Holy Place, beyond the second curtain or veil.

Thank You, Lord, that I can draw near to You by the blood of Jesus.
I proclaim that I take my place with Christ on the throne. I shall draw
near to the Most Holy Place. Amen.

Twelve Steps to a Good Year, Part 2 (audio)

By a New and Living Way

Let us draw near to the Most Holy Place.

The only furniture in the Most Holy Place, as it was designed by God, was the ark of the covenant, which was a box made of acacia wood and covered with gold. Its lid was called the mercy seat, or the place of propitiation. Inside were the two tablets of the Ten Commandments, but these were covered up by the mercy seat, indicating that through Christ's propitiation on our behalf, the broken law (the Ten Commandments that were broken) has been covered by His propitiation. On either end of the mercy seat was a cherub. The two cherubs faced one another, looking toward the center of the mercy seat with their wings stretched out over them and their wing tips touching over the center of the mercy seat.

The mercy seat was God's throne—He sits on a throne of mercy that covers the broken law. The two cherubs with their faces turned inward toward one another, their wing tips touching, represent the place of fellowship. So, this is a place of mercy and a place of fellowship—but it is also a throne, the seat of God as King.

In that piece of furniture there was no representation of God Himself, which was forbidden for the Israelites. But God did come in and take His place on that seat in the form of the *shekinah* glory—the visible, sensory presence of almighty God. The Most Holy Place was in total darkness; it had no natural or artificial illumination. But when the *shekinah* presence of God came in, then God was taking His place on the throne.

In Hebrews 10 we are invited into the Most Holy Place to *"draw near to God"* (verse 22 NIV). We are invited to take our place with Christ on the throne. We are to come by *"a new and living way"* (verse 20 NIV). This new and living way is Jesus.

Thank You, Lord, that I can draw near to You by the blood of Jesus.
I proclaim that I come to the Most Holy Place by Jesus, *"the new and living way."* I shall draw near to the Most Holy Place. Amen.

Twelve Steps to a Good Year, Part 2 (audio)

Four Requirements

Let us draw near to the Most Holy Place.

According to Hebrews 10:22, one must fulfill four requirements in order to approach the mercy seat and the throne in the Most Holy Place. First, one must have a *"sincere heart"*; second, one must have a *"full assurance of faith"*; third, one's heart must be *"sprinkled to cleanse* [him] *from a guilty conscience"*; and, fourth, one's body must be *"washed with pure water"* (NIV). Let's look very briefly at each of these.

A sincere heart: We approach God with our hearts, not with our heads. God is not the answer to an intellectual riddle, but He will meet a sincere, longing heart. We must come without pretense, exposing ourselves to God just as we are without hiding anything.

Full assurance of faith: Hebrews 11:6 says, *"But without faith it is impossible to please Him* [God], *for he who comes to God must believe."* We must come with absolute faith in God's faithfulness—not faith in our own abilities or righteousness.

Our hearts sprinkled from a guilty conscience: A guilty conscience results from committing wrong, sinful deeds. But through the sprinkling of the blood of Jesus, we have assurance that our evil deeds have been forgiven and that our hearts are pure from sin.

Our bodies washed with pure water: First John 5:6 says that Jesus came by water and by blood. In Hebrews 10:22, we see both these elements: the blood that sprinkles from an evil conscience and the water that washes our bodies. I believe that the water represents Christian baptism. In the New Testament, Christian baptism means sharing in the death, burial, and resurrection of Jesus Christ. So, the *"new and living way"* mentioned in Hebrews 10:20 is Jesus. We are to identify with all that He endured when He died for our sins and rose again.

Thank You, Lord, that I can draw near to You by the blood of Jesus. I proclaim that I come with a sincere heart, full assurance of faith, a heart sprinkled from a guilty conscience, and my body washed with pure water. I shall draw near to the Most Holy Place. Amen.

Twelve Steps to a Good Year, Part 2 (audio)

DECLARING GOD'S WORD

Identifying with Jesus

Let us draw near to the Most Holy Place.

Paul wrote to the church at Ephesus (and to us, as well),

> *But because of his great love for us, God, who is rich in mercy, made us alive with Christ even when we were dead in transgressions....And God raised us up with Christ and seated us with him in the heavenly realms in Christ Jesus.*
>
> (Ephesians 2:4–6 NIV)

Notice these three stages of identification with Jesus. First, we are made alive; second, we are raised up, or resurrected; and, third, we are seated with Him. Jesus is seated on the throne. So, what does it mean for us to be seated with Him? It means to be enthroned, to share the throne with Him.

Once we understand our identification with Jesus, we are invited to follow Him all the way. He is the *"new and living way"* (Hebrews 10:20). We can be made alive with Him, we can be resurrected with Him. But we need not stop there. We can be enthroned with Him.

Using the pattern of the tabernacle, I believe that the first curtain represents our sharing in the resurrection of Jesus. The second curtain that leads to the Most Holy Place represents what we enter through sharing in the ascension of Jesus. Jesus was not merely resurrected, but, subsequently, He also was raised up to heaven, to the throne. And that is where God wants us. God does not want us to stop short in this new and living way until we have reached the Most Holy Place, where we are sharing the throne with Jesus—seated with Him in heavenly places. That is our destination.

Let's make it our resolution not to stop short of the place where God wants us to come.

Thank You, Lord, that I can draw near to You by the blood of Jesus. I proclaim that I will not stop short of the place where God wants me to come. I shall draw near to the Most Holy Place. Amen.

Twelve Steps to a Good Year, Part 2 (audio)

Seven Times

Let us draw near to the Most Holy Place.

The Old Testament previews how Jesus was to pay the price and make the final sacrifice. This preview is found in the ordinance of the Day of Atonement, described in detail in Leviticus 16. The high priest was to go just once each year into the Most Holy Place, the Holy of Holies. He had to take two things: a censer filled with incense, which made an aromatic cloud that covered him and the mercy seat, and the blood of the sacrifice, offered on his own behalf.

Going thusly into the Most Holy Place, he had to sprinkle the blood seven times between the second veil, where he entered, and the front (or east) side of the mercy seat itself. So, there was an initial sprinkling of the blood seven times. I believe that this was an exact prophetic preview of how Jesus was to sprinkle His own blood on the way to the cross, as well as on the cross itself. The number seven indicates the work of the Holy Spirit—it is the number of completeness, or perfection, indicating a perfect work. The prophetic sprinkling was exactly fulfilled in the way that Jesus shed His blood: He shed His blood precisely seven times before the sacrifice was complete.

In that sevenfold shedding, Jesus' body was emptied of blood. He literally poured out His soul to death in these steps: (1) His sweat became blood (see, for example, Luke 22:44), (2) they struck Him in the face with fists and rods (see, for example, Luke 22:63–64), (3) they flogged Him with a Roman scourge (see, for example, Luke 18:33), (4) His beard was pulled out (see Isaiah 50:6), (5) thorns were pressed into His scalp (see, for example, Matthew 27:29), (6) His hands and feet were pierced with nails (see, for example, John 20:25), and (7) His side was pierced with a spear (see John 19:34).

Thank You, Lord, that I can draw near to You by the blood of Jesus. I proclaim that by sprinkling His blood seven times, Jesus made the sacrifice complete. I shall draw near to the Most Holy Place. Amen.

The Fullness of the Cross, Vol. 4: How to Appropriate the Blood (audio)
Extravagant Love (audio, booklet)

Life in the Blood

Let us draw near to the Most Holy Place.

In the Old Testament, the book of Leviticus contains the ordinances for Israel's Aaronic priesthood. The Lord said, *"For the life of the flesh is in the blood, and I have given it to you upon the altar to make atonement for your souls; for it is the blood that makes atonement for the soul"* (Leviticus 17:11).

That is a tremendous prophetic statement that was fulfilled fourteen centuries later in Jesus. The word that is translated *life* is the Hebrew word for soul (*nephesh*). It is not just the life of a human being that is in the blood, but it is also the soul. We all know that when the blood ceases to circulate, the life has gone. In a certain sense, life depends on the blood.

In the previous chapter of Leviticus, in the ordinances for the Day of Atonement, Moses told his brother, Aaron, the high priest, that he could go only once every year into the Most Holy Place, into the immediate presence of God. He had to enter holding in one hand a censer full of burning coals with incense on them to send up a cloud of fragrant smoke; in the other hand he had to hold the blood of the sin offering that had been slain in front of the tabernacle. If he did not have both the censer of fragrant incense and the blood of the sacrificial animal, death would be the consequence. There was no access to the presence of God without those two things.

The censer, with its fragrant incense, is a beautiful type that symbolizes worship. We never come into the immediate presence of God without worship. But we never come without blood, either, which speaks of atonement for our sins. These pictures in the Old Testament were prophetic types—previews of what would actually be fulfilled in the New Testament.

Thank You, Lord, that I can draw near to You by the blood of Jesus.
I proclaim that I come into the immediate presence of God with
worship and the blood of atonement. I shall draw near to the Most
Holy Place. Amen.

The Life-giver (audio)

The Lifeblood of Jesus

Let us draw near to the Most Holy Place.

When the priest entered the Most Holy Place with the incense and the blood, he had to sprinkle the blood seven times on the mercy seat, which was a picture of the atonement, and seven times in front of the mercy seat. God's ordinance was absolutely specific—not six times, not eight times, but seven times. Then, in Isaiah, we find a prophetic picture of the suffering of Jesus—the clearest picture in the Old Testament of Jesus' suffering for our sins.

> *Therefore I* [the LORD] *will divide Him* [Jesus] *a portion with the great, and He shall divide the spoil with the strong, because He poured out His soul unto death.* (Isaiah 53:12)

It is important for us to understand that the word in Isaiah 53:12 that is translated as *"soul"* is the same word that appears in Leviticus 17:11 and is translated as *"life"*: *"The life* [soul] *of the flesh* [every human being] *is in the blood."* When Jesus made atonement for our sins, He poured out His soul in His blood. His blood is the most precious blood in the universe because in that blood is the soul life of God, the Creator.

There is more power in one drop of the blood of Jesus than in all parts of the kingdom of Satan put together. The lifeblood of Jesus is the life of God the Creator—a life that is greater than the entire universe and all the creatures He ever created. That life is released only through the blood of Jesus. He became the Life-giver when He shed His blood. We should never turn away from the blood of Jesus. There is no other atonement for sin, and no other source of life. One of our big problems, brothers and sisters, is not meditating enough on the blood.

Thank You, Lord, that I can draw near to You by the blood of Jesus. I proclaim that life is released only through the blood of Jesus—the only source of life. I shall draw near to the Most Holy Place. Amen.

The Life-giver (audio)

WEEK **47**:

Let us hold fast our confession without wavering.

Let us hold fast the confession of our hope without wavering, for He who promised is faithful.

—Hebrews 10:23

NOVEMBER 19

The Importance of Hope

Let us hold fast our confession without wavering.

M ost Christians have heard much preaching about faith and love, but, in many cases, they have heard comparatively little about hope. Such was my own condition many years ago when I was in desperate need of help from God. I had heard many messages on faith and some preaching on love; but what I needed in that particular situation was hope, and the Holy Spirit had to take me directly to the Scripture because I had never heard a sermon about hope. It was there that the Holy Spirit met my need. For this reason, I am particularly concerned that people understand the importance of hope. I want you to grasp what hope is, how important it is, and how you may have it.

Hope is necessary if we are to maintain both faith and love. Unless we have hope, our faith will "leak out" and our love will fail. Hope is not optional; it is essential to the fullness of the Christian life.

People often say, "Where there's life, there's hope." I think there is a good deal of truth in that statement. But the opposite is also true: Where there's hope, there's life—and where there is no hope, there is no life. In my opinion, hopelessness is one of the saddest conditions in human experience. I can hardly think of anything sadder than being hopeless. Yet, countless people in our world today are completely hopeless. When I am sitting in an airport, taking a walk, or dining in a restaurant, and I look at the faces of other people, I find that many of them have a blank stare of hopelessness. But, thank God, we do not need to be hopeless.

Thank You, Lord, that You are faithful—You give me hope. I proclaim that where there is hope, there is life. I shall hold fast my confession without wavering. Amen.

Hope, Part 1 (audio)

DECLARING GOD'S WORD

Without Wavering

Let us hold fast our confession without wavering.

In Hebrews 3:1, we are admonished to make the right confession. Then, in Hebrews 4:14, we are told to *"hold fast our confession."* When the Bible calls Jesus our High Priest, we immediately know that it is our confession that enlists His ministry on our behalf.

In holding fast our confession, we must not change what we have said. We must make the words of our mouths agree with what the Word of God says. In Hebrews 10:23, the step that we are now considering, it says, *"Let us hold fast the confession of our hope without wavering."* Notice what has been added: *"without wavering."*

If we look through these passages of Hebrews in the order in which they appear, we find that, in respect to our confession, there are three successive stages. First, we make the confession; second, having made it, we hold it fast without changing it; and, third, we hold it fast without wavering.

Why was *"without wavering"* put in? To me, on the basis of logic and personal experience, it implies that when we make the right confession, we are going to encounter negative forces and pressures that will come against us. Even though we have made the right confession and we are holding it fast, there may come a time when it seems like all the forces of Satan and the powers of darkness are turned loose against us. The temptation is to let go of our confession. But the writer said, "Don't let go! Hold fast—without wavering." The darker the situation and the greater the problem, the more important it is to hold fast without wavering.

God is faithful. He is committed to His Word. Jesus is our High Priest. If we will only hold fast our confession without wavering, He will do His job as our High Priest.

Thank You, Lord, that You are faithful—You give me hope. I proclaim that I make my confession, do not change it, and hold it fast without wavering. I shall hold fast my confession without wavering. Amen.

Hope, Part 1 (audio)

A Realm That Does Not Change

Let us hold fast our confession without wavering.

There is a disconnect between faith and sight. The natural man walks by sight, trusting his senses and believing only what they tell him. But in the Christian life, the spiritual life, we should not trust our senses. Second Corinthians 5:7 tells us, *"For we walk by faith, not by sight."* We walk not by our senses, but by faith. Faith relates us to an unseen, eternal realm that never changes. The world of the senses is always changing—it is temporary, unstable, impermanent, and unreliable. Through faith, we relate to a different world—a world of eternal realities and eternal truths. As we relate to that world by faith, we hold fast our confession without wavering.

How we respond to the pressures God permits in our lives determines whether we trust our senses or our faith. If we change our confession because of the darkness, then we are going by our senses, for in faith there is no darkness. Faith does not rely on the senses; it sees with an inner spiritual eye into a realm that does not change and it trusts a High Priest who is unchangeable. Here is what James said about this issue:

> But when he [the believer] *asks, he must believe and not doubt, because he who doubts is like a wave of the sea, blown and tossed by the wind. That man should not think he will receive anything from the Lord; he is a double-minded man, unstable in all he does.* (James 1:6–8 NIV)

This passage describes the man who wavers. He started out ready to ask—believing, not doubting—but he did not hold fast without wavering. As a result, he is tossed to and fro, thrown about by the winds and waves. The remedy is to hold fast our confession without wavering.

Thank You, Lord, that You are faithful—You give me hope. I proclaim that I walk not by my senses, but by faith. I shall hold fast my confession without wavering. Amen.

Hope, Part 1 (audio)

DECLARING GOD'S WORD

Being Fully Persuaded

Let us hold fast our confession without wavering.

In connection with this principle of making the right confession and holding it fast without wavering, I want to look at the example of Abraham, as Paul portrayed him. Abraham is one of the best examples of someone who held fast without wavering. As Paul wrote,

> *Without weakening in his faith, he faced the fact that his body was as good as dead—since he was about a hundred years old— and that Sarah's womb was also dead.* (Romans 4:19 NIV)

Real faith faces facts. Any attitude that is not willing to look at the facts is not real faith. Abraham did not try to deceive himself; he did not imagine something differently from how it was. With his senses, he saw that his body was as good as dead, as was the womb of his wife, Sarah. But he did not trust solely in his senses. Paul continued,

> *Yet he did not waver through unbelief regarding the promise of God, but was strengthened in his faith and gave glory to God, being fully persuaded that God had power to do what he had promised. This is why "it was credited to him as righteousness."* (Romans 4:20–22 NIV)

Abraham is called *"the father of all those who believe"* (Romans 4:11), and we are exhorted to follow in the steps of Abraham's faith. (See verse 12.) We are required to walk that same path of faith. We are required to lay hold of the promise of God, to make our confession, to hold fast our confession without wavering, to refuse to be deterred by what our senses reveal, and to look beyond the seen things, peering into the unseen realm to see, by faith, our faithful High Priest, there at God's right hand.

Thank You, Lord, that You are faithful—You give me hope. I proclaim that I face the facts without wavering in unbelief. I shall hold fast my confession without wavering. Amen.

Hope, Part 1 (audio)

The Battle for the Promise

Let us hold fast our confession without wavering.

Whenever I have conducted a healing service, I have usually required the people to make the above confession, because it would qualify them for healing. Let me explain. If you have a problem in your kidneys, then you would confess, "Jesus Himself [remember, the emphasis is on Him] took my infirmities and bore my sicknesses; with His wounds, I am healed." Afterward, if you still have the problem in your kidneys, what do you do? Hold fast your confession. Do you still have the problem in your kidneys? Hold fast your confession without wavering. This is a battle. Believe me, I know from experience that pressing your way into healing can be a tremendous battle.

The writer of Hebrews said to the Hebrew Christians, *"You have not yet resisted to bloodshed, striving against sin"* (Hebrews 12:4). We are used to the idea that we have to strive against sin, but we sometimes forget that we have to strive against sickness, too. We must fight. We are soldiers. We do not lie down and let the devil walk over us, for easy surrender does not give glory to God.

In regard to holding fast our confession without wavering, let us not focus exclusively on physical healing, even though the need for it is something that touches almost all people. What about financial needs? For me—and this is not just a ritual—holding fast my confession is my way to release the treasures that God has in His storehouse for my ministry. God spoke to me and told me that He had made full provision for everything He would ask us to do. But to obtain the full provision, we had to believe and confess. And I make it personal. This confession is taken from 2 Corinthians 9:8: *"God is able to make all grace abound toward [us], that [we], always having all sufficiency in all things, may have an abundance for every good work."* Glory to God!

Thank You, Lord, that You are faithful—You give me hope. I proclaim that I fight for healing and provision—believing and confessing. I shall hold fast my confession without wavering. Amen.

The Fullness of the Cross, Vol. 1: How to Enter In (audio)

Unfailing Faith

Let us hold fast our confession without wavering.

We must emphasize the vital importance of faith. I say to you what Jesus said to Peter: *"I have prayed for you, that your faith should not fail"* (Luke 22:32). Faith is the basic requirement for belonging to God and being a child of Abraham, who is *"the father of circumcision to those who not only are of the circumcision, but who also walk in the steps of the faith which our father Abraham had while still uncircumcised"* (Romans 4:12). Abraham is more than just a figure—he is a pattern. He went ahead, laid out the pathway, and took certain steps. To be truly his descendants, we must walk in that pathway and follow in his steps. Let's look at the five steps of the faith of Abraham: (1) he accepted God's promise by faith alone, without evidence; (2) he recognized that he was incapable of producing the results on his own; (3) he focused on the promise without wavering, and this faith was reckoned to him as righteousness; (4) as a result, Sarah and he both received supernatural life in their bodies; and (5) thus, the promise was fulfilled, and God was glorified.

Those are the steps of the faith of our father Abraham—the pathway of faith that is set before every one of us. It is not some external ordinance but a lifetime walk of faith, following in the footsteps of Abraham. We must do as Abraham did. We have to accept God's promise just the way it is. We have to reckon that we are incapable of producing what God has promised in our lives. We have to focus on the promise and not on our own ability—or inability. And then, we will receive the supernatural grace and power of God released in our lives through our faith. In this way, the promise of God will be fulfilled in our lives.

Thank You, Lord, that You are faithful—You give me hope. I proclaim
that I walk in faith, fulfilling the basic requirement of belonging to
God and being a child of Abraham. I shall hold fast my confession
without wavering. Amen.

The Roman Pilgrimage, Vol. 1: Romans 4:1–4:26 (audio, video)

Faith/Present–Hope/Future

Let us hold fast our confession without wavering.

In Hebrews 11, we find the definition of faith—the only word explicitly defined in the Bible. *"Now faith is the substance of things hoped for, the evidence of things not seen"* (Hebrews 11:1). Here, we see a relationship between faith and hope. Faith is here and now; hope is for the future. Faith is a material thing—something so real that it is called a *substance*. It is in our hearts. On the basis of faith, we can have a legitimate hope for the future. But hope that is not based on legitimate faith is just wishful thinking.

> *If you confess with your mouth the Lord Jesus and believe in your heart that God has raised Him from the dead, you will be saved. For with the heart one believes unto...salvation.* (Romans 10:9–10)

In the New Testament, *believe* is a word of motion. It is not a static thing or an intellectual position. It is something in your heart that leads you to something new. *Faith* is a verb of motion: by *faith* we believe unto righteousness and salvation. You can have intellectual faith and never be changed. You can embrace all the doctrines of the Bible with your intellect but remain completely the same. But when you have faith in your heart, it leads to salvation.

Faith is in the present; hope is in the future. Biblical faith is in the heart; hope is in the mind. Paul spoke about both with an interesting picture: *"But let us who are of the day be sober, putting on the breastplate of faith and love, and as a helmet the hope of salvation"* (1 Thessalonians 5:8). Two items of armor are mentioned in this verse. Faith is a breastplate, which protects the heart, and hope is the helmet, which protects the head. Faith is in the heart; hope is in the mind.

Thank You, Lord, that You are faithful—You give me hope. I proclaim that I am putting on faith, the breastplate that protects my heart, and hope, the helmet that protects my mind. I shall hold fast my confession without wavering. Amen.

Laying the Foundation, Vol. 1: Through Repentance to Faith (audio, video)

Week 48:

Let us consider one another.

And let us consider one another in order to stir up love and good works.

—Hebrews 10:24

NOVEMBER 26

Bringing Out the Best

Let us consider one another.

And let us consider one another in order to stir up love and good works, not forsaking the assembling of ourselves together, as is the manner of some, but exhorting one another, and so much the more as you see the Day approaching. (Hebrews 10:24–25)

We will now look at the eighth "Let us" step in Hebrews, found in the above passage. Some English translations say, *"Let us consider how to stimulate one another."* But the order is reversed from the original Greek, which reads, "Let us consider one another, how to stimulate to love and good deeds." This rendering brings out the essence of this week's resolution to consider others. We should consider one another, always seeking to bring out the best in each other.

Many people today are shut up in prisons of self-centeredness. They are never truly happy; they never enjoy true peace. In fact, the more you worry and seek to please yourself, the more problems you have. One scriptural way to be released from that prison is to stop worrying about yourself all the time. Stop being concerned about yourself and start considering your fellow believers.

We are to follow Jesus' example and live out Paul's exhortation:

Do nothing from selfishness or empty conceit, but with humility of mind let each of you regard one another as more important than himself; do not merely look out for your own personal interests, but also for the interests of others. (Philippians 2:3–4 NASB)

The opposite of considering one another is looking out for *"your own personal interests."* Release comes through being more concerned about others than you are about yourself.

Thank You, Lord, that You help me to love others. I proclaim that I am more concerned about others than I am about myself. I shall consider others. Amen.

Twelve Steps to a Good Year, Part 2 (audio)

Emptying Ourselves

Let us consider one another.

In Philippians 2, Paul said that we need to follow Jesus' example. I always say that our attitudes determine our approaches, and our approaches determine the outcome. Here is the attitude we need to cultivate: *"Have this attitude in yourselves which was also in Christ Jesus, who, although He existed in the form of God, did not regard equality with God a thing to be grasped, but emptied Himself, taking the form of a bond-servant"* (Philippians 2:5–7 NASB). The Greek word translated *"bond-servant"* literally means "slave." So, we see that Jesus, who was Lord of all, emptied Himself and was willing to become a bondservant, a slave. We must imitate His attitude.

Paul penned a beautiful, parallel passage in Galatians:

> *For you were called to freedom, brethren; only do not turn your free-dom into an opportunity for the flesh* [do not gratify your own fleshly, selfish desires], *but through love serve one another. For the whole Law is fulfilled in one word, in the statement, "You shall love your neighbor as yourself."* (Galatians 5:13–14 NASB)

Looking outward at others is the way in which we free ourselves from indulging in our fleshly natures or yielding to selfishness. We are to serve one another in love. I believe that the Holy Spirit is emphasizing this loving, selfless attitude to God's people today. Many people talk about serving the Lord but never serve their fellow believers. I do not know how much you can really serve the Lord if you are not willing to serve your fellow believers, because the Lord comes to us in the members of His body. Our attitude toward those members is really our attitude toward the Lord Himself.

Thank You, Lord, that You help me to love others. I proclaim that I serve my fellow believers as a way of serving the Lord. I shall consider others. Amen.

Twelve Steps to a Good Year, Part 2 (audio)

Dethroning Ourselves

Let us consider one another.

I n connection with our being willing to serve others, I want to look at another passage from the apostle Paul—something that he wrote to the Corinthian Christians. By his background, Paul was a strict, observant, orthodox Jew. He was a Pharisee, and he had the qualifications to be a rabbi. His was the kind of righteousness that caused him to separate himself from other people, whom he regarded on a lower level or even despised.

But when he came to know Jesus, the most wonderful change took place in his nature. Bear in mind that the people of Corinth were basically the scum of the earth. In this epistle, Paul said that some of them had been homosexuals, some prostitutes, some drunkards, and some revilers. They were just not the best kind of people. Corinth was one of the major seaports of the ancient world, and, like many seaports, the city was filled with these sorts of people.

But let's look at this astonishing statement of Paul: *"For we do not preach ourselves but Christ Jesus as Lord, and ourselves as your bond-servants for Jesus' sake"* (2 Corinthians 4:5 NASB).

Here is this proud Pharisee saying, "We are your slaves for the sake of Jesus"—even to the likes of the people of Corinth!

Notice the three steps. First, dethrone self: *"not...ourselves."* Second, enthrone Christ: *"Christ Jesus as Lord."* Third, serve others: *"[we are] your bond-servants for Jesus' sake."* Those three steps are so important. By love, serve others. That's the message: escape from self-centeredness.

Thank You, Lord, that You help me to love others. I proclaim that I dethrone myself, enthrone Christ, and serve others. I shall consider others. Amen.

Twelve Steps to a Good Year, Part 2 (audio)

An Acquired Skill

Let us consider one another.

Serving is a skill that we have to acquire. It is not something that just happens, and it is certainly not ours by nature. For example, a server in a restaurant is a person who, in a sense, is called to serve. But a server needs to be trained. I have a friend who used to be a server, and he once explained to me all that is involved in being a *good* server. Once I understood the training process, I realized that it does not just happen; serving is a skill we have to acquire. We have to study others to find out what produces a positive response, not a negative one. We are to study others to provoke them to love and good deeds, not to the opposite. Serving requires practice, training, and discipline.

Serving also requires the right environment. After saying, *"Let us consider how to stimulate one another to love and good deeds"* (Hebrews 10:24 NASB), the writer of Hebrews went on to say, *"Not forsaking our own assembling together, as is the habit of some, but encouraging one another; and all the more, as you see the day drawing near"* (verse 25 NASB). We must learn to serve in the right environment, which is expressed in the words *"our own assembling together."* It means close, committed, regular fellowship.

In the next verse, the writer presented the disastrous alternative. Immediately after he warned us not to forsake our own assembling together, he said, *"For if we go on sinning willfully after receiving the knowledge of the truth, there no longer remains a sacrifice for sins, but a certain terrifying expectation of judgment"* (verses 26–27 NASB). The implication is that if we do not stay in the right environment—if we are not in close, committed, regular fellowship—we will go back to sinning. The only safe way is to stay in fellowship, consider other people, and learn to serve them joyfully.

Thank You, Lord, that You help me to love others. I proclaim that I am staying in fellowship, learning to serve, and focusing on considering other people. I shall consider others. Amen.

Twelve Steps to a Good Year, Part 2 (audio)

Considering Jesus First

Let us consider one another.

This eighth "Let us" passage says, in the original Greek, "Let us consider one another." (See Hebrews 10:24.) But I would like to look back to Hebrews 3:1, where the same word, *"consider,"* is used. It reads, *"Consider the Apostle and High Priest of our confession, Christ Jesus."* If we consider Jesus, we will end up considering one another. But it is important that we do it in that order. We consider Jesus first; then, we consider one another. It makes a great deal of difference whether I relate to you as just a person or as a person in Christ.

My mind goes back to an incident that happened while I was the principal of a college that trained teachers in East Africa. For every vacancy that allowed us to accept one student, there were at least ten suitable applicants. One girl actually walked twenty-four miles barefoot just to get an interview. You can hardly conceive the desperate hunger people in Africa had for getting an education. Education was the key to success in life, as they saw it.

One day, an elderly mother came to me on behalf of her son, a prospective student. He was not exactly suitable for the school, however, and we had not accepted him. His mother was pestering me to the point that I was growing annoyed with her. In Africa, they do not believe in democracy; they believe in the chief, the strong man. He is the one who matters. This woman kept telling me, "You are the great one; what you say goes." I got so irritated that I was about to give her a piece of my mind—and it was not my sanctified mind, either! That is when the Lord spoke to me, very gently, saying, *Remember, she's one of My children. Be careful how you treat her.* I repented. She really was a dear, precious woman, and a child of God. If we consider Jesus first, it will make all the difference in how we consider one another.

Thank You, Lord, that You help me to love others. I proclaim that I consider Jesus first, allowing this perspective to affect how I consider others. I shall consider others. Amen.

God's Last Word, Vol. 3: Hebrews 10:23–10:34 (audio)

Provocation—The Right Kind

Let us consider one another.

The King James Version of Hebrews 10:24 reads, *"And let us consider one another to provoke unto love and to good works."* This version uses the word *provoke,* a strong word that typically has a negative connotation. I think it was used deliberately in order to make us think. What do we usually provoke from other people? Anger or jealousy. But we are to provoke to *"love and to good works."*

The Greek word translated *"provoke"* is the same word from which the English word *paroxysm* is derived. Do you know what a paroxysm is? It is an absolutely uncontrollable outburst of emotion, such as anger, or even laughter.

Although the word *provoke* often suggests something bad, in this context, it is turned to the good, for we are to provoke one another to love and good works. And let me just point out that there are certain people whom you'll *have* to provoke if you want them to do the right thing. Moreover, you will have to consider *how* to provoke them.

This is one of my weaknesses. I don't like having to consider people's personalities. With a military background and a rather logical mind, it is sufficient for me just to tell the person to do something. But the Bible tells us to consider *how* to tell them, because if you want the right result from one person, you have to tell him in quite a different way from the way in which you might tell another person. Anybody who has children knows this is true—you cannot treat them all the same. You can scold one child and get the right result. But if you scold another child, you might just discourage or defeat him.

Thank You, Lord, that You help me to love others. I proclaim that I consider how to provoke others to love and good works. I shall consider others. Amen.

God's Last Word, Vol. 3: Hebrews 10:23–10:34 (audio)

DECEMBER 2

Right Fellowship

Let us consider one another.

There is one seemingly negative consequence of having fellowship with God and our fellow believers: we can no longer have the same sort of fellowship with unbelievers.

> *Do not be bound together with unbelievers; for what partnership have righteousness and lawlessness, or what fellowship has light with darkness? Or what harmony has Christ with Belial, or what has a believer in common with an unbeliever? Or what agreement has the temple of God with idols? For we are the temple of the living God.* (2 Corinthians 6:14–16 NASB)

The separation from unbelievers that Paul was speaking about is not primarily *physical*. We may find ourselves side-by-side with unbelievers every day—in our homes, in our workplaces, or in other activities of daily life. In such situations, our Christian testimony requires us to be friendly, courteous, and helpful. But we are not free to share with unbelievers that which is morally or spiritually impure or dishonoring to Christ. In this realm, we must follow Paul's exhortation in 2 Corinthians 6:17: *"Do not touch what is unclean."* If we are sensitive to the Holy Spirit, He will always warn us of these defiling contacts and show us how to protect ourselves from them.

However, the surest protection against wrong fellowship is right fellowship. As God's children, we are heirs to innumerable joys and blessings of which the world knows nothing. In fact, Paul told us that our Father God *"has blessed us with every spiritual blessing in the heavenly places in Christ"* (Ephesians 1:3). As we regularly share these blessings with the rest of God's family, we are no longer attracted by the tawdry, impure pleasures of a world that is walking in darkness.

Thank You, Lord, that You help me to love others. I proclaim that I have moved out of fellowship with darkness and into fellowship with God's family, my brothers and sisters in Christ. I shall consider others. Amen.

"Your Walk with God" (*New Wine* article)

Week 49:

Let us run the race with endurance.

Therefore we also, since we are surrounded by so great a cloud of witnesses, let us lay aside every weight, and the sin which so easily ensnares us, and let us run with endurance the race that is set before us.

—Hebrews 12:1

Success in the Race

Let us run the race with endurance.

The ninth "Let us" step from the book of Hebrews is found in the first verse of chapter 12:

> *Therefore, since we have so great a cloud of witnesses surrounding us, let us also lay aside every encumbrance, and the sin which so easily entangles us, and let us run with endurance the race that is set before us.* (Hebrews 12:1 NASB)

In English translations, there are two "let us" phrases in that one verse, which is a perfectly legitimate translation. But it just so happens that, in the original Greek, the first phrase, *"let us…lay aside every encumbrance,"* is not found in that form. Instead, it is a participle that reads like this: "Laying aside every encumbrance, let us run with endurance the race." The real "let us" phrase in the above verse, on which we will need to focus, is *"Let us run with endurance the race that is set before us."*

Here and elsewhere in the New Testament, the Christian life is compared to a race. This analogy implies a specific course marked out before us in advance. Success in the Christian life consists in completing the course in accordance with the rules of the competition.

In light of the fact that we are confronted with this race that is set before us, we need to see that there are four requirements for successfully completing the race. Each one of these requirements is found in the New Testament: (1) the right mental attitude, (2) self-control, (3) endurance, and (4) having our eyes fixed on Jesus. If we will keep these requirements in mind, we can finish the race and keep the faith.

Thank You, Lord, for helping me to *"press on."* I proclaim that I am maintaining the right mental attitude, practicing self-control, exhibiting endurance, and keeping my eyes on Jesus. By doing these things, I will finish the race and keep the faith. I shall run the race with endurance. Amen.

Twelve Steps to a Good Year, Part 3 (audio)

The Right Mental Attitude

Let us run the race with endurance.

One essential requirement for running a successful race is having a right mental attitude. This truth was exemplified by the words of Paul as he spoke about his relationship to Jesus Christ: *"That I may know Him, and the power of His resurrection and the fellowship of His sufferings, being conformed to His death; in order that I may attain to the resurrection from the dead"* (Philippians 3:10–11 NASB).

Paul had a specific objective. He did not run aimlessly. (See 1 Corinthians 9:26.) He had an aim before him. He knew what the goal was, which determined his mental attitude. He continued, *"Not that I have already obtained it, or have already become perfect* [complete], *but I press on in order that I may lay hold of that for which also I was laid hold of by Christ Jesus"* (verse 12 NASB). Paul's vision was that Christ had laid hold of him for a purpose; fulfilling that purpose meant that he would have to relate to this purpose. He had to be determined that the purpose of Christ would become his purpose.

> *Brethren, I do not regard myself as having laid hold of it yet; but one thing I do: forgetting what lies behind and reaching forward to what lies ahead, I press on toward the goal for the prize of the upward call of God in Christ Jesus.* (verses 13–14 NASB)

The phrase *"I press on"* occurs twice, once in verse 12 and once in verse 14. That is the mental attitude we need to share with Paul: "I press on. I have a goal. I have not yet arrived, but I know where I'm headed." The last time Paul used that phrase, he said, *"I press on toward the goal for the prize of the upward call of God in Christ Jesus."* There is a reward for those who successfully complete the race. Always keep the goal in mind, for we do not want to lose our God-appointed reward.

Thank You, Lord, for helping me to *"press on."* I proclaim that I am maintaining the proper mental attitude—keeping the goal in mind. I shall run the race with endurance. Amen.

Twelve Steps to a Good Year, Part 3 (audio)

The Condition of Self-control

Let us run the race with endurance.

Another condition for a successful race is self-control, and this condition is illustrated by the words Paul used in 1 Corinthians 9:24–25 to compare living the Christian life to competing in an athletic contest. This is an excellent parallel, and one that is still vivid for us today, because we are so often spectators of athletic contests in person and on television. The same principle still applies.

> *Do you not know that those who run in a race all run, but only one receives the prize? Run in such a way that you may win.*
> (1 Corinthians 9:24 NASB)

That is the objective. Then, Paul went on to state the condition:

> *And everyone who competes in the games exercises self-control in all things. They then do it to receive a perishable wreath* [the prize], *but we an imperishable.*   (verse 25 NASB)

If we are going to win the race, if we are going to win the prize, we must meet the condition of self-control. This truth is so obvious when we think in terms of athletics. Every athlete who succeeds as an athlete today has to exercise the most rigorous self-control. He has to go into training—controlling what he eats, how much sleep he gets, and the amount of exercise he has. He also has to control his psychology, building up the right kind of attitude. He cannot afford to give way to negative thoughts. He has to go into the competition with a positive attitude, believing he is going to achieve victory.

All this is equally true for us as Christians in our race. We cannot win the race without self-control.

Thank You, Lord, for helping me to *"press on."* I proclaim that I am exercising self-control in all things in order to win the prize. I shall run the race with endurance. Amen.

Twelve Steps to a Good Year, Part 3 (audio)

Cultivating Endurance

Let us run the race with endurance.

This confession tells us that another condition for victory in this race is stated in Hebrews 12:1: *"endurance."* It is one quality that is essential to our character, as Christians, if we are going to achieve real spiritual success and fulfillment. We must cultivate endurance.

What is the opposite of endurance? I think it is giving up, or quitting. Christians cannot afford to be quitters. When God commits us to something, we have to set our faces to fulfill it and go through with it. There is a close relationship between self-control and endurance. Without self-control, we will not achieve endurance. We must master our weaknesses; otherwise, every time we are tested in the area of endurance, some weakness—whether it is emotional, psychological, or physical—will get us down, and we will give up at the very point where we should have been holding on and enduring.

Yet another condition for a successful race is to have our eyes fixed on Jesus. As is stated in Hebrews, *"Fixing our eyes on Jesus, the author and perfecter of faith, who for the joy set before Him endured the cross"* (Hebrews 12:2 NASB).

We have to look continually to Jesus. In other words, we cannot run the race in self-reliance. Looking to Jesus means that He is our example, and we put our confidence in Him. He is the author—the beginning of our faith. He is the perfecter—the One who will bring us through to victory.

Thank You, Lord, for helping me to *"press on."* I proclaim that I do not give up, but fix my gaze on Jesus, the One who brings me through to victory. I shall run the race with endurance. Amen.

Twelve Steps to a Good Year, Part 3 (audio)

A Long, Deliberate Race

Let us run the race with endurance.

Where it says in Hebrews 12:1 to *"lay aside every weight,"* we must think in terms of this race. The runner empties his pockets and wears the lightest, most flexible clothing he can; he does not carry a single unnecessary ounce of weight. Some things that aren't exactly sins still act as weights that can burden us and hold us back. They exhaust our strength or lure us into spending too much time and attention on them.

Remember, this is not a short sprint—it is a long, deliberate race. The primary characteristic that is required is endurance. Many people start off the Christian life as if it were a dash. A little while later, they are panting beside the track; they are finished, and they have hardly begun the race. Ecclesiastes 9:11 wisely points out, *"The race is not to the swift, nor the battle to the strong."*

The following is the testimony of a victor—the apostle Paul:

I have fought the good fight, I have finished the course, I have kept the faith; in the future there is laid up for me the crown of righteousness, which the Lord, the righteous Judge, will award to me on that day; and not only to me, but also to all who have loved His appearing.　　　　(2 Timothy 4:7–8 NASB)

Paul knew that he had won the race. He had finished the course, and he knew that the prize was waiting for him. That is a glorious testimony. It can be the testimony of you and me, too, if we will only meet the conditions.

It isn't speed or strength but endurance that counts.

Thank You, Lord, for helping me to *"press on."* I proclaim that I *"lay aside every weight"* in preparation to finish a long, deliberate race. I shall run the race with endurance. Amen.

Twelve Steps to a Good Year, Part 3 (audio)

The Persevering Process

Let us run the race with endurance.

Let's consider some simple principles that will help us to cultivate endurance, reading first what Paul wrote in Romans 5:1–2: *"Therefore, having been justified by faith, we have peace with God through our Lord Jesus Christ, through whom also we have access by faith into this grace in which we stand, and rejoice in hope of the glory of God."* We rejoice because of what the future holds for us. Paul went on to say that we rejoice not only in the light of the future, but also in what the present offers: *"And not only in that, but we also glory in tribulations, knowing that tribulation produces perseverance; and perseverance, character; and character, hope"* (verses 3–4). Where verse 3 uses the word *"glory,"* the original Greek word means "to rejoice, boast, or exult." We should exult in tribulation because of what tribulation does. The *New American Standard Bible* says, *"Tribulation brings about perseverance; and perseverance, proven character; and proven character, hope."* Perseverance produces *proven* character in us. This is the heart of endurance—character that has stood the test. As Paul wrote, *"Now hope does not disappoint, because the love of God has been poured out in our hearts by the Holy Spirit who was given to us"* (Romans 5:5).

Love is a matter of character. In essence, we are dealing with the formation of our characters. We rejoice in tribulation, for tribulation is the only thing that produces perseverance. And perseverance produces proven character. I know men with whom I have walked and shared hardship, opposition, misrepresentation, and misunderstanding. But today, for me, their character is proven; I know I can trust them. In the midst of treachery and lawlessness, I want to know whom I can trust.

Thank You, Lord, for helping me to *"press on."* I proclaim that I rejoice in the tribulations that produce the character and hope I need to finish the race. I shall run the race with endurance. Amen.

Character That Stands the Test (Teaching Legacy Letter)

Until the End

Let us run the race with endurance.

One of the consistent themes of Hebrews is the danger of going back on your profession of faith in Christ. There are five distinct passages in Hebrews that warn us of the danger of going back. These are some of the most solemn words in Scripture. Therefore, one of the key words that Hebrews emphasizes is this word that we are looking at: *endurance.*

> *And we desire that each one of you show the same diligence to the full assurance of hope until the end, that you do not become sluggish, but imitate those who through faith and patience* [endurance] *inherit the promises.*　　　　　(Hebrews 6:11–12)

Faith and endurance. Some people will tell you that faith is all you need to claim God's promise. But that is not true. You need faith *and* endurance. It takes both. As the author of Hebrews continued, "*Therefore do not cast away your confidence, which has great reward. For you have need of endurance, so that after you have done the will of God, you may receive the promise*" (Hebrews 10:35–36).

The word *confidence* means that you have freedom of speech. You can talk boldly about Jesus—about what He has done for you and what He will do for you. You have done the will of God, but you have not yet received the promise. What do you need? Endurance. You need to hold out from the point where you did God's will and claimed the promise to the point where you actually receive the promise. Some people do the will of God and claim the promise, but they don't hold out. Then, they say that it didn't work. But it will not work without endurance. You need faith and endurance.

Thank You, Lord, for helping me to *"press on."* I proclaim that I endure to the end by faith, holding out to do God's will and claiming the promises. I shall run the race with endurance. Amen.

Character That Stands the Test (Teaching Legacy Letter)

WEEK 50:

Let us show gratitude.

Therefore, since we receive a kingdom which cannot be shaken, let us show gratitude, by which we may offer to God an acceptable service with reverence and awe.

—Hebrews 12:28 (NASB)

Grace and Thanks

Let us show gratitude.

The tenth "Let us" step in the book of Hebrews is found near the end of chapter 12:

> *Therefore, since we receive a kingdom which cannot be shaken, let us show gratitude, by which we may offer to God an acceptable service with reverence and awe; for our God is a consuming fire.*
> (Hebrews 12:28–29 NASB)

Where the version above says *"Let us show gratitude,"* the King James and *New King James* Versions say, *"Let us have grace"*—and it is important that we understand the connection between grace and thanks. The King James translation is a literal translation of the words—the phrase "to have grace" is commonly used in Greek to express the giving of thanks. This brings out the association between grace and thanks. This connection is also found in various modern Romance languages. In French, for instance, they say, *"Grâce à Dieu,"* which means "Thanks to God"; in Italian, it is *"grazie,"* and in Spanish, it is *"gracias."* All are taken from the same word for *grace*.

It is easy to see this connection between grace and thanks. In light of this fact, I want to tell you that you cannot have the grace of God in your life unless you practice giving thanks. Grace and thanks go together. There is nothing more ungracious than an unthankful person, whereas a thankful person will always experience the grace of God.

God requires two things of us as His people. First of all, He requires that we appreciate what He does for us. Second, He requires that we express our appreciation. It is important to understand our need to express appreciation to God.

Thank You, Lord, for all You have done for me. I proclaim that I appreciate what the Lord does for me, and I express that appreciation freely. I shall show gratitude. Amen.

Twelve Steps to a Good Year, Part 3 (audio)

DECEMBER 11

Stopping to Say "Thanks"

Let us show gratitude.

Some people are genuinely grateful to God but never take the time to tell God that they are. How would we feel if our children never thanked us for all that we've done for them? How would we feel if they never said "thank you" or showed their gratitude, if they just accepted everything we did for them as if it were by right, merely taking it for granted?

Unfortunately, that is how many of God's children treat Him—and it is not pleasing in His sight. We are required to appreciate what God does for us and to take the time to express our appreciation. One of my favorite verses is in Proverbs: *"In all your ways acknowledge Him* [God], *and He shall direct your paths"* (Proverbs 3:6).

I have learned by experience that if I pause at every stage in life to acknowledge God, I can be confident that He will continue to direct my path. You might ask, "How can I acknowledge God?" The simplest and best way is to thank Him—say "Thank You" for all He has done and for His faithfulness. You will get immediate assurance that He is going to continue to be faithful. Just as He has helped and guided you in the past, He will guide you in the future. But the key to this assurance is acknowledging Him by our thanksgiving.

When I was in East Africa, I discovered that in the language of my adopted African daughter's tribe, they had no word or phrase that meant "thank you." Can you imagine not being able to say "thank you"? I then realized that it is only where the Bible has come that people have learned to say "thank you." It is part of the grace of God.

Thank You, Lord, for all You have done for me. I proclaim that I will pause at every stage in life to acknowledge God by thanking Him. I shall show gratitude. Amen.

Twelve Steps to a Good Year, Part 3 (audio)

The Appropriate Response

Let us show gratitude.

We need to look at the background of this exhortation to be thankful as we read it in the epistle to the Hebrews, where we find the following rather solemn warning. The writer made a parallel application from the Old Testament, when God spoke to the people of Israel through Moses:

> *See to it that you do not refuse Him who is speaking. For if those did not escape when they refused him who warned them on earth, much less shall we* [believers in the New Testament] *escape who turn away from Him who warns from heaven. And His voice shook the earth then, but now He has promised, saying, "Yet once more I will shake not only the earth, but also the heaven." And this expression, "Yet once more," denotes the removing of those things which can be shaken, as of created things, in order that those things which cannot be shaken may remain.*
> (Hebrews 12:25–27 NASB)

Thankfulness is the appropriate response to the particular privileges and benefits that we have in God. We are not dependent on a shakable kingdom. We have an eternal kingdom, an unshakable kingdom, the kingdom of God Himself, the kingdom that is *"righteousness and peace and joy in the Holy Spirit"* (Romans 14:17 NASB). In the midst of all that is being shaken around us—all the distress, uncertainty, perplexity, confusion, hatred, division, war, and fear—we have an unshakable kingdom. We have peace, security, and purpose. What is the appropriate response? There is only one: it is thankfulness. *"Therefore, since we receive a kingdom which cannot be shaken, let us show gratitude"* (Hebrews 12:28); let us express our thanks to God.

Thank You, Lord, for all You have done for me. I proclaim that since I *"receive a kingdom which cannot be shaken,"* I will be thankful and show gratitude. I shall show gratitude. Amen.

Twelve Steps to a Good Year, Part 3 (audio)

DECLARING GOD'S WORD

The Release Thanksgiving Brings

Let us show gratitude.

Thankfulness, or gratitude, is the appropriate response to what God has done—and is still doing—for us. It is something that we owe to God, something we need to pay. But the expression of our appreciation also does something in our own spirits that nothing else can do.

I express it in this way: Thankfulness releases our spirits for acceptable worship and service. That is why the writer of Hebrews said, *"Let us show gratitude, by which we may offer to God an acceptable service with reverence and awe"* (Hebrews 12:28 NASB). Without gratitude, our services to God will not be acceptable. It is that "attitude of gratitude" that makes our services acceptable and releases our spirits. An unthankful person is bound up in himself. He is self-centered. He really cannot know true liberation. But thankfulness releases our spirits.

> *In everything give thanks; for this* [giving thanks] *is God's will for you in Christ Jesus. Do not quench the Spirit.*
>
> (1 Thessalonians 5:18–19 NASB)

That is a clear commandment: if we do not give thanks, we are being disobedient. We are also out of the will of God. In addition, failing to give thanks quenches the Spirit. The only release for the Spirit—to serve God acceptably—is through thanksgiving.

Then, notice the warning that concludes Hebrews 12: *"For our God is a consuming fire"* (verse 29). The writer was telling us, "We have to approach this holy, awe-inspiring God with the right attitude—with humble, thankful hearts."

Thank You, Lord, for all You have done for me. I proclaim that as I approach a holy, awe-inspiring God with a humble, thankful heart, that attitude releases my spirit for acceptable worship and service. I shall show gratitude. Amen.

Twelve Steps to a Good Year, Part 3 (audio)

The Necessity of Gratitude

Let us show gratitude.

L et's take a look at the situation of the world in these last days. We know that a shaking is coming. (See Hebrews 12:26–27.) Now, look at the disintegration of character, morality, and standards. Paul said,

> But mark this: There will be terrible times in the last days. People will be lovers of themselves, lovers of money, boastful, proud, abusive, disobedient to their parents, ungrateful, unholy, with-out love, unforgiving, slanderous, without self-control, brutal, not lovers of the good, treacherous, rash, conceited, lovers of plea-sure rather than lovers of God—having a form of godliness but denying its power. Have nothing to do with them.
>
> (2 Timothy 3:1–5 NIV)

This is a terrible list of the moral defects and character degen-eration that are going to mark the close of this age. I would predict that, if you go over that list again, you will find that most of these character defects are already conspicuous in our contemporary cul-ture. And, right there in the middle of the list, it says that people are "*disobedient to their parents, ungrateful, unholy, without love.*" Notice the association. The ungrateful are right next door to the unholy. You cannot be holy and remain ungrateful. Since our God is a consuming fire (see, for example, Hebrews 12:29), He requires that we serve Him with holiness, which is appropriate. We also have to serve Him with gratitude. We must come to Him with thankfulness.

Let us show gratitude so that we may serve Him acceptably, with reverence and godly fear. (See verse 28.)

Thank You, Lord, for all You have done for me. I proclaim that since our God is a consuming fire, I will serve Him with holiness and gratitude. I shall show gratitude. Amen.

Twelve Steps to a Good Year, Part 3 (audio)

Giving Thanks to God

Let us show gratitude.

To be thankful is a direct command of Scripture; if we are not thankful, we are being disobedient. (See 1 Thessalonians 5:18.) Thankfulness, like most important attitudes of the Christian life, originates in the will, not in the emotions. We do not have to *feel* thankful in order to *be* thankful. Those who have children train them to say "thank you." In Britain, children are expected to say "thank you" even before they receive anything. It is simply a matter of proper conduct.

God often deals with us in that way, requiring us to say "thank you" before we actually receive something. Oftentimes, if we wait to receive it first, we will not get it.

> And let the peace of God rule in your hearts, to which also you were called in one body; and be thankful. Let the word of Christ dwell in you richly in all wisdom, teaching and admonishing one another in psalms and hymns and spiritual songs, singing with grace in your hearts to the Lord. And whatever you do in word or deed, do all in the name of the Lord Jesus, giving thanks to God the Father through Him. (Colossians 3:15–17)

This passage makes two demands of us: to do all things in the name of the Lord Jesus, and to give thanks while doing them. These instructions apply to every task, whether it's scrubbing the kitchen floor, cleaning the bathroom, driving the car, or writing a letter.

That gives us a pretty good gauge of right and wrong. If there is anything that we cannot honestly do in the name of the Lord Jesus, giving thanks all the while, then we'd better not do it. This method cuts away a whole list of do's and don'ts. It is a basic principle to guide our words and actions.

Thank You, Lord, for all You have done for me. I proclaim that I will do all things in the name of the Lord Jesus, giving thanks to God the Father while I am doing them. I shall show gratitude. Amen.

Thankfulness (audio)

Fulfilling God's Will

Let us show gratitude.

Thankfulness is a way of expressing the peace of Christ that rules in our hearts, an expression of the Word of Christ dwelling richly within us. Giving thanks is a principle that should guide all that we do. (See Colossians 3:15–17.) Let's look at three short but no less important verses, starting with 1 Thessalonians 5:16–18: *"Rejoice always, pray without ceasing, in everything give thanks; for this is the will of God in Christ Jesus for you."* There are three simple instructions in those verses: rejoice always, pray without ceasing, and in everything give thanks. Concerning the giving thanks in everything, Paul said, "This is God's will for you in Christ Jesus." When we are not giving thanks, we are not fulfilling the will of God. In other words, we are out of God's will. How important it is to understand that!

The second thing I want to say about thankfulness, or thanksgiving, is that it is an essential expression of the fullness of the Spirit. Paul wrote, *"Do not quench the Spirit"* (verse 19). Here is what he said to the Ephesians: *"So then do not be foolish, but understand what the will of the Lord is. And do not get drunk with wine, for that is dissipation, but be filled with the [Holy] Spirit"* (Ephesians 5:17–18 NASB).

Paul provided us with a negative, followed by a positive, regarding the will of the Lord. If we do not understand these truths about God's will, then we are foolish. Each exhortation is equally valid. It is wrong for a Christian to get drunk with wine, but it is equally wrong for a Christian *not* to be filled with the Holy Spirit. Sometimes, as religious people, we focus so much on the negative—not filling ourselves with wine so that we become drunk—that we forget about the positive—being filled with the Holy Spirit. We need to be filled with the Spirit.

Thank You, Lord, for all You have done for me. I proclaim that by giving thanks, I am fulfilling the will of God and expressing the fullness of the Spirit. I shall show gratitude. Amen.

Thanksgiving (audio)

DECLARING GOD'S WORD

WEEK 51:

Let us go forth to Him outside the camp.

*Therefore let us go forth to Him, outside the camp,
bearing His reproach.*

—Hebrews 13:13

Bearing His Reproach

Let us go forth to Him outside the camp.

The eleventh "Let us" resolution of Hebrews is in chapter 13:

> *Therefore Jesus also, that He might sanctify the people through His own blood, suffered outside the gate. Hence, let us go out to Him outside the camp, bearing His reproach. For here we do not have a lasting city, but we are seeking the city which is to come.*
> (Hebrews 13:12–14 NASB)

This passage deals with our attitude and relationship to this present world. It is telling us that our home is not in this world. We have no enduring place in this world. The world rejected Jesus. It drove Him out of the city and crucified Him outside the gate.

The Scripture always emphasizes the fact that Jesus' crucifixion took place outside the city wall. Jesus was rejected. He was put out of society; the world did not want Him. And the way in which the world treated Jesus, sooner or later, and in one way or another, is going to be the way in which the world will treat you and me, as believers. We must be willing to go out to Him—to the place of crucifixion, rejection, and shame—bearing His reproach. Elsewhere in Hebrews, it says that the reproach of Christ amounts to greater riches than all the treasures of Egypt. (See Hebrews 11:26.) So, His reproach becomes our glory.

Then, the writer gave a beautiful reason: *"For here we do not have a lasting city."* Other people may think that this world is permanent, but we know that it is not. *"But we are seeking the city which is to come."* I like this translation because it says *the* city. There is one specific city that is the destination and the home of all true believers. It is where we really belong.

Thank You, Lord, that You are calling me to leave this world behind.
I proclaim that I am willing to go out to Jesus *"outside the city wall,"*
bearing His reproach. I shall go forth to Him outside the camp.
Amen.

Twelve Steps to a Good Year, Part 3 (audio)

DECLARING GOD'S WORD

A City He Has Prepared

Let us go forth to Him outside the camp.

I n the eleventh chapter of Hebrews, the writer listed a kind of honor roll of many faithful saints of the Old Testament. Then, he said,

> All these died in faith, without receiving the promises, but having seen them and having welcomed them from a distance, and having confessed that they were strangers and exiles on the earth. For those who say such things make it clear that they are seeking a country of their own. And indeed if they had been thinking of that country from which they went out, they would have had opportunity to return. But as it is, they desire a better country, that is a heavenly one. Therefore God is not ashamed to be called their God; for He has prepared a city for them. (Hebrews 11:13–16 NASB)

These forerunners in the faith—men and women who are our examples in so many ways—confessed that they were strangers and exiles on this earth. They did not really belong; they were seeking a country of their own.

There are multitudes of refugees in our world today who are going through the agony of having no permanent place of their own. The people in Hebrews, too, were seeking a place of their own—but not in this world. If they had wanted to, they could have gone back to the place from which they came. Abraham, for instance, could have returned to Ur of the Chaldeans. But he had his mind set forward; he was not looking backward. They desired a better country—that is, a heavenly one. Then, we read that beautiful sentence, *"Therefore God is not ashamed to be called their God."* When we identify ourselves with God—with His preparation of a city for us—then He is proud to be our God. He has prepared a city—for them, for us.

Thank You, Lord, that You are calling me to leave this world behind. I proclaim that I am a stranger and an exile on this earth, seeking the city that God has prepared for me. I shall go forth to Him outside the camp. Amen.

Twelve Steps to a Good Year, Part 3 (audio)

Identification with the Cross

Let us go forth to Him outside the camp.

Commitment to Jesus requires identification with His cross and going out to the place where He was crucified. This commitment rules out two things: pleasing self and pleasing the world.

> *Brethren, join in following my example, and observe those who walk according to the pattern you have in us. For many walk, of whom I often told you, and now tell you even weeping, that they are enemies of the cross of Christ, whose end is destruction, whose god is their appetite, and whose glory is in their shame, who set their minds on earthly things.* (Philippians 3:17–19 NASB)

Paul was speaking of people who merely profess to be Christians, enemies of the cross who claim to be followers of Christ. They indulge themselves and set their minds on the things of this world. The principle of the cross—death to self and to the things of the flesh—has not been applied in their lives. Even in the church, many people profess allegiance to Christ but reject His cross. Their end is destruction.

By our identification with the cross of Jesus, we also rule out pleasing this world. James wrote these stern words to professing believers: "*You adulterous people, don't you know that friendship with the world is hatred toward God? Anyone who chooses to be a friend of the world becomes an enemy of God*" (James 4:4 NIV). James called these people "*adulterous.*" Becoming part of the bride of Christ, the church, requires a spiritual commitment—the bride must be single-hearted, totally committed and devoted to Jesus. If that devotion to Jesus is infiltrated by the love of this world, then we are spiritual adulterers. We are not being faithful to the Bridegroom, Jesus Christ. To be a friend of the world is to commit spiritual adultery.

Thank You, Lord, that You are calling me to leave this world behind. I proclaim that I apply this principle of the cross—death to self and to the things of the flesh. I shall go forth to Him outside the camp.
Amen.

Twelve Steps to a Good Year, Part 3 (audio)

DECLARING GOD'S WORD

The Mark of Separation

Let us go forth to Him outside the camp.

In the gospel of John, Jesus issued this statement:

> *If the world hates you, keep in mind that it hated me first. If you belonged to the world, it would love you as its own. As it is, you do not belong to the world, but I have chosen you out of the world. That is why the world hates you.* (John 15:18–19 NIV)

When the world "loves us as its own," that is a pretty sure sign that we do not belong to Jesus. We need to give heed to that warning. What, then, should our attitude be in light of this? Paul expressed it well in Galatians 6:14: *"But may it never be that I should boast, except in the cross of our Lord Jesus Christ, through which the world has been crucified to me, and I to the world"* (NASB).

May we never boast or put confidence in anything but the cross of the Lord. Not in education, religion, or denomination—none of these things. We can safely boast only in the cross of the Lord Jesus Christ, where Jesus won a total, permanent, irreversible victory over all the forces of evil. Through the cross, *"the world has been crucified to me, and I to the world."* The cross is the mark of separation between the people of God and the world. When we accept the principle of the cross in our lives, we no longer belong to this world. Jesus gave us this beautiful promise of victory: *"I have told you these things, so that in me you may have peace. In this world you will have trouble. But take heart! I have overcome the world"* (John 16:33 NIV).

We are going to have trouble—but Jesus has overcome the world! Through Him, we, too, can overcome the world, if we are willing to go forth to Him—outside the camp, bearing His reproach.

Thank You, Lord, that You are calling me to leave this world behind. I proclaim that I accept the cross as a mark of separation between the people of God and the world—a world to which I no longer belong. I shall go forth to Him outside the camp. Amen.

Twelve Steps to a Good Year, Part 3 (audio)

His Banishment: Our Acceptance

Let us go forth to Him outside the camp.

In the sixteenth chapter of Leviticus, we read about the Day of Atonement, specifically about the scapegoat. This day involved two goats. One goat was a sin offering, and it was killed. The other goat, which was called *azazel*, or *"scapegoat"* (Leviticus 16:8), was led away into the wilderness. It was led off into an uninhabited land to wander there hopelessly and die of thirst. It never returned.

Jesus was the scapegoat in the figure of the Day of Atonement. He was banished from the presence of Almighty God. Jesus is actually typified by both goats. As the sin offering, He died on the cross. But as the scapegoat, He was banished from the presence of God, enduring our rejection for us. The opposite of banishment is acceptance. That is stated in Ephesians 1:6: *"He made us accepted in the Beloved."*

We must all understand that we are accepted. Again, one of the most common problems that people have in modern America is the feeling of rejection. In any given congregation, I can guarantee that there are several people who are struggling with feelings of rejection. In most cases, these feelings are due to their parents—growing up, they may have never believed that their parents really wanted them, and so they never learned to feel accepted. They go through life feeling rejected, unhappy, unable to integrate with other people, and unable to show love, because they have never experienced love.

I have learned by experience that one of the great keys to helping such people is to impart to them the assurance that they are accepted by God. It is also comforting to know that He Himself knows the pain of rejection, for no one else was as utterly rejected as He when He died on the cross for our sins.

Thank You, Lord, that You are calling me to leave this world behind. I proclaim that because Jesus was banished from the presence of Almighty God, I am *"accepted in the Beloved."* I shall go forth to Him outside the camp. Amen.

Full Salvation and How to Enter In, Part 2 (audio)

Accepting *"the Arm of the Lord"*

Let us go forth to Him outside the camp.

Isaiah 53 begins with a warning about the danger that this prophetic message, given to Isaiah by God, will be met by many with unbelief: *"Who has believed our report? And to whom has the arm of the LORD been revealed?"* (Isaiah 53:1).

The Lord's Servant, described in earlier verses (see Isaiah 52:13–15) and foretold in this prophecy, is described in the above verse as *"the arm of the LORD."* This phrase denotes God's power intervening on behalf of His people. It indicated ahead of time that through Jesus Christ Himself, God would intervene to bring salvation to His people. All this was fulfilled in Jesus. He came to reveal God and to bring His salvation and healing to everyone. Peter, an eyewitness of the earthly ministry of Jesus, summed it up: *"God anointed Jesus of Nazareth with the Holy Spirit and with power, who went about doing good and healing all who were oppressed by the devil, for God was with Him"* (Acts 10:38).

The gospel of John applies Isaiah's prophecy directly to Jesus:

> But although He had done so many signs [miracles] *before them,*
> *they did not believe in Him, that the word of Isaiah the prophet*
> *might be fulfilled, which he spoke:* "Lord, who has believed our
> report? And to whom has the arm of the LORD been revealed?"
> (John 12:37–38)

We must hold fast to our belief in Him who fulfilled the Old Testament prophecies. Even many of those who witnessed firsthand the miracles of Jesus were incredulous. Let us not demand signs and wonders, which do not guarantee belief, but let us maintain faith in the One who earned our salvation, the greatest miracle of all.

Thank You, Lord, that You are calling me to leave this world behind. I proclaim that although many of Jesus' own people rejected Him, I receive Him as *"the arm of the Lord"* who brings salvation. I shall go forth to Him outside the camp. Amen.

Three Messages for Israel (booklet)

"No Form Nor Comeliness"

Let us go forth to Him outside the camp.

Isaiah 53:2 gives a prophetic description of Jesus' early years on earth: *"For He shall grow up before Him as a tender plant, and as a root out of dry ground. He has no form or comeliness; and when we see Him, there is no beauty that we should desire Him."* From youth to adulthood, Jesus grew up like a sturdy plant, upright and God-fearing in all His ways. This fact is also described in Luke 2:40: *"And the Child grew and became strong in spirit, filled with wisdom; and the grace of God was upon Him."* At the same time, Jesus was *"a root out of dry ground."* He came forth as God's messenger to Israel at a period of prolonged spiritual poverty. Israel had not received any prophetic revelation for nearly three hundred years. This prophetic silence was broken only by John the Baptist, then Jesus Himself, who both proclaimed the coming of God's kingdom.

Jesus had no special outward splendor that would reveal His true identity to people. They saw in Him nothing more than the son of Joseph the carpenter. (See Matthew 13:54–55.) When Peter acknowledged Him as the Messiah and Son of God, Jesus said that this revelation came not through Peter's natural senses; rather, it was given to him by God the Father. (See Matthew 16:17.) The prophecy continues, *"He is despised and rejected by men, a Man of sorrows [pains] and acquainted with grief [disease]. And we hid, as it were, our faces from Him; He was despised, and we did not esteem Him"* (Isaiah 53:3). Jesus did not seek the favor of the wealthy. Instead, He devoted Himself tirelessly to helping the poor and the suffering. He faced pain and disease, eventually taking upon Himself the pain and disease of the whole human race. Hanging on the cross in shame and agony, He became *"like one from whom men hide their face"* (Isaiah 53:3 NASB).

Thank You, Lord, that You are calling me to leave this world behind. I proclaim that although Jesus was despised and rejected by men, I receive Him and esteem Him as Messiah, the Son of God. I shall go forth to Him outside the camp. Amen.

Three Messages for Israel (booklet)

Week 52:

Let us continually offer up a sacrifice of praise.

Therefore by Him let us continually offer the sacrifice of praise to God, that is, the fruit of our lips, giving thanks to His name.

—Hebrews 13:15

Lips That Give Thanks

Let us continually offer up a sacrifice of praise.

This is the twelfth and final "Let us" resolution from the book of Hebrews: "*Through Him [Jesus] then, let us continually offer up a sacrifice of praise to God, that is, the fruit of lips that give thanks to His name*" (Hebrews 13:15 NASB). To me, this resolution is very appropriate and beautiful because it is something we are instructed to keep on doing. If we continually offer up a sacrifice of praise to God, all year long, it will make all the difference as to what the year holds for each of us.

This final step of offering up a sacrifice of praise to God relates directly, and in a practical way, to the two previous steps, which were, "Let us show gratitude" and "Let us go forth to Him outside the gate."

Gratitude naturally leads to praise. There are many passages in the Bible in which thanksgiving is related to praise. One of the most beautiful is Psalm 100:4: "*Enter into His gates with thanksgiving, and into His courts with praise.*" The first step in gaining access to God is thanksgiving; the second step is praise. Thanksgiving leads to praise. It finds expression in praise, and it flows out in praise.

The step just before this one, "Let us go forth to Him outside the camp," brings us release from the two slaveries of pleasing self and pleasing the world. Again, this step is directly related to offering the sacrifice of praise. You might not see it at first, but there are two hindrances to spontaneous, free-flowing praise in our lives: love of self and love of the world. As long as our affections are centered in ourselves or in the world, we are not really free to praise God. The cross removes these two hindrances and sets us free to praise God.

Thank You, Lord. I give You praise. I proclaim that I remove all hindrances and that I offer up praise to God—"*the fruit of lips that give thanks to His name.*" I shall continually offer up a sacrifice of praise. Amen.

Twelve Steps to a Good Year, Part 3 (audio)

DECEMBER 25

Liberated by the Cross

Let us continually offer up a sacrifice of praise.

The cross of Jesus removes the hindrances of pleasing ourselves and pleasing the world. Then, when we are no longer affected by what happens to ourselves, we cease to be significantly affected by our moods, problems, or apparent adversity. What goes on in the world around us no longer affects us.

We may sit and listen to the news, and, afterwards, get up thinking that the situation in the world is pretty bad—there are crises, disasters, crime, immorality. But we need to see that the world does not dominate us, that it does not dominate our thinking. We are in the world but not of the world. When we are released from slavery to the world—when the world no longer controls our thinking and we have been liberated by the cross in our inner attitude toward the world—then there is nothing left to hinder our praise.

We do not praise God just when things are going right in the world or with ourselves. We praise God because *He is worthy to be praised.* Our liberated spirits are not entangled with self-love and the love of the world.

You can find out a lot about a person when you study how much praising he does. Is he a slave to the old man, or has he entered into the resurrected life of the new man? The old man is a grumbler. When we hear a person grumbling, we know that is the old man speaking. But the new man is a praiser. Which are you? The old man says, "I can't take this any longer," "Things are getting too bad," "Nobody treats me right," "What's wrong with the world?" The new man says, "Hallelujah! Praise the Lord! I'm free. I'm a child of God. Heaven is my home. God loves me."

Which of these attitudes is yours?

Thank You, Lord. I give You praise. I proclaim that I have been liberated by the cross to give praise to God, for He is worthy to be praised. I shall continually offer up a sacrifice of praise. Amen.

Twelve Steps to a Good Year, Part 3 (audio)

A Costly Sacrifice

Let us continually offer up a sacrifice of praise.

L et's look at a verse from the book of Proverbs that points to the importance of what we say with our mouths:

> *Death and life are in the power of the tongue, and those who love it will eat its fruit.* (Proverbs 18:21)

Two things come from the use of the tongue: death and life. If we grumble, or if we are negative or self-centered, our tongues will bring forth death. But if we are liberated from all of that negativity and are walking in the praise and worship of God, our tongues will bring forth life. Additionally, whatever fruit our tongues bring forth, whether sweet or bitter, we are going to eat of it.

Let's go back to our pattern verse for this week. I'd like to bring out one more important point from it. The writer said,

> *Through Him* [Jesus] *then, let us continually offer up a sacrifice of praise to God.* (Hebrews 13:15 NASB)

One very significant word in this verse is *"sacrifice."* Praise is a sacrifice. According to the principles of Scripture, a sacrifice requires a death. In the Old Testament sacrifices, nothing was ever offered to God that had not passed through death. So, we see that the sacrifice of praise requires a death—the death of the old man. The old man cannot praise God as He deserves to be praised. There has to be a death.

Again, we know that a sacrifice costs us something; thus, praise is costly. Let me put it this way: we need to praise God most when we least feel like it. Praise cannot depend on our feelings. It is a sacrifice of our spirits.

Thank You, Lord. I give You praise. I proclaim that praise is a sacrifice, praise is costly, and, whether I feel like it or not, I give God praise. I shall continually offer up a sacrifice of praise. Amen.

Twelve Steps to a Good Year, Part 3 (audio)

DECEMBER 27

Contagious Praise

Let us continually offer up a sacrifice of praise.

Let's look at the example of King David in Psalm 34. The introduction to this psalm says, *"A psalm of David when he feigned madness before Abimelech* [or Achish], *who drove him away and he departed"* (NASB). At this time in his life, David was a fugitive from his own country. King Saul was trying to kill him, so David had to leave his familiar surroundings.

He went to the court of a Gentile king for refuge, but the king suspected him of being an enemy. In order to save his own life, he had to feign madness. The historic book of 1 Samuel tells us that he scratched at the door and slobbered on his beard. (See 1 Samuel 21:10–15.) That was the situation. But what was David's reaction?

> *I will bless the LORD at all times; His praise shall continually be in my mouth. My soul shall make its boast in the LORD; the humble shall hear it and rejoice. O magnify the LORD with me, and let us exalt His name together.* (Psalm 34:1–3 NASB)

Right there, in the midst of such a terrible situation, with his life hanging in the balance and the shame of having to feign madness, David praised the Lord. That is the sacrifice of praise. When he was at his lowest, David decided to go on boasting in the Lord. When there was nothing else to boast about, he decided to boast in the Lord.

Then, David went on, *"O magnify the LORD with me, and let us exalt His name together."* Praise is contagious. If we learn to praise God in this way, others will join in. But grumbling is contagious, too. If we grumble, we will attract fellow grumblers. We must learn to offer the sacrifice of praise to God continually.

Thank You, Lord. I give You praise. I proclaim that regardless of my circumstances, I give God the sacrifice of praise, boasting in the Lord. I shall continually offer up a sacrifice of praise. Amen.

Twelve Steps to a Good Year, Part 3 (audio)

DECEMBER 28

Praise in the Desert

Let us continually offer up a sacrifice of praise.

When I was serving in the British army during World War II, I was stationed in the deserts of North Africa. One negative aspect of desert living conditions is that they tend to provoke murmuring and complaining. This happened with Israel many times, and it often brought God's judgment and disfavor upon them. I got so weary of the desert, the food, and the blaspheming British soldiers that I began to complain. When I did this, I lost the sense of God's presence and blessing.

I decided to set aside a special day to fast and to ask God why His presence seemed to have withdrawn from me. I said, "God, why are You not near to me? Why do I have to continue this monotonous, wearisome life in the desert?" By evening, God had given me the answer. He spoke to me very clearly, saying, "Why have you not thanked Me? Why have you not praised Me?" As I meditated on what God said, I realized that I had lost the sense of His presence because I had become unthankful.

In due course, the Holy Spirit directed me to various passages along this line, including 1 Thessalonians 5:16–19: *"Rejoice always; pray without ceasing; in everything give thanks; for this is God's will for you in Christ Jesus. Do not quench the Spirit"* (NASB). Again, the implication is that if we do not rejoice always, pray without ceasing, and give thanks in everything, we are quenching the Holy Spirit! By murmuring and complaining instead of praising and giving thanks, I had quenched the Holy Spirit in my life.

God expects us to continually offer up a sacrifice of praise from our lips—not just inwardly from our hearts. We have to make our praise vocal by giving thanks to the name of the Lord!

Thank You, Lord. I give You praise. I proclaim that I do not quench the Spirit but rejoice always, pray without ceasing, and give thanks in everything. I shall continually offer up a sacrifice of praise. Amen.

Pages from My Life's Book: Discipled in the Desert (audio)

DECLARING GOD'S WORD

The Mark of Thankfulness

Let us continually offer up a sacrifice of praise.

As we have seen, thankfulness is a direct command of Scripture and an indispensable mark of being filled with the Holy Spirit. These facts lead to two practical conclusions that apply to each of us personally: first, an unthankful Christian is disobedient; second, an unthankful Christian is not full of the Holy Spirit.

Thanksgiving is also a requirement for entering God's presence, as we read in Psalm 100:4–5: *"Enter His gates with thanksgiving, and His courts with praise. Give thanks to Him; bless His name. For the* LORD *is good; His lovingkindness is everlasting, and His faithfulness to all generations"* (NASB). Two essential stages in our approach to God are entering the gates with thanksgiving and entering the courts with praise.

Again, the psalmist also gave three specific reasons that we should thank God. First, *"the* LORD *is good"*; second, *"His lovingkindness is everlasting"*; and, third, *"His faithfulness [is] to all generations."* Each of these is permanent and unchanging. God is always good; His lovingkindness is everlasting; His faithfulness is to all generations. The primary reasons for giving thanks to God never depend on our feelings or circumstances. We may feel up one day, down the next; sometimes we are encouraged, other times discouraged. But there is no reason to change our attitude of thankfulness to God.

In order to approach God on the basis of these three eternal facts, we need to change our focus. We need to look away from things that irritate, discourage, or provoke us, looking instead at the eternal things, which we see through eyes of faith. When we come to God with the right focus, we are in a position to hear from God and to receive from Him.

Thank You, Lord. I give You praise. I proclaim that I enter Your gates with thanksgiving, and Your courts with praise, because You are good, and Your lovingkindness is everlasting. You are faithful. I shall continually offer up a sacrifice of praise. Amen.

Thanksgiving (audio)

December 30

Praise Silences the Devil

Let us continually offer up a sacrifice of praise.

Praise is a spiritual weapon that we can use to silence the devil. There is perhaps no more important fact in the Bible than this. From the point of view of practical Christian living, God has given you a way to silence the devil's mouth. Psalm 8:2 says, *"Out of the mouth of babes and nursing infants You have ordained strength, because of Your enemies, that You may silence the enemy and the avenger."* The psalmist, addressing God, was speaking about *"enemies"* in the plural and *"the enemy and the avenger"* in the singular. *"The enemy and the avenger"* is none other than the devil himself; *"enemies"* are the evil spirits that are Satan's instruments against us. Because of Satan and his evil spirits, God has ordained strength that we might silence the devil.

This verse was quoted by Jesus in the gospel of Matthew. The quotation is a revelation of the full meaning of this passage. In this scene, Jesus is in the temple, healing the sick, and the children are running to and fro, crying, *"Hosanna to the Son of David!"* (Matthew 21:15). This upsets the religious leaders, so they say to Jesus, "Do You hear what they are saying?" Jesus then gives us this revelation: *"Yes. Have you never read, 'Out of the mouth of babes and nursing infants You have perfected praise'?"* (verse 16). Where the psalmist said, *"You have ordained strength,"* Jesus said, *"You have perfected praise."* So, we get a simple, direct inference. The "ordained strength" of God's people in battle is "perfected praise." God has made it possible for us to silence the devil and all his evil spirits by perfect praise.

As "babes and infants," if we will but praise God perfectly, out of our mouths will come forth a weapon that silences the devil. And God will be glorified.

Thank You, Lord. I give You praise. I proclaim that by my *"perfected praise,"* I silence the devil and glorify God. I shall continually offer up a sacrifice of praise. Amen.

Spiritual Conflict, Vol. 4: Strategy for Conquest: Triumphant Praise (audio)

Invoking God's Blessing

Let us continually offer up a sacrifice of praise.

The climax of the priestly blessing that Aaron and his descendants were instructed to pronounce on the people of Israel came with these words: *"So they shall put My name on the children of Israel, and I will bless them"* (Numbers 6:27).

Often, the most effective prayers we can offer on behalf of others are prayers of praise and thanksgiving, invoking the name of the Lord Jesus on them. When we put the name of Jesus on those for whom we are praying, we invoke God's blessing on them. Few of us realize how much we uplift people in their spirits when we simply praise God for them. It is a major part of our ministry as intercessors.

"Praying Hyde" was an outstanding missionary in the Punjab in India in the last century, when India was still under British rule. Hyde's ministry was prayer; everything else was secondary. Early on, he came across an Indian evangelist whom he considered ineffective and cold. As he began to pray about this man, he said, "Lord, You know—" he was going to say, "—how cold Brother So-and-so is." But the Holy Spirit stopped him with Proverbs 30:10: *"Do not slander a servant to his master"* (NIV).

So, Brother Hyde changed his approach. He began to think of everything good in that man's life and to thank God for him. Within a few months, that man became outstandingly successful as an evangelist. What changed him? Not being accused in prayer, but being the object of thanksgiving.

God has taught me that if I cannot thank Him for somebody, I probably have no right to pray for that person. I had better not pray at all because my prayer may do more harm than good. As Numbers 6:27 says, *"So they shall put My name on the children of Israel, and I will bless them."*

Thank You, Lord. I give You praise. I proclaim that I do not *"slander a servant"* but instead invoke God's blessing on him or her. I shall continually offer up a sacrifice of praise. Amen.

Husbands and Fathers (book)

About the Author

Derek Prince (1915–2003) was born in Bangalore, India, into a British military family. He was educated as a scholar of classical languages (Greek, Latin, Hebrew, and Aramaic) at Eton College and Cambridge University in England and later at Hebrew University, Israel. As a student, he was a philosopher and self-proclaimed atheist. He held a fellowship (equivalent to a professorship) in ancient and modern philosophy at King's College, Cambridge.

While in the British Medical Corps during World War II, Prince began to study the Bible as a philosophical work. Converted through a powerful encounter with Jesus Christ, he was baptized in the Holy Spirit a few days later. This life-changing experience altered the whole course of his life, which he thereafter devoted to studying and teaching the Bible as the Word of God.

Discharged from the army in Jerusalem in 1945, he married Lydia Christensen, founder of a children's home there. Upon their marriage, Derek immediately became father to Lydia's eight adopted daughters—six Jewish, one Palestinian Arab, and one English. Together, the family saw the rebirth of the state of Israel in 1948. In the late 1950s, the Princes adopted another daughter while Derek was serving as principal of a college in Kenya.

In 1963, the Princes immigrated to the United States and pastored a church in Seattle, Washington. Stirred by the tragedy of John F. Kennedy's assassination, Derek began to teach Americans how to intercede for their nation. In 1973, he became one of the founders of Intercessors for America. His book *Shaping History through Prayer and Fasting* has awakened Christians around the world to their responsibility to pray for their governments. Many consider underground translations of this book as having been instrumental in the fall of communist regimes in the former USSR, East Germany, and Czechoslovakia.

Lydia Prince died in 1975, and Derek married Ruth Baker (a single mother to three adopted children) in 1978. He met his second wife, like the first, while he was serving the Lord in Jerusalem. Ruth died in December 1998 in Jerusalem, where the Princes had lived since 1981.

Until a few years before his own death in 2003 at the age of eighty-eight, Prince persisted in the ministry God had called him to as he traveled the world, imparting God's revealed truth, praying for the sick and afflicted, and sharing his prophetic insights into world events in the light of Scripture. He pioneered teaching on such groundbreaking themes as generational curses, the biblical significance of Israel, and demonology.

He is the author of more than fifty books, six hundred audio teachings, and one hundred video teachings, many of which have been translated and published in more than one hundred languages. His radio program, now known as *Derek Prince Legacy Radio*, began in 1979 and has been translated into over a dozen languages. Derek's main gift of explaining the Bible and its teaching in a clear, simple way has helped build a foundation of faith in millions of lives. His nondenominational, nonsectarian approach has made his teaching equally relevant and helpful to people from all racial and religious backgrounds, and his teaching is estimated to have reached more than half the globe.

Internationally recognized as a Bible scholar and spiritual patriarch, Derek Prince established a teaching ministry that spanned six continents and more than sixty years. In 2002, he said, "It is my desire—and I believe the Lord's desire—that this ministry continue the work, which God began through me over sixty years ago, until Jesus returns."

Declaring God's Word

With its international headquarters in Charlotte, North Carolina, Derek Prince Ministries continues to reach out to believers in over 140 countries with Derek's teaching, fulfilling the mandate to keep on "until Jesus returns." This is accomplished through the outreaches of more than thirty Derek Prince Ministries International offices around the world, including primary work in Australia, Canada, China, France, Germany, the Netherlands, New Zealand, Norway, Russia, South Africa, Switzerland, the United Kingdom, and the United States. For current information about these and other worldwide locations, visit www.derekprince.org.